lonely planet

INDIA

TOP SIGHTS, AUTHENTIC EXPERIENCES

Anirban Mahapatra, ... own,
Mark Elliott, Pau... ,
Daniel McCrohan, ... ohn Noble,
Kevin Raub, Sa... Singh, Iain Stewart

Contents

Plan Your Trip

India's Top 12 4
Need to Know 16
Hotspots For... 18
Essential India 20
Month by Month 22
Get Inspired 25
Itineraries 26
Family Travel 32

Delhi 35
...at a Glance 36

Red Fort 38
Old Delhi's Bazaars 42
Qutab Minar 44
Walking Tour: Lutyens' Delhi 46
Sights 48
Tours 51
Shopping 51
Eating 52
Drinking & Nightlife 57
Information 58
Getting There & Away 58
Getting Around 59
Where to Stay 61

Agra & the Taj Mahal 63
...at a Glance 64

Taj Mahal 66
Fatehpur Sikri 74
Agra Fort 78
Sights 82
Eating 83
Information 83
Getting There & Away 83
Getting Around 83

Jaisalmer 85
...at a Glance 86

Jaisalmer Fort 88
Camel Safaris 90
Sights 94
Shopping 95
Eating 96
Drinking & Nightlife 96
Getting There & Away 96
Getting Around 97

Jaipur 99
...at a Glance 100

Amber Fort 102
City Palace 104
Walking Tour: Pink City 106
Sights 108
Activities 109
Shopping 110
Eating 111
Drinking & Nightlife 111
Information 112
Getting There & Away 113
Getting Around 113

Ranthambhore National Park 114

Mumbai 117
...at a Glance 118

Bazaar District 120
Dining in Mumbai 122
Bollywood 124
Walking Tour: Architectural Mumbai 126
Sights 128
Shopping 131
Eating 131
Drinking & Nightlife 133
Information 134
Getting There & Away 134
Getting Around 135

Ajanta & Ellora 137
...at a Glance 138

Ajanta Caves 140
Ellora Caves 144
Aurangabad 150
Sights 150
Tours 151
Eating 151
Drinking & Nightlife 153
Information 153
Getting There & Away 153
Getting Around 153

External boundaries shown reflect the requirements of the Government of India.

CHINA
TIBET
Lhasa
NEPAL
KATHMANDU
SIKKIM
Gangtok
THIMPHU
BHUTAN
ARUNACHAL PRADESH
Itanagar
DARJEELING p213
Siliguri
ASSAM
Guwahati (Gaulhati)
NAGALAND
Kohima
Patna
BIHAR
MEGHALAYA
Shillong
Imphal
VARANASI p229
BANGLADESH
MANIPUR
DHAKA
TRIPURA
Aizawl
MYANMAR
JHARKHAND
MIZORAM
Ranchi
WEST BENGAL
Kolkata (Calcutta)
Chittagong
Mouths of the Ganges
ODISHA
Bhubaneswar
NAY PYI TAW
THAILAND
Bheemunipatnam
Visakhapatnam
Yangon
Bay of Bengal
Port Blair
Andaman & Nicobar Islands (India)
Andaman Sea

Welcome to India

With its sumptuous mix of traditions, spiritual beliefs, festivals, architecture and landscapes, India will blaze brightly in your memories long after you've left its shores.

From snow-dusted Himalayan peaks to sun-splashed southern beaches, India has a bounty of outdoor attractions. You can spy tigers on jungle safaris, laze in shimmering coastal retreats, trek amid dizzying high mountains, or inhale pine-scented air on forest walks. Scattered amid such natural treasures is a wealth of architectural gems, from serene temples straddling pancake-flat plains to crumbling forts overlooking plunging ravines.

Spirituality is the ubiquitous thread in India's rich cultural tapestry. An amazing array of sacred sites pays testament to the country's inclusive religious history. And then there are its innumerable colourful festivals – from stellar city parades to simple village harvest fairs.

Indian cuisine, meanwhile, is a delicious smorgasbord of regionally distinct recipes. Spices lie at the heart of Indian cooking, flavouring everything from marinated meats, lavish *thalis* (plate meals), simple vegetarian curries and deep-sea delights. There's also a tempting array of street food, from spicy samosas and kebabs to *kulfi* (firm ice cream) and lassi (yoghurt drink).

With its ability to thrill and confound at once, India can throw up a few unexpected surprises along the way. This can be challenging, but embracing India's unpredictability will also see you imbibe its soul. Don't be exasperated – just go with the flow!

You can spy tigers on jungle safaris, laze in shimmering coastal retreats, trek amid dizzying high mountains, or inhale pine-scented air on forest walks.

Holi festival (p22)

KABUL
AFGHANISTAN
ISLAMABAD
JAMMU & KASHMIR
Srinagar
Kargil
Leh
Jammu
McLeod Ganj p258
MANALI p245
Amritsar
PUNJAB
Shimla
Chandigarh
UTTARAKHAND
Dehra Dun
PAKISTAN
HARYANA
Moradabad
DELHI p35
Bikaner
AGRA & THE TAJ MAHAL
JAISALMER p85
JAIPUR p99
Bharatpur
Kanpur
Barmer
Jodhpur
Ajmer
Gwalior
Karachi
RAJASTHAN
Ranthambhore National Park p114
Udaipur
Bhuj
Gulf of Kachchh
Gandhinagar
Bhopal
MADHYA PRADESH
GUJARAT
Rajkot
Indore
Junagadh
Surat
Malegaon
Ajanta
Nagpur
Gulf of Khambhat
Ellora
AJANTA & ELLORA p137
Aurangabad
MUMBAI p117
MAHARASHTRA
TELANGANA
ARABIAN SEA
Sangareddi
Hyderabad
Kolhapur
Kalaburgi (Gulbarga)
Panaji (Panjim)
Dharwad
Hampi p210
GOA p155
Ballari (Bellary)
ANDHRA PRADESH
Davangere
Bengaluru (Bangalore)
Mangaluru (Mangalore)
MYSURU p195
Salem
Lakshadweep (India)
Coimbatore
Thrissur (Trichur)
TAMIL NADU
Trichy
Lakshadweep Sea
KERALA p173
Madurai
Thiruvananthapuram (Trivandrum)
0 500 km
0 250 miles

Goa 155
...at a Glance 156

Old Goa Day Trip......158
Goa's Beaches 160
Yoga by the Sea 164
Panaji (Panjim)...........166
Palolem.......................167
Anjuna.........................170

Kerala 173
...at a Glance 174

Backwater Boat Trips 176
Ayurvedic Resorts 178
Kerala's Beaches 180
Kathakali 182
Thiruvananthapuram (Trivandrum).............184
Kovalam......................185
Alappuzha (Alleppey)...................187
Kochi (Cochin) 189

Mysuru 195
...at a Glance 196

Mysuru City Tour.....198
Mysuru........................ 202
Kodagu (Coorg) 205
Bengaluru 206

Hampi 210

Darjeeling 213
...at a Glance 214

Tea Experience 216
Singalila Ridge Trek 218
Sights..........................222
Shopping 225
Eating...........................225
Drinking & Nightlife....226
Information.................226
Getting There & Away.........................227
Getting Around...........227

Varanasi 229
...at a Glance 230

The Ghats 232
Sights.......................... 236
Tours 237
Shopping 237
Eating........................... 239
Drinking & Nightlife... 240
Information................. 241
Getting There & Away.. 242
Getting Around...........242

Manali 245
...at a Glance 246

Manali Adventure Activities 248
Sights...........................252
Shopping 253
Eating...........................253
Drinking & Nightlife....256
Information.................257
Getting There & Away...257
Getting Around...........257

Tibetan Culture in McLeod Ganj 258

In Focus

India Today 264
History 266
The Way of Life........... 277
Understanding Hinduism 280
Delicious India............282
Architecture & the Arts 285
Landscape & Wildlife 288

Survival Guide

Directory A–Z 292
Transport 308
Language.................... 313
Index 316
Symbols & Map Key.......................322

Jawahar Circle, Jaipur (p99)
TAPASR / SHUTTERSTOCK ©

Plan Your Trip
India's Top 12

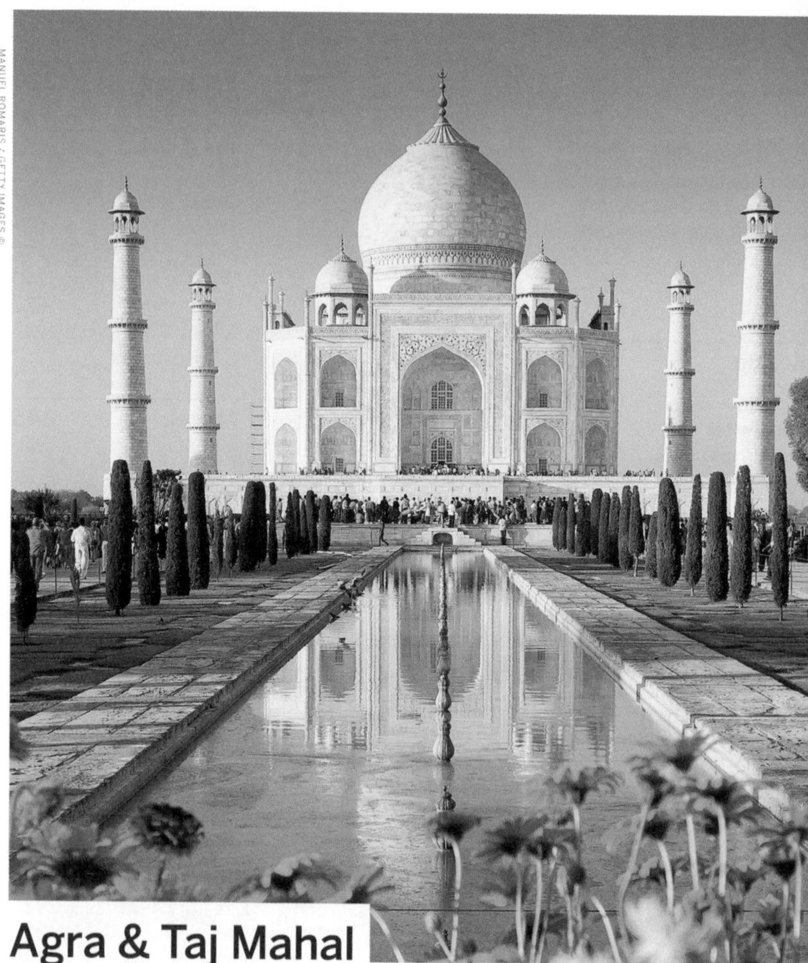
MANUEL ROMARIS / GETTY IMAGES ©

Agra & Taj Mahal

A timeless monument to love

The exquisite tomb of an emperor's beloved wife, the Taj Mahal (p66) is arguably the world's most beautiful building, and has been enshrined in the writings of Tagore and Kipling. Built by Emperor Shah Jahan in adoration of his third wife, Mumtaz Mahal, this white-marble mausoleum is inlaid with calligraphy, precious stones and floral designs. It represents the pinnacle of Mughal architecture and romance. Left: Taj Mahal (p66) and reflecting pool; Right: Interior of Taj Mahal

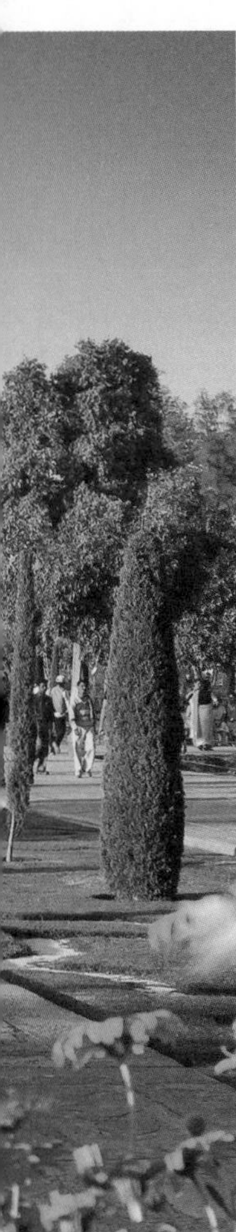

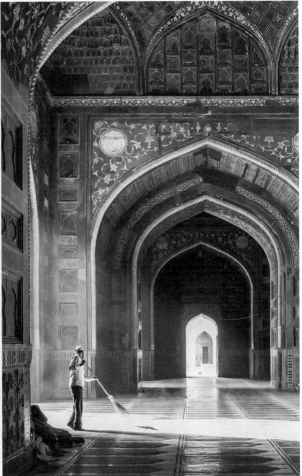

ALEXANDER RESHNYA / SHUTTERSTOCK ©

1

Jaipur

An enthralling city with regal heritage

Jaipur (p99) encapsulates the chaotic and colourful magic of Rajasthan (the land of kings), of which it is the state capital. It's a city of seething bazaars selling everything from brocaded saris to sparkling jewellery to meenakari enamelwork, honking traffic, awe-inspiring palaces and massive fortresses. In between seeing all the sights, there's wonderful shopping, fine dining and even balloon flights over the majestic Amber Fort. Top: Hawa Mahal (p108); Bottom: City Palace (p104)

2

RCHPHOTO / GETTY IMAGES ©

Kerala

Drifting lazily on shimmering lagoons

Visiting Kerala (p173) is like heading into a dream. Go on a slow cruise through the state's tropical backwaters, comprising 900km of interconnected rivers, lakes, canals and lagoons lined by coconut groves and picturesque villages. Navigate the serene waterways on a teak-and-thatch houseboat – watch the sun sink behind the trees as you sip a gin and tonic and snack on succulent Keralan seafood, and you'll forget all about life on land for a while.

3

Varanasi

City of life and death

Welcome to one of India's most-revered sacred cities. Pilgrims flock here to worship, take a holy dip in the Ganges River, or cremate loved ones. Hindus believe the Ganges' waters cleanse away sins, and dying here is deemed particularly propitious as it offers liberation from the life-and-death cycle. Varanasi (p229) will sweep you into its dizzying spiritual whirlwind – just take a deep breath and immerse yourself in pondering the meaning of life, death… and beyond.

Goa

Palm-fringed tropical beach paradise

With palms nodding on one side of the sugar-white sands and powder-blue waves lapping on the other, the coastline of Goa (p155) is lined with beautiful beaches and has a hedonistic atmosphere like nowhere else in India. It's not quite an undiscovered paradise, though: this cool coastal strip bustles with fellow travellers, beach-shack eateries and myriad water sports. Goa appeals to social animals and fans of creature comforts who like their seafood fresh and their holidays easy. Right: Vagator Beach (p161)

NARVIKK / GETTY IMAGES ©

SAIKO3P / GETTY IMAGES ©

Delhi

Fantastic empires, fine food, fabulous shopping

India's throbbing capital (p35) bears the remnants of former empires, from Mughal tombs to British-era mansions. There's so much to see here, from the splendour of Old Delhi to the architectural wonders of the Qutab Minar and Mehrauli. Add the many fine eateries, superb museums, a pulsating entertainment-and-nightlife scene and some amazing shopping along the way, and it's easy to see why Delhi mesmerises so many. Above: Pouring hot milk for chai

6

SKREIDZELEU / SHUTTERSTOCK ©

Mumbai

India's eclectic film-star city

Mumbai (p117) absorbs influences into her midst and inventively makes them her own. Architecturally, the art deco and modern towers lend the city its cool, but it's the dramatic flourishes of its Victorian-era structures that are the essence of Mumbai's visual magic. Today, the city is gathering culinary threads from around the world and leads India in the creativity of its restaurants. It's the country's capital of cinema, fashion and nightlife. Above: Chhatrapati Shivaji Maharaj Terminus (p129)

7

Darjeeling

Tea time at a classic hill station

One of many British-founded mountain retreats known as hill stations, Darjeeling (p213) sits over a steep Himalayan ridge staring at the world's third-highest mountain, Khangchendzonga. It's a cool escape where you can visit estates growing the tea that has spread Darjeeling's name around the world. If you're the energetic type, you can also put on your hiking boots and trek some spectacular trails in the shadow of soaring Himalayan peaks.

SEREE TANSRISAWAT / SHUTTERSTOCK ©

MARC GUITARD / GETTY IMAGES ©

9 Jaisalmer

Castles and camels in the desert

A gigantic, golden sandcastle rising like a mirage from the deserts of Rajasthan, 12th-century Jaisalmer (p85) is a fantastical structure and a small town in itself, elegantly blending with the toffee-gold hues of its desert environs. It rises above a city whose narrow lanes conceal magnificent *havelis* (traditional, ornately decorated residences) carved from the same golden-honey sandstone. Take a camel safari outside town to experience the full desert magic. Far left: Jain temple (p89), Jaisalmer Fort; Left: Camel decorated for Desert Festival (p96)

Manali

10

Himalayan haunt for thrill seekers and easy-goers

The green valleys and snowy peaks of this scenic Himalayan hill town (p245) – located north of Delhi – are a canvas for different kinds of travellers to paint their perfect holiday picture. Trek, ski, raft, mountain-bike or paraglide in the mountains, valleys, forests and rivers that surround the settlement. Or chill out with fellow travellers at the relaxed hippie-hangout in town. Top: Rafting on Beas River (p250); Bottom left: Skiing (p250); Bottom right: Paragliding (p251)

MAZZZUR / GETTY IMAGES ©

Ajanta & Ellora

Stunning millennia-old works of sacred art

Renunciation of the worldly life was never so serenely sophisticated. The temples, monasteries and prayer halls here were carved out of rock faces by Buddhist, Hindu and Jain monks at Ajanta and Ellora (p137) thousands of years ago. They weren't just places of worship and retreat but supreme artistic homages to the divine; few works from ancient times match the conception and execution of Ajanta's murals and Ellora's sculptures. Above: Kailasa Temple (p146), Ellora

ARUN SAMBHU MISHRA / SHUTTERSTOCK ©

Mysuru

India's past and future on a platter

Also called Mysore, Mysuru (p195) is home to one of the most glittering of all India's princely palaces. This southern town encompasses many faces of India, from bygone regal splendour to a booming IT industry that spills over from neighbouring Bengaluru (Bangalore). Most importantly, Mysuru is home to the dazzling annual Dussehra festival, featuring a 10-day carnival that ends with a riotous parade passing through town. Above: Dussehra Festival (p204)

12

Plan Your Trip
Need to Know

When to Go

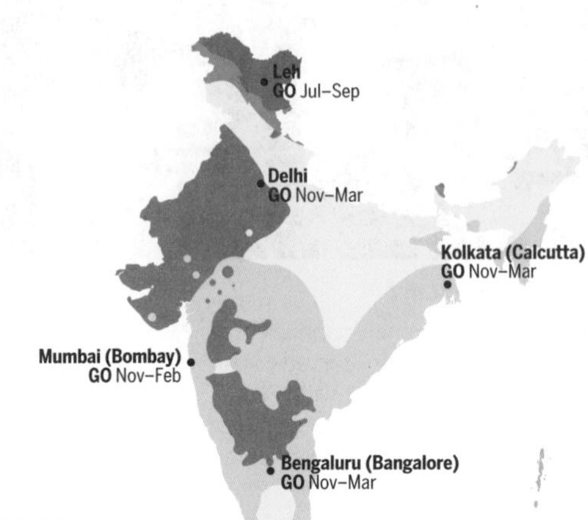

High Season (Dec–Mar)

- Warm days, cool nights. Peak tourists, peak prices.
- Cold or freezing conditions from December to February at altitude.
- Temperatures climb steadily from February.

Shoulder (Jun–Nov)

- Passes to Ladakh and Himalaya open June to September.
- Monsoon rains persist through to September.
- Southeastern coast and southern Kerala see heavy rain October to December.

Low Season (Apr–Jun)

- April is hot; May to June scorching. Competitive hotel prices.
- From June, the monsoon brings draining humidity.
- Beat the heat (but not the crowds) in the cool hills.

Currency

Indian rupee (₹)

Language

Hindi and English (official)

Visas

Required for most visitors; e-Visa (valid 60 days) available for more than 150 nationalities. Longer trips require a standard six-month tourist visa.

Money

ATMs widely available; carry cash as backup, especially in remote regions. Don't accept damaged banknotes: they won't be accepted by others.

Mobile Phones

Roaming connections excellent in urban areas, poor in the countryside and the Himalaya. Local prepaid SIMs widely available. India operates on the GSM network at 900MHz, the world's most common; mobile phones from most countries will work on the subcontinent.

Time

India Standard Time (GMT/UTC plus 5½ hours)

Daily Costs

Budget: Less than ₹3000

- Dorm bed: ₹400–₹600
- Double room in budget hotel: ₹400–₹1000
- All-you-can-eat thali (plate meal): ₹100–₹300
- Bus/train tickets: ₹300–₹500

Midrange: ₹3000–₹10,000

- Double hotel room: ₹1500–₹5000
- Meal in midrange restaurant: ₹600–₹1500
- Admission to historic sight/museum: ₹500–₹1500
- Local taxi/autorickshaw: ₹500–₹2000

Top End: More than ₹10,000

- Deluxe hotel room: ₹5000–₹24,000
- Meal at superior restaurant: ₹2000–₹5000
- First-class train travel: ₹1000–₹8000
- Hire car and driver: from ₹2000 per day

Useful Websites

Incredible India (www.incredibleindia.org) Official India tourism site.
Lonely Planet (www.lonelyplanet.com/india) Destination information, the Thorn Tree travel forum and more.
Templenet.com Temple talk.
Rediff News (www.rediff.com/news) Portal for India-wide news.
TheAlternative.in Green and socially conscious take on travel and Indian life.

Opening Hours

The following are guidelines and may vary:
Banks (nationalised) 10am to 2pm/4pm Monday to Friday, to noon/1pm/4pm Saturday; closed second and fourth Saturday
Bars and clubs noon to 12.30am
Post offices 9.30am to 5pm Monday to Saturday
Restaurants 8am to 10pm, or lunch (noon to 3pm) and dinner (7pm to 10/11pm)
Shops 10am to 7pm or 8pm, some closed Sunday
Museums/Sights Often closed Monday

Arriving in India

Indira Gandhi International Airport (Delhi) Express metro to New Delhi station ₹60. Frequent 24-hour AC buses to Kashmere Gate station ₹50. Taxis to centre from ₹450; Uber and Ola Cabs cheaper (add ₹150 to fares for airport parking/entry).
Chhatrapati Shivaji Maharaj International Airport (Mumbai) Non-AC/AC taxis ₹670/810 to Colaba and Fort, ₹400/480 to Bandra. Train (avoid 6am-to-11am rush hour): autorickshaw (₹18 per km) to Andheri station, then Churchgate or CST train (₹10, 45 minutes). Off-peak UberGo ₹250 to Bandra Kurla Complex, ₹260 to Bandra (W), ₹460 to Fort, ₹560 to Colaba.
Kempegowda International Airport (Bengaluru) AC taxis to centre ₹750 to ₹1000; Uber/Ola ₹550 to ₹650. Frequent AC Vayu Vajra buses ₹170 to ₹260.
Chennai International Airport Metro to centre ₹50 to ₹70. Taxis ₹450 to ₹600; Ola cheaper.

Getting Around

Transport in India is frequent and inexpensive, though not always fast. Consider domestic flights or sleeper trains as alternatives to long, uncomfortable bus rides.

Air Flights are available to most major centres and state capitals; cheap flights on offer with budget airlines.

Train Frequent services to most destinations; inexpensive tickets available, even on sleeper trains.

Bus Buses go everywhere; some destinations are served 24 hours, but longer routes have just one or two buses a day.

For more on **getting around**, see p308 

Plan Your Trip
Hotspots for...

DMITRY RUKHLENKO / SHUTTERSTOCK ©

Architecture

Towering temples, opulent palaces, massive forts, mesmerising mosques: India's empires and cultures have created some of the world's most stunning buildings.

Agra (p63)
Agra is home to the Taj Mahal and the massive Agra Fort, with the elegant Fatehpur Sikri nearby.

Taj Mahal (p66)
Simply the most beautiful building in the world.

Delhi (p35)
Eight historical empires have bequeathed Delhi a plethora of forts, mosques, temples and more.

Red Fort (pictured; p38)
A superb Mughal palace in a citadel.

Ellora (p144)
Ellora's stunning cave temples were carved out of sheer rock faces over centuries by monks.

Kailasa Temple (p146)
The world's largest monolithic rock sculpture.

DICKYSINGH / GETTY IMAGES ©

Outdoors

Hiking the Himalaya, searching for tigers in dense jungles or swimming in warm tropical seas – your options for immersion in nature are endless.

Manali (p245)
The adventure capital of the north: trekking, paragliding, skiing, rafting, biking – it's all here.

Hamta Pass Trek (p249)
A four-day hike from the Kullu Valley to Chatru.

Ranthambhore Tiger Reserve (pictured; p114)
These wild jungles offer some of the best tiger sightings and plenty of other wildlife, too.

Jeep Safaris (p115)
Views are best from 4WD jeeps; book ahead.

Goa (p155)
Legendary for beach-based hedonism, Goa's sunset-facing strands also offer plenty of water sports.

Palolem (p167)
Goa's safest swimming beach.

Cuisine

From kebabs to curries and thalis, India is a spicy riot of flavours, whether you're eating at a street stall or an elegant modern restaurant.

AJP / SHUTTERSTOCK ©

Mumbai (p117)
Flavours from across India meet and complement global culinary trends.

Masala Library (p133)
Cutting-edge modern Indian cuisine.

Delhi (p35)
The capital proffers an increasingly fine and diverse choice of regional and international food.

Bukhara (p54)
Meaty Northwest Frontier cuisine.

Kerala (p173)
With coconuts, spices and rich seafood pickings, this state has a flavourful cuisine.

Villa Maya (p185)
Superb seafood in a Dutch mansion.

Spirituality

The devotion on display in sacred sites and the spectacle of colourful festivals show the deep spiritual current running through most Indians.

CHERYLRAMALHO / SHUTTERSTOCK ©

Varanasi (p229)
Hindus come to wash away their sins, achieve *moksha* (liberation from rebirth) and cremate the dead.

The Ghats (pictured; p232)
Washing and cremating by the Ganges.

McLeod Ganj (p258)
Home to the Dalai Lama and Tibetans in exile, this town has a strong Buddhist vibe.

Tsuglagkhang Complex (p259)
Two Tibetan temples and a monastery.

Delhi (p35)
Delhi is adorned with many architecturally superb and atmospheric places of worship.

Hazrat Nizam-ud-din Dargah (p48)
Shrine of a Sufi saint.

Plan Your Trip
Essential India

PIKOSO.KZ / SHUTTERSTOCK ©

Activities

With fantastic variations in landscape, terrain, topography and climate, India presents endless options for a host of outdoor activities. In the mountainous north, you can go trekking, paragliding, skiing, rafting and mountaineering. In India's many protected areas, you can take jungle safaris seeking tigers, elephants, leopards, birds and other wildlife. Along the southern beaches you can go diving, surfing, kayaking, swimming or dolphin-spotting, and in Kerala you can cruise inland waterways on houseboats. And in this birthplace of yoga and ayurveda, there are innumerable opportunities to practise different forms of yoga, meditation and healing.

Shopping

India's exuberant bazaars and tantalising shops offer a treasure trove of goodies, including fabulously patterned textiles, finely crafted woodwork, chunky silver bangles, delicate gemstone jewellery and a tremendous mix of village creations. The array of arts and handicrafts is vast, with every region – sometimes every village – having its own unique traditions.

Note that government-run emporiums, fair-trade cooperatives, department stores and modern shopping centres charge fixed prices. Anywhere else you may need to bargain, as initial asking prices can be highly inflated.

The first 'rule' to haggling is don't show too much interest in an item. Second, resist purchasing the first thing that takes your fancy. Wander around several shops and check their prices. Decide how much you would be happy paying, and then express a casual interest. If you have no idea of the going rate, try slashing the asking price by half. From there, you and the vendor can work up and down in small increments until you reach a deal. You'll find that many shopkeepers lower their so-called 'final price' if you head out of the store saying you'll 'think about it'.

GREY COLOR / SHUTTERSTOCK ©

Eating

India serves food suited to every palate and pocket. From sizzling street food stands, where crowds wait impatiently for freshly prepared batches of sensational snacks, to fantastic fine-dining restaurants where desserts are brought out on a bed of dry ice –the country has it all. In between is a mass of regular eateries churning out honed-for-generations specialities. Restaurants in main cities and tourism hubs usually embrace a range of international as well as Indian cuisines. This is perhaps the world's best country for vegetarian travel, with tasty, nourishing, meat-free food available virtually everywhere.

Drinking & Nightlife

There's a wide choice of bars and nightclubs in India's large cities, catering to a glamorous mix of local men and women. However, in many smaller towns, the only nightlife you're likely to find is the possibility of drinking alcohol at a restaurant, if that, and any bars will be patronised only by men.

★ Best Indian Meals

Bukhara (p54)

Indian Accent (p55)

Peshawri (p122)

Trishna (p123)

Villa Maya (p185)

Entertainment

Cultural events featuring music, dance and theatre, and more-contemporary live-music gigs mostly take place in larger cities. Entertainment in smaller places centres on the year-round whirl of festivals, with music, costumes, parades and dance. Annual festivals featuring Indian classical dance and music also happen in many places.

From left: Jewel boxes; thali.

Plan Your Trip
Month by Month

GSK919 / SHUTTERSTOCK ©

January

Post-monsoon cool lingers, with downright cold in the mountains. Pleasant weather and several festivals make it a popular time to travel (book ahead!).

Republic Day

Republic Day commemorates the founding of the Republic of India on 26 January 1950. The biggest celebrations are in Delhi, which holds a huge military parade along Rajpath, and the Beating of the Retreat ceremony three days later.

February

A good time to be in India, with balmy weather in most non-mountainous areas.

Carnival in Goa

The four-day party preceding Lent is particularly big in Goa. Sabado Gordo (Fat Saturday) starts it off with elaborate parades, and the revelry continues with street parties, concerts and general merry-making. Can also fall in March.

Taj Mahotsav

This 10-day carnival of culture, cuisine and crafts is Agra's biggest party. Held at Shilpgram, the festival features more than 400 craft makers from all over India, a potpourri of folk and classical music and dance, and enough regional food to induce a curry coma.

March

The last month of the travel season, March is full-on hot in most of the country, with rains starting in the Northeast.

Holi

One of North India's most ecstatic festivals; Hindus celebrate the beginning of spring according to the lunar calendar by throwing coloured water and *gulal* (powder) at anyone within range. Upcoming dates: 9 March 2020, 28 March 2021.

Above: Grand Parade, Carnival, Goa

AMIT KG / SHUTTERSTOCK ©

Wildlife Watching

With water sources drying out, animals venture into the open to find refreshment: your chance to spot elephants, deer and, if you're lucky, tigers and leopards. Visit www.sanctuaryasia.com for detailed info.

April

The heat has officially arrived in most places, which means you can get deals and avoid tourist crowds. It's peak time for visiting Darjeeling.

Easter

The Christian holiday marking the Crucifixion and Resurrection of Jesus Christ is celebrated simply in Christian communities with prayer and good food, particularly in Goa and Kerala. Upcoming dates for Easter Sunday: 12 April 2020, 4 April 2021.

Rama's Birthday

During Rama Navami, which lasts anywhere from one to nine days, Hindus celebrate Rama's birth with processions, music, fasting and feasting, and enactments of scenes from the Ramayana.

★ Best Festivals

Holi, February or March

Ganesh Chaturthi, August or September

Onam, August or September

Navratri & Dussehra, September or October

Diwali, October or November

May

It's hot almost everywhere. Hill stations are hopping, though, and in the mountains it's premonsoon trekking season.

Eid al-Fitr

Muslims celebrate the end of Ramadan with three days of festivities. Prayers, shopping, gift-giving and, for women and girls,

Above: Military parade on Republic Day, Delhi

mehndi (henna designs) may all be part of the celebrations. Upcoming dates: 24 May 2020, 13 May 2021.

August

Monsoon is going strong. Tropical areas such as Kerala and Goa feature lush, green jungle, and it's often raining only a few hours a day.

Independence Day

This public holiday on 15 August commemorates India's independence from Britain in 1947. The biggest celebrations are in Delhi, where the Prime Minister addresses the nation from the Red Fort.

Krishna's Birthday

Janmastami celebrations range from fasting to *puja* (prayers), and offering sweets to drawing elaborate *rangoli* (rice-paste designs) outside the home. Upcoming dates: 11 August 2020, 30 August 2021.

Onam

Onam is Kerala's biggest cultural event, when the entire state celebrates the golden age of mythical King Mahabali for 10 days. Upcoming dates: 30 August 2020, 21 August 2021.

September

The rain is now petering out (with temperatures still relatively high). The second trekking season begins mid-month in the Himalaya.

Ganesh's Birthday

Hindus celebrate the 10-day Ganesh Chaturthi – the celebration of the birth of the much-loved elephant-headed god – with verve, particularly in Mumbai. Clay idols of Ganesh are ceremonially immersed in rivers, tanks (reservoirs) or the sea. Upcoming dates: 22 August 2020, 10 September 2021.

October

The travel season starts to kick off in earnest. October heralds giant festivals and mostly good weather.

Navratri

The exuberant Hindu 'Festival of Nine Nights' leading up to Dussehra celebrates the goddess Durga in all her incarnations. Upcoming dates: 17 October 2020, 7 October 2021.

Dussehra

Colourful Dussehra celebrates the victory of the Hindu god Rama over the demon king Ravana and the triumph of good over evil. Mysuru brims over with a lavish carnival. Upcoming dates: 25 October 2020, 14 October 2021.

November

The climate is blissful in most places – hot but not uncomfortably so – but the southern monsoon is sweeping Kerala.

Diwali (Festival of Lights)

In the lunar month of Kartika, Hindus celebrate Diwali for five days. On the auspicious day, people exchange gifts, light fireworks, and light lamps to welcome Lord Rama home from exile. Upcoming dates: 14 November 2020, 4 November 2021.

Film Fiesta

Held in Goa in late November, the International Film Festival of India – the country's largest film festival – draws Bollywood's finest for premieres, parties, screenings and ceremonies. See https://iffigoa.org for details.

December

December is peak tourist season for a reason: you're guaranteed glorious weather (except for the chilly mountains), the humidity's low, the mood is festive and the beach rocks.

Camel Safaris

The cool winter is the time to mount a camel and ride through the Rajasthani desert. Setting out from Jaisalmer, you can explore the Thar Desert and sleep under a sky full of stars.

Plan Your Trip
Get Inspired

Read

Midnight's Children (1981) Salman Rushdie's allegory about Independence and Partition.

A Fine Balance (1995) Rohinton Mistry's beautifully written, tragic tale set in Mumbai.

White Tiger (2008) Aravind Adiga's novel about class struggle in globalised India.

A Suitable Boy (1993) Vikram Seth's opus of romance, family secrets and political intrigue.

Shantaram (2003) Gregory David Roberts' vivid experiences of his life in India. A traveller favourite!

The God of Small Things (1997) Poignant tale of passion and caste in Kerala, by Arundhati Roy.

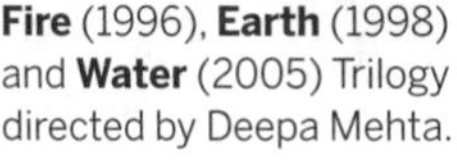

Watch

Fire (1996), **Earth** (1998) and **Water** (2005) Trilogy directed by Deepa Mehta.

Pather Panchali (1955) Haunting masterpiece from Satyajit Ray.

Pyaasa (Thirsty; 1957) and **Kaagaz Ke Phool** (Paper Flowers; 1959) For a taste of Guru Dutt nostalgia.

Gandhi (1982) Richard Attenborough classic starring Ben Kingsley as Gandhi.

Newton (2017) Brilliant indie spanning democracy, bureaucracy and insurgency in tribal India, by Amit V. Masurkar.

Dhobi Ghat (2011) Understated, absorbing tale touching on many levels of Mumbai and Indian life, directed by Kiran Rao.

Listen

Taal (AR Rahman; 1999) Feel-good Bollywood music.

Aashiqui (Nadeem-Shravan; 1990) Filmi romance with a *ghazal* twist.

Sajda (Jagjit Singh and Lata Mangeshkar; 1987) Haunting, beautiful *ghazal* devotional songs.

Live at the Monterey International Pop Festival (Ravi Shankar; 1967) A stellar performance from India's sitar maestro.

Call of the Valley (Shivkumar Sharma, Brij Bhushan Kabra and Hariprasad Chaurasia; 1967) Soulful strains evoking rural life in Kashmir.

Afternoon Ragas (Nikhil Banerjee; 1970) Moody music by yet another sitar heavyweight.

Above: Chhatrapati Shivaji Maharaj Terminus, Mumbai (p129)

Plan Your Trip

Five-Day Itineraries

Northern Magic

This action-packed three-city trip combines India's historic and modern capital Delhi, with Agra, home of the glorious Taj Mahal, and the holy city of Varanasi – India at its most intense.

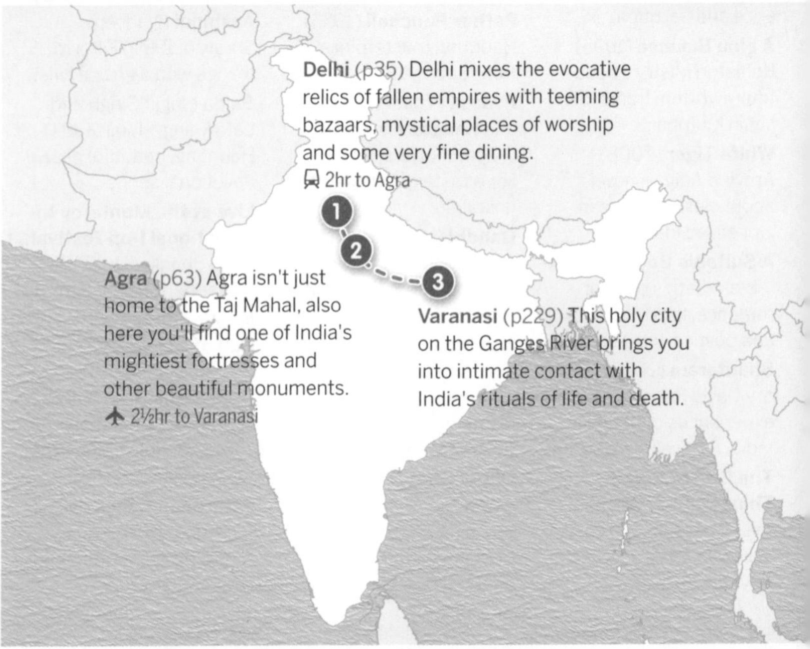

Delhi (p35) Delhi mixes the evocative relics of fallen empires with teeming bazaars, mystical places of worship and some very fine dining.

2hr to Agra

Agra (p63) Agra isn't just home to the Taj Mahal, also here you'll find one of India's mightiest fortresses and other beautiful monuments.

2½hr to Varanasi

Varanasi (p229) This holy city on the Ganges River brings you into intimate contact with India's rituals of life and death.

Rajasthan Ramble

Head out west to the colourful state of Rajasthan, realm of maharajas, palaces, tiger-prowled jungles and massive desert forts, where history can never quite be disentangled from legend.

1 Jaipur (p99) Jaipur's city palace and magnificent Amber Fort preside over a city that offers some of India's best shopping.
3hr to Sawai Madhopur

2 Ranthambhore National Park (p114) Jungle safaris with serious chances of sighting wild tigers.
3hr to Jaipur, then 12hr to Jaisalmer

3 Jaisalmer (p85) The fabled Jaisalmer Fort rises like a mirage out of deserts whose mystique is best explored on a camel safari.

Plan Your Trip
10-Day Itinerary

Southern Odyssey

Soak up Mumbai's city vibes, take a trip to the ancient rock-cut architecture of Ellora, then head south for a spot of beach bliss in Goa, before moving on down to Kerala for a backwaters cruise from Alappuzha (Alleppey).

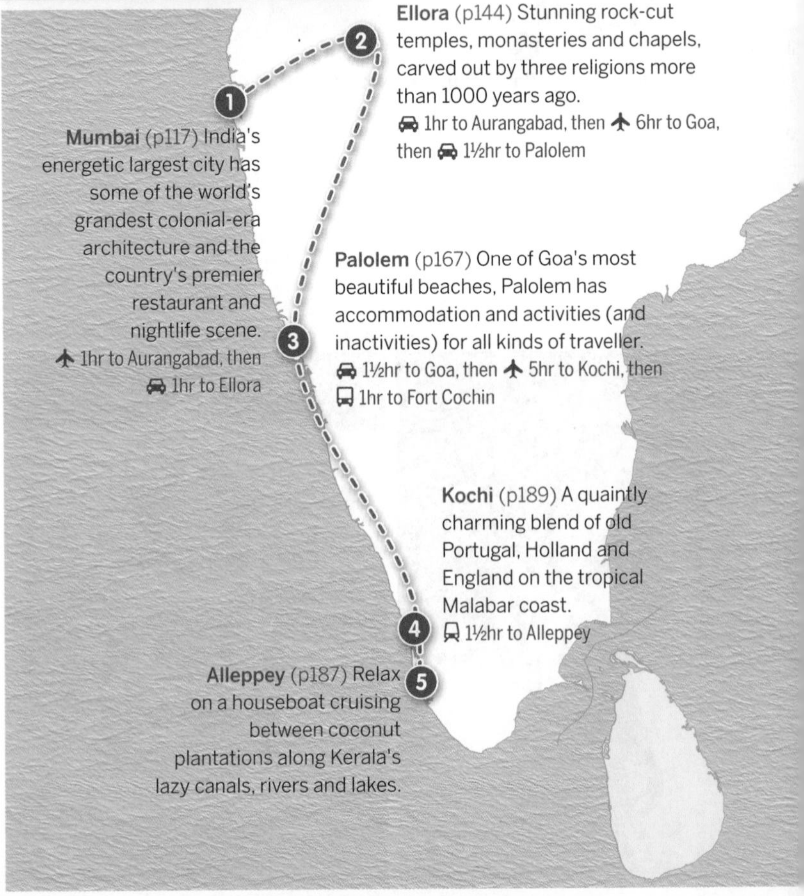

Ellora (p144) Stunning rock-cut temples, monasteries and chapels, carved out by three religions more than 1000 years ago.
1hr to Aurangabad, then 6hr to Goa, then 1½hr to Palolem

Mumbai (p117) India's energetic largest city has some of the world's grandest colonial-era architecture and the country's premier restaurant and nightlife scene.
1hr to Aurangabad, then 1hr to Ellora

Palolem (p167) One of Goa's most beautiful beaches, Palolem has accommodation and activities (and inactivities) for all kinds of traveller.
1½hr to Goa, then 5hr to Kochi, then 1hr to Fort Cochin

Kochi (p189) A quaintly charming blend of old Portugal, Holland and England on the tropical Malabar coast.
1½hr to Alleppey

Alleppey (p187) Relax on a houseboat cruising between coconut plantations along Kerala's lazy canals, rivers and lakes.

2

FROM LEFT: LU YANG / SHUTTERSTOCK ©; DAN BACIU / SHUTTERSTOCK ©; OLGA_V / SHUTTERSTOCK ©

Two-Week Itinerary

Mountains, Cities & Beaches

Internal flights can get you quickly around India and maximise your time in its most special destinations, from the Himalaya to the southern beaches via cities of the Ganges plain.

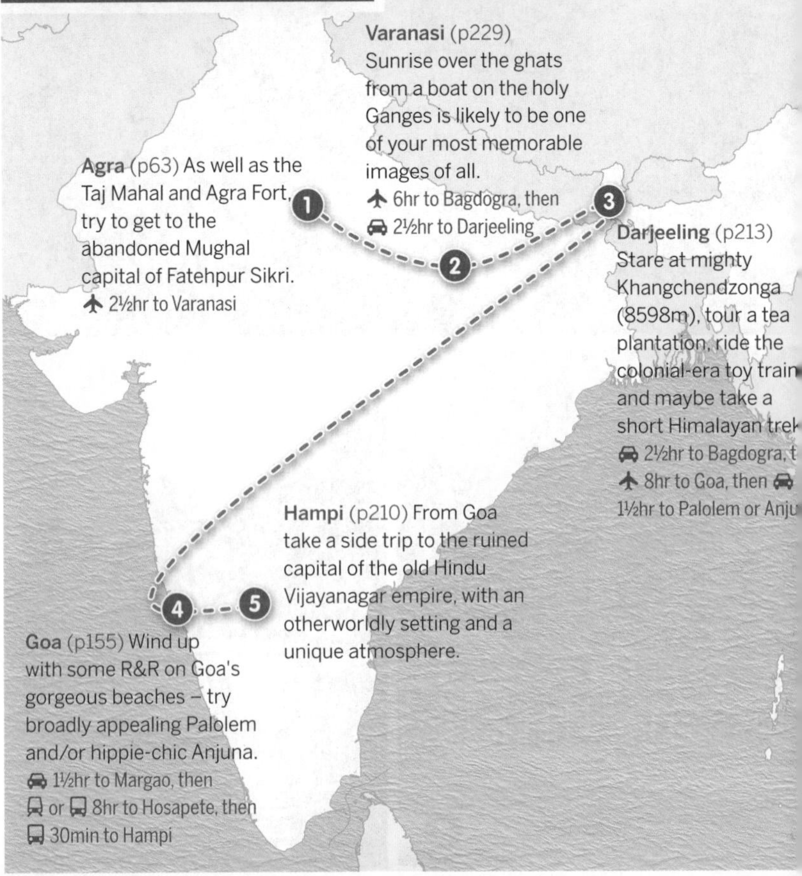

Agra (p63) As well as the Taj Mahal and Agra Fort, try to get to the abandoned Mughal capital of Fatehpur Sikri.
✈ 2½hr to Varanasi

Varanasi (p229) Sunrise over the ghats from a boat on the holy Ganges is likely to be one of your most memorable images of all.
✈ 6hr to Bagdogra, then 🚗 2½hr to Darjeeling

Darjeeling (p213) Stare at mighty Khangchendzonga (8598m), tour a tea plantation, ride the colonial-era toy train and maybe take a short Himalayan trek
🚗 2½hr to Bagdogra, t
✈ 8hr to Goa, then 🚗 1½hr to Palolem or Anju

Goa (p155) Wind up with some R&R on Goa's gorgeous beaches – try broadly appealing Palolem and/or hippie-chic Anjuna.
🚗 1½hr to Margao, then 🚌 or 🚆 8hr to Hosapete, then 🚌 30min to Hampi

Hampi (p210) From Goa take a side trip to the ruined capital of the old Hindu Vijayanagar empire, with an otherworldly setting and a unique atmosphere.

2

FROM LEFT: CHRIS PIASON / SHUTTERSTOCK ©, ANANDOART / GETTY IMAGES ©, TRAVELWILD / SHUTTERSTOCK ©

3

5

Plan Your Trip
Family Travel

FOTOSUNNY / SHUTTERSTOCK ©

Fascinating and thrilling: India will be even more astounding for children than for their wide-eyed parents. Its scents, sights and sounds make for an unforgettable adventure and one that most kids will take in their stride.

You (and your kids) may have to get used to being the centre of attention. Locals will thrill at taking a photograph beside your bouncing baby. If this becomes tiring or disconcerting, you can always politely decline.

On the Road

- Indian travel can be arduous at times. Plan easy, fun days to break or follow longer journeys.
- Pack plenty of diversions (iPads or laptops with downloaded movies, audiobooks, old-fashioned story books, local toys).
- If you're hiring a car and driver (a sensible, flexible option) and require safety capsules, child restraints or booster seats, bring these with you or make this absolutely clear to the hiring company as early as possible. If necessary, don't be afraid to tell your driver to slow down and drive responsibly.

Fun Forms of Transport

Autorickshaw Bump thrillingly along in these child-scale vehicles.

Toy Train to Darjeeling Ride the cute little steam train past colourful mountain villages and rushing waterfalls.

Houseboat, Alappuzha (Alleppey) Go boating along Kerala's beautiful backwaters, with interesting stops en route.

Eating

- In regions such as Rajasthan, Himachal Pradesh, Goa, Kerala, or the big cities, you'll find it easy to feed your brood. Major cities and more touristy towns always offer a range of international cuisines.
- Easy portable snacks such as bananas, samosas, *puri* (puffy dough pockets), white-bread sandwiches and packaged biscuits are widely available.

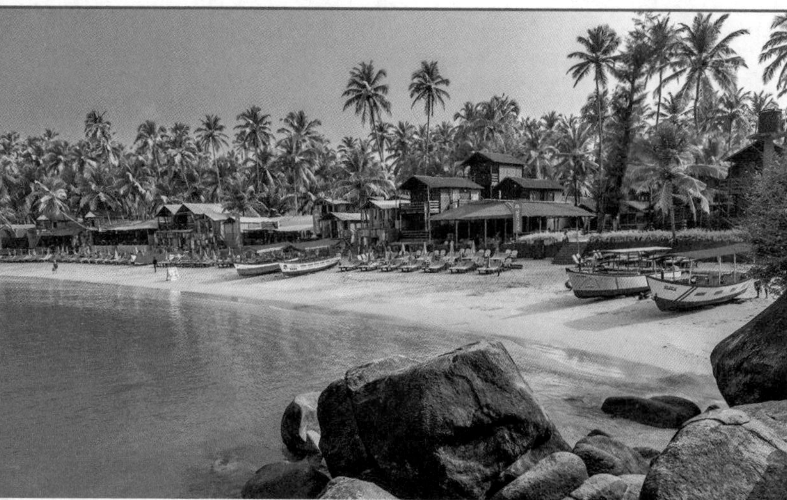

NEJDET DUZEN / SHUTTERSTOCK ©

- Many children will delight in paneer (unfermented cheese) dishes, simple dhal (mild lentil curry), buttered naan (tandoori bread) and pilau (rice dish) – and few can resist the finger food fun of a vast South Indian dosa (paper-thin lentil-flour pancake).

★ Best for Kids

Camel Safaris (p90)

Ranthambhore National Park (p114)

Palolem, Goa (p167)

Taj Mahal (p66)

Kerala houseboats (p176)

Health

- Access to healthcare is better in traveller-frequented parts of the country, where it's almost always easy to track down a doctor at short notice.
- Diarrhoea can be very serious in young children. Seek medical help if it is persistent or accompanied by fever; rehydration is essential.

What to Take

You can get these items in many parts of India, too:

- Nappies, nappy cream, extra bottles, wet wipes, infant formula and canned, bottled or rehydratable food.
- A fold-up baby bed or the lightest possible travel cot you can find (hotel cots may prove precarious).
- A backpack is a better option than a stroller/pushchair, as ootpaths are often scarce.
- Insect repellent, mosquito nets, hats, sunscreen.

From left: Masala dosa with chutneys; Palolem Beach (p162), Goa

DMITRY RUKHLENKO / SHUTTERSTOCK ©

DELHI

AL-JADEED
M.MURSALEE
& SONS

M.S. Collection
Fancy Suits, Dupatta & Dress Material
1354, BAZAR CHITLI QABAR JAMA MASJID DELHI-6

0 4 km
0 2 miles

Connaught Place
Colonial-era colonnade with midrange shops, eateries and bars, wrapped around a chaotic-feeling central hub.

New Delhi
Tree-lined boulevards, expensive real estate, parks, upscale hotels and grand, Raj-era buildings.

South Delhi
A nice escape from the mayhem of the city centre, with the boutique shops, cafes and restaurants of Hauz Khas and Shahpur Jat Village.

Indira Gandhi International Airport

QUTAB MINAR COMPLEX

ndira Gandhi International Airport (p58)

Arriving in Delhi

Indira Gandhi International Airport Terminal 1: Indian low-cost airlines. Terminal 3: other flights. Fixed-price taxis, the metro and AC buses all run into the city.

There are three main railway stations:

New Delhi station Near Paharganj.

Delhi station (Delhi Junction) in Old Delhi.

Nizamuddin station South of Sunder Nagar, southeast of the centre.

Where to Stay

Delhi's innumerable hotels range from wallet-friendly dives to lavish five-star properties. Wherever you are on the scale, it's wise to book ahead and tell the hotel your expected arrival time. Most places offer airport pickup, if arranged in advance. See Where to Stay (p61) for more information on the city's main accommodation areas.

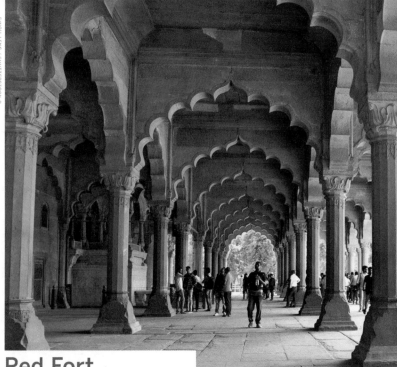

SINGH_LENS / SHUTTERSTOCK ©

Red Fort

The defining monument of Mughal Delhi. The massive Red Fort still conjures up vivid pictures of Mughal splendour at its peak, despite the depredations of time and human spoils.

Founded by Emperor Shah Jahan and surrounded by a magnificent 18m-high wall, this fort took 10 years to construct (1638–48) and is rumoured to have had the decapitated bodies of prisoners built into the foundations for luck. It once overlooked the Yamuna River, which has now shrunk to some distance away. A tree-lined waterway, known as *nahr-i-bihisht* (river of paradise), once ran out of the fort and along Chandni Chowk, fed by the Yamuna.

The last Mughal emperor Bahadur Shah Zafar was flushed from the Red Fort in 1857, tried seven months later by the British, and exiled to Burma (Myanmar) for his role in the First War of Independence. The British then destroyed buildings and gardens inside the fortress walls and replaced them with barrack blocks for the colonial army.

Great For...

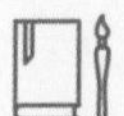

☑ Don't Miss

Diwan-i-Khas, a pavilion described by past poets as paradise on earth.

Interior of Red Fort

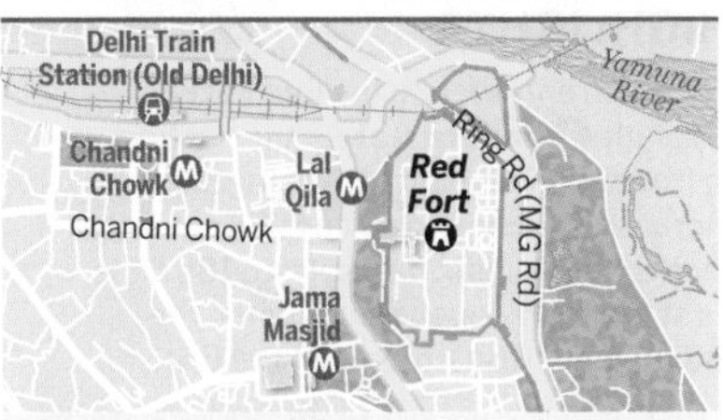

Need to Know

Map p50; Indian/foreigner ₹50/600, with card payment ₹35/550, video ₹25, audio guide in Hindi/English or Korean ₹69/118; dawn-dusk Tue-Sun; Chandni Chowk

Take a Break

Head to the Gali Parathe Wali (p53) lane for fresh *paratha* (flaky bread).

★ Top Tip

The audio-guide tour, by the acclaimed Narrowcasters, brings the site to life.

Entering through the **Lahore Gate** (Map p50; included in Red Fort), you pass through **Chatta Chowk** (Covered Bazaar; Map p50), formerly an imperial bazaar glittering with silk and jewels for royal women. Today's wares are rather more mundane souvenirs. Eastward, the arched **Naubat Khana** (Map p50) or 'Drum House' once accommodated royal musicians and served as parking for royal horses and elephants. Beyond is the **Diwan-i-Am** (Map p50), the arcaded sandstone hall of public audience, where the emperor greeted guests from a throne on the marble platform, which is backed by fine pietra-dura (inlaid stone) work that features Orpheus, incongruously, and is thought to be Florentine.

South of the public area of the Diwan-i-Khas, you reach the private royal quarters. The emperor lived and slept in the **Khas Mahal** (Special Palace; Map p50), shielded from prying eyes by lace-like carved marble screens. The cooling *nahr-i-behisht* flowed through here to an elegant lotus-shaped fountain in the **Rang Mahal** (Palace of Colour; Map p50), home to the emperor's chief wife. The **Mumtaz Mahal** (Map p50) is thought to have been built for Arjumand Banu Begum (also known as Mumtaz Mahal), the wife for whom Shah Jahan built the Taj Mahal.

The wonderfully decorated **Diwan-i-Khas** (Map p50), or Hall of Private Audience, was used for bowing and scraping to the emperor.

Further north, the **Shahi Burj** (Emperor's Tower; Map p50), a three-storey octagonal tower, was Shah Jahan's favoured work-place, where he planned the running of his empire. In front are the remains of an elegant formal garden.

Red Fort

HIGHLIGHTS

The main entrance to the Red Fort is through **1 Lahore Gate** – the bastion in front of it was built by Aurangzeb for increased security. You can still see bullet marks on the gate, dating from 1857, the First War of Independence, when the Indian army rose up against the British.

Walk through the Chatta Chowk (Covered Bazaar), which once sold silks and jewellery to the nobility; beyond it lies Naubat Khana, a part white-plaster, part russet-red building, which houses Hathi Pol (Elephant Gate), so called because visitors used to dismount from their elephants or horses here as a sign of respect. From here it's straight on to the **2 Diwan-i-Am**, the Hall of Public Audiences.

Behind this are the private palaces, the **3 Khas Mahal** and the **4 Diwan-i-Khas**. Entry to this Hall of Private Audiences, the fort's most expensive building, was only permitted to the officials of state. The artificial stream the Nahr-i-Bihisht (Stream of Paradise) used to run a cooling channel of water through all these buildings.

Nearby is the **5 Moti Masjid (Pearl Mosque)** and south is the Mumtaz Mahal, which before renovations housed the Museum of Archaeology, or you can head north, where the Red Fort gardens are dotted by palatial pavilions and old British barracks. Here you'll find the **6 Baoli**, a spookily deserted water tank, though you can no longer climb down into it. Another five minutes' walk – across a road, then a railway bridge – brings you to the island fortress of Salimgarh.

(Note that many of the fort buildings were closed for renovations at the time of research, but the pavilions can be viewed from outside, and most structures are expected to reopen once the renovations are complete.)

TOP TIPS

- To avoid crowds, get here early or late in the day; avoid weekends and public holidays.
- Bring the fort to life with the excellent audio guide, available at the ticket office.

Baoli
The Red Fort step well is seldom visited and is a hauntingly deserted place, even more so when you consider its chambers were used as cells by the British from August 1942.
Salimgarh
6
Museum on India's Struggle for Freedom (closed for renovations)
Chatta Chowk
Lahore Gate
Lahore Gate is particularly significant, as it was here that Jawaharlal Nehru raised the first tricolour flag of independent India in 1947.
1

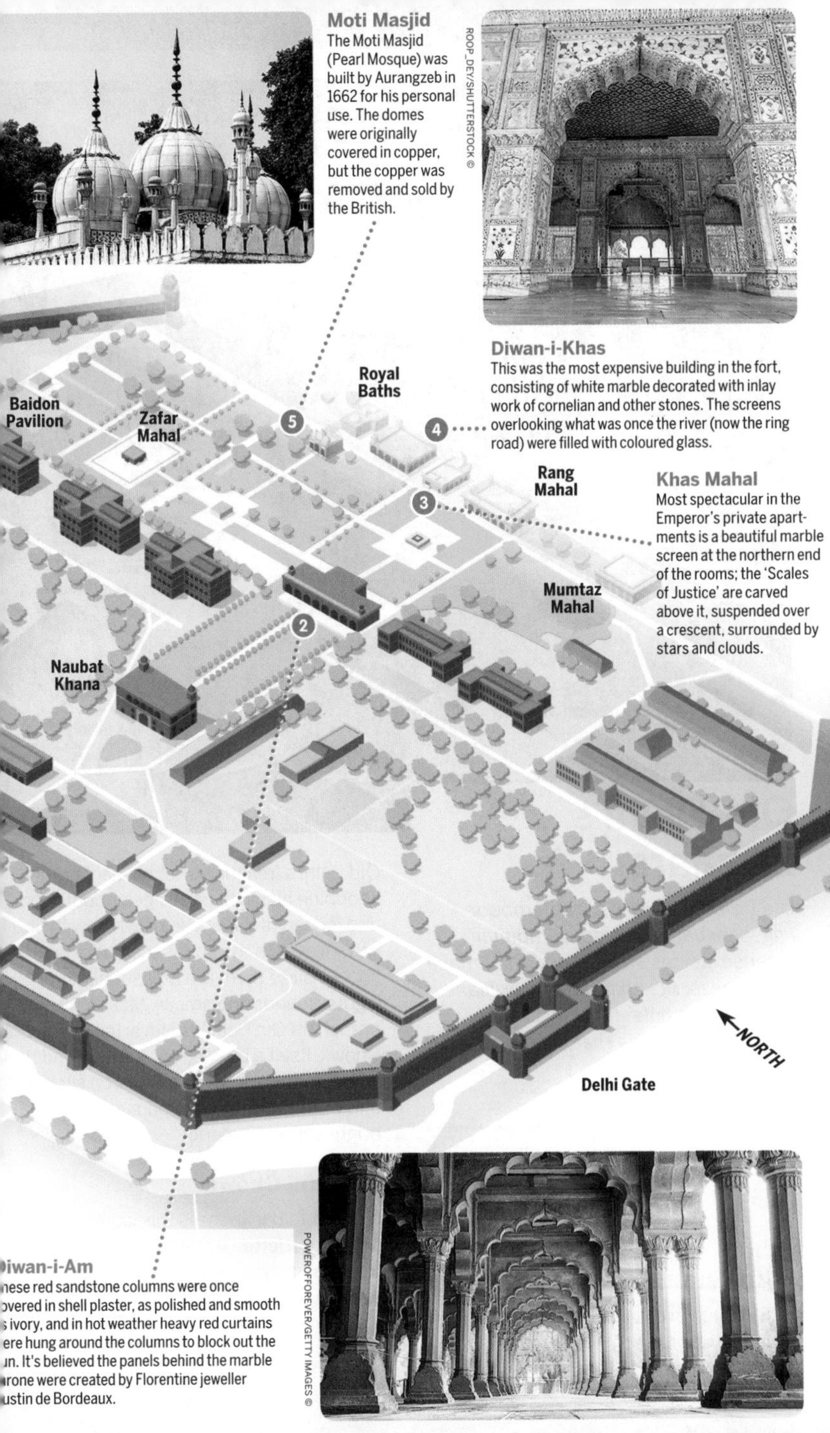

Moti Masjid
The Moti Masjid (Pearl Mosque) was built by Aurangzeb in 1662 for his personal use. The domes were originally covered in copper, but the copper was removed and sold by the British.

Diwan-i-Khas
This was the most expensive building in the fort, consisting of white marble decorated with inlay work of cornelian and other stones. The screens overlooking what was once the river (now the ring road) were filled with coloured glass.

Khas Mahal
Most spectacular in the Emperor's private apartments is a beautiful marble screen at the northern end of the rooms; the 'Scales of Justice' are carved above it, suspended over a crescent, surrounded by stars and clouds.

iwan-i-Am
nese red sandstone columns were once overed in shell plaster, as polished and smooth s ivory, and in hot weather heavy red curtains ere hung around the columns to block out the un. It's believed the panels behind the marble rone were created by Florentine jeweller ustin de Bordeaux.

Old Delhi's Bazaars

Old Delhi's bazaars are a bamboozling, sensual whirlwind, combining incense, spices strong enough to make you sneeze, rickshaw fumes, brilliant colours, and hole-in-the-wall shops packed with goods that shimmer and glitter.

Great For...

☑ Don't Miss

The sight of the giant jars of pickles and chutneys in the spice market.

Old Delhi's frenetic street bazaars are the shopping highlight of this neighbourhood, and indeed of Delhi. They sparkle with life, as well as with the goods they have on offe and a visit to them is a brilliant blend of sights, sounds and smells. Most of them branch off Old Delhi's main artery, Chandni Chowk, itself a busy street market, and the sell everything from embroidered slippers and wedding bangles to paper kites and bright yellow turmeric.

Chandni Chowk

Old Delhi's backbone is this iconic shopping strip, dotted by temples, snarled by traffic and crammed with stores selling everything from street food to clothing, electronics and break-as-soon-as-you-buy-them novelties.

Dried fruit shop, Chandni Chowk

EMAD ALJUMAH / GETTY IMAGES ©

Tiny bazaars lead off the main drag, so you can dive off and explore these small lanes, which glitter with jewellery, decorations, paper goods and more. For silver jewellery, head for **Dariba Kalan** (Map p50; approx 10am-8pm; M Lal Qila), the alley near the Sisganj Gurdwara. Off this lane, the **Kinari Bazaar** (Map p50; 11am-8pm; M Jama Masjid), literally 'trimmings market', is a blaze of colour famous for *zardozi* (gold embroidery), temple trim and wedding turbans.

Running south from the old Town Hall, **Nai Sarak** (Map p50; approx 10am-8pm; M Jama Masjid) is lined with stalls selling saris, shawls, chiffon and *lehengas* (long skirts with a waist cord), while nearby **Ballimaran** (Map p50; 10am-8pm; M Chandni Chowk) has sequinned slippers and fancy, curly-toed *jootis* (traditional slip-on shoes).

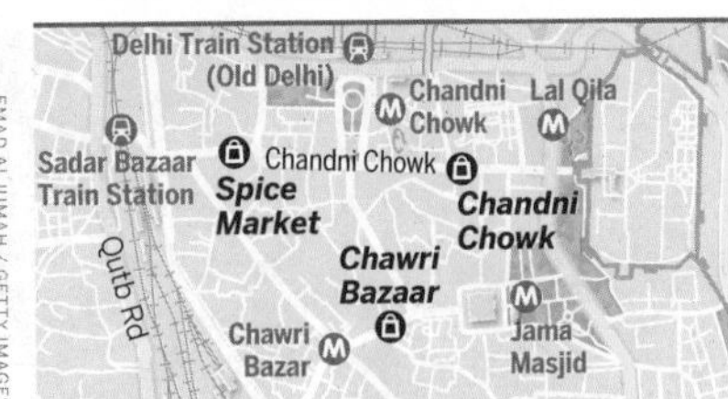

Need to Know

Most areas operate between 10am and 8pm. Some shops close on Sunday.

Take a Break

Stop into clean, bright **Haldiram's** (Map p50; 1454/2 Chandni Chowk; mains ₹70-180; 9.30am-10.45pm; M Chandni Chowk) for top-notch dosas (paper-thin lentil-flour pancakes).

★ Top Tip

Best visiting time is midmorning or late afternoon, when the streets are less busy.

Spice Market

Khari Baoli means 'salty step-well', but there's no well here any more, just Delhi's nose-numbing wholesale **Spice Market** (Gadodia Market; Map p50; Khari Baoli; M Chandni Chowk), ablaze with piles of scarlet-red chillis, ginger and turmeric roots, peppercorns, cumin, coriander seeds, cardamom, dried fruit and nuts. It seems little has changed here for centuries, as labourers hustle through the narrow lanes with huge sacks of herbs and spices on their heads. Deeper inside the market, it's so spicy that everyone can't help coughing and sneezing.

You can buy small packets of items, despite it being a wholesale market.

Chawri Bazaar

For gorgeous wrapping paper and wedding cards, head to **Chawri Bazaar** (Map p50; 10am-7pm; M Chawri Bazar), leading west from the Jama Masjid.

Cloister columns, Quwwat ul-Islam Mosque

Qutab Minar

If you only have time to visit one of Delhi's ancient ruins, make sure it's this complex centred on the soaring Qutab Minar, erected by Delhi's first Muslim sultan, Qutb-ud-din Aibak.

Great For...

☑ Don't Miss

The stonework on the walls of the **Quwwat-ul-Islam Masjid**.

The Afghan Qutb-ud-din Aibak raised the Qutab Minar in 1193 to proclaim his triumph over the Hindu city of Qila Rai Pithora (Lal Kot), which he razed to the ground to build the Qutab Minar and his nearby capital Mehrauli. Qutb-ud-din's successor Altamish is entombed in a magnificent sandstone-and-marble mausoleum covered in Islamic calligraphy, while Ala-ud-din Khilji's sprawling madrasa (Islamic college) and tomb (early 14th century) stand in ruins at the rear of the complex.

Qutab Minar

The Qutab Minar itself is an unmissable, soaring Afghan-style victory tower and minaret, ringed by intricately carved sandstone bands bearing verses from the Quran. It stands nearly 73m high and tapers from a 15m-diameter base to a mere 2.5m at

Qutab Minar

TUNART / GETTY IMAGES ©

Need to Know

Map p56; ☎011-26643856; Indian/foreigner ₹40/600, with card payment ₹35/550; ⏰dawn-dusk; Ⓜ Qutab Minar

Take a Break

Treat yourself to creative Mediterranean at surprising, stylish **Olive** (Map p56; ☎011-29574443; Bhulbhulaiya Rd, behind Qutab Minar, Mehrauli; pizza from ₹950, meze platters from ₹1500; ⏰noon-midnight; Ⓜ Qutab Minar).

★ Top Tip

For the most atmosphere, visit at dawn before the crowds arrive.

the top. Qutb-ud-din only completed the first of its five storeys before his unlucky death (impaled on his saddle while playing polo). His successors completed the job. The tower was struck by lightning in the 14th century, after which Feroz Shah had it repaired in marble.

Quwwat-ul-Islam Masjid

At the foot of the Qutab Minar stands the **Quwwat-ul-Islam Masjid** (Might of Islam Mosque; Map p56), the first mosque built in India. An inscription over its east gate states that it was constructed with materials obtained from demolishing '27 idolatrous temples'. Its walls are studded with sun disks, *shikharas* (spires) and other recognisable pieces of Hindu and Jain masonry.

In the courtyard stands a 6.7m-high **iron pillar** (Map p56) that is much more ancient than any of the surrounding monuments. It hasn't rusted in 1600 years, due to both the dry atmosphere and its incredible purity. The exquisite marble-and-sandstone Alai Darwaza gatehouse was added in 1310.

Alai Minar

Sultan Ala-ud-din Khilji wanted to build a second tower of victory, twice as high as Qutab Minar. Construction only reached the first level before the sultan died, and the project with him. The 27m-high plinth can be seen just north of the Qutab Minar.

Walking Tour: Lutyens' Delhi

This stroll takes you through the imperial city built to serve as British India's capital from 1911 onwards. It was designed by English architect Edwin Lutyens.

Start Connaught Place
Distance India Gate
Duration 3–4 hours

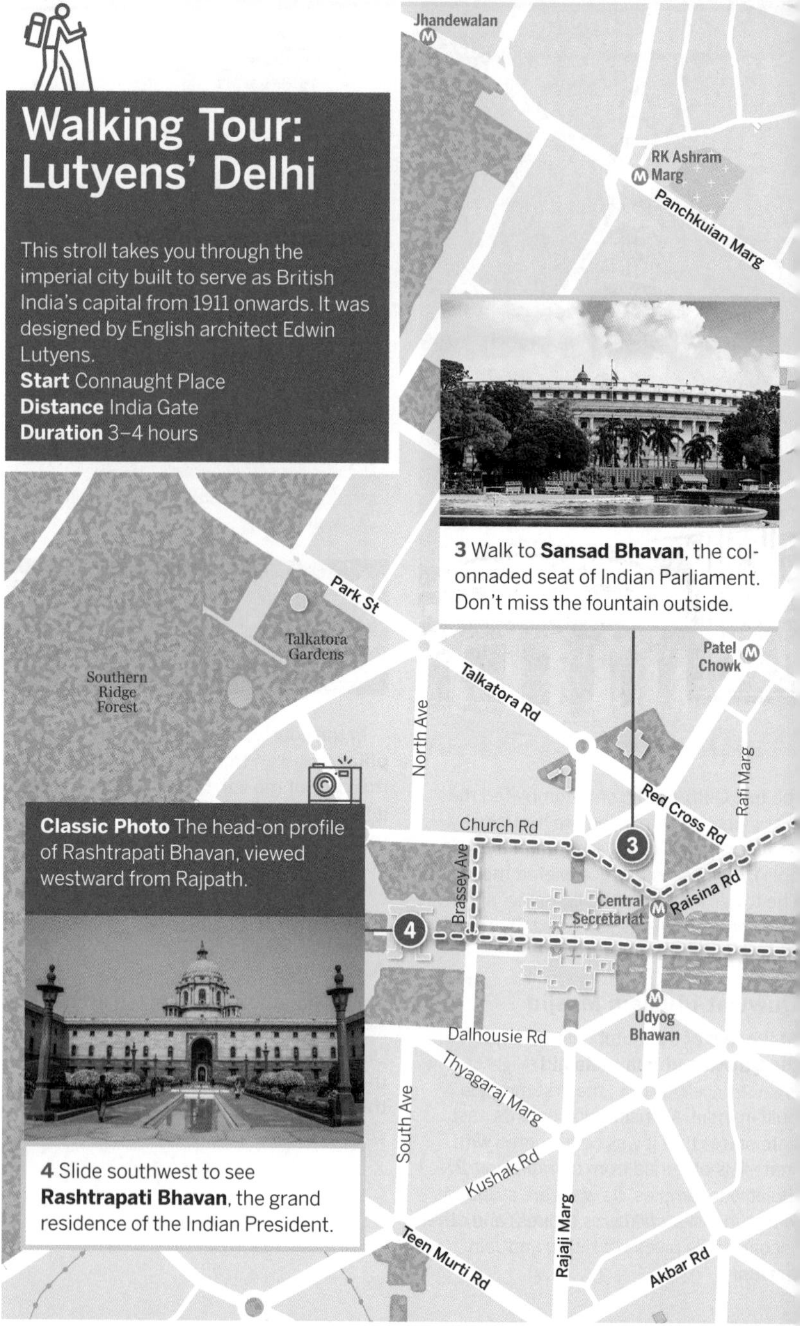

3 Walk to **Sansad Bhavan**, the colonnaded seat of Indian Parliament. Don't miss the fountain outside.

Classic Photo The head-on profile of Rashtrapati Bhavan, viewed westward from Rajpath.

4 Slide southwest to see **Rashtrapati Bhavan**, the grand residence of the Indian President.

Jhandewalan
RK Ashram Marg
Panchkuian Marg
Park St
Talkatora Gardens
Southern Ridge Forest
Talkatora Rd
North Ave
Patel Chowk
Rafi Marg
Red Cross Rd
Church Rd
Brassey Ave
Central Secretariat
Raisina Rd
Udyog Bhawan
Dalhousie Rd
Thyagaraj Marg
South Ave
Kushak Rd
Rajaji Marg
Teen Murti Rd
Akbar Rd

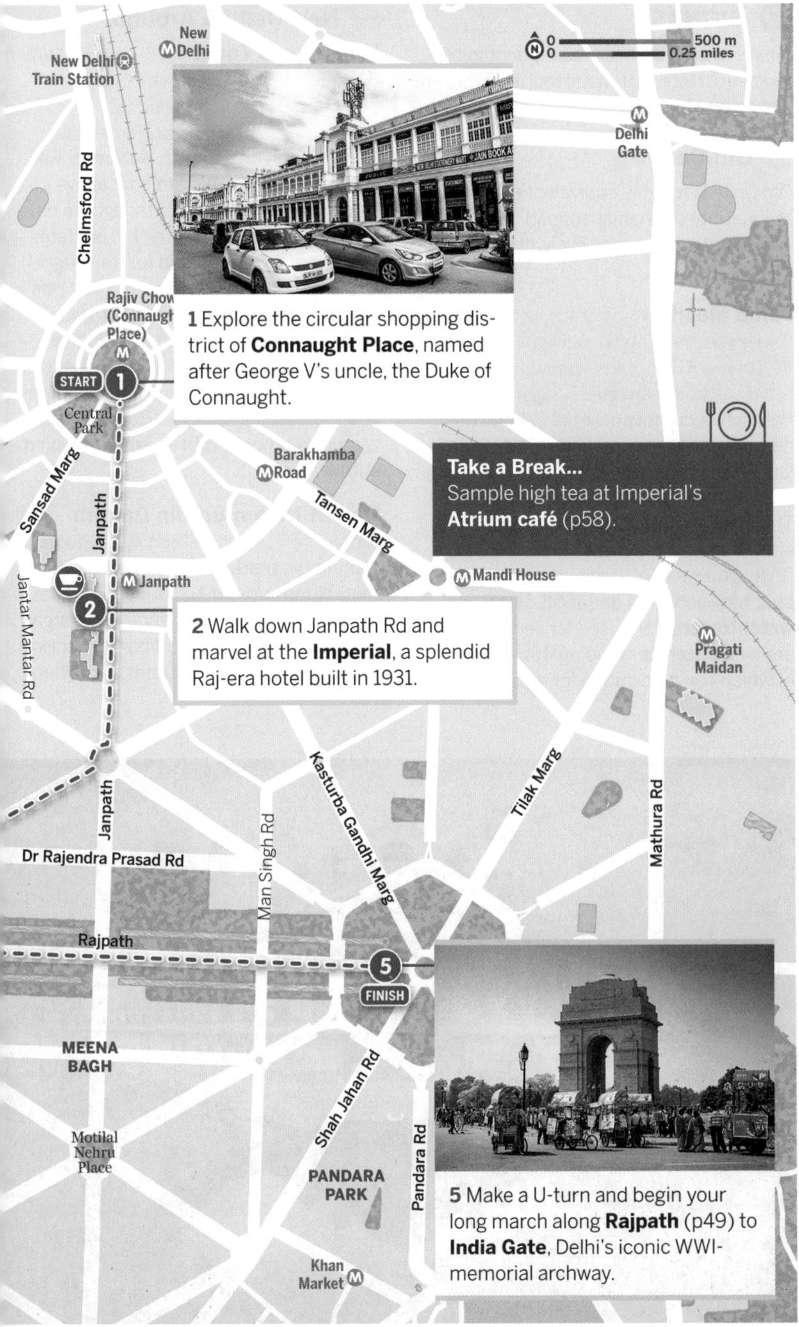

1 Explore the circular shopping district of **Connaught Place**, named after George V's uncle, the Duke of Connaught.

Take a Break...
Sample high tea at Imperial's **Atrium café** (p58).

2 Walk down Janpath Rd and marvel at the **Imperial**, a splendid Raj-era hotel built in 1931.

5 Make a U-turn and begin your long march along **Rajpath** (p49) to **India Gate**, Delhi's iconic WWI-memorial archway.

SIGHTS

Most sights in Delhi are easily accessible by metro. Note that many tourist sights are closed on Mondays.

Old Delhi

Old Delhi is roughly equivalent to the Mughal city of Shahjahanabad. The easiest way to get around is by cycle rickshaw or on foot.

Jama Masjid Mosque

(Friday Mosque; Map p50; camera & video each ₹300, tower ₹100; ⏲non-Muslims 8am-1hr before sunset, minaret 9am-5.30pm; Ⓜ Jama Masjid) A beautiful pocket of calm at the heart of Old Delhi's mayhem, the capital's largest mosque is built on a 10m elevation. It can hold a mind-blowing 25,000 people. The marble and red-sandstone structure, known also as the 'Friday Mosque', was Shah Jahan's final architectural triumph, built between 1644 and 1658. The four **watchtowers** were used for security. There are two **minarets** standing 40m high, one of which can be climbed for amazing views.

New Delhi & Around

Humayun's Tomb Monumen

(Map p55; Mathura Rd; Indian/foreigner ₹40/600, with car payment ₹35/550, video ₹25; ⏲dawn-dusk; Ⓜ JLN Stadium, Hazrat Nizam-uddin) Humayun's tomb is sublimely well proportioned, seeming to float above its symmetrical gardens. It's thought to have inspired the Taj Mahal, which it predates by 60 years. Constructed for the Mughal emperor in the mid-16th century by Haji Begum, Humayun's Persian-born wife, the tomb marries Persian and Mughal elements. The arched facade is inlaid with bands of white marble and red sandstone, and the building follows strict rules of Islamic geometry, with an emphasis on the number eight.

Hazrat Nizam-ud-din Dargah Shrine

(Map p55; off Lodi Rd; ⏲24hr; Ⓜ JLN Stadium) Visiting the marble shrine of Muslim Sufi saint Nizam-ud-din Auliya is Delhi's most mystical, magical experience. The dargah is hidden away in a tangle of bazaars selling rose petals, attars (perfumes) and offer-

Humayun's Tomb

ings, and on some evenings you can hear the *qawwali* (Sufi devotional singing), amid crowds of devotees. The ascetic Nizam-ud-din died in 1325 at the ripe old age of 92. His doctrine of tolerance made him popular not only with Muslims, but with adherents of other faiths, too.

Crafts Museum Museum

(Map p55; ☎011-23371641; Bhairon Marg; Indian/foreigner ₹20/200; ⏰10am-5pm Tue-Sun; Ⓜ Pragati Maidan) Much of this lovely museum is outside, including tree-shaded carvings and life-size examples of village huts from various regions of India. Displays celebrate the traditional crafts of India, with some beautiful textiles on display indoors, such as embroidery from Kashmir and cross-stitch from Punjab. Highlights include a huge wooden 18th-century temple chariot from Maharashtra. Artisans sell their products in the rear courtyard. The museum also includes the excellent Cafe Lota (p54) and a very good shop.

Rajpath Area

(Map p55; Ⓜ Central Secretariat) Rajpath (Kingsway) is a vast parade linking India Gate to the offices of the Indian government. Built on an imperial scale between 1914 and 1931, it was designed by Edwin Lutyens and Herbert Baker and underlined the ascendance of the British rulers. Yet just 16 years later, the Brits were out on their ears and Indian politicians were pacing the corridors of power.

National Museum Museum

(Map p55; ☎011-23019272; www.nationalmuseumindia.gov.in; Janpath; Indian/foreigner ₹20/650, camera ₹20/300; ⏰10am-6pm Tue-Sun, free guided tour 10.30am & 2.30pm Tue-Fri, 10.30am, 11.30am, 2.30pm & 3pm Sat & Sun; Ⓜ Udyog Bhawan) This glorious, if dusty, museum is full of treasures. Mind-bogglingly ancient, sophisticated figurines from the Harappan civilisation, almost 5000 years old, include the remarkable *Dancing Girl*, and there are also some fine ceramics from the even-older Nal civilisation. Other items include Buddha relics, exquisite jewellery, miniature paintings, medieval woodcarvings, textiles and musical instruments. Don't miss the immense, five-tier wooden temple chariot built in South India in the 19th century.

Gandhi Memorial

Gandhi Smriti (Map p55; ☎011-23012843; 5 Tees Jan Marg; ⏰10am-5pm Tue-Sun, closed 2nd Sat of month; Ⓜ Lok Kalyan Marg), the poignant memorial to Mahatma Gandhi, is in Birla House, where he was shot dead on the grounds by a Hindu zealot on 30 January 1948, after campaigning against intercommunal violence.

The house itself is where Gandhi spent his last 144 days. The exhibits include film footage, modern art, and rooms preserved just as Gandhi left them. The small clothes shop within the grounds sells garments made from *khadi*, homespun cotton that was championed by Gandhi during the Independence movement.

World Peace Gong, Gandhi Smriti
SAIKO3P / SHUTTERSTOCK ©

Lodi Garden Park

(Map p55; Lodi Rd; ⏰6am-8pm Oct-Mar, 5am-8pm Apr-Sep; Ⓜ Khan Market, Jor Bagh) Delhi's loveliest escape was originally named after the wife of the British Resident, Lady Willingdon, who had two villages cleared in 1936 in order to landscape a park containing the Lodi-era tombs. Today, these lush, tree-shaded gardens – a favoured getaway for Delhi's elite, local joggers and courting couples – help protect more than 100

Old Delhi
0 500 m
0 0.25 miles
Zorawar Singh Marg
Delhi Train Station (Old Delhi)
Prepaid Autorickshaws
Ring Rd (MG Rd)
Lothian Cemetery
Shyama Prasad (SP) Mukherjee Marg
Mahatma Gandhi Park
Chandni Chowk
Red Fort
Sadar Bazaar Train Station
Church Mission Rd
HC Sen Rd
Lal Qila
Khari Baoli
Chandni Chowk
Kinari Bazaar
Lal Kuan Bazaar Rd
Bazaars
Esplanade Rd
Qutb Rd
OLD DELHI
Nai Sarak
Chel Puri
Meena Bazaar
Netaji Subhash Park
Lambi Gali
Jama Masjid
Shanti Vana Rd
Car Parts Bazaar
Chawri Bazar
PARDA BAGH
Matya Mahal
Dakhni Rai St
Chitli Qabar Rd
Netaji Subhash Marg
DARYAGANJ
Arya Samaj St
Sitaram Bazaar
International Tourist Bureau
Daya Nand Rd
Prepaid Autorickshaw Booth
New Delhi
Hindi Park
Ansari Rd
Shim Tur (300m)
Asaf Ali Rd
New Delhi Train Station
Ramlila Grounds
Main Bazaar
Delhi Gate
Ansari Rd
Jawaharlal Nehru Marg
Chelmsford Rd
State Entry Rd
Bhavbuti Rd
Radial Rd 5
Basant Rd
Turkman Rd
Bahadur Shah Zafar Marg
PAHARGANJ
Basant La
Kumar Tourist Taxi Service
Minto Bridge Train Station
Shankar Market
Deen Dayal Upadhyaya Marg
Central Park
Rajiv Chowk (Connaught Place)
Shivaji Bridge Train Station
Kotla Marg
Prepaid Autorickshaw Booth
Kamala (350m); State Emporiums (350m)
Prepaid Autorickshaw Booth
Barakhamba Road
ITO
India Tourism Delhi
Tilak Bridge Train Station
Vivekanda Rd
Janpath
Hailey Rd
Wakil La
Sikandra Rd
Mandi House
Pragati Maidan
Janpath La

Old Delhi

Sights

1	Chatta Chowk	D2
2	Diwan-i-Am	D2
3	Diwan-i-Khas	D2
4	Jama Masjid	C3
5	Khas Mahal	D2
6	Lahore Gate	D2
7	Mumtaz Mahal	D2
8	Naubat Khana	D2
9	Rang Mahal	D2
10	Red Fort	D2
11	Shahi Burj	D1
14	Chawri Bazaar	B3
15	Dariba Kalan	C2
16	Kinari Bazaar	C2
17	Nai Sarak	B2
18	Spice Market	A2

Shopping

12	Ballimaran	B2
13	Central Cottage Industries Emporium	A6

Eating

19	Haldiram's	C2
20	Hotel Saravana Bhavan	A6
21	Karim's	C3
22	PT Gaya Prasad Shiv Charan	B2
23	Rajdhani	A6

Drinking & Nightlife

	1911	(see 24)
24	Atrium, Imperial	A6
25	Unplugged	A5

species of trees and 50 species of birds and butterflies, as well as half a dozen fabulously captivating 15th-century **Mughal monuments**.

South Delhi

Mehrauli Archaeological Park Park

(Map p56; dawn-dusk; M Qutab Minar) FREE There are extraordinary riches scattered around Mehrauli, with more than 440 monuments – from the 10th century to the British era – dotting a forest and the village itself behind the forest. In the forest, most impressive are the time-ravaged **tombs** of Balban and Quli Khan, his son, and the **Jamali Khamali mosque**, attached to the tomb of the Sufi poet Jamali. To the west is the 16th-century **Rajon ki Baoli**, Delhi's finest step-well.

TOURS

DelhiByCycle Cycling

(9811723720; www.delhibycycle.com; per person ₹1850; 6.30-10am) Founded by a Dutch journalist, these cycle tours are the original and the best, and a thrilling way to explore Delhi. Tours focus on specific neighbourhoods – Old Delhi, New Delhi, Nizamuddin, and the banks of the Yamuna – and start early to miss the worst of the traffic. The price includes chai and breakfast. Helmets and child seats available.

Salaam Baalak Trust Walking

(SBT; 011-23586416; www.salaambaalaktrust.com; suggested donation ₹400; 10am-noon) This 30-year-old charity was founded by the mother of film director Mira Nair, following her 1988 hit film about the life of street children, *Salaam Bombay!* It offers two-hour 'street walks' around Paharganj, guided by former street kids. They tell you their own, often-shocking, stories and take you to a couple of the trust's 'contact points' near New Delhi train station.

SHOPPING

Connaught Place Area

Central Cottage Industries Emporium Arts & Crafts

(Map p50; 011-23326790; Janpath; 10am-7pm; M Janpath) This government-run multilevel store is a wonderful treasure trove of fixed-price, India-wide handicrafts. Prices are higher than in the state emporiums, but the selection of woodcarvings, jewellery, pottery, papier mâché, stationery, brassware, textiles (including shawls), toys, rugs, beauty products and miniature paintings makes it a glorious one-stop shop for beautiful crafts.

Shopping at Shahpur Jat

Shahpur Jat Village (Map p56; ⏰10am-7pm Mon-Sat; Ⓜ Hauz Khas, Green Park) Located within the boundaries of the ruined walls of **Siri Fort** (Map p56; Ⓜ Hauz Khas, Green Park) (the second of Delhi's seven historic cities), this urban village contains an artsy collection of high-end clothing boutiques, health-conscious cafes and no-frills eateries, many of which are hidden amongst a network of graffiti-splattered alleyways. It's one of Delhi's more intriguing places to shop.

Clothing store, Shahpur Jat

HINDUSTAN TIMES / CONTRIBUTOR / GETTY IMAGES ©

State Emporiums Handicrafts

(Baba Kharak Singh Marg; ⏰11am-1.30pm & 2-6.30pm Mon-Sat; Ⓜ Shivaji Stadium) Handily in a row are these regional treasure-filled emporiums. They may have the air of torpor that often afflicts governmental enterprises, but shopping here is like travelling around India – top stops include Kashmir, for papier mâché and carpets; Rajasthan, for miniature paintings and puppets; Uttar Pradesh, for marble inlay work; Karnataka, for sandalwood sculptures; and Odisha, for stone carvings.

Kamala Arts & Crafts

(Baba Kharak Singh Marg; ⏰10am-7pm Mon-Sat; Ⓜ Rajiv Chowk) Crafts, curios, textiles and homewares from the Crafts Council of India, designed with flair and using traditional techniques but offering some contemporary, out-of-the-ordinary designs.

New Delhi & Around

Khan Market Market

(Map p55; ⏰approx 10.30am-8pm Mon-Sat; Ⓜ Khan Market) Khan Market is Delhi's most-upmarket shopping enclave, the most expensive place to rent a shop in India, and is favoured by the elite and expats. Its boutiques focus on fashion, books and homewares, and it's also a good place to eat and drink.

South Delhi

Dilli Haat Arts & Crafts

(Map p56; Aurobindo Marg; Indian/foreigner ₹30/100; ⏰10.30am-10pm Mar-Nov, 11am-9pm Dec-Feb; Ⓜ INA) Right beside INA metro station, this popular, but somewhat stage-managed, open-air food-and-crafts market is a cavalcade of colour and sells regional handicrafts from all over India; bargain hard. At the far end are food stands where you can sample cuisine from every corner of the country. Beware impostors; this is the only real Dilli Haat in Delhi.

Hauz Khas Village Handicrafts, Clothing

(Map p56; Hauz Khas Fort Rd; ⏰11am-7pm Mon-Sat; Ⓜ IIT) This arty little enclave has narrow lanes crammed with boutiques selling designer Indian clothing, handicrafts, contemporary ceramics, handmade furniture and old Bollywood posters. Intriguingly, it's located beside numerous 13th- and 14th-century **ruins** (Map p56; ⏰dawn-dusk; Ⓜ IIT), as well as a forested **deer park** (Map p56; Hauz Khas; ⏰5am-8pm; to 7pm winter; Ⓜ IIT, Green Park) FREE and a lake. Standout eating and drinking options include **Naivedyam** (Map p56; ☎011-26960426; dishes ₹150-200, thalis ₹275-380; ⏰11am-11pm; Ⓜ Green Park) and **Hauz Khas Social** (Map p56; www.socialoffline.in/HauzKhasSocial; 12 Hauz Khas Village; ⏰11am-12.30am; Ⓜ Green Park).

EATING

Creative cuisine at Delhi's modern-Indian restaurants now sits alongside purveyors

Khan Market

of traditional delights. Reservations are recommended for high-end restaurants.

 Old Delhi

PT Gaya Prasad Shiv Charan — Street Food $

(Map p50; 34 Gali Paranthe Wali; parathas ₹60-70; 7am-10pm; M Jama Masjid) This winding lane off Chandni Chowk has been dishing up its namesake *paratha* fresh off the *tawa* (hotplate) for generations, originally serving pilgrims at the time of the Mughals. Walk down it from Chandni Chowk, take two turns and you'll find this, the most popular *paratha* joint of many. Stuffings include green chilli, almond, banana and more.

Karim's — Mughlai $$

(Map p50; Gali Kababyan; mains ₹120-400; 9am-12.30am; M Jama Masjid) Down a narrow alley off a lane leading south from Jama Masjid, Karim's has been delighting carnivores since 1913. Expect meaty Mughlai treats such as mutton *burrah* (marinated chops), delicious mutton Mughlai, and the breakfast mutton-and-bread combo *nahari*. Numerous branches, including at **Nizamuddin West** (Map p55; 168/2 Jha House Basti; dishes ₹120-400; 1-3pm & 6.30-11pm Tue-Sat; M JLN Stadium), but this no-frills, multiroomed courtyard location is the oldest and best.

Shim Tur — Korean $$

(3rd fl, Navrang Guesthouse, Tooti Gali; meals ₹200-500; 10.30am-11pm; M Ramakrishna Ashram Marg) The Korean food is fresh and authentic here; try the *bibimbap* (rice bowl with vegetables, egg and pickles; ₹270). But it takes determination to find this place: take the turning for the Hotel Rak International, opposite which is the grotty, unsigned Navrang Guesthouse. Follow the signs to its rooftop and you'll find the small, bamboo-lined, softly lit terrace.

Connaught Place Area

Hotel Saravana Bhavan — South Indian $$

(Map p50; 46 Janpath; dishes ₹95-210, thalis ₹210; 8am-11pm; M Janpath) Fabulous dosas, *idlis* and other South Indian delights.

Cheap Bhawan Bites

Kautilya Marg, a road in Delhi's diplomatic enclave, is lined with state *bhawans*, which act like consulates for the different states of India, and some of them open their staff canteens to the public for breakfast, lunch and dinner. The food is always cheap (around ₹100 for a lunchtime platter), filling (usually unlimited refills) and fabulously authentic (they tend only to use genuine, regionally sourced ingredients). **Gujarat Bhawan** (11 Kautilya Marg, Chanakyapuri; breakfast ₹60, thalis ₹110-140; 7.30-10.30am, 12.30-3pm & 7.30-10pm; ; Lok Kalyan Marg) is a good choice at No 11, but there are also houses for Bihar, Tamil Nadu and Karnataka, among others. Further east is the unusual **Nagaland House** (Map p55; 29 Dr APJ Abdul Kalam Rd; thalis ₹120-200; 7-9am, noon-3pm & 7.30-10pm; Lok Kalyan Marg), a *bhawan* with especially friendly staff that serve pork specialities from the far-off north-eastern state of Nagaland.

Traditional thali

MATYAS REHAK / SHUTTERSTOCK ©

With queues coming out the door, this is the biggest and the best of Delhi's Saravana Bhavan branches, and you can see dosas being made in the back.

Also offers great South Indian coffee.

Rajdhani Indian $$$

(Map p50; 011-43501200; 18 N-Block, Connaught Place; thalis ₹525; noon-3.30pm & 7-11pm; ; Rajiv Chowk) Thalis fit for a king. Treat yourself with food-of-the-gods vegetarian thalis that encompass a fantastic array of Gujarati and Rajasthani dishes.

New Delhi & Around

Pandara Market Indian

(Map p55; Pandara Rd; noon-1am; Khan Market) This small, but enduring food market, made up of a dozen or so restaurants and ice-cream shops, set around a quiet square, is the go-to place for excellent Mughlai and Punjabi food. Prices and standards are high. For quality food, try **Gulati** (Map p55; www.gulatirestaurant.in; Pandara Market; mains ₹450-650; noon-midnight; Khan Market), **Havemore** (Map p55; 011-23387171; Pandara Market; mains ₹350-850; 11am-1am; ; Khan Market), **Pindi** (Map p55; 9818739131; Pandara Market; mains ₹350-650; 11am-1am; Khan Market) or **Chicken Inn** (Map p55; www.chickeninn.co; Pandara Market; mains ₹350-850; noon-midnight; Khan Market). For traditional sweets and ice cream, try **Krishna di Kulfi** (Map p55; Pandara Market; snacks ₹80-120; 7am-midnight; Khan Market).

Cafe Lota Modern Indian $$

(Map p55; Crafts Museum; dishes ₹215-415; 8am-9.30pm; Pragati Maidan) Bamboo slices the sunlight into flattering stripes at this outdoor restaurant offering a modern take on delicious Indian cooking from across the regions. Sample its fish and (sweet potato) chips, or *palak patta chaat* (crispy spinach, potatoes and chickpeas with spiced yoghurt and chutneys), as well as amazing desserts and breakfasts. It's great for kids.

Bukhara Indian $$$

(011-26112233; ITC Maurya, Sardar Patel Marg; mains ₹1500-3000; 12.30-2.45pm & 7-11.30pm; Durgabai Deshmukh South Campus) One of Delhi's best (and most expensive) restaurants, this hotel eatery with low seating and crazy-paving walls serves wow-factor Northwest Frontier–style

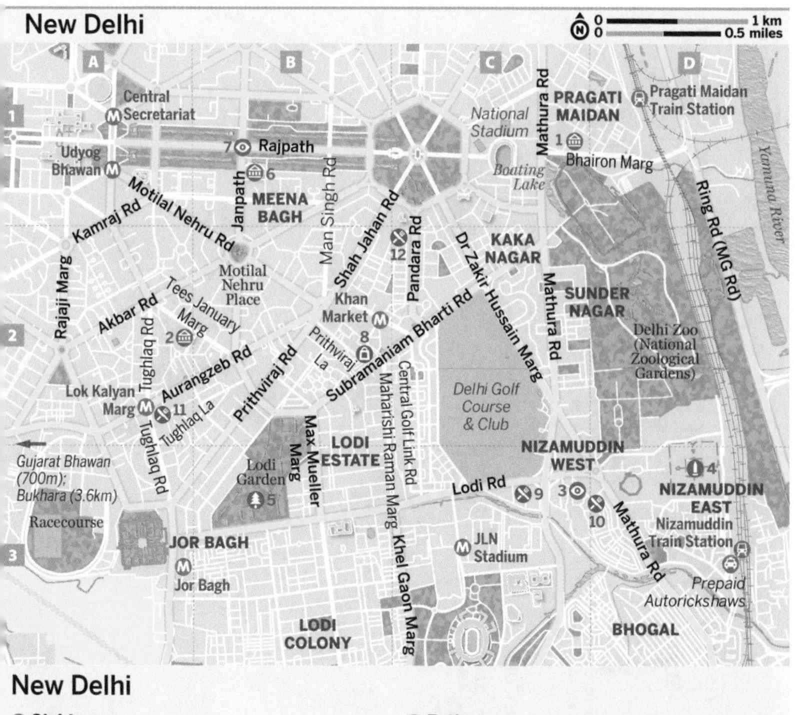

New Delhi

Sights

1 Crafts Museum C1
2 Gandhi Smriti A2
3 Hazrat Nizam-ud-din Dargah C3
4 Humayun's Tomb D3
5 Lodi Garden B3
6 National Museum B1
7 Rajpath B1

Shopping

8 Khan Market B2

Eating

Cafe Lota .... (see 1)
Chicken Inn .... (see 12)
Gulati .... (see 12)
Havemore .... (see 12)
9 Indian Accent C3
10 Karim's D3
Krishna di Kulfi .... (see 12)
11 Nagaland House A2
12 Pandara Market C2
Pindi .... (see 12)

:uisine, with silken kebabs and its famous 3ukhara dhal. Reservations are essential. :xpect long waits.

ndian Accent Indian **$$$**

Map p55; 011-26925151; https://indian ccent.com/newdelhi; Lodhi Hotel, Lodi Rd; ishes ₹500-1750, tasting menu veg/nonveg ₹3600/3900; noon-2.30pm & 7-10.30pm; JLN Stadium) Inside luxury **Lodhi** (www. helodhi.com) hotel, though privately run, Indian Accent is one of the capital's top dining experiences. Chef Manish Mehrotra works his magic using seasonal ingredients married in surprising and beautifully creative combinations. The tasting menu is astoundingly good, with wow-factor combinations such as tandoori bacon prawns or paper dosa filled with wild mushroom and water chestnuts. Dress smart. Book ahead.

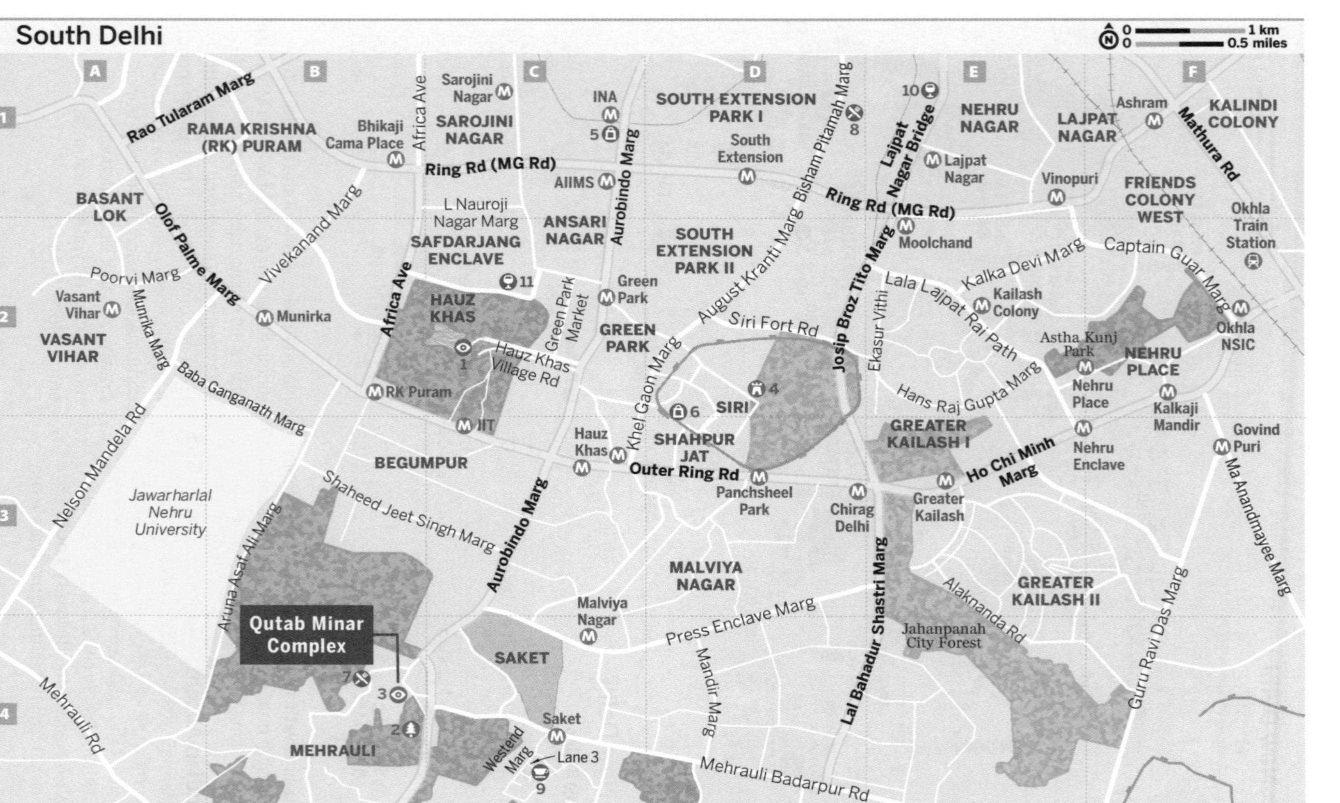
South Delhi
1 km
0.5 miles
A
B
C
D
E
F
1
2
3
4
Rao Tularam Marg
RAMA KRISHNA (RK) PURAM
Bhikaji Cama Place
Africa Ave
Sarojini Nagar
SAROJINI NAGAR
INA
5
Aurobindo Marg
SOUTH EXTENSION PARK I
South Extension
Bisham Pitamah Marg
8
10
Lajpat Nagar Bridge
NEHRU NAGAR
Lajpat Nagar
LAJPAT NAGAR
Ashram
Mathura Rd
KALINDI COLONY
Ring Rd (MG Rd)
AIIMS
Vinopuri
FRIENDS COLONY WEST
Okhla Train Station
BASANT LOK
Olof Palme Marg
Vivekanand Marg
L Nauroji Nagar Marg
SAFDARJANG ENCLAVE
ANSARI NAGAR
SOUTH EXTENSION PARK II
August Kranti Marg
Josip Broz Tito Marg
Moolchand
Captain Guar Marg
Kalka Devi Marg
Lala Lajpat Rai Path
Poorvi Marg
Vasant Vihar
VASANT VIHAR
Munirka Marg
Munirka
11
HAUZ KHAS
Green Park Market
Green Park
GREEN PARK
Siri Fort Rd
Ekasur Vithi
Kailash Colony
Okhla NSIC
Astha Kunj Park
NEHRU PLACE
Nehru Place
Kalkaji Mandir
1
Hauz Khas Village Rd
Baba Ganganath Marg
RK Puram
IIT
Khel Gaon Marg
6
SIRI
4
Hans Raj Gupta Marg
GREATER KAILASH I
Nehru Enclave
Govind Puri
Nelson Mandela Rd
BEGUMPUR
Hauz Khas
SHAHPUR JAT
Outer Ring Rd
Panchsheel Park
Chirag Delhi
Greater Kailash
Ho Chi Minh Marg
Ma Anandmayee Marg
Jawarharlal Nehru University
Shaheed Jeet Singh Marg
Aruna Asaf Ali Marg
MALVIYA NAGAR
Lal Bahadur Shastri Marg
Alaknanda Rd
GREATER KAILASH II
Guru Ravi Das Marg
Malviya Nagar
Press Enclave Marg
Jahanpanah City Forest
Qutab Minar Complex
SAKET
7
3
Mandir Marg
Mehrauli Rd
2
MEHRAULI
Saket
Westend Marg
Lane 3
9
Mehrauli Badarpur Rd

South Delhi

Sights

1 Hauz Khas C2
Hauz Khas Deer Park .... (see 1)
Iron Pillar .... (see 3)
2 Mehrauli Archaeological Park B4
3 Qutab Minar Complex B4
Quwwat-ul-Islam Masjid .... (see 3)
4 Siri Fort D2

Shopping

5 Dilli Haat C1
Hauz Khas Village .... (see 1)
6 Shahpur Jat Village D2

Eating

Naivedyam .... (see 1)
7 Olive B4
8 Swagath D1

Drinking & Nightlife

9 Blue Tokai C4
10 Ek Bar E1
Hauz Khas Social .... (see 1)
11 Piano Man Jazz Club C2

South Delhi

Swagath South Indian $$$

(Map p56; 011-49981100; www.swagath.in; 14 Block A Defence Colony Market; dishes ₹400-700, seafood ₹600-1300; 11.30am-11.30pm; M Lajpat Nagar) Famous for its top-notch Mangalorean seafood, such as pomfret, prawns or lobster, this busy multilevel restaurant is often jam-packed and also has regular South and North Indian dishes.

DRINKING & NIGHTLIFE

Connaught Place Area

Unplugged Bar

(Map p50; 011-33107701; 23 L-Block, Connaught Place; beers/cocktails from ₹145/400; noon-midnight; M Rajiv Chowk) There's nowhere else like this in Connaught Place. You could forget you were in CP, in fact, with the big courtyard garden, wrought-iron chairs and tables, and swing seats, all under the shade of a banyan tree hung with basket-weave lanterns. There's live music on Wednesday, Friday, Saturday and Sunday evenings: anything from alt-rock to electro-fusion.

1911 Bar

(Map p50; Imperial Hotel, Janpath; 11am-12.45am; M Janpath) The Imperial, built in the 1930s, resonates with bygone splendour. This bar is a more recent addition, but still riffs on the Raj. Here you can sip the perfect cocktail (₹1000) amid designer-clad clientele, against a backdrop of faded photos and murals of maharajas.

South Delhi

Blue Tokai Cafe

(Map p56; www.bluetokaicoffee.com; Champa Gali, Lane 3, West End Marg, Saket; coffee from ₹100, snacks ₹150-300; 9am-10pm; ; M Saket) Found in a magically unexpected art enclave called Champa Gali, down a lane beside the fake Dilli Haat shopping centre ('Delhi Haat'), Blue Tokai is one of a few cool cafes here – but it's the one the coffee aficionados come to. Beans are ground on-site and you can get serious caffeine hits such as nitrogen-infused cold brew.

Ek Bar Bar

(Map p56; D17, 1st fl, Defence Colony; 5pm-1am; M Lajpat Nagar) On the upper floors of a building in the exclusive area of the Defence Colony, this place has stylish, kooky decor in deep, earth-jewel colours, serious mixology (cocktails from ₹475) showcasing Indian flavours (how about a gin and tonic with turmeric?), modern Indian bar snacks, nightly DJs, and a see-and-be-seen crowd.

Piano Man Jazz Club Club

(Map p56; http://thepianoman.in; B-6 Commercial Complex, Safdarjung Enclave; noon-3pm & 7.30pm-12.30am; M Green Park) The real thing, this popular, atmospheric place with proper musos is a dim-lit speakeasy with some excellent live jazz performances.

High Tea at the Imperial

Is there anything more genteel than high tea at the **Atrium** (Map p50; Imperial Hotel, Janpath; 8am-11.30pm; M Janpath)? Sip tea from bone-china cups and pluck dainty sandwiches and cakes from tiered stands, while discussing the latest goings-on in Shimla and Dalhousie. High tea is served in the Atrium from 3pm to 6pm daily (₹1500 plus tax).

Masala tea with cinnamon

SONELLY / SHUTTERSTOCK ©

INFORMATION

DANGERS & ANNOYANCES

Delhi has, unfortunately, a deserved reputation for being unsafe for women. Precautions include never walking around in deserted places, even during daylight hours; keeping an eye on your route; and taking special care after dark – such as commuting via a reputable cab company or driver.

TOUTS

Taxi-wallahs at the airport and around tourist areas frequently act as touts for hotels, claiming that your hotel is full, poor value, dangerous, burnt down or closed, or that there are riots in Delhi. Men who approach you at Connaught Place run similar scams to direct you to shops and tourist agents.

TRAIN STATION HASSLE

Touts at New Delhi train station endeavour to steer travellers away from the legitimate **International Tourist Bureau** (ITB; Map p50; 011-23405156; 1st fl, New Delhi Train Station; 6am-10pm; M New Delhi) and into private travel agencies where they earn a commission. You're particularly vulnerable when arriving tired at night.

FAKE TOURIST OFFICES

Many Delhi travel agencies claim to be tourist offices, even branding themselves with official-looking logos. There is only one India Tourism Delhi office; ask for a list of recommended agents.

TOURIST INFORMATION

India Tourism Delhi (Government of India; Map p50; 011-23320008, 011-23320005; www.incredibleindia.org; 88 Janpath; 9am-6pm Mon-Fri, to 2pm Sat; M Janpath) This official tourist office is a useful source of advice on Delhi, getting out of Delhi, and visiting surrounding states.

GETTING THERE & AWAY

AIR

Indira Gandhi International Airport (01243376000; www.newdelhiairport.in; M IGI Airport) is about 14km southwest of the centre. International and domestic flights use Terminal 3. Ageing Terminal 1 is reserved for low-cost carriers. Free shuttle buses (present your boarding pass and onward ticket) run between the two terminals every 20 minutes, but can take a while. Leave at least three hours for transfers to be safe.

BUS

Practically all state-run services for nearby states leave from the large **Kashmere Gate Inter State Bus Terminal** (ISBT; 011-23860290; M Kashmere Gate) in Old Delhi, accessible by metro (exit gate 7). Tickets for AC buses can be booked in advance, though, either in person a day or two before, or through a travel agent or some hotels.

TRAIN

Delhi has three train stations: Old Delhi (DLI), New Delhi (NDLS), and Nizamuddin (HNZ). Make sure you know which station your train is leaving from. All three have metro stations outside them.

New Delhi Railway Station (btwn Ajmeri Gate & Main Bazaar, Paharganj; 24hr; M New Delhi) is the largest and best-connected of Delhi's train stations. It's the best option for foreign travellers wanting to buy train tickets, thanks to its very helpful International Tourist Bureau. Its ticket office is reserved solely for foreign travellers, and you have to show a foreign passport to even be allowed inside.

GETTING AROUND

TO/FROM THE AIRPORT

Pre-arranged pickups Hotels offer prearranged airport pickup, usually more expensive than arranging a taxi yourself. However, it may be worth it to ease your arrival. You'll pay extra to cover the airport parking fee (up to ₹220) and ₹100 charge for the driver to enter the arrivals hall.

Metro The Airport Express line (www.delhimetrorail.com) runs every 10 to 15 minutes from 5.15am to 11.40pm, completing the journey from Terminal 3 to New Delhi train station in around 30 minutes (International/domestic terminal to New Delhi, ₹60/50).

Bus AC buses run from outside Terminal 3 to Kashmere Gate Inter State Bus Terminal (Delhi's main bus station) every 10 minutes, via the Red Fort, LNJP Hospital, New Delhi Station Gate 2, Connaught Place, Parliament St and Ashoka Rd.

Taxi In front of the arrivals buildings at Terminal 3 and Terminal 1 are **Delhi Traffic Police Prepaid Taxi counters** (complaints 56767, women's helpline 1091; www.delhitrafficpolice.nic.in) offering fixed-price taxi services. You can also book a prepaid taxi at the **Megacabs counter** (011-41516171, bookings 9090909090; www.megacabs.com) at both the international and domestic terminals. Taxi-app services such as **Uber** (www.uber.com/in/en) and **Ola Cabs** (www.olacabs.com) tend to offer cheaper rates than any other types of taxi in Delhi.

METRO

Delhi's **metro** (www.delhimetrorail.com; single journey ₹10-60) is fast and efficient, with signs and arrival/departure announcements in Hindi and English. Trains run from around 6am to 11pm and the first carriage in the direction of travel is reserved for women only.

Metro station

Tokens (₹10 to ₹60) are sold at metro stations. A metro smart card (₹50 deposit plus ₹100 minimum initial top-up) gets you 10% off all journeys (20% outside the peak hours of 8am to noon and 5pm to 9pm). There are also tourist cards (one-day card ₹200 plus ₹50 deposit; three-day card ₹500 plus ₹50 deposit).

Because of security concerns, all bags are X-rayed and passengers must pass through an airport-style scanner.

TAXI

Local taxis (recognisable by their black-and-yellow livery) have meters but, as in autorickshaws, these are effectively ornamental as most drivers refuse to use them; negotiate a price before you start your trip.

Taxis typically charge twice the autorickshaw fare. Note that fares vary as fuel prices go up and down. From 11pm to 5am there's a 25% surcharge for autorickshaws and taxis.

Kumar Tourist Taxi Service (Map p50; 011-23415930; www.kumarindiatours.com; 14/1 K-Block, Connaught Place; 8am-9pm) is a reliable company; a day of Delhi sightseeing costs from ₹3000 (an eight-hour and 80km limit applies).

Metropole Tourist Service (011-24310313, 9810277699; www.metrovista.co.in; 224 Defence Colony Flyover Market; 8am-6.30pm; M Jangpura) is another reliable and long-running taxi service, and decent value, too.

AUTORICKSHAW & E-RICKSHAW

Autorickshaws Delhi's signature green-and-yellow autorickshaws are everywhere. You never have to worry about finding one – drivers will find you! They have meters that are never used, so negotiate the fare clearly before you start your journey. As a guide, Paharganj to Connaught Place should cost around ₹30.

Delhi Traffic Police run a network of prepaid autorickshaw booths. There are 24-hour booths outside the three main train stations: **New Delhi** (Map p50; outside New Delhi Railway Station, Paharganj side; 24hr; M New Delhi), **Old Delhi** (Map p50; outside Old Delhi Railway Station; 24hr; M Chandni Chowk) and **Nizamuddin** (Map p55; outside Nizamuddin Railway Station). Other booths are outside the **India Tourism Delhi** (Map p50; 88 Janpath; 11am-8.30pm; M Janpath, Rajiv Chowk) office and at **Central Park** (Map p50; Central Park, Connaught Place; M Rajiv Chowk).

E-rickshaws Delhi's ever-expanding fleet of golf-cart-lookalike e-rickshaws (electric rickshaws) offer a more environmentally friendly alternative. Many of them are shared rickshaws, plying fixed routes for very cheap individual fares, but many can also be hired privately. Fares should be roughly the same as autorickshaws.

Where to Stay

Delhi hotels range from the cheap and cheerless to the ostentatiously luxurious. It's wise to book ahead for midrange or top-end places. Budgeteers will have no problem getting rooms on the fly.

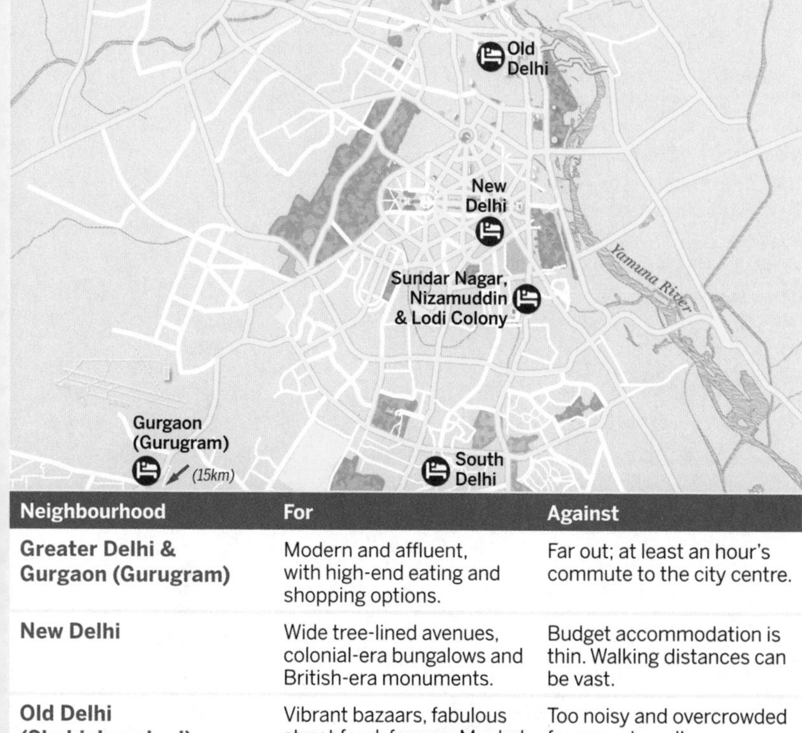

Neighbourhood	For	Against
Greater Delhi & Gurgaon (Gurugram)	Modern and affluent, with high-end eating and shopping options.	Far out; at least an hour's commute to the city centre.
New Delhi	Wide tree-lined avenues, colonial-era bungalows and British-era monuments.	Budget accommodation is thin. Walking distances can be vast.
Old Delhi (Shahjahanabad)	Vibrant bazaars, fabulous street food, famous Mughal monuments. Paharganj, Delhi's Backpacker Central, is nearby.	Too noisy and overcrowded for some travellers.
South Delhi	Delhi's most leafy, quiet and affluent neighbourhoods.	Options are pricey. You'll be relying on taxis and autorickshaws more than in other areas.
Sunder Nagar, Nizamuddin & Lodi Colony	A diverse area featuring colonial-era bungalows and slums. Decent choice of midrange places.	Parts of the area are far from the centre with sparse transport links.

AGRA & THE TAJ MAHAL

In This Chapter

Taj Mahal 66
Fatehpur Sikri 74
Agra Fort 78
Sights 82
Eating 83
Information 83
Getting There & Away 83
Getting Around 83

Agra & the Taj Mahal at a Glance...

The Taj Mahal rises from Agra's haze as though from a dream. You've seen it in pictures, but experiencing it in person you'll understand that it's not just a famous monument, but a love poem composed of stone.

For 130 years, Agra was the centre of India's great Mughal empire, and its legacy lives on in beautiful artwork, mouth-watering cuisine and magnificent architecture. The Taj is one of three places here with Unesco World Heritage status: the Agra Fort and the Fatehpur Sikri palace complex complete a superb trio of sights.

Two Days in Agra

Try to be at the **Taj Mahal** (p107) for dawn, a magical time to watch the rising sun's rays light up the monument's marble facade. Later, explore **Agra Fort** (p117) and indulge with dinner at **Pinch of Spice** (p83).

On day two, take a trip out to **Fatehpur Sikri** (p74), and return for a second visit to the Taj, possibly in the moonlight.

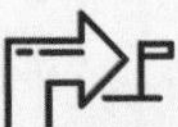

Four Days in Agra

On day three enjoy a different view of the Taj Mahal from the exquisitely carved 'Baby Taj', the **Itimad-ud-Daulah** (p82), before diving into a matchless local-eating experience at **Mama Chicken** (p83). On day four, head 10km out of town to see **Akbar's Mausoleum** (p82), and return for a final visit to the Taj itself.

Previous page: Yamuna River boat passing the Taj Mahal (p66)

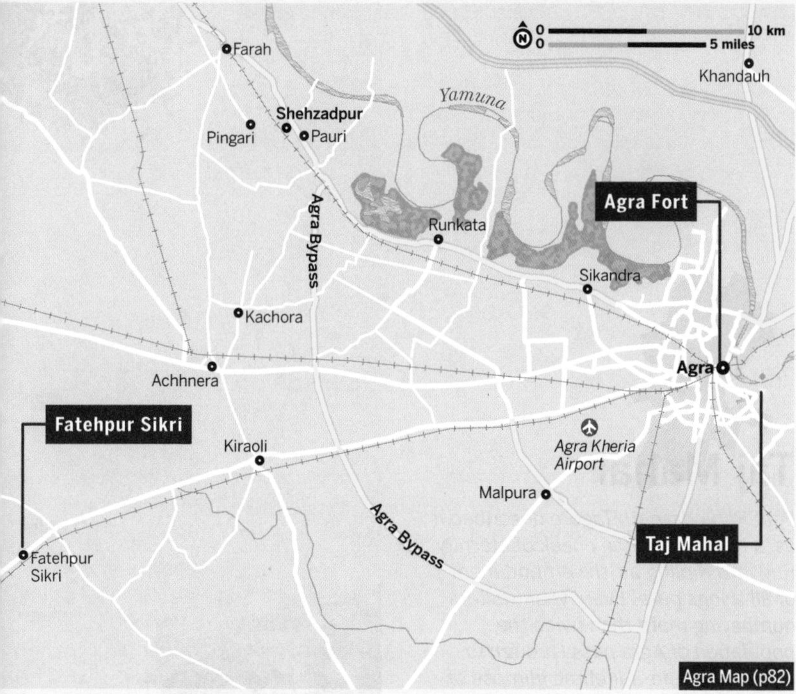

0 10 km
0 5 miles
Farah
Khandauh
Yamuna
Shehzadpur
Pingari
Pauri
Agra Bypass
Agra Fort
Runkata
Sikandra
Kachora
Agra
Achhnera
Fatehpur Sikri
Kiraoli
Agra Kheria Airport
Malpura
Agra Bypass
Taj Mahal
Fatehpur Sikri
Agra Map (p82)

Arriving in Agra

Agra Cantonment station The main train station, west of the centre; trains to/from Delhi, Mumbai and elsewhere.

Agra Fort station Near the fort; for most trains to/from Rajasthan and Varanasi.

ISBT Bus Stand Luxury buses to/from Delhi and Varanasi.

Idgah Bus Stand Buses to/from Delhi, Jaipur and Fatehpur Sikri.

Where to Stay

The main place for budget accommodation is the bustling area of Taj Ganj, immediately south of the Taj, while there's a high concentration of midrange hotels further south, along and near Fatehabad Rd. Sadar Bazaar, an area boasting good-quality restaurants, offers another option. Top-end places are scattered around all these areas.

Taj Mahal

Poet Rabindranath Tagore described it as 'a teardrop on the cheek of eternity'; Rudyard Kipling as 'the embodiment of all things pure'. Every year, visitors numbering more than twice the population of Agra pass through to catch a once-in-a-lifetime glimpse of what is widely considered the most beautiful building in the world.

Great For...

Need to Know

0562-2330498; www.tajmahal.gov.in; Indian/foreigner ₹50/1100, mausoleum ₹200, video ₹25; dawn-dusk Sat-Thu

★ Top Tip

Sunrise is magical, and the most comfortable time to visit, with far fewer crowds.

The Taj was built by the Mughal emperor Shah Jahan as a memorial for his third wife, Mumtaz Mahal, who died giving birth to their 14th child in 1631. The death of Mumtaz left the emperor so heartbroken that his hair is said to have turned grey virtually overnight. Construction of the Taj began the following year. Although the main building is thought to have been built in eight years, the whole complex was not completed until 1653.

Not long after it was finished Shah Jahan was overthrown by his son Aurangzeb and imprisoned in Agra Fort (p117), where for the rest of his days he could only gaze out at his creation through a window. Following his death in 1666, Shah Jahan was buried here alongside his beloved Mumtaz.

In total, some 20,000 people from India and Central Asia worked on the building. Specialists were brought in from as far away as Europe to produce the exquisite marble screens and pietra dura made with thousands of semiprecious stones.

Entry

Note: the Taj is **closed every Friday** to anyone not attending prayers at the mosque.

The Taj can be accessed through the **west**, south and east gates. Tour groups tend to enter through the east and west gates, with separate queues for women and men. The south gate was closed to visitors in 2018 for security concerns but can be used to exit the Taj. The east gate generally has shorter queues. Once you get your ticket, you can skip ahead of the lines of Indians waiting to get in – one perk of your pricey entry fee. It's possible to buy your tickets online in advance at

View of the Taj Mahal from Mehtab Bagh

tps://asi.payumoney.com (you'll get a 50 discount for your troubles), but you on't save much time as you still have to in the main security queue. A ticket that cludes entrance to the mausoleum itself osts ₹200 extra.

Cameras and videos are permitted, ut you can't take photographs inside the ausoleum itself. Tripods are banned. Remember to retrieve your free 500ml bottle water and shoe covers (included in the j ticket price). If you keep your ticket, you get small entry-fee discounts when visiting Agra Fort, Fatehpur Sikri, Akbar's Tomb or the Itimad-ud-Daulah on the same day. Bags much bigger than a money pouch are not allowed inside; free bag storage is available. Any food or tobacco will be confiscated when you go through security, as will pens.

★ Top Taj Viewpoints

Inside the Taj grounds

From Mehtab Bagh

From the south bank of the Yamuna

From a Taj Ganj rooftop cafe

From Agra Fort

ROOP_DEY / SHUTTERSTOCK ©

Rickshaw Rumble

When taking an auto- or cycle-rickshaw to the Taj, make sure you're clear which gate you want to go to when negotiating the price. Otherwise, almost without fail, riders will take you to the roundabout at the south end of Shahjahan Gardens Rd – where expensive tongas (horse-drawn carriages) or camels wait to take tour groups to the west gate – and claim that's where they thought you meant. Only nonpolluting autos can go within a 500m radius of the Taj because of pollution rules, but they can get a lot closer than this.

Inside the Grounds

The **ornamental gardens** are set out along classical Mughal *charbagh* (formal Persian garden) lines – a square quartered by watercourses, with an ornamental marble plinth at its centre. When the fountains are not flowing, the Taj is beautifully reflected in the water.

The Taj Mahal itself stands on a raised marble platform at the northern end of the ornamental gardens, with its back to the Yamuna River. Its raised position means that the backdrop is only sky – a master stroke of design. Purely decorative 40m-high white **minarets** grace each corner of the platform. After more than three centuries they are not quite perpendicular, but they may have been designed to lean slightly outwards so that in the event of an earthquake they would fall away from the

Take a Break

Café Coffee Day (www.cafecoffeeday.com; 21/101 Taj East Gate; coffee ₹110-135; 6am-8pm) has proper coffee in AC comfort just outside the East Gate.

precious Taj. The red-sandstone **mosque** to the west is an important gathering place for Agra's Muslims. The identical building to the east, the **jawab**, was built for symmetry.

The central Taj structure is made of semitranslucent white marble, carved with flowers and inlaid with thousands of semiprecious stones in beautiful patterns. A perfect exercise in symmetry, the four identical faces of the Taj feature impressive vaulted arches embellished with pietra dura scrollwork and quotations from the Quran in a style of calligraphy using inlaid jasper. The whole structure is topped off by four small domes surrounding the famous bulbous central dome.

Directly below the main dome is the **Cenotaph of Mumtaz Mahal**, an elaborate false tomb surrounded by an exquisite perforated marble screen inlaid with dozens of different types of semiprecious stones. Beside it, offsetting the symmetry of the Taj, is the **Cenotaph of Shah Jahan**, who was interred here with little ceremony by his usurping son Aurangzeb in 1666. Light is admitted into the central chamber by finely cut marble screens. The real tombs of Mumtaz Mahal and Shah Jahan are in a locked basement room below the main chamber and cannot be viewed.

Taj Museum

Within the Taj complex, on the western side of the gardens, is the small but excellent **Taj Museum** (10am-5pm Sat-Thu) FREE, housing a number of original Mughal miniature paintings, including a pair of 17th-century ivory portraits of Emperor Shah Jahan and his beloved wife Mumtaz Mahal. It also has some very well-preserved gold and silver coins dating from the same period, plus architectural drawings of the Taj and some nifty celadon plates, said to split into pieces or change colour if the food served on them contains poison.

Moonlight Magic

For five nights around the full moon the **Taj by Moonlight** (Indian adult/child ₹510/500, foreigner ₹750/500; closed Fri & Ramadan) is open to groups of 50 people in a series of eight 30-minute time slots between 8.30pm and 12.30am. You can only view the Taj from the entry gate viewing area and you only get 30 minutes there, making this an expensive option – but some people love it. The later time slots are best for moonlight views.

Tickets must be bought a day in advance from the **Archaeological Survey of India office** (ASI; 0562-2227261; www.asiagracircle.in; 22 The Mall; 10am-6pm Mon-Fri); see its website for details. (Note: this office is known as the Taj Mahal Office by some rickshaw riders.) You need to go through security clearance at the Shilpgram **Tourist Facilitation Centre** (Taj East Gate Rd; 9.30am-5pm Sat-Thu) first, before being taken by security on an electric bus to the eastern gate.

Pishtaq (arched recesses) on exterior of Taj Mahal

Myths & Legends

Black Taj

The story goes that Shah Jahan planned to build a negative image of the Taj Mahal in black marble on the opposite side of the river as his own mausoleum, and that work began before he was imprisoned by his son Aurangzeb in Agra Fort. Extensive excavations at Mehtab Bagh have found no trace of any such construction.

Craftsmen Mutilations

Legend has it that on completion of the Taj, Shah Jahan ordered the hands of the project's craftsmen to be chopped off, preventing them from ever building anything as beautiful again. Some even say he went so far as to have their eyes gouged out.

Thankfully, no historical evidence supports either story.

Protecting the Taj

Dust and air pollution have tarnished the surface of the Taj over the years, giving it a brownish hue. More recently, a greenish tint began to appear, due to the excrement of millions of insects that breed in the polluted Yamuna River and are drawn to the Taj's white-ish walls. In an effort to restore the marble to some of its earlier glory, a mud-pack cleanse was developed, based on a traditional recipe used by Indian women to restore their own facial radiance, and applied in 2017 and 2018.

☑ Don't Miss

The pietra dura (marble inlay work) inside the *pishtaq* (arched recesses) on the outer walls.

Taj Mahal

TIMELINE

1631 Emperor Shah Jahan's beloved third wife, Mumtaz Mahal, dies in Buhanpur while giving birth to their 14th child. Her body is initially interred in Buhanpur itself, where Shah Jahan is fighting a military campaign, but is later moved, in a golden casket, to a small building on the banks of the Yamuna River in Agra.

1632 Construction of a permanent mausoleum for Mumtaz Mahal begins.

1633 Mumtaz Mahal is interred in her final resting place, an underground tomb beneath a marble plinth, on top of which the Taj Mahal will be built.

1640 The white-marble mausoleum is completed.

1653 The rest of the Taj Mahal complex is completed.

1658 Emperor Shah Jahan is overthrown by his son Aurangzeb and imprisoned in Agra Fort.

1666 Shah Jahan dies. His body is transported along the Yamuna River and buried underneath the Taj, alongside the tomb of his wife.

1908 Repeatedly damaged and looted after the fall of the Mughal empire, the Taj receives some long-overdue attention as part of a major restoration project ordered by British viceroy Lord Curzon.

1983 The Taj is awarded Unesco World Heritage Site status.

2002 Having been discoloured by pollution in more recent years, the Taj is spruced up with an ancient recipe known as multani mitti – a blend of soil, cereal, milk and lime once used by Indian women to beautify their skin.

Today More than three million tourists visit the Taj Mahal each year. That's more than twice the current population of Agra.

ARIS ABDULLAH/SHUTTERSTOCK ©

Pishtaqs
These huge arched recesses are set into each side of the Taj. They provide depth to the building while their central, latticed marble screens allow patterned light to illuminate the inside of the mausoleum.

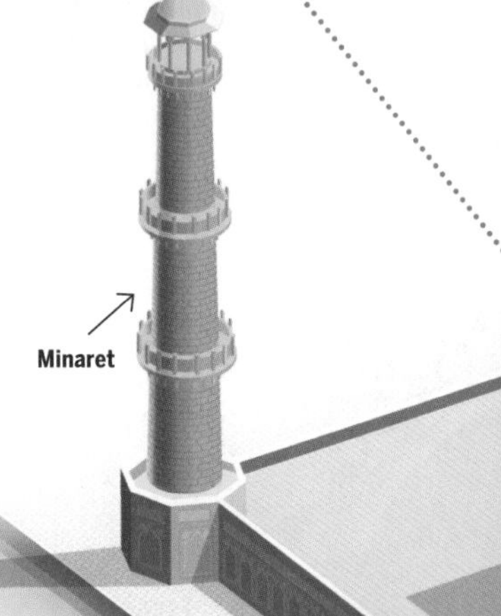

Marble Relief Work
Flowering plants, thought to be representations of paradise, are a common theme among the beautifully decorative panels carved onto the white marble.

FABIOLM/GETTY IMAGES ©

GO BAREFOOT

Help the environment by entering the mausoleum barefoot instead of using the free disposable shoe covers.

LIGHT THE WAY

Use the torch on your smartphone to fully appreciate the translucency of the white marble and semi-precious stones.

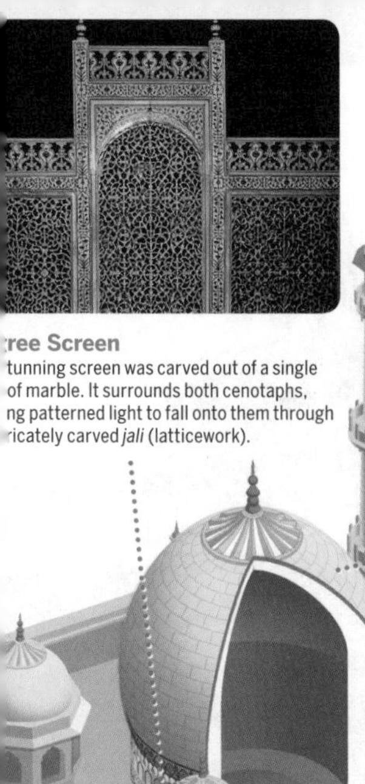

ree Screen

tunning screen was carved out of a single of marble. It surrounds both cenotaphs, ng patterned light to fall onto them through ricately carved *jali* (latticework).

PJHPIX/SHUTTERSTOCK ©

Central Dome

The Taj's famous central dome, topped by a brass finial, represents the vault of heaven, a stark contrast to the material world, which is represented by the square shape of the main structure.

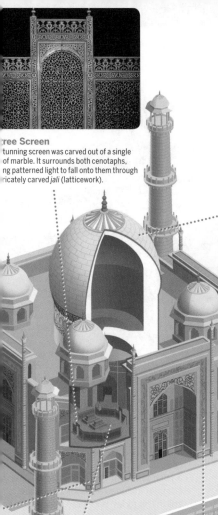

Yamuna River

NORTH →

Pietra Dura

It's believed that 35 different precious and semi-precious stones were used to create the exquisite pietra dura (marble inlay work) found on the inside and outside of the mausoleum walls. Again, floral designs are common.

Calligraphy

The strips of calligraphy surrounding each of the four pishtaqs get larger as they get higher, giving the impression of uniform size when viewed from the ground. There's also calligraphy inside the mausoleum, including on Mumtaz Mahal's cenotaph.

otaphs

enotaphs of taz Mahal and Jahan, decorated pietra dura inlay are actually tombs. The real are located in derground vault d to the public.

COLOR CHASER/SHUTTERSTOCK ©

FRENTUSHA/GETTY IMAGES ©

RUSLANKALN / GETTY IMAGES ©

Fatehpur Sikri

This Indo-Islamic architectural masterpiece, 40km west of Agra, was capital of the Mughal empire between 1572 and 1585. It was abandoned shortly after the 1605 death of its creator, Emperor Akbar.

Great For...

☑ Don't Miss

The wonderfully intricate carving on the little Rumi Sultana palace.

Akbar built his capital near the village of Sikri because the Sufi saint Shaikh Salim Chishti had correctly predicted the birth o an heir to the Mughal throne. The imperia complex included a stunning mosque, still in use today, and three palaces, one for each of Akbar's favourite wives – one believed to have been a Hindu, one a Muslim and one a Christian. Water shortages were apparently the reason for its early abandonment.

Palaces & Pavilions

Now a pristinely manicured garden, the **Diwan-i-Am** (Hall of Public Audience) was an open courtyard where Akbar presided over trials.

The **Pachisi Courtyard** was designed for playing the game of ludo – the large, cross-shaped game board is visible in

the middle. In the southeast corner is the most intricately carved structure in the whole complex, the tiny but elegant **Rumi Sultana**, which was said to be the palace built for Akbar's Turkish Muslim wife. At the courtyard's north end, the **Diwan-i-Khas** (Hall of Private Audience) is centred on a magnificently carved central column.

Just west of the Pachisi Courtyard is the impressive **Panch Mahal**, a pavilion with five storeys that decrease in size until the top consists of only a tiny kiosk. Continuing anticlockwise will bring you to the **Ornamental Pool**. Heading west from here reveals the **Palace of Jodh Bai**, and the one-time home of Akbar's Hindu wife, said to be his favourite. Just outside is the **Palace of the Christian Wife**, used by Akbar's Goan wife Mariam.

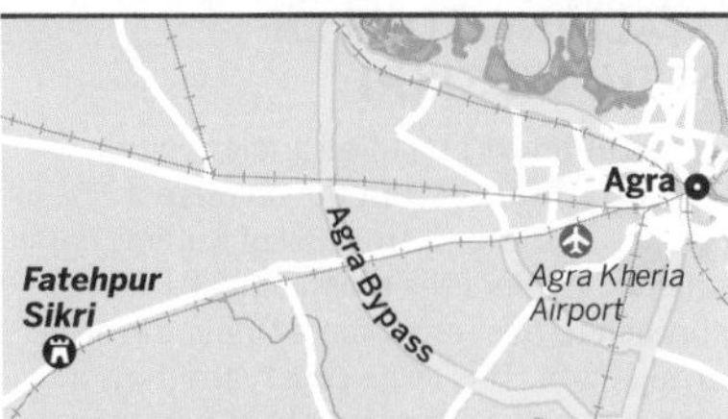

Need to Know

Indian/foreigner ₹50/610, video ₹25; dawn-dusk

Take a Break

You can get a decent, inexpensive meal at **Hotel Goverdhan** (9412526585; www.hotelfatehpursikriviews.com; Agra Rd; s/d with AC ₹1400/1600, without ₹1000/1200;), about 200m east of the bus stand.

★ Top Tip

The red-sandstone palace walls are at their most atmospheric and photogenic near sunset.

Jama Masjid

This beautiful, immense mosque was completed in 1571. The main entrance, at the top of a flight of stone steps, is through the spectacular 54m-high **Buland Darwaza** (Victory Gate), built to commemorate Akbar's military victory in Gujarat. Inside is the stunning white-marble **tomb of Shaikh Salim Chishti**, completed in 1581.

Getting to Fatehpur Sikri

From the Fatehpur **bus stand**, buses run to Agra's **Idgah Bus Stand** (0562-2420324; Idgah Rd) every half-hour (₹45, one hour) until 6pm.

A return taxi from Agra costs from ₹1500 for a day trip, but clarify that this includes toll and parking charges. A one-way taxi to Delhi or Jaipur costs ₹4000.

Fatehpur Sikri

A WALKING TOUR OF FATEHPUR SIKRI

You can enter this fortified ancient city from two entrances, but the northeast entrance at Diwan-i-Am (Hall of Public Audiences) offers the most logical approach to this remarkable Unesco World Heritage Site. This large courtyard (now a garden) is where Emperor Akbar presided over the trials of accused criminals.

Once through the ticket gate, you are in the northern end of the 1 **Pachisi Courtyard**. The first building you see is 2 **Diwan-i-Khas** (Hall of Private Audiences), the interior of which is dominated by a magnificently carved central stone column. Pitch south and enter 3 **Rumi Sultana**, a small but elegant palace built for Akbar's Turkish Muslim wife.

It's hard to miss the 4 **Ornamental Pool** nearby – its southwest corner provides Fatehpur Sikri's most photogenic angle, perfectly framing its most striking building, the five-storey Panch Mahal, one of the gateways to the Imperial Harem Complex, where the 5 **Lower Haramsara** once housed more than 200 female servants.

Wander around the Palace of Jodh Bai and take notice of the towering ode to an elephant, the 21m-high 6 **Hiran Minar**, in the distance to the northwest. Leave the palaces and pavilions area via Shahi Darwaza (King's Gate), which spills into India's second-largest mosque courtyard at 7 **Jama Masjid**. Inside this immense and gorgeous mosque is the sacred 8 **Tomb of Shaikh Salim Chishti**. Exit through the spectacular 9 **Buland Darwaza** (Victory Gate), one of the world's most magnificent gateways.

JAN S/SHUTTERSTOCK ©

Buland Darwaza

Most tours end with an exit through Jama Masjid's Victory Gate. Walk out and take a look behind you: Behold! The magnificent 15-storey sandstone gate, 54m high, is a menacing monolith to Akbar's reign.

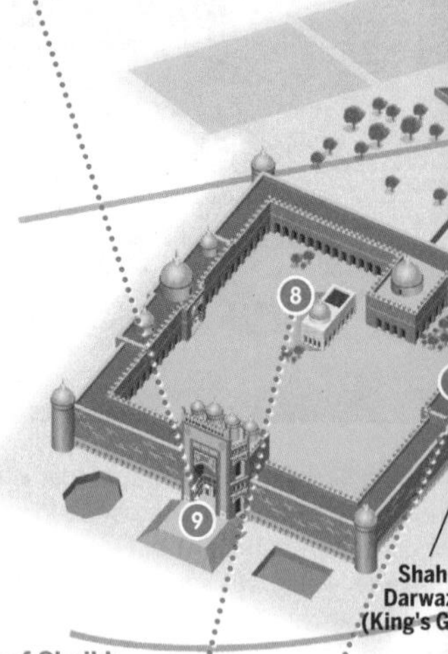

Tomb of Shaikh Salim Chishti

Each knot in the strings tied to the 56 carved white marble designs of the interior walls of Shaikh Salim Chishti's tomb represents one wish of a maximum three.

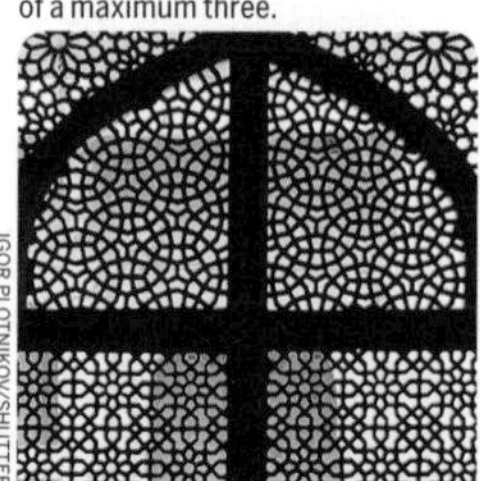

IGOR PLOTNIKOV/SHUTTERSTOCK ©

Jama Masjid

The elaborate marbl inlay work throughou the Jama Masjid complex is said to ha inspired similar work 82 years later at the Taj Mahal in Agra.

DUSHI82/SHUTTERSTOCK ©

CECOLUSSI/GETTY IMAGES ©

ROOP_DEY/SHUTTERSTOCK ©

Diwan-i-Khas

Emperor Akbar modified the central stone column inside Diwan-i-Khas to call attention to a new religion he called Din-i-Ilahi (God is One). The intricately carved column features a fusion of Hindu, Muslim, Christian and Buddhist imagery.

ran Minar

's bizarre, seldom-visited tower off the north-
st corner of Fatehpur Sikri is decorated with
ndreds of stone representations of elephant
ks. It is said to be the place where Minar,
oar's favourite execution elephant, died.

Pachisi Courtyard

Under your feet just past Rumi Sultana is the Pachisi Courtyard where Akbar is said to have played the game *pachisi* (an ancient version of ludo) using slave girls in colourful dress as pieces.

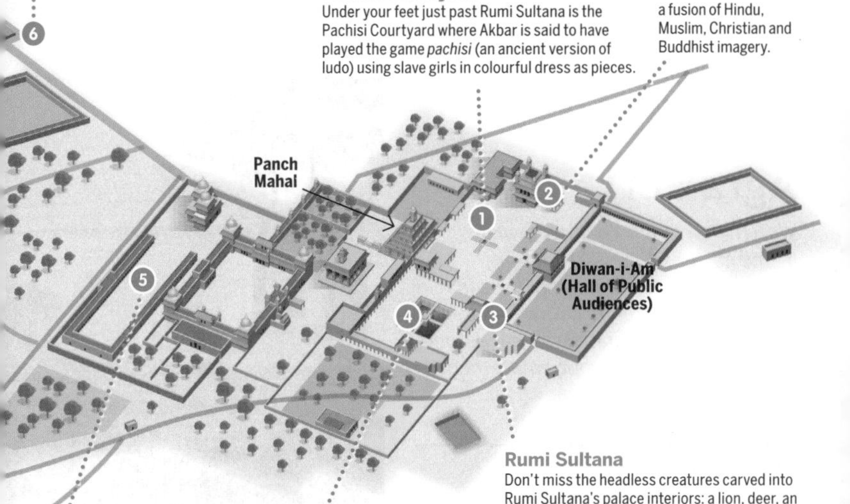

6

Panch Mahal

1

2

Diwan-i-Am (Hall of Public Audiences)

5

4

3

Rumi Sultana

Don't miss the headless creatures carved into Rumi Sultana's palace interiors: a lion, deer, an eagle and a few peacocks were beheaded by jewel thieves who swiped the precious jewels that originally formed their heads.

Ornamental Pool

Tansen, said to be the most gifted Indian vocalist of all time and one of Akbar's treasured nine *Navaratnas* (Gems), would be showered with coins during performances from the central platform of the Ornamental Pool.

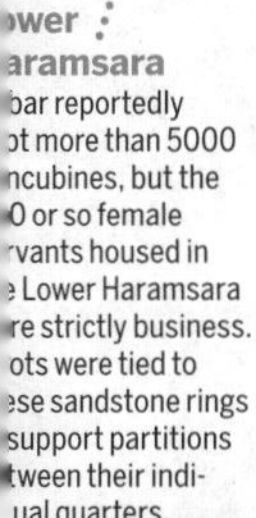

ower aramsara

bar reportedly
ot more than 5000
ncubines, but the
0 or so female
rvants housed in
e Lower Haramsara
re strictly business.
ots were tied to
ese sandstone rings
support partitions
tween their indi-
ual quarters.

CANAN KAYA/SHUTTERSTOCK ©

Anguri Bagh courtyard (p81)

Agra Fort

With the Taj Mahal overshadowing it, one can easily forget that Agra has one of the finest Mughal forts in India. Walking through courtyard after courtyard of this palatial red-sandstone and marble fortress, your amazement grows as the scale of what was built here begins to sink in.

Great For...

Need to Know

Lal Qila; Indian/foreigner ₹50/650, video ₹25; dawn-dusk

★ Top Tip

If the Shish Mahal is still closed, you can glimpse its sparkling mirrors through cracks in the doors.

MIKADUN / SHUTTERSTOCK ©

Construction along the bank of the Yamuna River was begun by Emperor Akbar in 1565 on the site of an earlier fort. Further additions were made, particularly by his grandson Shah Jahan, using his favourite building material – white marble. The fort was built primarily as a military structure, but Shah Jahan transformed it into a palace, and later it became his gilded prison for eight years after his son Aurangzeb seized power in 1658.

The ear-shaped fort's colossal double walls rise more than 20m and measure 2.5km in circumference. The Yamuna River originally flowed along the straight eastern edge of the fort, and the emperors had their own bathing ghats here. It contains a maze of buildings, forming a city within a city, including vast underground sections, though many of the structures were destroyed over the years by Nadir Shah, the Marathas, the Jats and finally the British, who used the fort as a garrison. Even today, much of the fort is used by the military and is off-limits to the general public.

The **Amar Singh Gate** to the south is the sole entry point to the fort these days and where you buy your entrance ticket. Its dogleg design was meant to confuse attackers who made it past the first line of defence – the crocodile-infested moat.

Following the processional way you reach a gateway and the huge red-sandstone **Jehangir's Palace** on the right. In front of the palace is **Hauz-i-Jehangir**, a huge bowl carved out of a single block of stone, which was used for bathing. The palace was probably built by Akbar for his son Jehangir. With tall stone pillars and corner brackets, it blends Indian and Central Asian archi-

Khas Mahal interior

tectural styles, a reminder of the Mughals' Turkestani cultural roots.

Further along the eastern edge of the fort you'll find the **Khas Mahal**, a beautiful marble pavilion and pool that formed the living quarters of Shah Jahan. Taj views are framed in the ornate marble grills.

The large courtyard here is **Anguri Bagh**, a garden that has been brought back to life in recent years. In the courtyard is an innocuous-looking entrance – now locked – that leads down a flight of stairs into a two-storey labyrinth of underground rooms and passageways where Akbar used to keep his 500-strong harem. On the northeast corner of the courtyard you can get a glimpse of the **Shish Mahal** (Mirror Palace), with walls inlaid with tiny mirrors.

Just to the north of the Khas Mahal is the **Mathamman (Shah) Burj**, the wonderful white-marble octagonal tower and palace where Shah Jahan was imprisoned for eight years until his death in 1666, and from where he could gaze out at the Taj Mahal, the tomb of his wife. When he died, Shah Jahan's body was taken from here by boat to the Taj. Higher up is the now-closed **Mina Masjid**, which served as Shah Jahan's private mosque.

In the large courtyard, along the eastern wall of the fort, is **Diwan-i-Khas** (Hall of Private Audience), which was reserved for important dignitaries or foreign representatives. The hall once housed Shah Jahan's legendary Peacock Throne, inset with precious stones – including the famous Koh-i-noor diamond. Overlooking the river and the distant Taj Mahal is **Takhti-i-Jehangir**, a huge slab of black rock with an inscription around the edge.

Following the north side of the courtyard, a door leads to the tiny but exquisite white-marbled **Nagina Masjid** (Gem Mosque), built in 1635 by Shah Jahan for the ladies of the court.

A hidden doorway near the mosque exit leads down to the scallop-shaped arches of the large, open **Diwan-i-Am**, used by Shah Jahan for domestic government business. It features a beautifully decorated throne room where the emperor listened to petitioners. To the north is the **Moti Masjid**, now off-limits to visitors. From here head back to the Amar Singh gate.

You can walk to the fort from Taj Ganj via the leafy Shah Jahan Park, or take an autorickshaw for ₹80. Food is not allowed into the fort. The fort opens 30 minutes before sunrise; the ticket office opens 15 minutes before that. Last entry is 30 minutes before sunset.

☑ Don't Miss

The **Mathamman (Shah) Burj**, from where the imprisoned Shah Jahan gazed out at his creation, the Taj Mahal.

ATHIKHOM SAENGCHAI / SHUTTERSTOCK ©

Take a Break

For restaurants, head to Taj Ganj or the Sadar Bazaar area of town.

SIGHTS

Akbar's Mausoleum Historic Building

(Indian/foreigner ₹30/310, video ₹25; dawn-dusk) This outstanding sandstone and marble tomb commemorates the greatest of the Mughal emperors. The huge courtyard is entered through a stunning gateway decorated with three-storey minarets at each corner and built of red sandstone strikingly inlaid with white-, yellow- and blue-marble geometric and floral patterns. The interior vestibule of the tomb is decorated with painted alabaster, creating a contrast to the plain inner tomb. The unusual upper pavilions are closed. Look for deer in the surrounding gardens.

Itimad-ud-Daulah Historic Building

(Indian/foreigner ₹30/310, video ₹25; dawn-dusk) Nicknamed the Baby Taj, the exquisite tomb of Mizra Ghiyas Beg should not be missed. This Persian nobleman was Mumtaz Mahal's grandfather and Emperor Jehangir's *wazir* (chief minister). His daughter, Nur Jahan, who married Jehangir, built the tomb between 1622 and 1628,

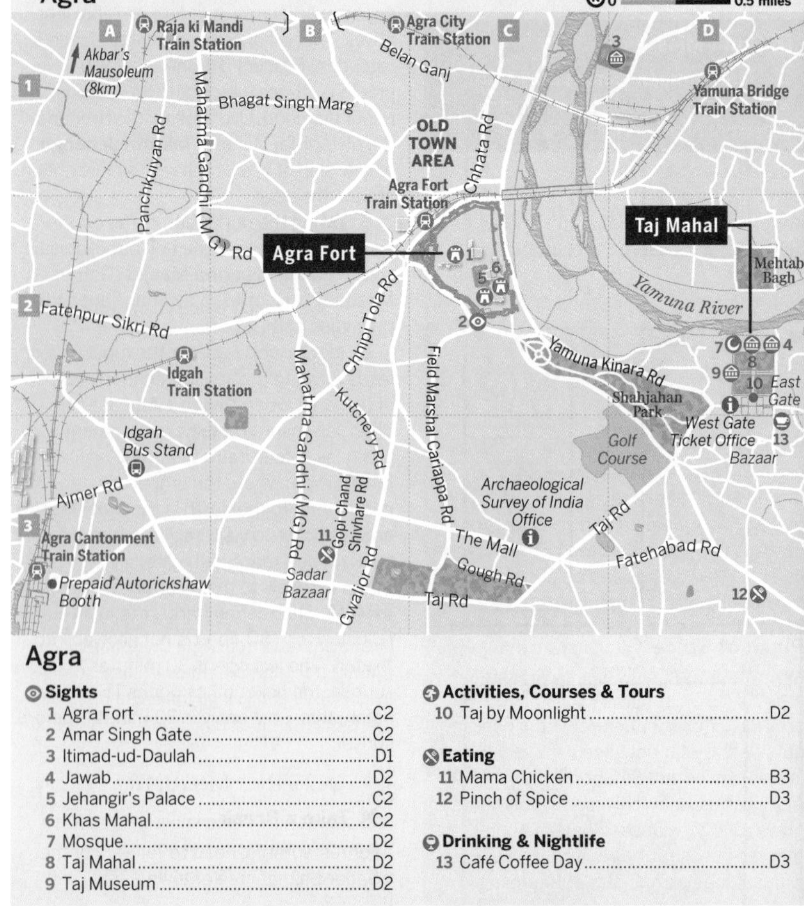

Agra

Sights

1 Agra Fort C2
2 Amar Singh Gate C2
3 Itimad-ud-Daulah D1
4 Jawab D2
5 Jehangir's Palace C2
6 Khas Mahal C2
7 Mosque D2
8 Taj Mahal D2
9 Taj Museum D2

Activities, Courses & Tours

10 Taj by Moonlight D2

Eating

11 Mama Chicken B3
12 Pinch of Spice D3

Drinking & Nightlife

13 Café Coffee Day D3

Ceiling, Akbar's Mausoleum

in a style similar to the tomb she built for Jehangir near Lahore in Pakistan.

EATING

Mama Chicken Dhaba $$
(Stall No 2, Sadar Bazaar; rolls ₹40-190, mains ₹230-290; noon-midnight) This fabulous *dhaba* (casual eatery) is a must: duelling veg and nonveg glorified street stalls employ 24 cooks during the rush, each of whom handles outdoor tandoors, grills or pots. They whip up outrageously good 'franky' rolls (like a flatbread wrap), chicken curries, naan breads and chicken tandoori *momos* (Tibetan dumplings).

Pinch of Spice Modern Indian $$$
(www.pinchofspice.in; 1076/2 Fatehabad Rd; mains ₹375-450; noon-11.30pm) This modern North Indian superstar is the best spot outside five-star hotels to indulge yourself in rich curries and tandoori kebabs. The *murg boti masala* (chicken tikka in a spicy gravy) and the *paneer lababdar* (unfermented cheese cubes in a spicy red gravy with sauteed onions) are outstanding.

INFORMATION

UP Tourism (0562-2421204; www.up-tourism.com; Agra Cantonment Train Station; 6.30am-9.30pm) The friendly train-station branch inside the Tourist Facilitation Centre on Platform 1 offers helpful advice and is where you can book day-long bus tours of Agra.

GETTING THERE & AWAY

BUS

From the **ISBT Bus Stand** (0562-2603536), AC Volvo buses go to Delhi (₹553 to ₹582, 4 hours, six daily) and Varanasi (₹1500, 11 hours, 7pm).

TRAIN

Most trains leave from **Agra Cantonment (Cantt) train station**, although some services to Varanasi and Jaipur go from Agra Fort station. Trains run to Delhi all day.

GETTING AROUND

Just outside Agra Cantonment train station is the **prepaid autorickshaw booth** (24hr). Always agree on the fare before entering the rickshaw.

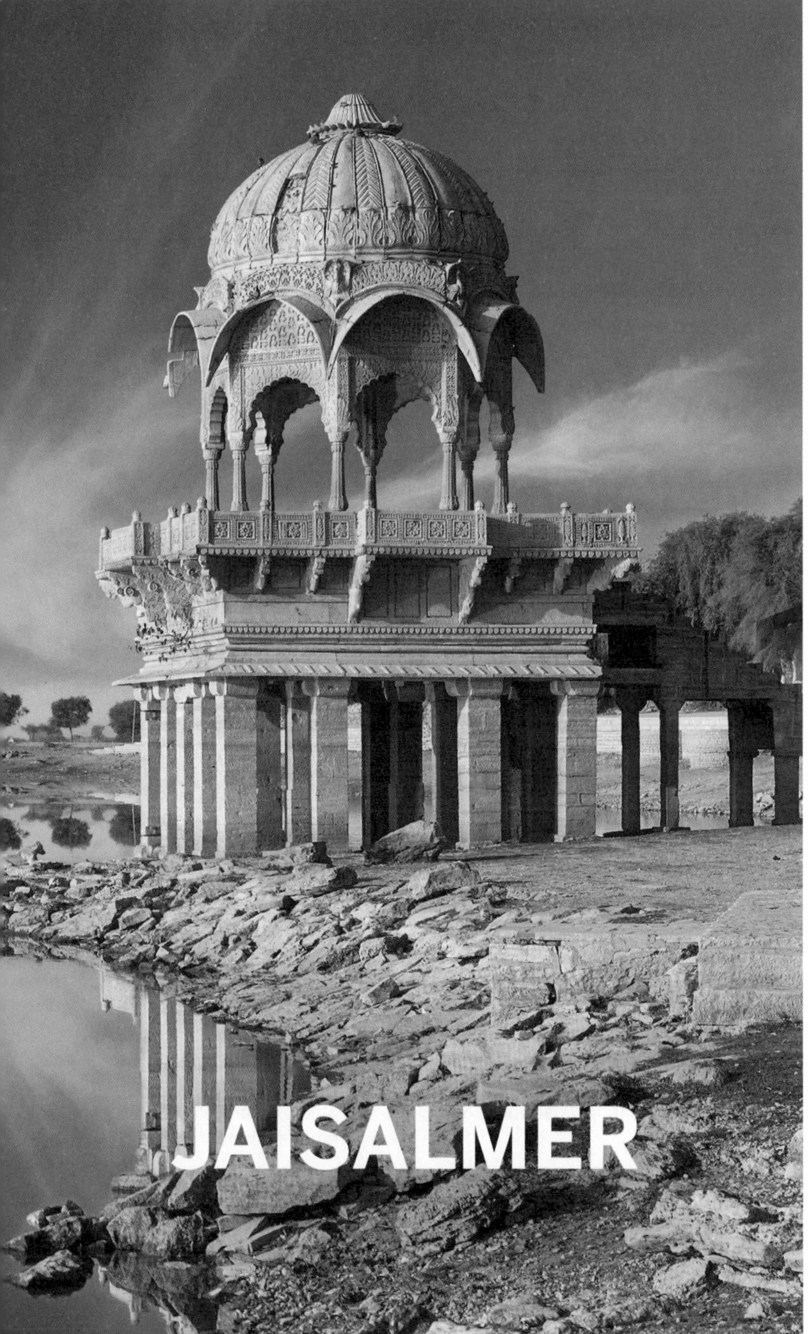

JAISALMER

In This Chapter

Jaisalmer Fort 88
Camel Safaris 90
Sights 94
Shopping 95
Eating 96
Drinking & Nightlife 96
Getting There & Away 96
Getting Around 97

Jaisalmer at a Glance...

Jaisalmer's fort is a breathtaking sandcastle rising from the plains like a mirage from a bygone era. No place better evokes exotic camel-train trade routes and desert mystery. Ninety-nine bastions encircle the fort's twisting lanes. Beneath the ramparts, the old city's narrow streets conceal magnificent havelis (traditional, ornately decorated residences) carved from the same golden-honey sandstone – hence Jaisalmer's designation as the Golden City.

Two Days in Jaisalmer

On day one organise an overnight **camel safari** (p90) to start the same afternoon. Wander the city at leisure, followed by lunch, before heading into the desert for your safari. You will return from safari in the morning, which will leave plenty of time for a detailed exploration of fascinating **Jaisalmer Fort** (p89) on day two.

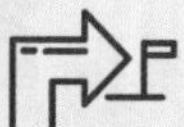

Four Days in Jaisalmer

On day three visit the **Patwa-ki-Haveli** (p94) and other *havelis*, browse the shops and have a dinner with Rajasthani music and dancing at **Desert Boy's Dhani** (p96). Enjoy a second exploration of the fort (including a palace visit if you haven't already made one) on day four, and bid farewell with dinner at a rooftop restaurant.

Previous page: Gadi Sagar temple on Gadi Sagar lake (p94)

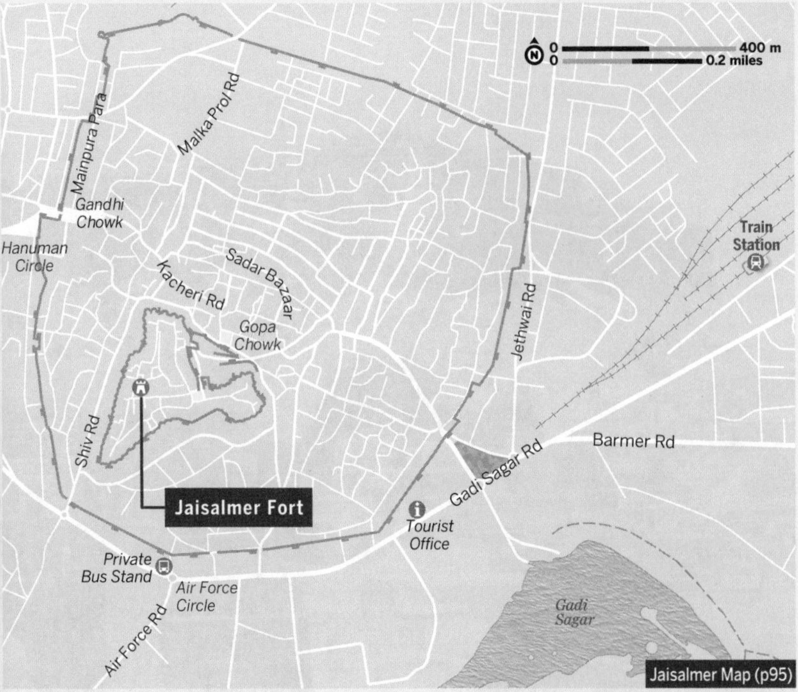

0 400 m
0 0.2 miles
Mainpura Para
Malka Prol Rd
Gandhi Chowk
Hanuman Circle
Sadar Bazaar
Kacheri Rd
Gopa Chowk
Jethwai Rd
Train Station
Shiv Rd
Barmer Rd
Gadi Sagar Rd
Jaisalmer Fort
Tourist Office
Private Bus Stand
Air Force Circle
Air Force Rd
Gadi Sagar
Jaisalmer Map (p95)

Arriving in Jaisalmer

Jaisalmer Airport 5km south of town, with connections to Delhi, Jaipur and Mumbai.

Train station On the eastern edge of town, with trains to Delhi.

Main bus stand South of the fort, with buses to Jaipur.

Where to Stay

While staying in the fort might appear to be Jaisalmer's most atmospheric choice, habitation inside the fort – driven in no small part by tourism – is damaging the monument irreparably. Fortunately, there's a wide choice of good places to stay outside the fort. You'll get massive discounts between April and August, when Jaisalmer is hellishly hot.

Jaisalmer Fort

Jaisalmer's massive fort is not just a fairy-tale desert citadel but also a fascinatingly alive urban centre with about 4000 residents. It is honeycombed with narrow lanes lined with houses and temples.

Great For...

☑ **Don't Miss**

The 360-degree panorama over fort, city and desert from the palace rooftop.

Founded in 1156 by the Bhati Rajput ruler Jaisal, Jaisalmer Fort was the focus of a number of battles between the Bhatis, the Mughals of Delhi and the Rathores of Jodhpur, but the Bhatis ruled Jaisalmer right through to Independence in 1947. Along with its palace, temples and houses, the fort is home to a large number of handicraft shops, guesthouses and restaurants.

Fort Palace

Towering over the fort's main square, and partly built on top of the Hawa Pol (the fourth fort gate), is the former rulers' elegant seven-storey **palace** (Indian/foreigner incl audio guide ₹100/500, camera ₹100; ⏲8am-6pm, from 9am Nov-Mar). Highlights of the tour include the mirrored and painted Rang Mahal (the bedroom of the 18th-century ruler Mulraj II), a gallery of finely wrought

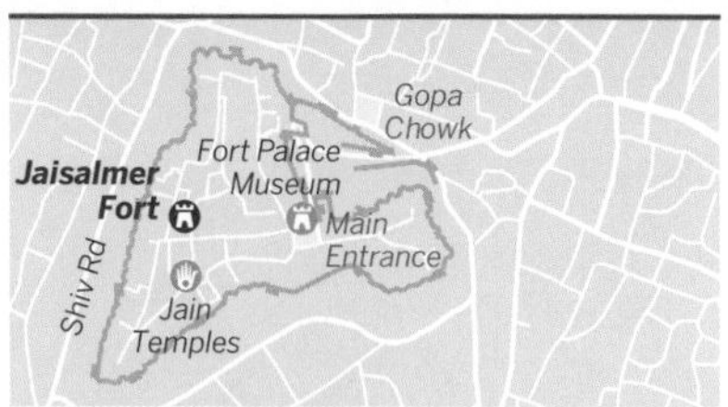

Need to Know

Entry to the fort is through the First Fort Gate, on its east side.

Take a Break

Sun Set Palace (Vyas Para; mains ₹110-240; 8am-10pm;) serves good Indian vegetarian dishes on an airy terrace.

★ Top Tip

The worthwhile 1½-hour audio-guide tour (in six languages) is included with entry. Leave ₹2000 deposit and ID.

15th-century sculptures donated to the rulers by the builders of the fort's temples, and the spectacular 360-degree views from the rooftop.

Jain Temples

Within the fort walls is a maze-like, interconnecting treasure trove of seven beautiful yellow sandstone **Jain temples** (Indian/foreigner ₹50/200; Chandraprabhu, Rikhabdev & Gyan Bhandar 8am-noon, other temples 11am-noon), dating from the 15th and 16th centuries. The temples' intricate carving has an extraordinary quality because of the soft, warm stone. Shoes and all leather items must be removed before entering.

A Castle Built on Sand

A decade ago, three of Jaisalmer Fort's ancient bastions had collapsed and the whole structure was in danger of being undermined by leaks from its antique drainage system. The main problem: material progress, in the form of piped water for the fort's inhabitants. Much-needed conservation works have since been done – most importantly the renewal of the fort's drainage system, repaving of the streets and repair works inside the palace.

Though things have improved, some conservationists still believe the fort's structure is in danger, highlighted by a collapse of a wall being restored in 2016. Calls remain for the fort's inhabitants, and those who work in the fort, to be removed. The fort's current population (around 4000) has been established since the 1960s; before then, the fort's inhabitants numbered in the few hundreds, made up mostly of royal family and their workers, plus monks and priests connected to the fort's temples. Visitors should be aware of the fort's fragile nature and conserve resources, especially water, as much as possible.

Camel Safaris

Trekking around by camel is the most evocative and fun way to sample Thar Desert life – and camping out in the desert, huddling around a tiny fire beneath the stars and listening to the camel drivers' songs, is a magical experience. Most trips now include 4WD rides to get you to less-frequented areas.

Great For...

Lodhruva
Thar Desert
Jaisalmer
Sam
Khuri

Need to Know

Competition between safari organisers is intense and standards vary. Check a few operators before deciding.

★ Top Tip

The camel drivers expect a tip at the trip's end: up to ₹100 per day is welcomed.

VIXIT / SHUTTERSTOCK ©

Trekking around the Thar Desert on a camel is a lot of fun, but don't expect great seas of dunes. The Thar is mostly arid scrubland sprinkled with villages and wind turbines, with dune areas popping out here and there. You'll often come across children herding flocks of sheep or goats, whose neck bells tinkle in the desert silence.

Which Safari?

Most hotels and guesthouses are very happy to arrange your camel safari. While many provide a good service, some may cut corners and take you for the kind of ride you didn't have in mind. You can also organise a safari directly with one of the specialist agencies in Jaisalmer, since these depend exclusively on safari business.

The best-known dunes, at **Sam**, 40km west of Jaisalmer, are crowded in the evening and have more of a carnival atmosphere. The dunes near **Khuri**, 48km southwest of Jaisalmer, are also quite busy at sunset, but quiet the rest of the time.

Typical rates are between ₹1200 and ₹2500 per person for a one-day, one-night trip (leaving one morning and returning the next, with the camel riding usually done in two-hour batches, one before lunch, one after). Rates should include 4WD transfers, meals, mineral water, blankets and sometimes a thin mattress. Check that there will be one camel for each rider. Always get everything down in writing. Costs are normally lower (₹1100 to ₹1600 per person) if you leave Jaisalmer in the afternoon and return the following morning.

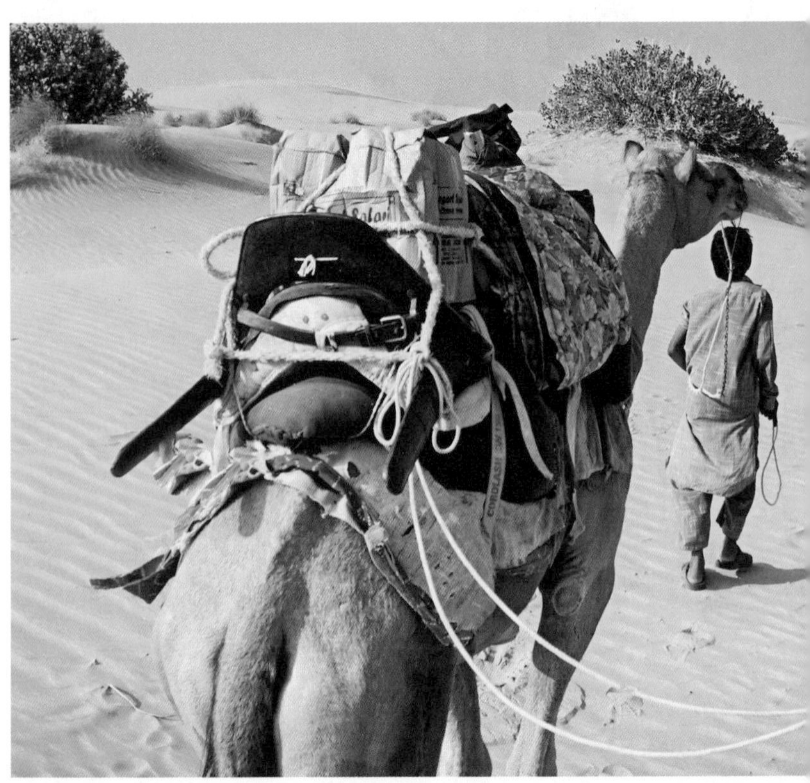

Sahara Travels Tours

(☎02992-252609, 9414319921; www.saharatravelsjaisalmer.com; Gopa Chowk; ⏲6am-8pm) Run by the son of the late LN Bissa (aka Mr Desert), this place is very professional and transparent. Prices for an overnight trip (9am to 11am the following day) are ₹2100 per person, all inclusive. A cheaper overnight alternative that avoids the mid-day sun starts at 2pm and finishes at 11am for ₹1650.

Thar Desert Tours Tours

(☎9414365333; www.tharcamelsafarijaisalmer.com; Gandhi Chowk; ⏲8.30am-7.30pm) This well-run operator charges ₹1300 per person per day including water and meals, adjusting prices depending on trip times. It limits tours to five people maximum, and we also receive good feedback about them. Customers pay 80% upfront.

Trotters Tours

(☎9828929974; www.trottersjaisalmer.net; Gopa Chowk; ⏲5.30am-9.00pm) This company is transparently run with a clear price list showing everything on offer, including trips to 'off-the-beaten-track' areas as well as cheaper jaunts to Sam or Khuri. Prices for an overnight trip (6.30am to 11am/5.30pm the following day) are ₹2250 to ₹2450 per person, all inclusive.

☑ Don't Miss

An overnight safari, with a night on some dunes, is a minimum to get a feel for the experience.

ELENA-STUDIO / GETTY IMAGES ©

What to Take

A wide-brimmed hat, long trousers, long-sleeved shirt, insect repellent, toilet paper, a torch (flashlight), sunscreen, sports bras for women, water bottle, sleeping bag, and some cash (for a tip to the camel men, if nothing else) are recommended.

In the Desert

At resting points during the safari, the camels are unsaddled and hobbled. They'll often have a roll in the sand before walking away to browse on nearby shrubs, while the camel drivers brew chai or prepare food. The whole crew rests in the shade of thorn trees.

Take care of your possessions, particularly on the return journey. Any complaints you do have should be reported, either to the **Superintendent of Police** (☎02992-252233), or the **tourist office** (☎02992-252406; Gadi Sagar Rd; ⏲9.30am-6pm) post inside the First Fort Gate and on the Gadi Sagar access road.

Take A Break

There's always a long lunch stop during the hottest part of the day.

SIGHTS

Patwa-ki-Haveli Historic Building

(Indian/foreigner ₹50/200; 9am-6pm) The biggest fish in the *haveli* pond is Patwa-ki-Haveli, which towers over a narrow lane, its intricate stonework like honey-coloured lace. Divided into five sections, it was built between 1800 and 1860 by five Jain brothers who made their fortunes in brocade and jewellery. It's all very impressive from the outside; however, the first of the five sections, the privately owned **Kothari's Patwa-ki-Haveli Museum** (Indian/foreigner ₹100/250; 9am-6pm), richly evokes 19th-century life and is the only one worth paying entry for.

Thar Heritage Museum Museum

(9414150762; Main Rd, Artists Colony; ₹100; 10am-8pm) This private museum has an intriguing assortment of Jaisalmer artefacts, from turbans, musical instruments, fossils and kitchen equipment, to displays on birth, marriage, death and opium customs. It's brought alive by the guided tour you'll get from its founder, local historian and folklorist LN Khatri. Look for the snakes and ladders game that acts as a teaching guide to Hinduism's spiritual journey.

Desert Cultural Centre & Museum Museum

(02992-253723; Gadi Sagar Rd; museum ₹50, camera ₹50, combined museum & puppet show ₹100; 9am-6pm, puppet shows 6.30-8.30pm) This interesting little museum tells the history of Rajasthan's princely states and has exhibits on traditional Rajasthani culture. Features include Rajasthani music (with video), textiles, a *kavad* (a brightly painted wooden mobile story box), and a *phad* (scroll painting) depicting the story of the Rajasthani folk hero Pabuji. It also hosts nightly half-hour **puppet shows** with English commentary. The ticket includes admission to the Jaisalmer Folklore Museum.

Gadi Sagar Lake

This stately tank, southeast of the city walls, was Jaisalmer's vital water supply until 1965, and because of its importance it is surrounded by many small temples and

Lace-like stone carvings, Patwa-ki-Haveli

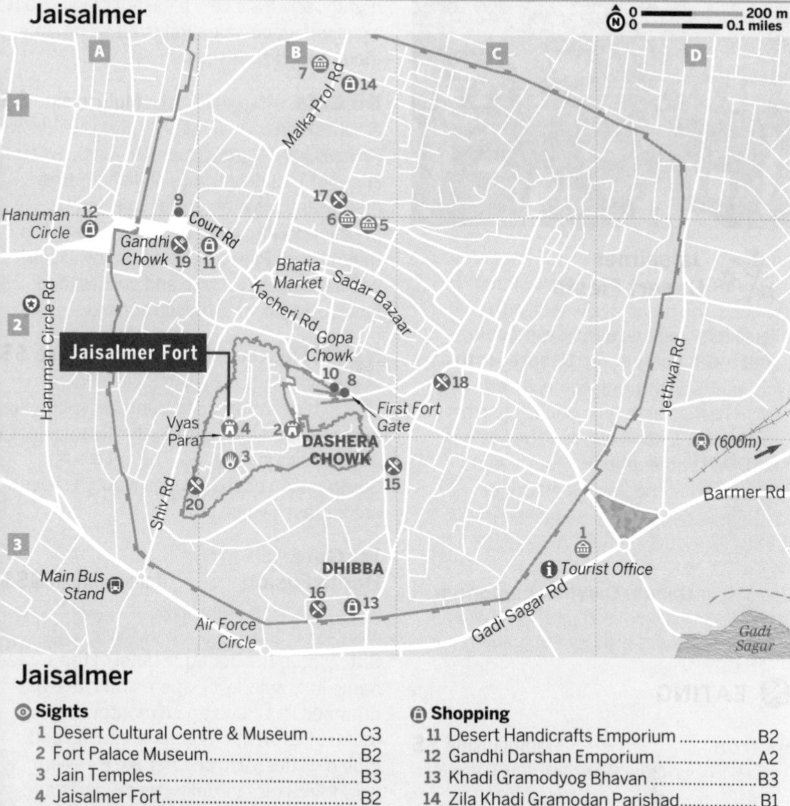

Jaisalmer

Sights

1 Desert Cultural Centre & Museum C3
2 Fort Palace Museum B2
3 Jain Temples B3
4 Jaisalmer Fort B2
5 Kothari's Patwa-ki-Haveli Museum B2
6 Patwa-ki-Haveli B2
7 Thar Heritage Museum B1

Activities, Courses & Tours

8 Sahara Travels B2
9 Thar Desert Tours A1
10 Trotters B2

Shopping

11 Desert Handicrafts Emporium B2
12 Gandhi Darshan Emporium A2
13 Khadi Gramodyog Bhavan B3
14 Zila Khadi Gramodan Parishad B1

Eating

15 1st Gate Home Fusion B3
16 Desert Boy's Dhani B3
17 KB Cafe B1
18 Natraj Restaurant C2
19 Saffron A2
20 Sun Set Palace A3

shrines. The tank was built in 1367 by Maharawal Gadsi Singh, taking advantage of a natural declivity that already retained some water. It's a waterfowl favourite in winter, but can almost dry up before the monsoon.

SHOPPING

Jaisalmer is famous for its stunning embroidery, bedspreads, mirrorwork wall hangings, oil lamps, stonework and antiques. Watch out when purchasing silver items: the metal is sometimes adulterated with bronze.

There are several good *khadi* (homespun cloth) shops where you can find fixed-price tablecloths, rugs and clothes, with a variety of patterning techniques including tie-dye, block printing and embroidery. Try **Zila Khadi Gramodan Parishad** (Malka Prol Rd; ⏲10am-6pm Mon-Sat), **Khadi Gramodyog Bhavan** (Dhibba; ⏲10am-6pm

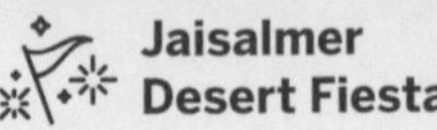

Jaisalmer Desert Fiesta

Jaisalmer celebrates its desert culture with the action-packed **Desert Festival** (Jan/Feb), featuring camel races, camel polo, folk music, snake charmers, turban-tying contests, and the famous Mr Desert competition. Many events take place at the Sam Sand Dunes.

Masked revellers, Jaisalmer Desert Festival

Mon-Sat) or **Gandhi Darshan Emporium** (near Hanuman Circle; 11am-7pm Fri-Wed).

EATING

Saffron Multicuisine $$

(Hotel Nachana Haveli, Goverdhan Chowk; mains ₹245-385, thali veg/nonveg ₹385/545; 7am-11pm) On the spacious roof terrace of Hotel Nachana Haveli, the veg and nonveg food here is excellent. It's a particularly atmospheric place in the evening, with private and communal lounges and more formal seating arrangements. The Indian food is hard to beat, though the Italian isn't too bad either. Alcohol is served and the thali is generous.

Desert Boy's Dhani Indian $$

(Dhibba Para; mains ₹120-350, thali ₹350-450; 11am-4pm & 7-11pm;) A walled-garden restaurant where tables are spread around a large, stone-paved courtyard shaded by a spreading tree. There's also traditional cushion seating undercover and in an AC room. Rajasthani music and dance is performed from 8pm to 10pm nightly, and it's a very pleasant place to eat excellent, good-value Rajasthani and other Indian veg dishes.

KB Cafe Multicuisine $$

(02992-253833; www.killabhawan.com; Patwa-ki-haveli Chowk; mains ₹160-380; 8am-9pm;) This delightfully stylish rooftop restaurant sits atop one of Jaisalmer's premier boutique hotels with views to the magnificent Patwa-ki-haveli. Enjoy excellent vegetarian pasta, pizza and curries, and finish off with an espresso coffee.

Natraj Restaurant Multicuisine $$

(Aasani Rd; mains ₹120-310; 8am-10.30pm;) This rooftop restaurant has satisfying pure veg food that is consistently excellent and the service is good. The delicious South Indian dosas (large savoury crepes) are fantastic value.

1st Gate Home Fusion Italian, Indian $$$

(02992-254462, 9462554462; First Fort Gate; mains ₹360-500; 7.30am-10.30pm;) Sitting atop the boutique hotel of the same name, this split-level, open-air terrace has dramatic fort views and a mouthwatering menu of authentic vegetarian Italian and Indian dishes. Also on offer are excellent wood-fired pizzas, delicious desserts and good strong Italian coffee. Wine (by the bottle or glass), beer and cocktails are available.

DRINKING & NIGHTLIFE

As the sun sets and the floodlights paint the bastions in bright light and dark shadows, head to a rooftop to enjoy a cold beer, wine or lassi. Most hotels have a rooftop restaurant affording fort views and there are several independent restaurants on the approach to the fort near the first gate.

GETTING THERE & AWAY

AIR

In 2018 SpiceJet (www.spicejet.com) commenced daily flights to/from Ahmedabad, Jaipur,

Dosa with curry and coconut chutney

Delhi and Mumbai from Jaisalmer's new airport, 5km south of town.

BUS

RSRTC buses leave from the **main bus stand** (Shiv Rd). There are two or three services to Jaipur (seat/sleeper ₹420/550, 11 hours).

TRAIN

The **train station** (ticket office 8am-8pm Mon-Sat, to 1.45pm Sun) is located on the eastern edge of town, just off the Jodhpur road. There's a reserved ticket booth for foreigners. There are three train services to Delhi (sleeper/3AC ₹450/1205, 18 hours), at 1am, 1.25am and 4.45pm via Jaipur.

GETTING AROUND

It costs around ₹50 from the train station to Gandhi Chowk, north of the fort.

It's possible to hire taxis or 4WDs from the stand on Hanuman Circle Rd. To Khuri, the Sam Sand Dunes or Lodhruva, expect to pay from ₹1200 return including a wait of about an hour.

10

JAIPUR

In This Chapter

Amber Fort 102
City Palace 104
Walking Tour: Pink City 106
Sights 108
Activities 109
Shopping 110
Eating 111
Drinking & Nightlife 111
Information 112
Getting There & Away 113
Getting Around 113

Jaipur at a Glance...

Enthralling, historical Jaipur is the gateway to India's most flamboyant state, Rajasthan. The city's colourful, chaotic streets ebb and flow with a heady brew of old and new. Amid the mayhem, the splendours of Jaipur's majestic past stand tall. The City Palace still houses the former royal family, while the surrounding arid hills provide the setting for the fairy-tale grandeur of Amber Fort, Jaipur's star attraction.

Two Days in Jaipur

Dive into the beating heart of the **Pink City** to explore its frenetic bazaars, the iconic **Hawa Mahal** (p108), the fascinating **Jantar Mantar** (p108) and **City Palace** (p103). Wind up with dinner at classic **Niro's** (p111).

On your second day, explore magnificent **Amber Fort** (p101) then return for dinner at **Peacock Rooftop Restaurant** (p111) and more rooftop action at **Blackout club** (p112).

Four Days in Jaipur

On day three investigate the newer and outlying parts of Jaipur, including the **Central Museum** (p108), **Nahargarh** (p113) and some of the excellent shops, including **Jaipur Modern** (p110).

Soar away on a **Sky Waltz** (p109) balloon flight on day four, before returning to the Pink City's bazaars and winding down with an ayurvedic massage at **Kerala Ayurveda Kendra** (p110).

Previous page: Hawa Mahal (p108)
WAJ / SHUTTERSTOCK ©

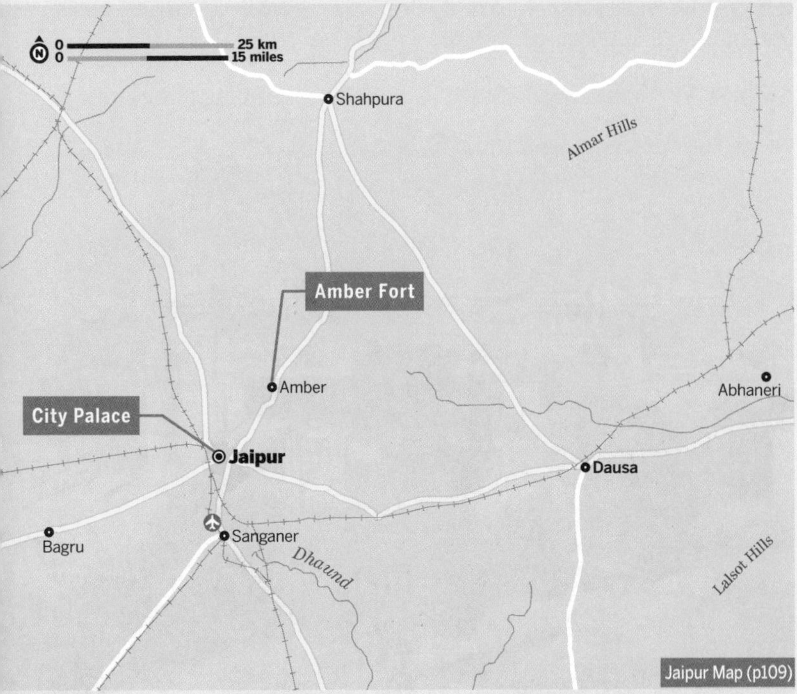

Jaipur Map (p109)

Arriving in Jaipur

Jaipur International Airport Select international flights to hubs in Asia and the Middle East, and domestic connections.

Train station Trains to/from Sawai Madhopur (for Ranthambore National Park), Agra and Delhi.

Main bus station Government buses to/from Delhi.

Where to Stay

Travellers are spoiled for choice in all budget categories. Many hotels will pick you up from the bus or train station if you ring ahead, saving you from persistent touts. From May to September, most midrange and top-end hotels drop prices by 25% to 50%.

BANANA REPUBLIC IMAGES / SHUTTERSTOCK ©

Amber Fort

The magnificent, formidable, honey-hued fort of Amber (pronounced 'amer'), an ethereal example of Rajput architecture, rises from a rocky mountainside about 11km northeast of Jaipur, and is the city's must-see sight.

Great For...

☑ **Don't Miss**

The delicate and quirky marble-relief panels in the Jai Mandir, depicting insects and flowers.

This magnificent fort comprises an extensive palace complex, built from pale-yellow and-pink sandstone and white marble. You can trudge up from the road in about 10 minutes, or take a 4WD (₹450 return for five passengers, including a one-hour wait time).

Entrances

Walking up the hill, you'll enter Amber Fort through the **Suraj Pol** (Sun Gate), which leads to the **Jaleb Chowk** (Main Courtyard), where returning armies would display their war booty to the populace. Women could view this area from the veiled windows of the palace. The ticket office is directly across the courtyard from the Suraj Pol. If you arrive by car, enter through the **Chand Pol** (Moon Gate) on the opposite side of Jaleb Chowk.

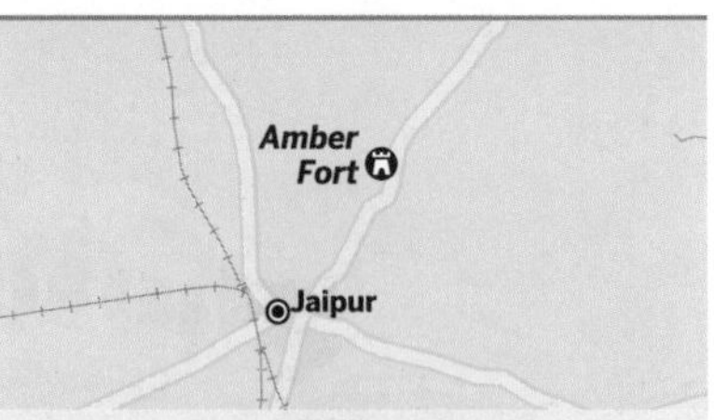

Need to Know

Indian/foreigner ₹100/500, night entry ₹100, guide ₹200, audio guide ₹200-250; 8am-6pm, night entry 7-9pm

Take a Break

Find cafes and restaurants in the complex, or street stalls in the town below.

★ Top Tip

Hiring a guide or audio guide is highly recommended: there are few signs and many blind alleys.

Siladevi Temple

From Jaleb Chowk, an imposing stairway leads up to the main palace, but first it's worth taking the steps just to the right, which lead to the small **Siladevi Temple**, with its gorgeous silver doors featuring repoussé (raised relief) work.

Diwan-i-Am

The main stairway from Jaleb Chowk takes you to the second courtyard and the **Diwan-i-Am** (Hall of Public Audience), which has a double row of columns, each topped by an elephant-shaped capital, and latticed galleries above.

Ganesh Pol & Royal Halls

The maharaja's apartments are set around the third courtyard. You enter through the fabulous **Ganesh Pol**, decorated with beautiful frescoed arches. The **Jai Mandir** (Hall of Victory) is noted for its inlaid panels and multimirrored ceiling. Opposite is the **Sukh Niwas** (Hall of Pleasure), with an ivory-inlaid sandalwood door and a channel that once carried cooling water through the room.

Amber's History

Amber Fort was built by the Kachhwaha Rajputs from Gwalior, in present-day Madhya Pradesh. Construction, financed with war booty, began in 1592 under Maharaja Man Singh, the Rajput commander of Mughal emperor Akbar's army. The fort was later extended and completed by the Jai Singhs before they shifted their capital to Jaipur.

Mubarak Mahal

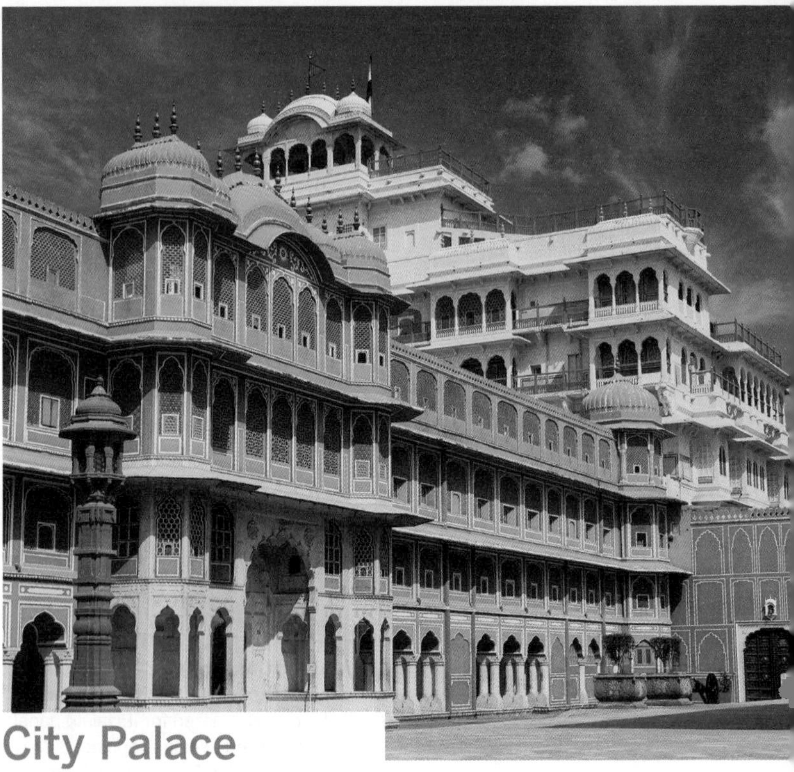

City Palace

This fascinating complex of courtyards, gardens and buildings, a striking blend of Rajasthani, Mughal and European architecture, stands right at the heart of the Old City.

Great For...

☑ Don't Miss

The two enormous urns in the Diwan-i-Khas, reputedly the world's largest silver objects.

The palace's outer wall was built by Jaipur's 18th-century founder Jai Singh II. The palace within has been enlarged and adapted with buildings added right up to the 20th century.

Mubarak Mahal

Entering through Virendra Pol, you'll see the **Mubarak Mahal**, built in the late-19th century for Maharaja Madho Singh II as a reception centre for dignitaries. It forms part of the **Maharaja Sawai Mansingh II Museum**, containing royal costumes and superb shawls. One remarkable exhibit is Sawai Madho Singh I's capacious clothing; it's said he was a cuddly 2m tall, 1.2m wide and 250kg.

ɪacock Gate, Pitam Niwas Chowk

DON MAMMOSER / SHUTTERSTOCK ©

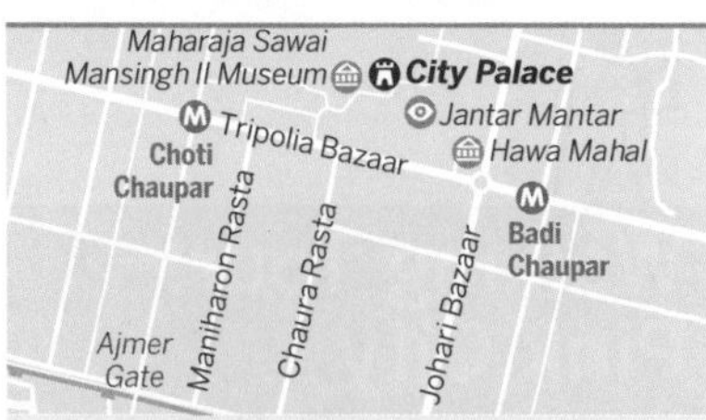

Need to Know

0141-4088888; www.royaljaipur.in; Indian/foreigner incl camera ₹130/500, guide from ₹300, audio guide ₹200, Royal Grandeur tour Indian/foreigner ₹2500/3000; 9.30am-5pm

Take a Break

The all-vegetarian LMB (p111) serves top-class thalis and sweets.

★ Top Tip

Foreigners' tickets (valid two days) cover the Royal Gaitor, Cenotaphs of the Maharanis, and Jaigarh in Amber.

ɪrmoury

he **Armoury** in the **Anand Mahal Sileg hana** (the Maharani's Palace) has one f India's best collections of weapons. lany of the ceremonial items are elegantly ngraved and inlaid, belying their grisly urpose.

ɪiwan-i-Khas (Sarvatobhadra)

ɪt the centre of the **Sarvatobhadra** court-ard is a pink-and-white, marble-paved gal-ɪry that served as the **Diwan-i-Khas** (Hall f Private Audience), where maharajas vould consult their ministers. You'll see two normous **silver vessels** here, each 1.6m all and reputedly the largest silverware in ne world.

Diwan-i-Am Art Gallery

Within the lavish **Diwan-i-Am** (Hall of Public Audience), this gallery's exhibits include a copy of the entire Bhagavad Gita handwritten in tiny script, and miniature copies of other Hindu scriptures.

Pitam Niwas Chowk & Chandra Mahal

Towards the palace's inner courtyard is **Pitam Niwas Chowk**. Four gates here represent the seasons – **Peacock Gate** (autumn), **Lotus Gate** (summer), **Green Gate** (spring) and **Rose Gate** (winter). Beyond is the **Chandra Mahal**, residence of the current royal family, where you can take a 45-minute guided tour of select areas.

Walking Tour: Pink City

Jaipur's Old City was painted pink in 1876 to welcome the Prince of Wales. This walk visits the major monuments tucked amidst this bustling area.

Start New Gate
Distance 4.5km
Duration 3-5 hours

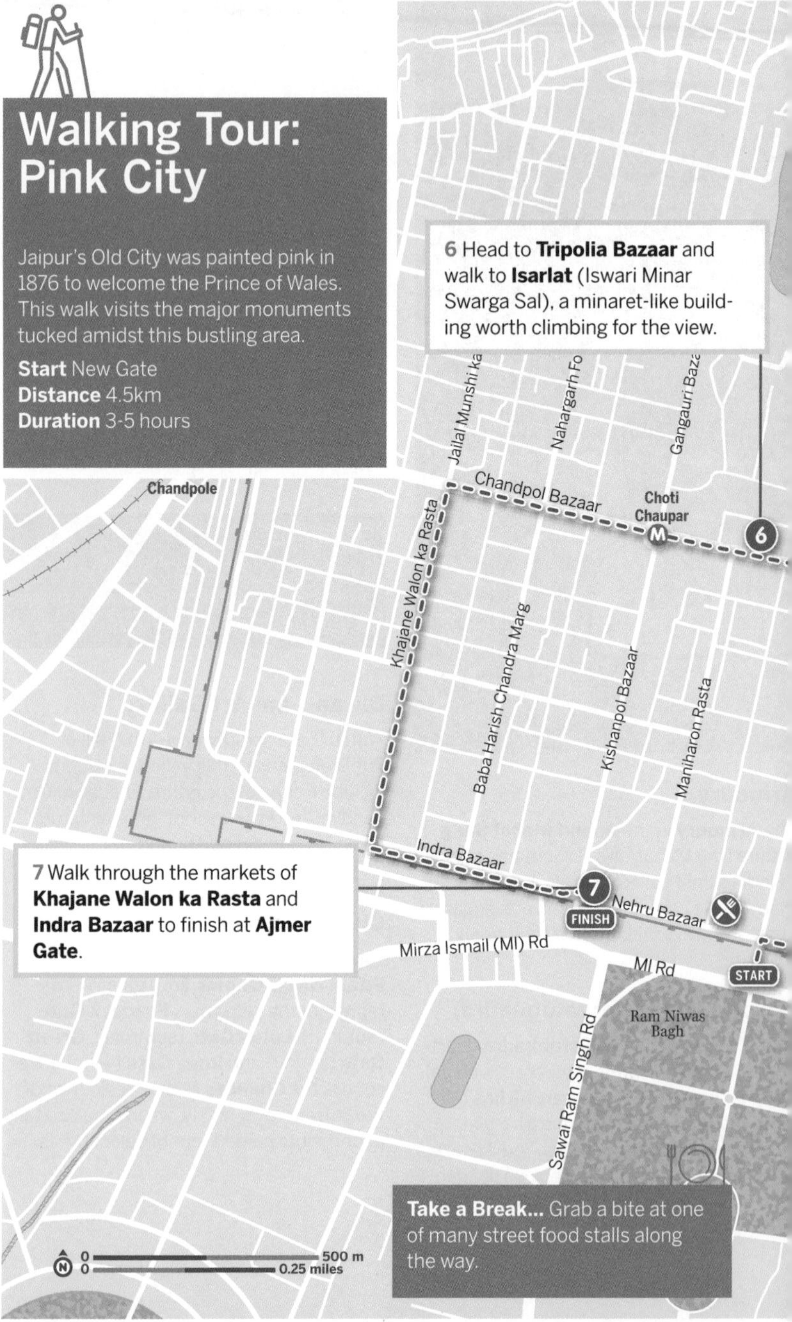

6 Head to **Tripolia Bazaar** and walk to **Isarlat** (Iswari Minar Swarga Sal), a minaret-like building worth climbing for the view.

7 Walk through the markets of **Khajane Walon ka Rasta** and **Indra Bazaar** to finish at **Ajmer Gate**.

Take a Break... Grab a bite at one of many street food stalls along the way.

Jailal Munshi ka
Nahargarh Fo
Gangauri Baza
Chandpole
Chandpol Bazaar
Choti Chaupar
Khajane Walon ka Rasta
Baba Harish Chandra Marg
Kishanpol Bazaar
Maniharon Rasta
Indra Bazaar
FINISH
Nehru Bazaar
Mirza Ismail (MI) Rd
MI Rd
START
Ram Niwas Bagh
Sawai Ram Singh Rd
0 500 m
0 0.25 miles

4 To the west is the **City Palace** (p104), an amazing collection of palaces, galleries, gateways and courtyards.

5 Hop across to **Jantar Mantar** (p108), the royal observatory, resembling a collection of bizarre sculptures.

Classic Photo The beehive geometric facade of Hawa Mahal viewed from across the road.

3 Walk north to **Hawa Mahal** (p108), built in 1799 to enable royal ladies to watch street life.

2 Turn left into **Johari Bazaar**, where jewellers sell highly glazed meenakari (enamelwork).

1 Entering from New Gate, turn right into **Bapu Bazaar**, selling fabric and shoes, a favourite with Jaipur's women.

Tripolia Bazaar
Badi Chaupar
Chaura Rasta
Johari Bazaar
Bapu Bazaar
Agra Rd

SIGHTS

Old City (Pink City)

Hawa Mahal Historic Building

(Palace of the Winds; Sireh Deori Bazaar; Indian/foreigner incl camera ₹50/200, guide ₹200, audio guide ₹177; ⏲9am-5.30pm) Jaipur's most-distinctive landmark, the Hawa Mahal is an extraordinary pink-painted, delicately honeycombed hive that rises a dizzying five storeys. It was constructed in 1799 by Maharaja Sawai Pratap Singh to enable ladies of the royal household to watch the life and processions of the city. The top offers stunning views over Jantar Mantar and the City Palace in one direction and over Sireh Deori Bazaar in the other.

Jantar Mantar Historic Site

(Indian/foreigner ₹50/200, guide ₹200, audio guide ₹100; ⏲9am-4.30pm) Adjacent to the City Palace is Jantar Mantar, an observatory begun by Jai Singh II in 1728. Built for measuring the heavens, the name is derived from the Sanskrit *yanta mantr*, meaning 'instrument of calculation', and in 2010 it was added to India's list of Unesco World Heritage Sites. Paying for a local guide is highly recommended if you wish to learn how each fascinating instrument works.

Other Areas

Central Museum Museu

(Albert Hall; J Nehru Marg; Indian/foreigner ₹40/300, audio guide Hindi/English ₹118/177; ⏲9.30am-5pm Tue-Sun) This museum is housed in the spectacularly florid Albert Hall, located south of the Old City. The building was designed by Sir Swinton Jacob, and combines some elements of English and North Indian architecture, as well as huge friezes celebrating the world's great cultures. It was known as the pride of the new Jaipur when it opened in 1887. The grand old building hosts an eclectic array of tribal dress, dioramas, sculptures, miniature paintings, carpets, musical instruments and even a Egyptian mummy.

Intricate carving, Royal Gaitor

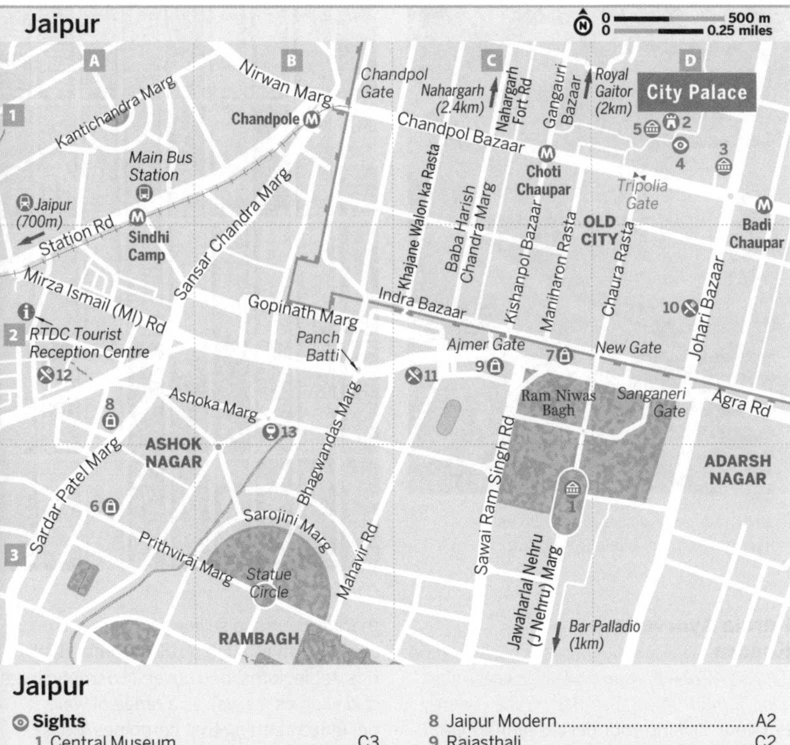

Jaipur

Sights
1 Central Museum C3
2 City Palace D1
3 Hawa Mahal D1
4 Jantar Mantar D1
5 Maharaja Sawai Mansingh II Museum D1

Shopping
6 Anokhi A3
7 Gem-Testing Laboratory C2
8 Jaipur Modern A2
9 Rajasthali C2

Eating
10 LMB D2
11 Niro's C2
12 Peacock Rooftop Restaurant A2

Drinking & Nightlife
13 Blackout B2

Royal Gaitor Historic Site

(Gatore ki Chhatriyan; Indian/foreigner ₹20/30; 9am-5pm) The royal cenotaphs, just outside the city walls, beneath Nahargarh, feel remarkably undiscovered and are an appropriately restful place to visit. The stone monuments are beautifully and intricately carved. Maharajas Pratap Singh, Madho Singh II and Jai Singh II, among others, are honoured here. Jai Singh II has the most impressive marble cenotaph, with a dome supported by 20 carved pillars.

ACTIVITIES

Sky Waltz Ballooning

(9560387222; www.skywaltz.com; Indian adult/child ₹12,000/7000, foreigner adult/child US$280/165) Sky Waltz offers spectacular early-morning balloon flights over Amber Fort and the surrounding countryside. The package includes pickup and drop-off from your Jaipur hotel, hot refreshments, watching the balloon inflation, and the hour-long flight itself.

ROBERT F COOKE / SHUTTERSTOCK ©

From left: hot-air ballooning (p109); bracelets at a market stall; Peacock Rooftop Restaurant

Kerala Ayurveda Kendra Ayurveda

(☎0141-4022446; www.keralaayurvedakendra.com; 32 Indra Colony, Bani Park; ⏰9am-9pm) Is Jaipur making your nerves jangle? Get help through ayurvedic massage and therapy. Treatments include *sirodhara* (₹1750/2800 for 50/90 minutes), where medicated oil is steadily streamed over your forehead to reduce stress, tone the brain and help with sleep disorders. Massages (male therapist for male clients and female for female clients) cost from ₹900 for 50 minutes.

SHOPPING

Jaipur is a shopper's paradise. Commercial buyers come here from all over the world to stock up on the amazing range of jewellery, gems, textiles and crafts that come from all over Rajasthan. You'll have to bargain hard, particularly around major tourist sights.

Anokhi Clothing, Textiles

(www.anokhi.com; 2nd fl, KK Sq, C-11 Prithviraj Marg; ⏰10am-8pm) Anokhi is a classy, upmarket boutique selling stunning high-quality textiles such as block-printed fabrics, tablecloths, bed covers, cosmetic bags and scarves, as well as a range of well-designed clothing that combines Indian and Western influences. There's a wonderful organic cafe on the premises and a decent bookshop in the same building.

Rajasthali Arts & Crafts

(MI Rd; ⏰11am-7.30pm Mon-Sat) This state-government-run emporium, opposite Ajmer Gate, is packed with quality Rajasthani artefacts and crafts, including enamelwork, embroidery, pottery, woodwork, jewellery, puppets, block-printed sheets, miniatures, brassware, mirrorwork and more. Scout out prices here before launching into the bazaar; items can be cheaper at the markets, but the quality is often higher at the state emporium for not much more money.

Jaipur Modern Fashion & Accessories

(☎0141-4112000; www.jaipurmodern.com; 51 Sardar Patel Marg, C-Scheme; ⏰11am-9pm) This contemporary showroom offers local arts and crafts, clothing, homewares, stationery and fashion accessories. The staff are relaxed (no hard sell here) and if you are not in the mood to shop, there's a great cafe serving organic South Indian coffee and Mediterranean snacks.

EATING

Peacock Rooftop Restaurant Multicuisine $$

(0141-2373700; Hotel Pearl Palace, Hari Kishan Somani Marg; mains ₹150-390; 7am-11pm) This multilevel rooftop restaurant at the Hotel Pearl Palace gets rave reviews for its excellent yet inexpensive cuisine (Indian, Chinese and continental) and fun ambience. The attentive service, whimsical furnishings and romantic view towards Hathroi Fort make it a first-rate restaurant. In addition to the dinner menu, there are healthy breakfasts and great-value burgers, pizzas and thalis for lunch.

LMB Indian $$

(0141-2565844; Johari Bazaar; mains ₹230-390; 8am-11pm;) Laxmi Misthan Bhandar, LMB to you and me, is a vegetarian restaurant in the Old City that's been going strong since 1954. A welcoming air-conditioned refuge from frenzied Johari Bazaar, LMB is also an institution with its singular decor, attentive waiters and extensive sweet counter. Now it is no longer sattvik (pure vegetarian), you can order meals with onion and garlic.

Niro's Indian $$$

(0141-2374493; www.nirosindia.com; MI Rd; mains ₹400-580; 10am-11pm;) Established in 1949, Niro's is a long-standing favourite on MI Rd that, like a good wine, only improves with age. Escape the chaos of the street by ducking into its cool, clean, mirror-ceilinged sanctum to savour veg and nonveg Indian cuisine with professional service. Classic Chinese and continental food is available, but the Indian menu is definitely the pick.

DRINKING & NIGHTLIFE

Bar Palladio Bar

(0141-2565556; www.bar-palladio.com; Narain Niwas Palace Hotel, Narain Singh Rd; cocktails

Jaipur Gems

Jaipur is famous for precious and semiprecious stones. The main gem-dealing area is around Pahar Ganj in the Old City. Here you can see stones being cut and polished in workshops tucked off narrow backstreets.

To receive an authenticity certificate (and thus avoid being scammed), you can deposit your gems at the **gem-testing laboratory** (☎0141-2568221; www.gtljaipur.info; Rajasthan Chamber Bhawan, MI Rd; ⏰10am-4pm Mon-Sat) between 10am and 4pm, then return the following day between 4pm and 5pm to pick up the certificate. The service costs ₹1050 per stone, or ₹1650 for same-day service (if deposited before 1pm).

from ₹600; ⏰6-11pm) This cool bar-restaurant has an extensive drinks list and an Italian food menu (mains ₹360 to ₹420). The vivid blue theme of the romantic Orientalist interior flows through to candlelit outdoor seating, making this a very relaxing place to sip a drink, snack on bruschetta and enjoy a conversation. **Il Teatro** is an occasional live-music event at the bar – see the website for dates.

Blackout — Club

(☎0141-3319497; www.facebook.com/blackoutjaipur; Hotel Golden Oak, Ahinsa Circle, C-Scheme; cocktails from ₹250; ⏰1pm-2am) This popular spot is spread over three levels, including the rooftop, which boasts great views of the city. There's ample seating, good food, a DJ and a dance floor. It's more of a restaurant during the week and a club on the weekends. Thursday night (from 8pm) is Ladies Night, with free cocktails for women.

ℹ INFORMATION

RTDC Tourist Office (☎0141-5110598; www.rajasthantourism.gov.in; Paryatan Bhavan, Sanjay Marg; ⏰9.30am-6pm Mon-Sat) has maps and

Autorickshaw

brochures on Jaipur and Rajasthan. Branches at the **airport** (☎0141-2725708; ⏰9am-5pm Mon-Fri) and the **train station** (☎0141-2315714; Platform 1; ⏰24hr).

GETTING THERE & AWAY

AIR

You can fly into Jaipur from Europe and the US via Delhi. A few direct flights connect Bangkok and hubs in the Gulf.

BUS

State buses leave from the **main bus station** (www.rsrtc.rajasthan.gov.in; Station Rd; left luggage per bag per 24hr ₹20). Half-hourly deluxe buses for Delhi leave from Platform 3. Seats can be booked in advance from the **reservation office** (☎0141-5116032; Main Bus Station; ⏰8am-6pm).

TRAIN

The **reservation office** (☎enquiries 131, reservations 135; ⏰8am-2pm & 3-8pm) is to your left as you enter Jaipur train station. Services include:

Agra sleeper ₹205, 3½ to 4½ hours, nine services daily

Delhi sleeper ₹135, 4½ to six hours, at least nine services daily

Jaisalmer sleeper ₹350, 12 hours, three services daily

Ranthambhore NP (Sawai Madhopur) sleeper ₹180, two to three hours, at least nine services daily

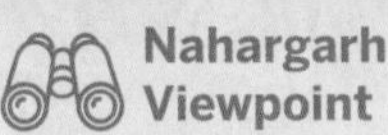

Nahargarh Viewpoint

Built in 1734 and extended in 1868, the sturdy **Nahargarh** (Tiger Fort; Indian/foreigner ₹50/200; ⏰10am-5pm) overlooks the city from a sheer ridge to the north. The story goes that the fort was named after Nahar Singh, a dead prince whose restless spirit was disrupting construction. Whatever was built in the day crumbled in the night. The prince agreed to leave on condition that the fort was named for him. The views are glorious and there's a restaurant that's perfect for a cold beer.

View of Jaipur from Nahargarh

GETTING AROUND

Autorickshaw drivers at the bus and train stations are pushy – bargain hard.

If you have the apps, both Uber and Ola operate in Jaipur and offer cheaper services than rickshaws.

Male tiger

Ranthambhore National Park

India has about 70% of the world's wild tigers, and Ranthambhore is one of your best chances of spotting these majestic beasts in their native habitat: a thrilling experience to say the least.

Great For...

☑ Don't Miss

Historic Ranthambhore Fort, with its hilltop panoramas, is a great complement to tiger spotting.

Ranthambhore's 1334 sq km of wild jungle scrub is home to around 60 to 67 tigers. Spotting any is partly a matter of luck, so allow time for two or three safaris to maximise your chances. Even if no tigers appear, there's plenty of other wildlife to see, including more than 300 bird species. At the park's centre is the 10th-century Ranthambhore Fort, scattered around which are ancient temples and mosques, hunting pavilions, crocodile-filled lakes and vine-covered *chhatris* (cenotaphs). The park was a royal hunting ground until 1970, a curious 15 years after it had become a sanctuary.

The park's gateway town is Sawai Madhopur, about 150km southeast of Jaipur. From here it's 10km to the first park gate, and another 3km to the main gate.

Peacock

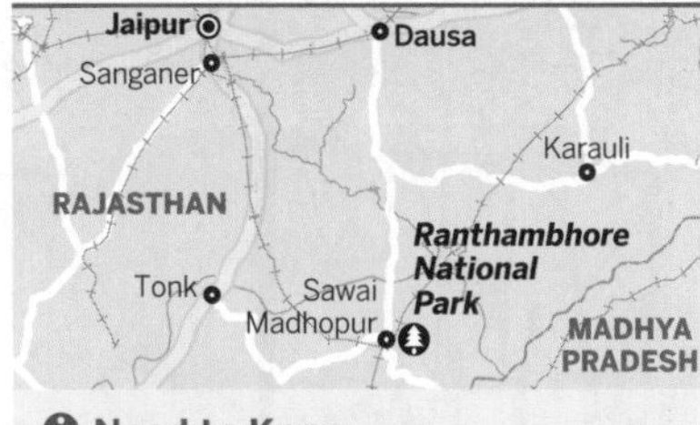

Need to Know

www.rajasthanwildlife.in; Oct-Jun)

Take a Break

Between safaris it's easiest to eat at your hotel. Most hotels offer full-board packages.

★ Top Tip

Book your safaris several months in advance, as they fill up quickly.

Safaris

Safaris start between 6am and 7am and between 2pm and 3.30pm, depending on the time of year. Each safari lasts for around three hours. Mornings can be exceptionally chilly in the open vehicles, so bring warm clothes.

The best option is to travel by **gypsy** (six-person, open-topped 4WD; Indian/foreigner ₹974/1714). You still have a chance of seeing a tiger from a **canter** (20-seat, open-topped truck; ₹617/1357), but other passengers can be rowdy.

Be aware that the rules for booking safaris (and prices) are prone to change. You can book online through the park's official website (www.rajasthanwildlife.in), or go in person to the safari booking office. And to be sure of bagging a seat in a vehicle, start queuing at least an hour (if not two) before the safaris are due to begin – meaning a very early start for morning safaris!

Booking with agencies and hotels is much simpler, but be aware that they add commission (₹100 to ₹800 per person per safari) to the official rates. The area's nicest accommodation is stretched out along Ranthambhore Rd, between Sawai Madhopur and the park.

Getting There & Away

Sawai Madhopur is poorly served by buses. Sawai Madhopur Junction train station (near Hammir Circle, which leads to Ranthambhore Rd) has services to/from Agra (Agra Fort Station; sleeper ₹200, six hours, three daily), Delhi (2nd-class/sleeper/3AC ₹140/260/660, 5½ to eight hours, 13 daily) and Jaipur (2nd-class seat/sleeper/3AC ₹95/180/560, two hours, 11 to 13 daily).

Many hotels will pick you up from the train station for free if you call ahead.

CHURCHGATE
CHURCHGATE
3037
2

MUMBAI

In This Chapter

Bazaar District ... 120
Dining in Mumbai ... 122
Bollywood ... 124
Walking Tour:
Architectural Mumbai ... 126
Sights ... 128
Shopping ... 131
Eating ... 131
Drinking & Nightlife ... 133
Information ... 134
Getting There & Away ... 134
Getting Around ... 135

Mumbai at a Glance...

Massive Mumbai, formerly Bombay, is full of dreamers, hard-labourers, starlets, gangsters, fisherfolk, millionaires and millions of other people. It's India's financial powerhouse and fashion epicentre, home to India's most-prolific film industry and has some of Asia's biggest slums.

Mumbai's furious energy and punishing pollution are challenging, but far from threatening. It contains some splendid colonial-era architecture, and you'll uncover unique bazaars, hidden temples and India's premier restaurants and nightlife.

Two Days in Mumbai

Begin at **Chhatrapati Shivaji Maharaj Vastu Sangrahalaya** museum (p128), before lunch at **Samrat** (p131). Tour the **Gateway of India** (p128) and **Taj Mahal Palace** (p128), then fine-dine at **Bastian** (p122).

On day two visit unique **Crawford Market** (p121). Hip Lower Parel district beckons for dinner and craft beers at **Thirsty City 127** (p133).

Four Days in Mumbai

After exploring **Marine Dr** (p129), return for lunch in the artsy **Kala Ghoda** district. In the evening, head north for exquisite seafood at **Trishna** (p123), followed by bar action in Bandra.

On day four visit the atmospheric **Mahalaxmi Dhobi Ghat** (p128). Call it a night after exploring modern Indian fare at **Masala Library** (p133).

Previous page: Chhatrapati Shivaji Maharaj Terminus (p134)

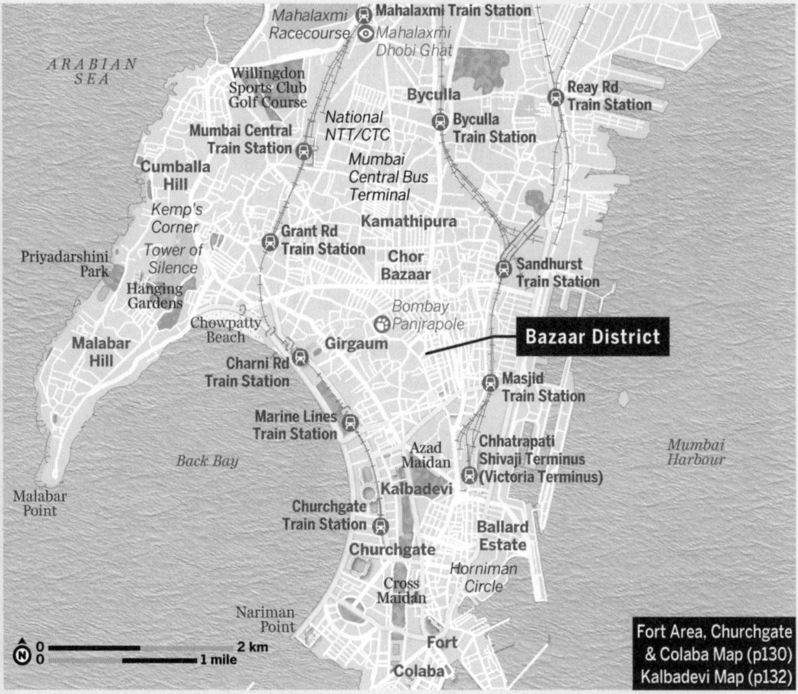

Mahalaxmi Racecourse
Mahalaxmi Train Station
Mahalaxmi Dhobi Ghat
ARABIAN SEA
Willingdon Sports Club Golf Course
Byculla
Reay Rd Train Station
National NTT/CTC
Byculla Train Station
Mumbai Central Train Station
Mumbai Central Bus Terminal
Cumballa Hill
Kemp's Corner
Kamathipura
Grant Rd Train Station
Chor Bazaar
Tower of Silence
Priyadarshini Park
Sandhurst Train Station
Hanging Gardens
Bombay Panjrapole
Chowpatty Beach
Bazaar District
Malabar Hill
Girgaum
Charni Rd Train Station
Masjid Train Station
Marine Lines Train Station
Azad Maidan
Chhatrapati Shivaji Terminus (Victoria Terminus)
Mumbai Harbour
Back Bay
Malabar Point
Kalbadevi
Churchgate Train Station
Ballard Estate
Churchgate
Horniman Circle
Cross Maidan
Nariman Point
0 2 km
0 1 mile
Fort
Colaba

Fort Area, Churchgate & Colaba Map (p130)
Kalbadevi Map (p132)

Arriving in Mumbai

Chhatrapati Shivaji Maharaj International Airport handles both international and domestic flights.

Chhatrapati Shivaji Terminus (CST) Trains to/from the east and south and a few to/from the north.

Mumbai Central station (BCT) Trains to/from the north.

Where to Stay

Mumbai has the most-expensive accommodation in India; you'll never feel like you're getting your money's worth. Always book ahead as demand is high and places can fill up quickly. Compact Colaba has the liveliest tourist scene and many budget options. Neighbouring Fort area is convenient for train stations. Most top-end places are along Marine Dr or in the western suburbs.

Flower stall, Bhuleshwar Market

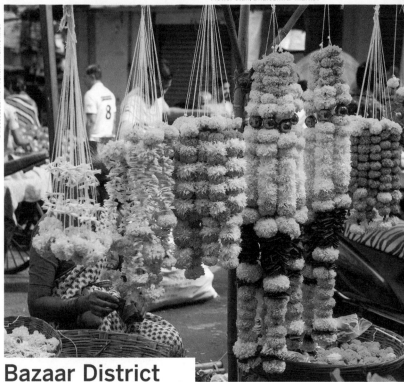

Bazaar District

Mumbai's main market district is one of Asia's most fascinating, an incredibly dense combination of humanity and commerce that's a total assault on the senses.

Great For...

☑ Don't Miss

If you're in Crawford Market during Alphonso mango season (May to June), be sure to indulge.

You can buy just about anything in Mumbai's fabulous markets, but most of the fun is simply taking in the street life and investigating the souk-like lanes of the shopping districts. The markets merge into each other in an amoeba-like mass, but there are some key landmarks to orientate yourself.

Chor Bazaar

Chor Bazaar (Map p132; Mutton St, Kumbharwada; ⏲10am-9pm) is known for antiques, though be wary of reproductions. The main area of activity is Mutton St, where shops specialise in these 'antiques' and miscellaneous junk. Dhabu St, to the east, is lined with fine leather goods.

Shrine to Hanuman, Zaveri Bazaar

Crawford Market

Mumbai's largest market, **Crawford Market** (Map p132; Mahatma Jyotiba Phule Mandai; cnr DN & Lokmanya Tilak Rds, Fort; ⌚10am-8pm, to noon Sun), contains the last whiff of British Bombay before the tumult of the central bazaars begins. Bas-reliefs by Rudyard Kipling's father, Lockwood Kipling, adorn the Norman Gothic exterior. Fruit and vegetables, meat and fish are mainly traded; it's also a touristy spot to stock up on spices.

Zaveri Bazaar

Wander the narrow lanes of Mumbai's **jewellery market** (Map p132; 94 Sheikh Memon St, Bhuleshwar) in search of gems, jewels and gold – 65% of India's gold trade emerges from here. Notable jewellers include Tribhovandas Bhimji Zaveri, Dhirajlal Bhimji Zaveri, Tanishq, Keertilals, Dwarkadas Chandumal and UTZ.

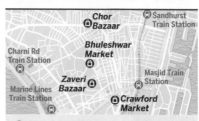

Need to Know

The markets are open daily, about 10am to 9pm. Some individual shops close on Sunday.

Take a Break

Stop into **Badshah Snacks & Drinks** (Map p132; www.badshahcolddrinks.com; 52/156 Umrigar Bldg, Lokmanya Tilak Marg, Lohar Chawl; snacks & drinks ₹38-240; ⌚7am-12.30am) for its famous *falooda* (rose-flavoured drink).

★ Top Tip

You need at least two to three hours to explore the market district thoroughly.

Bhuleshwar Market

One of Mumbai's most frenetic and fascinating markets, **Bhuleshwar Market** (Map p132; cnr Sheikh Memon St & M Devi Marg, Bhuleshwar; ⌚10am-9pm) is an everything-and-the-kitchen-sink-type shopping thoroughfare that is known for hoarding everything from cloths and textiles, goldwork, flowers and everyday household items. It also is home to **Bombay Panjrapole** (Map p132; ☎022-22425493; www.bombaypanjrapole.org.in; Panjrapole Marg, Bhuleshwar; ⌚7am-6pm), an animal shelter.

Vada pav, a deep-fried spiced lentil-ball sandwich

SUBODHSATHE / GETTY IMAGES ©

Dining in Mumbai

Mumbai is India's culinary capital, with flavours from all over India colliding with international trends. You can feast like a maharaja or snack on an infinite array of street foods.

Great For...

☑ Don't Miss

Vada pav (deep-fried spiced lentil-ball sandwich), Mumbai's No. 1 street snack.

Top Dining Experiences

Bastian Seafood **$$$**

(www.facebook.com/bastianmumbai; B/1, New Kamal Bldg, Linking Rd, Bandra (W); mains for 2 ₹1100-3200; ⌚noon-3pm & 7pm-midnight; 📶) All the praise bestowed upon this trendy seafooder is indisputably warranted. Chinese-Canadian chef Boo Kwang Kim and his culinary sidekick, American-Korean Kelvin Cheung, have forged an East-meets-West gastronomic dream. Go with the market-fresh side menu: choose your catch (prawns, fish, mud crab or lobster) then pick from an insanely difficult list of impossibly tasty pan-Asian sauces.

Peshawri North Indian **$$$**

(☎022-28303030; www.itchotels.in; ITC Maratha, Sahar Rd, Andheri (E); mains ₹1600-3225; ⌚12.45-2.45pm & 7-11.45pm) Make this

Bhelpuri with coriander and tamarind chutney

SUBODHSATHE / GETTY IMAGES ©

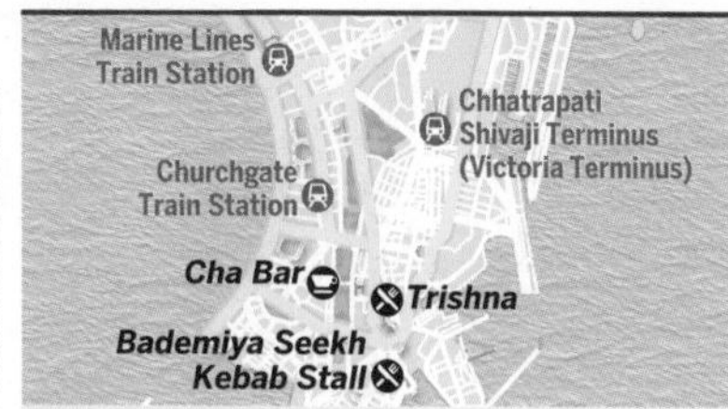

Need to Know

Reservations are always a good idea, and sometimes essential, at high-end and hip restaurants.

Take a Break

Sip organic, ayurvedic and exotic teas at **Cha Bar** (Map p130; 3 Dinsha Vachha Marg, Churchgate; ⌚11am-8pm).

★ Top Tip

North Mumbai is home to the city's trendiest dining, centred on Bandra West and Juhu.

Northwest Frontier restaurant, outside the international airport, your first or last stop in Mumbai. It's a carbon-copy of Delhi's famous Bukhara (p54), with the same menu and decor. Folks flock here for the dhal *bukhara*, a 24-hour simmered black dhal (₹945), but don't miss the kebabs. Try the Murgh Malai (marinated tandoor-grilled chicken) and *raan* (slow-roasted lamb hock).

Trishna Seafood **$$$**

(Map p130; ☎022-22703214; Ropewalk Ln, Kala Ghoda; mains ₹460-1830; ⌚noon-3.30pm & 6.30pm-midnight) Behind a modest entrance on a quiet Kala Ghoda lane is this often-lauded, intimate South Indian seafood restaurant. It's not a trendy place – the decor is old school, the seating a little cramped and the menu perhaps too long – but the cooking is superb. Witness the Hyderabadi fish tikka, jumbo prawns with green-pepper sauce, and the outstanding king crab and lobster dishes.

Street Food

Mumbai's street cuisine is vaster than many Western culinary traditions. Stalls get started in late afternoon, when chai complements much of the fried deliciousness.

Most street food is vegetarian. Chowpatty Beach is a great place to try Mumbai's famous *bhelpuri* (puffed rice tossed with fried rounds of dough, lentils, onions, herbs and chutneys). Stalls offering samosas, *pav bhaji* (spiced vegetables and bread), *vada pav* (deep-fried spiced lentil-ball sandwich), *bhurji pav* (scrambled eggs and bread) and *dabeli* (a mixture of potatoes, spices, peanuts and pomegranate, also on bread) are spread throughout the city.

For a meaty meal, Mohammed Ali and Merchant Rds in Kalbadevi are famous for kebabs. In Colaba, **Bademiya Seekh Kebab Stall** (Map p130; www.bademiya.com; Tulloch Rd; 5pm-4am) is a late-night Mumbai rite of passage, renowned for its chicken tikka rolls.

DREAMPICTURES / GETTY IMAGES ©

Bollywood

Mumbai is the glittering epicentre of India's gargantuan Hindi-language film industry, entrancing the nation with more than 1000 films a year.

Great For...

☑ Don't Miss

To experience Bollywood blockbusters in situ, **Eros cinema** (p126) is the place.

The Lumiere brothers screened the first film ever shown in India at the Watson Hotel in Mumbai in 1896. Beginning with the 1913 silent epic *Raja Harishchandra* (with an all-male cast, some in drag) and the first talkie, *Lama Ara* (1931), Bollywood now churns out more than 1000 films a year.

Every part of India has its regional film industry, but Bollywood continues to entrance the nation with its escapist formula, in which all-singing, all-dancing lovers fight and conquer the forces keeping them apart. Bollywood stars can attain near godlike status in India.

Bollywood Tours

You can see the stars' homes as well as a film/TV studio with **Bollywood Tours** (Map p132; ☎9820255202; www.bollywoodtours.in; 8 Lucky House, Goa St, Fort; per person half-/full-day

tour ₹8140/12,580; ⏲9am-6pm Mon-Fri, to 5pm Sat), but you're not guaranteed to see a dance number and you may spend much of it in traffic.

Indian Hippy

Indian Hippy (☎8080822022; www.hippy.in; hippy.in@gmail.com; 17C Sherly Rajan Rd, off Carter Rd, Bandra (W); portraits ₹7500-15,000; ⏲by appointment) will put your name in lights, with custom-designed Bollywood posters hand-painted on canvas by the original studio artists (a dying breed since the advent of digital illustrating). Bring or email a photo and your imagination (or let staff guide you). Also sells vinyl LP record clocks, vintage posters and all manner of frankly bizarre Bollywood-themed products. Ships worldwide.

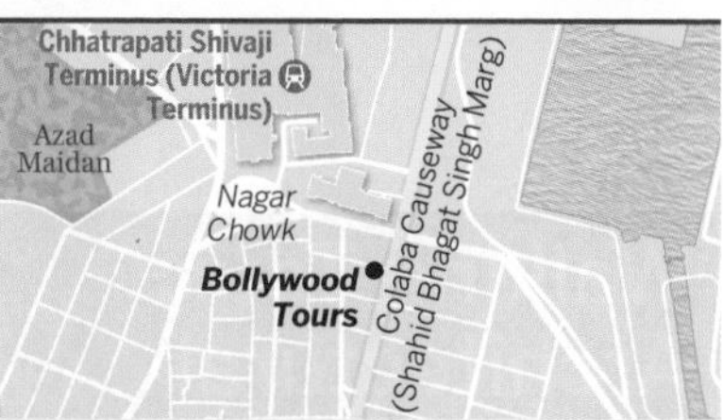

Need to Know

Star-spotting is a popular pastime in Mumbai's posher hotels, restaurants and clubs.

Take a Break

Drop into **Mini Market/Bollywood Bazaar/Super Sale** (☎9820032923; 33/31 Mutton St, Kumbharwada; ⏲11am-8pm Sat-Thu) for vintage Bollywood posters and other movie ephemera.

★ Top Tip

Film fans should check out the week-long **Mumbai Film Festival** (MFF; www.mumbaifilmfestival.com; ⏲Oct/Nov).

Extra, Extra!

Studios sometimes want Westerners as extras to add a whiff of international flair (or provocative dress, which locals often won't wear) to a film. If you're game, just hang around Colaba where studio scouts, recruiting for the following day's shooting, will find you (as will gaggles of scammers).

A day's work, which can be up to 16 hours, pays around ₹500 (more for speaking roles). You'll get lunch, snacks and (usually) transport. The day can be long and hot with loads of standing around the set; not everyone has a positive experience.

Complaints range from lack of food and water to dangerous situations and intimidation when extras don't comply with the director's orders. Others describe the behind-the-scenes peek as a fascinating experience. Before agreeing to anything, always ask for the scout's identification and go with your gut feeling.

Walking Tour: Architectural Mumbai

Mumbai's defining visual feature is its distinctive mix of colonial-era architecture, including gorgeous art deco creations from the 1920s and '30s.

Start Gateway of India
Distance 3.5km
Duration 1¾ hours

7 Cross the Oval Maidan for the art deco beauties along its west side, especially **Eros cinema** (www.eroscinema.co.in; Maharshi Karve Rd, Churchgate).

Churchgate Train Station
Cross Maidan
Veer Nariman Rd
FINISH
Oval Maidan
Bhaurao Patil Marg
Maharshi Karve Rd
Madame Cama Rd
Wodehouse Rd (Nathalal Parekh Marg)
Back Bay

6 Backtrack past Flora Fountain and south to the august High Court and the ornate **University of Mumbai** (www.mu.ac.in; Bhaurao Patil Marg).

Take a Break... Stop for the legendary breakfasts at **Pantry** (ground fl, Yashwanth Chambers, Military Square Ln, B Bharucha Marg, Kala Ghoda; 8.30am-11pm).

0 — 500 m
0 — 0.25 miles

Chhatrapati Shivaji Terminus (Victoria Terminus)

5 Ahead lies stately **Horniman Circle**, an arcaded ring of 1860s buildings around a beautifully kept botanical garden.

4 Continue to Flora Fountain and turn east down Veer Nariman Rd to **St Thomas' Cathedral** (3 Veer Nariman Rd, Churchgate; 7am-6pm).

Classic Photo The Chhatrapati Shivaji Maharaj Vastu Sangrahalaya, a blend of Islamic, Hindu and British styles fronted by tall palms.

Mahatma Gandhi (MG) Rd

Sir P Mehta Rd

Homi Modi St

Nagindas Master Rd

M Samachar Marg

Shahid Bhagat Singh Marg

K Dubash Marg

MB Marg

PJ Ramchandani Marg (Strand Rd)

START

3 Continue up Mahatma Gandhi (MG) Rd, passing the glorious **Chhatrapati Shivaji Maharaj Vastu Sangrahalaya** museum (p128).

2 Walk to **Regal Circle** to admire buildings like the art deco Regal Cinema.

1 Start at the **Gateway of India** (p128), with the world-famous Taj Mahal Palace hotel behind it.

Heritage Walks of Mumbai

Fiona Fernandez' *Ten Heritage Walks of Mumbai* (₹395) has walking tours of the city, with fascinating historical background. The **Indiatourism office** (www.incredibleindia.com; ground fl, Air India Bldg, Vidhan Bhavan Marg, Nariman Point; ⌚8.30am-6pm Mon-Fri, to 2pm Sat) can provide a list of approved multilingual guides; official prices are ₹1600/2000 per half-/full day for up to five people.

SIGHTS

Gateway of India Monument

(Map p130; Apollo Bunder, Colaba) This bold basalt arch of colonial triumph faces out to Mumbai Harbour from the tip of Apollo Bunder. Incorporating Islamic styles of 16th-century Gujarat, it was built to commemorate the 1911 royal visit of King George V, but wasn't completed until 1924. Ironically, the British builders of the gateway used it just 24 years later to parade the last British regiment as India marched towards independence.

Taj Mahal Palace, Mumbai Landmark

(Map p130; https://taj.tajhotels.com; Apollo Bunder) Mumbai's most famous landmark, this stunning hotel is a fairy-tale blend of Islamic and Renaissance styles, and India's second-most-photographed monument. It was built in 1903 by the Parsi industrialist JN Tata, supposedly after he was refused entry to nearby European hotels on account of being 'a native'. Dozens were killed inside the Taj Mahal Palace when it was targeted during the 2008 terrorist attacks, and images of its burning facade were beamed worldwide. The fully restored hotel reopened on Independence Day 2010.

Chhatrapati Shivaji Maharaj Vastu Sangrahalaya Museum

(Map p130; Prince of Wales Museum; www.csmvs.in; 159-161 MG Rd, Fort; Indian/foreigner ₹83/500, mobile/camera ₹50/100; ⌚10.15am-6pm) Mumbai's biggest and best museum,

From left: Marine Drive; Chhatrapati Shivaji Maharaj Vastu Sangrahalaya; Gateway of India and Taj Mahal Palace, Mumbai

PATEL SANKET M / SHUTTERSTOCK ©

Chhatrapati Shivaji Maharaj Vastu Sangrahalaya displays a mix of India-wide exhibits. The domed behemoth, an intriguing hodgepodge of Islamic, Hindu and British architecture, is a flamboyant Indo-Saracenic design by George Wittet (who also designed the Gateway of India). Its vast collection includes impressive Hindu and Buddhist sculpture, terracotta figurines from the Indus Valley, Indian miniature paintings and some particularly vicious-looking weaponry.

Chhatrapati Shivaji Maharaj Terminus Historic Building

(Map p132; Victoria Terminus) Imposing, exuberant and overflowing with people, this monumental train station is the city's most extravagant Gothic building and an aphorism of colonial-era India. It's a meringue of Victorian, Hindu and Islamic styles whipped into an imposing Dalí-esque structure of buttresses, domes, turrets, spires and stained glass.

Marine Drive Waterfront

(Map p130; Netaji Subhashchandra Bose Rd; ⌚24hr) Built on reclaimed land in 1920 and a part of Mumbai's recently crowned Victorian Gothic and Art Deco Ensembles Unesco World Heritage Site, Marine Dr arcs along the shore of the Arabian Sea from Nariman Point past Girgaum Chowpatty and continues to the foot of Malabar Hill. Lined with flaking art deco apartments, it's one of Mumbai's most popular promenades and sunset-watching spots. Its twinkling night-time lights have earned it the nickname 'the Queen's Necklace'.

Mumbai's Washing Well

The 140-year-old **Mahalaxmi Dhobi Ghat** (Bapurao Jagtap Marg, Mahalaxmi; ⌚4.30am-dusk) is Mumbai's biggest human-powered washing machine: every day hundreds of people beat the dirt out of thousands of kilograms of soiled Mumbai clothes and linen in 1026 open-air troughs. The best view is from the bridge across the railway tracks near Mahalaxmi train station.

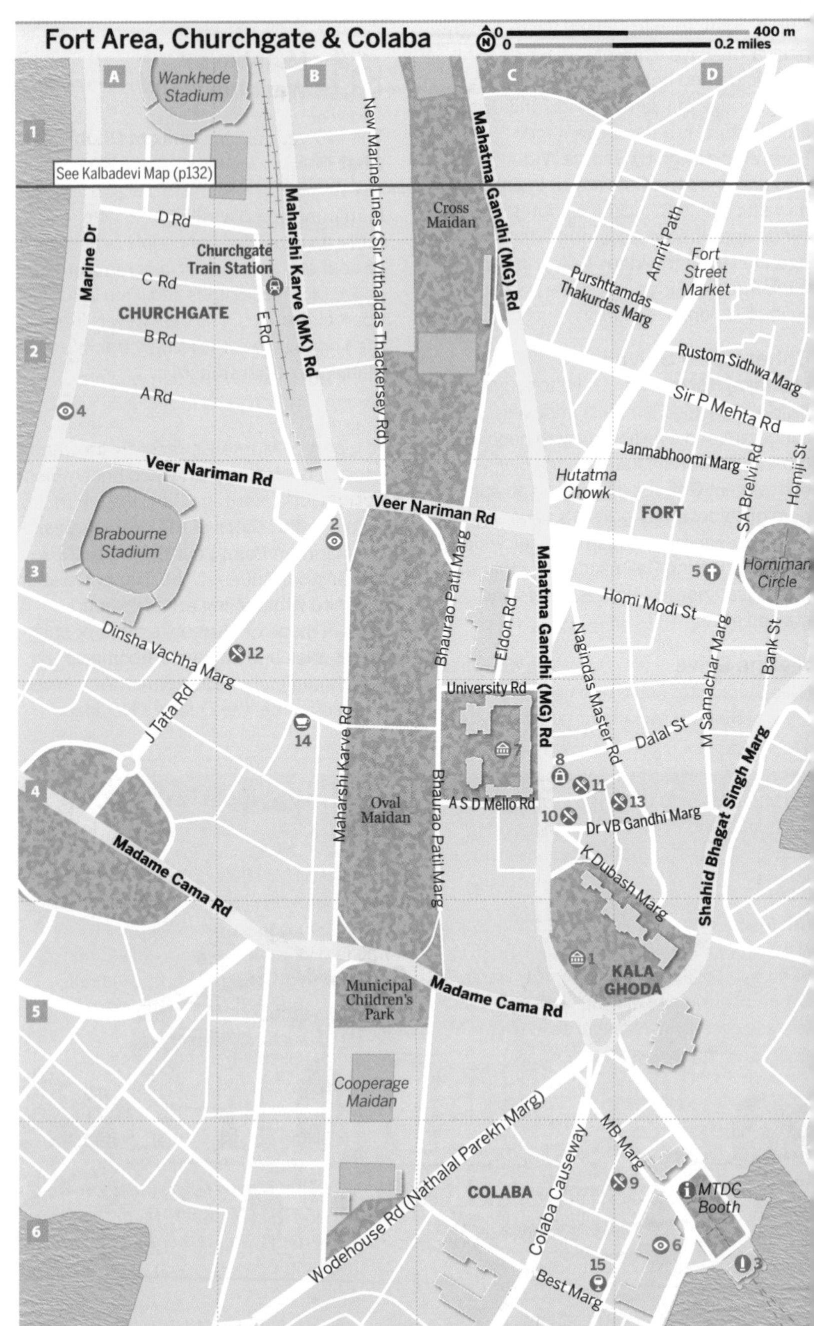
Fort Area, Churchgate & Colaba
0 400 m
0 0.2 miles
A
B
C
D
1
2
3
4
5
6
Wankhede Stadium
See Kalbadevi Map (p132)
D Rd
C Rd
B Rd
A Rd
E Rd
Marine Dr
Churchgate Train Station
CHURCHGATE
Maharshi Karve (MK) Rd
New Marine Lines (Sir Vithaldas Thackersey Rd)
Cross Maidan
Mahatma Gandhi (MG) Rd
Amrit Path
Fort Street Market
Purshttamdas Thakurdas Marg
Rustom Sidhwa Marg
Sir P Mehta Rd
Janmabhoomi Marg
SA Brelvi Rd
Homji St
Hutatma Chowk
FORT
Veer Nariman Rd
Veer Nariman Rd
Brabourne Stadium
Horniman Circle
Homi Modi St
Bhaurao Patil Marg
Eldon Rd
Nagindas Master Rd
M Samachar Marg
Bank St
Dinsha Vachha Marg
J Tata Rd
University Rd
Dalal St
Shahid Bhagat Singh Marg
Maharshi Karve Rd
Oval Maidan
A S D Mello Rd
Bhaurao Patil Marg
Dr VB Gandhi Marg
K Dubash Marg
Madame Cama Rd
KALA GHODA
Municipal Children's Park
Madame Cama Rd
Cooperage Maidan
Wodehouse Rd (Nathalal Parekh Marg)
Colaba Causeway
MB Marg
COLABA
MTDC Booth
Best Marg
1
2
3
4
5
6
7
8
9
10
11
12
13
14
15

Fort Area, Churchgate & Colaba

Sights

1 Chhatrapati Shivaji Maharaj Vastu Sangrahalaya ... C5
2 Eros ... B3
3 Gateway of India ... D6
4 Marine Dr ... A2
5 St Thomas' Cathedral ... D3
6 Taj Mahal Palace, Mumbai ... D6
7 University of Mumbai ... C4

Shopping

8 Fabindia ... C4

Eating

9 Bademiya Seekh Kebab Stall ... D6
10 Khyber ... C4
11 Pantry ... C4
12 Samrat ... B3
13 Trishna ... D4

Drinking & Nightlife

14 Cha Bar ... B4
15 Social ... C6

SHOPPING

ulture Shop Design

/ww.kultureshop.in; 241 Hill Rd, Bandra (W); 11am-8pm) Behold Bandra's – and Mumai's – coolest shop, featuring graphic art ıd illustrations sourced from a global army Indian artists. You'll find thought-rovoking and conceptually daring T-shirts, t prints, coffee mugs, notebooks, station-y and other cutting-edge objets d'art.

lay Clan Gifts & Souvenirs

/ww.theplayclan.com; Shop 1 & 2, Royal Opera ouse, Parmanand Marg, Girguam; 11am-7pm) itschy, design-y goods such as stylish nbroidered T-shirts, funky coffee mugs ıd coasters, and superhip graphic art, cluding beaded embroidered art and ustrative wood prints that are pricey but ıique.

abindia Clothing, Homewares

lap p130; www.fabindia.com; Jeroo Bldg, 137 G Rd, Kala Ghoda; 10am-9pm) Ethically ourced cotton and silk fashions and home-ares in everybody's favourite modern-eets-traditional Indian shop.

EATING

amrat Gujarati $$

lap p130; www.prashantcaterers.com/samrat; em Court Bldg, J Tata Rd, Churchgate; thali nch/dinner ₹345/450; noon-11pm) Samrat as an à la carte menu but opt for the mous Gujarati thali – a cavalcade of ste and texture, sweetness and spice that includes numerous curries and chutneys, curd, rotis and other bits and pieces. Samrat is air-conditioned and beer is available.

Khyber Mughlai $$$

(Map p130; 022-40396666; www.khyberrestaurant.com; 145 MG Rd; mains ₹590-1110; 12.30-4pm & 7.30-11.30pm) The much-acclaimed Khyber has a Northwest Frontier–themed design that incorporates murals that depict turbaned Mughal royalty, lots of exposed brickwork

Mumbai's Dabba-Wallahs

A small miracle of logistics, Mumbai's 5000 dabba-wallahs (literally 'food-container people'; also called tiffin wallahs) work tirelessly to deliver hot lunches to office workers throughout the city (and to the poor later on in the evenings, a 2015 initiative).

Lunch boxes are picked up each day from restaurants and homes and carried on heads, bicycles and trains to a centralised sorting station. A sophisticated system of numbers and colours (many wallahs don't read) identifies the destination of each lunch. More than 200,000 meals are delivered – always on time, come (monsoon) rain or (searing) shine.

Kalbadevi
0 400 m
0 0.2 miles
A
B
C
D
1
2
3
4
5
6
KAMATHIPURA
Mahalaxmi Dhobi Ghat (2.2km)
Maulana Azad Rd
Mutton St
Dhabu St
Grant Rd
OPERA HOUSE
Sir JJ Rd
Jail Rd
6
CHOR BAZAAR
4
Sardar V Patel Rd
KHOTACHIWADI
V Patel Marg
Bazaar District
Merchant Rd
1
Jagannath Shankarsheth Marg (JSS Marg)
Meheralli Rd
Dr Jaikar Marg
BHULESHWAR
3
Sheikh Memon St
Abdul Rehman St
Mohammed Ali Rd
Play Clan (800m)
Kalbadevi Rd
7
Masjid Train Station
GIRGAUM
Marine Dr
8
5
Gymkhanas
MRA Marg
Lokmanya Tilak Rd
Marine Lines Train Station
KALBADEVI
Maharshi Karve (MK) Rd
Dr Dadabhai Naoroji Rd
Mahatma Gandhi (MG) Rd
New Marine Lines (Sir Vithaldas Thackersey Rd)
Back Bay
Cross Maidan
Azad Maidan
Chhatrapati Shivaji Terminus (Victoria Terminus)
MTDC Booth
Wankhede Stadium
Colaba Causeway (SBS Marg)
See Fort Area, Churchgate & Colaba Map (p130)
2

Kalbadevi

Sights
1 Bombay Panjrapole B3

Activities, Courses & Tours
2 Bollywood Tours D6

Shopping
3 Bhuleshwar Market C3
4 Chor Bazaar C2
5 Crawford Market D4
6 Mini Market/Bollywood Bazaar/Super Sale C2
7 Zaveri Bazaar C4

Eating
8 Badshah Cold Drinks C4

and oil lanterns – just the sort of place where an Afghan warlord might feel right at home. The meat-centric menu features gloriously tender kebabs, rich curries and lots of tandoori favourites that are slow-roasted in the Khyber's famous red-masala sauce.

Masala Library Modern Indian **$$$**
(☎022-66424142; www.masalalibrary.co.in; ground fl, First International Financial Centre, G Block, BKC Rd, Bandra (E); mains ₹575-1250, tasting menu ₹2500-2700, with wine ₹4250-4450; ⏰noon-2.15pm & 7-11pm) Daring and imaginative Masala Library dangles the contemporary Indian carrot to foodies and gastronauts, challenging them to rethink their notions of subcontinental cuisine. The tasting menus are an exotic culinary journey – try wild-dehydrated-mushroom chai with truffle-oil crumbs; langoustine *moilee* (seafood curry) with gunpowder mash, *jalebi* caviar and a betel-leaf fairy floss to finish.

DRINKING & NIGHTLIFE

Social Bar
(Map p130; www.socialoffline.in; ground fl, Glen Rose Bldg, BK Boman Behram Marg, Apollo Bunder, Colaba; ⏰9am-1.30am; 📶) Colaba is the best of the locations of the hip Social chain, which combines a restaurant/bar with a collaborative work space. The happening bar nails the cocktails (from ₹295) – the Acharroska is the perfect marriage of Indian pungency and Brazilian sweetness.

Thirsty City 127 Bar
(www.facebook.com/pg/thirstycity127; Todi Mills, Mathuradas Mill Compound, Tulsi Pipe Rd, Lower Parel; ⏰6pm-1.30am Tue-Sun; 📶) The former space of Mumbai's first microbrewery has been revamped into a slick craft beer and cocktail destination under the direction of Indian beer maven/visual artist Vir Kotak. The striking space catches attention with copper-plated fermentation tanks, and velvet and turquoise banquettes, but the swill reigns: eight taps (solid Neipa, Kölsch, Hefeweizen etc served in Teku glassware) and cocktails (₹800) themed by beer ingredients.

Toto's Garage Bar
(☎022-26005494; 30th Rd, Bandra (W); ⏰6pm-1am) A highly sociable, down-to-earth local

Craft-Brew Mumbai

While certainly late to the craft-brew boozefest, Mumbai has finally embraced hop-heavy IPAs, roasty, chocolatey porters and refreshing saisons, thanks to the city's very own craft-beer wallah, American expat Greg Kroitzsh. Kroitzsh opened Mumbai's first microbrewery, the now-shuttered Barking Deer, in 2013, and the taps began flowing in Mumbai. The city's signature brew has quickly become Belgian Wit – citrusy and refreshing, it's a perfect accompaniment for hot and humid Mumbai.

From left: Dabba-wallahs (p131); *dabeli* (p123); Mumbai taxi ride

dive done up in a car-mechanic theme, where you can go in your dirty clothes, drink draught beer (₹200 a glass) and listen to classic rock. Check out the upended VW Beetle above the bar. It's always busy and caters to all kinds.

INFORMATION

MTDC Tourist Office (Maharashtra Tourism Development Corporation; 022-22845678; www.maharashtratourism.gov.in; 4th fl, Apeejay House, 3 Dinsha Vachha Marg, Churchgate; 9am-5.30pm Mon-Sat, closed 2nd & 4th Sat of month) The MTDC's head office has helpful staff and lots of pamphlets and information about Maharashtra; it also facilitates bookings for MTDC hotels.

This is the only MTDC office of note that accepts credit cards. Additional booths of interest to tourists are at **Apollo Bunder** (022-22841877; www.maharashtratourism.gov.in; Apollo Bunder, Colaba; 9am-3pm Tue-Sun) and **Chhatrapati Shivaji Maharaj Terminus** (022-22622859; www.maharashtratourism.gov.in; Chhatrapati Shivaji Maharaj Terminus, Fort; 10am-5.30pm Mon-Sat, closed 2nd & 4th Sat of month).

GETTING THERE & AWAY

AIR

Mumbai's carbon-neutral **Chhatrapati Shivaji Maharaj International Airport** (022-66851010; www.csia.in; Santa Cruz (E)), situated about 30km from the city centre, handles all international arrival flights in Terminal 2 (T2), while domestic flights operate out of both the T2 and the older Terminal 1 (T1), also known locally as Santa Cruz Airport, which is located 5km away.

Mumbai's M-Indicator

Mumbai's **M-Indicator** (http://m-indicator.soft112.com) is an invaluable app for catching Mumbai public transportation – from train schedules to rickshaw fares, it covers the whole shebang.

TRAIN

Central Railway (www.cr.indianrailways.gov.in) – handling services to the east, south, plus a few trains to the north – operates from Chhatrapati Shivaji Terminus (CST), also known as Victoria Terminus (VT). **Western Railway** (www.wr.indianrailways.gov.in) has services to the north from Mumbai Central train station, usually called Bombay Central (BCT).

GETTING AROUND

TO/FROM THE AIRPORT

TERMINAL 2

Prepaid Taxi Set-fare taxis cost ₹670/810 (non-AC/AC; including one piece of luggage) to Colaba and Fort and ₹400/480 to Bandra.

Taxi An off-peak UberGo from the airport is ₹260 to Bandra and ₹560 to Colaba. A ₹105 pickup fee is automatically embedded into the fare.

TERMINAL 1

Taxi There's a prepaid taxi counter in the arrivals hall. A non-AC/AC taxi with one bag costs ₹570/695 to Colaba or Fort and ₹295/350 to Bandra (a bit more at night). An off-peak UberGo from the airport runs ₹220 to Bandra Kurla Complex or Bandra (W), ₹400 to Fort and ₹425 to Colaba.

TAXI & AUTORICKSHAW

Mumbai's black-and-yellow taxis are the most convenient way to get around southern Mumbai. The minimum fare is ₹22 (for up to 1.5km); a 5km trip costs about ₹80. Autorickshaws are the name of the game north of Bandra. The minimum fare is ₹18, up to 1.5km; a 3km trip is about ₹36 during daylight hours.

AJANTA & ELLORA

In This Chapter

Ajanta Caves 140
Ellora Caves 144
Aurangabad.......................................150
Sights 150
Tours 151
Eating.. 151
Drinking & Nightlife...........................153

Ajanta & Ellora at a Glance...

The remote caves of Ajanta and Ellora, located in Maharashtra, are stunning galleries of ancient art, featuring rock-cut sculptures, and shrines with natural-dye paintings. The Ellora caves were chipped out by generations of Buddhist, Hindu and Jain monks between roughly AD 600 and 1000. The Buddhist caves at Ajanta are even older: the earliest ones date to around the 2nd century BC. Note that Ajanta is closed on Mondays and Ellora on Tuesdays.

Two Days in Ajanta & Ellora

Start early from Aurangabad to visit **Daulatabad Fort** (p152) en route to **Ellora** (p113). Explore Ellora and return to Aurangabad.

Start early again on day two for the longer trip to **Ajanta** (p141). When you get back to Aurangabad, reward yourself with a thali dinner at **Bhoj** (p152).

Four Days in Ajanta & Ellora

Instead of returning to Aurangabad at the end of day two, stay at the **MTDC Ajanta Tourist Resort** (p143), allowing for a second caves visit before returning to Aurangabad. On day four visit the **Bibi-qa-Maqbara** (p150) and **Aurangabad Caves** (p150).

Previous page: Ellora Caves (p144)

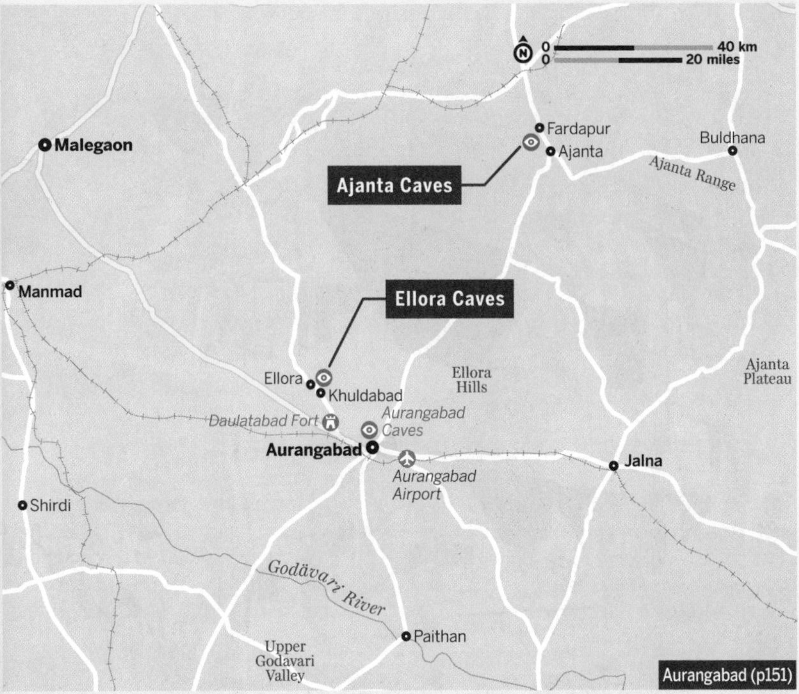

0 40 km
0 20 miles
Malegaon
Fardapur
Ajanta
Buldhana
Ajanta Range
Ajanta Caves
Manmad
Ellora Caves
Ellora
Khuldabad
Ellora Hills
Ajanta Plateau
Daulatabad Fort
Aurangabad Caves
Aurangabad
Aurangabad Airport
Jalna
Shirdi
Godävari River
Paithan
Upper Godavari Valley
Aurangabad (p151)

Arriving in Ajanta & Ellora

The usual jumping-off point for both places is Aurangabad, which has frequent bus connections with both sites. Aurangabad has daily flights from Delhi and Mumbai, and four daily trains from Mumbai.

Where to Stay

There are just a few reasonable overnight options near the cave sites, including the **MTDC Ajanta Tourist Resort** (p143) in Fardapur and **Hotel Kailas** (p149) at Ellora. There's a far bigger range of options for all budgets, at better prices than you might expect, in Aurangabad.

Ajanta Caves

Superbly set in a remote river valley 105km northeast of Aurangabad, the remarkable cave temples of Ajanta were among the earliest monastic institutions to be constructed in India.

Great For...

☑ **Don't Miss**

Cave 16 at Ajanta, with some of the finest paintings.

Ajanta's caves line a steep face of a horseshoe-shaped gorge on the Waghore River. Five of the caves are *chaityas* (prayer halls) while others are *viharas* (monasteries). Caves 8, 9, 10, 12, 13 and part of 15 are early Buddhist caves, while the others date from around the 5th century AD (Mahayana period). In the austere early-Buddhist school, the Buddha was never represented directly but always alluded to by a symbol such as the footprint or wheel of law.

Ajanta's 'Frescoes'

Few other paintings from ancient times match the artistic excellence and fine execution of the renowned 'frescoes' (actually temperas) adorning many of the Ajanta caves' interiors.

The paintings in most caves remain finely preserved and many attribute this to

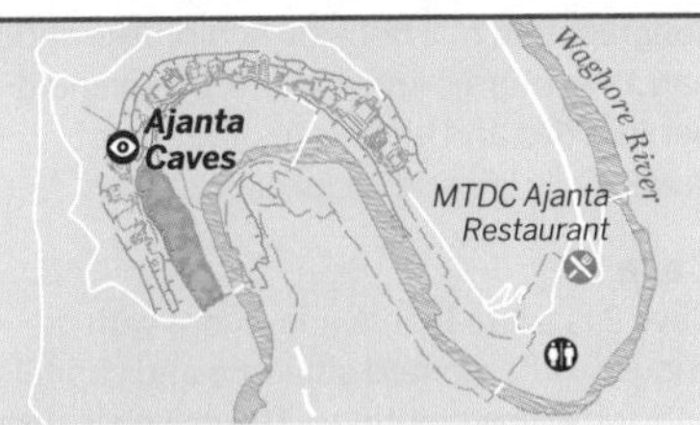

Need to Know

Indian/foreigner ₹40/600, video ₹25, authorised guide ₹1600; 9am-5.30pm Tue-Sun

Take a Break

MTDC Ajanta Restaurant (www.maharashtratourism.gov.in; Ajanta Caves; mains ₹160-480, thalis ₹150-320; 9am-6pm Tue-Sun), by the ticket office, serves vegetarian thalis and cold drinks.

★ Top Tip

To avoid midday crowds, stay overnight in Fardapur or start early from Aurangabad.

their relative isolation from humanity for centuries. However, it would be a tad optimistic to say that decay hasn't set in.

It's believed the natural pigments for these paintings were mixed with animal glue and vegetable gum to bind them to the dry surface. Many caves have small, craterlike holes in their floors, which acted as palettes during paint jobs.

Flash photography is prohibited within the caves. Rows of tiny, pigment-friendly lights help to illuminate minute details, but you'll need long exposures for photographs.

Ajanta Lost & Found

It was Ellora's rise that brought about Ajanta's downfall and historians believe the site was abandoned once the focus shifted to Ellora. As the Deccan forest claimed and shielded the caves, Ajanta remained deserted for about a millennium. But in 1819, a British hunting party led by officer John Smith stumbled upon them purely by chance.

Viewpoints

Two lookouts offer picture-perfect views of the whole horseshoe-shaped gorge. The first is a short walk beyond the river, crossed by a bridge below Cave 8. A further 40-minute uphill walk (not to be attempted during the monsoon) leads to the lookout from where the British party first spotted the caves.

Major Caves

Cave 1

Cave 1, a Mahayana *vihara*, was one of the last to be excavated and is the most beautifully decorated. This is where you'll find a rendition of the *Bodhisattva Padmapani*, the most famous and iconic of the Ajanta artworks. A veranda in front leads to a large congregation hall housing sculptures and narrative murals known for their splendid perspective and elaborate detailing of dress, daily life and facial expressions.

Cave 2

Cave 2 is a late Mahayana *vihara* with deliriously ornamented columns and capitals and some fine paintings. The ceiling is decorated with geometric and floral patterns. The murals depict scenes from the Jataka tales, including Buddha's mother's dream of a six-tusked elephant, which heralded his conception.

Cave 4

Cave 4 is the largest *vihara* at Ajanta and is supported by 28 pillars. Although never completed, the cave has some impressive sculptures, such as the four statues surrounding a huge central Buddha. There are also scenes of people fleeing from the 'eight great dangers' to the protection of Avalokitesvara.

Cave 10

Cave 10 is thought to be the oldest cave (200 BC) and was the first one to be spotted by the British hunting party. It is the largest *chaitya* whose facade has collapsed. The paintings inside have been damaged, in some cases by graffiti dating from soon after their rediscovery. One of the pillars to the right bears Smith's engraved name, his mark left here for posterity.

Cave 16

Cave 16, a *vihara,* contains some of Ajanta's finest paintings and is thought to have been the original entrance to the entire complex. The best known of these paintings is of the 'dying princess', Sundari. She was the wife

Cave sculpture

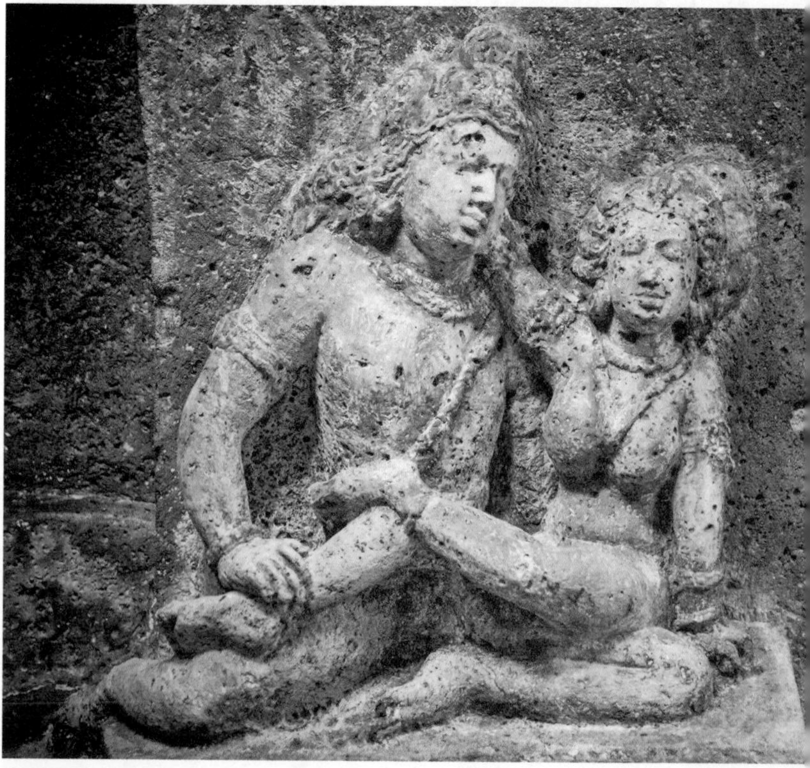

of the Buddha's half-brother Nanda, and she is said to have fainted at the news that her husband was renouncing the material life (and her) in order to become a monk.

Cave 17

With carved dwarfs supporting the pillars, cave 17 has Ajanta's best-preserved and most-varied paintings. Famous images include a princess applying make-up, a seductive prince using the old trick of plying his lover with wine, and the Buddha returning home from his enlightenment to beg from his wife and astonished son.

★ Top Tip

During busy periods, viewers are allotted 15 minutes within the caves, which have to be entered barefoot (socks/shoe covers allowed; flip-flops will make your life a lot easier).

KEVIN STANDAGE / SHUTTERSTOCK ©

Cave 19

Cave 19, a magnificent *chaitya,* has a remarkably detailed facade; its dominant feature is an impressive horseshoe-shaped window. Two fine, standing Buddha figures flank the entrance. Inside is a three-tiered dagoba with a figure of the Buddha on the front. Outside the cave, to the west, sits a striking image of the Naga king with seven cobra hoods around his head. His wife, hooded by a single cobra, sits by his side.

Cave 26

A largely ruined *chaitya,* cave 26 is now dramatically lit and contains some fine sculptures that shouldn't be missed. On the left wall is a huge figure of the reclining Buddha, lying back in preparation for nirvana. Other scenes include a lengthy depiction of the Buddha's temptation by Maya.

Getting to Ajanta

Buses from Aurangabad will drop you at Fardapur T-junction, 4km from the site. After paying an 'amenities' fee (₹10), walk to the departure point for the buses (with/without AC ₹22/16), running half-hourly until 5pm.

Taxis from Fardapur cost between ₹1500 and 2500 to Aurangabad.

★ MTDC Ajanta Tourist Complex

Located just behind the shopping 'plaza' and the bus stand, the five **cottages** (☎02438-244230; www.maharashtratourism.gov.in; d with/without AC ₹2130/1790) nestled in grassy lawns have some charm, though they could be better maintained. Note there's no restaurant.

Kailasa Temple (p146)

Ellora Caves

Ellora's stunning cave temples, 30km from Aurangabad, served as monasteries, chapels or temples for Buddhists, Hindus and Jains and were embellished with a profusion of sculptures. In their midst stands the awesome Kailasa Temple – the world's largest monolithic sculpture – hewn from a cliff face over 150 years by thousands of labourers.

Great For...

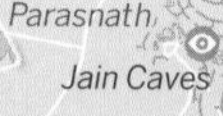

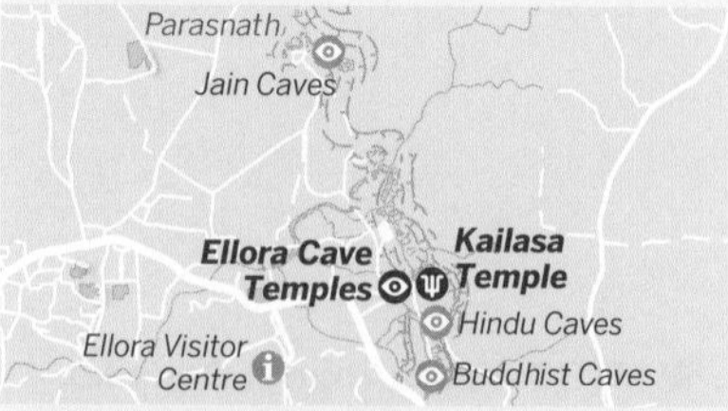

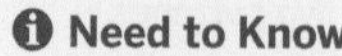

Need to Know

Ellora Cave Rd; Indian/foreigner ₹40/600; 6am-6pm Wed-Mon

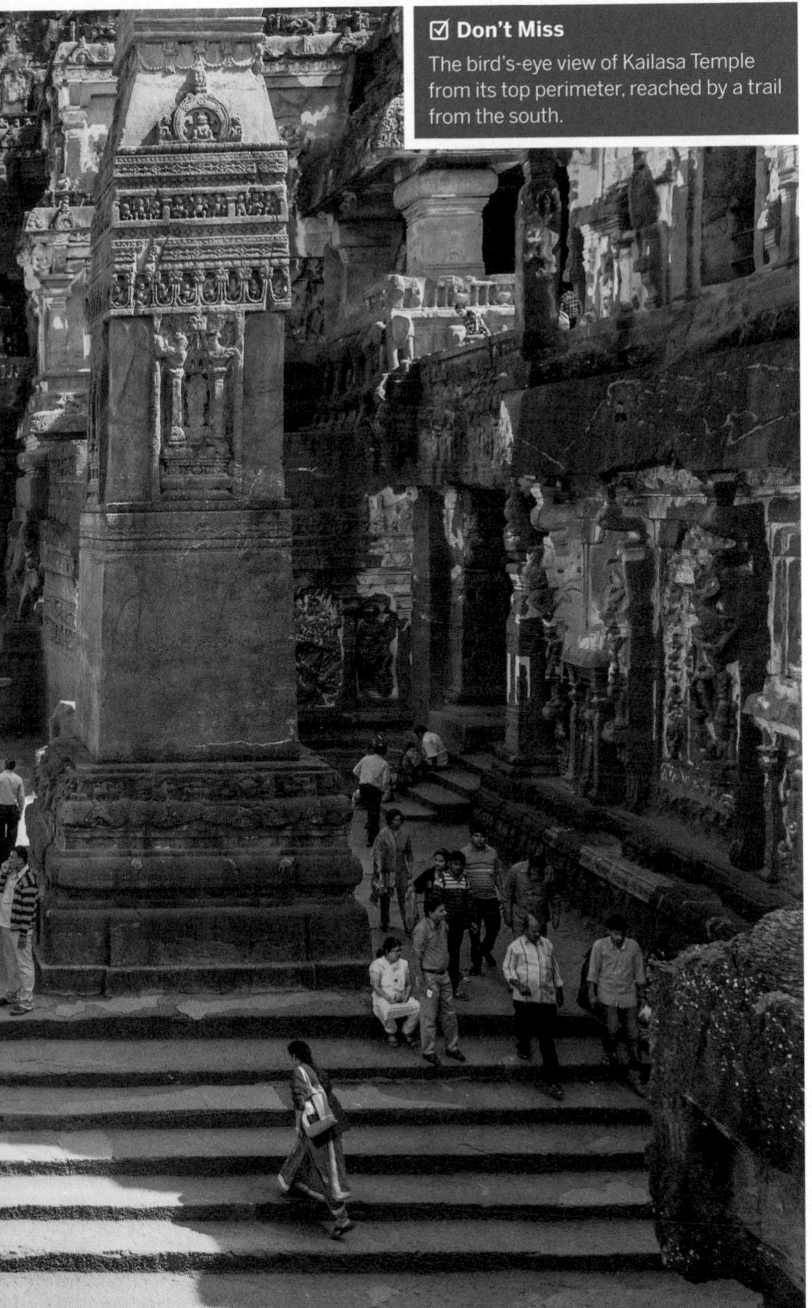

☑ **Don't Miss**

The bird's-eye view of Kailasa Temple from its top perimeter, reached by a trail from the south.

PAUL PRESCOTT / SHUTTERSTOCK ©

Ellora has 34 caves in all: 12 Buddhist (AD 600–800), 17 Hindu (AD 600–900) and five Jain (AD 800–1000) – though the exact time scales of their construction are the subject of academic debate.

Unlike the caves at Ajanta, carved into a sheer rock face, the Ellora caves line a 2km-long escarpment, whose gentle slope allowed architects to build elaborate courtyards in front of the shrines and adorn them with sculptures of a surreal quality.

The established academic theory is that Ellora represents the renaissance of Hinduism under the Chalukya and Rashtrakuta dynasties, the subsequent decline of Indian Buddhism and a brief resurgence of Jainism under official patronage. However, due to the absence of inscriptions, accurately dating most of Ellora's monuments is impossible, and some scholars argue that some Hindu temples predate the Buddhist group. What is certain is that their coexistence at one site indicates a lengthy period of religious tolerance.

Visitor Centre & Guides

Ellora's impressive **visitor centre** (NH211; ⌚9am-5pm Wed-Mon), 750m west of the site, is well worth dropping by. It features modern displays and information panels, a 15-minute video and a Kailasa Temple gallery (with diorama). Official guides can be hired at the ticket office in front of the Kailasa Temple for ₹1370 (up to five people). They have an extensive knowledge of cave architecture so are worth the investment.

Kailasa Temple

One of India's greatest monuments, this astonishing temple (Cave 16), carved from

Kailasa Temple

solid rock, was built by King Krishna I in AD 760 to represent Mt Kailasa (Kailash), Shiva's Himalayan abode. To say that the assignment was daring would be an understatement. Three huge trenches were bored into the sheer cliff face, a process that entailed removing 200,000 tonnes of rock by hammer and chisel, before the temple could begin to take shape and its remarkable sculptural decoration could be added.

Covering twice the area of the Parthenon in Athens and being half as high again, Kailasa is an engineering marvel that was

Take a Break

MTDC Ellora Restaurant & Beer Bar (www.maharashtratourism.gov.in; Ellora Cave Rd; mains/thali from ₹80/150; 9am-5pm), within the temple complex, is an easy place for lunch.

LEONID ANDRONOV / SHUTTERSTOCK ©

executed straight from the head with zero margin for error. Modern draughtspeople might have a lesson or two to learn here.

The temple houses several intricately carved panels, depicting scenes from the Ramayana, the Mahabharata and the adventures of Krishna. Also worth admiring are the immense monolithic pillars that stand in the courtyard, flanking the entrance on both sides, and the southeastern gallery that has 10 giant and fabulous panels depicting the different avatars (incarnations of a deity) of Lord Vishnu.

After you're done with the main enclosure, bypass the hordes of snack-munching day trippers to explore the temple's many dank, bat urine–soaked corners with their numerous forgotten carvings.

Buddhist Caves

Calm and contemplation infuse the 12 Buddhist caves, which stretch to the south of Kailasa. All are Buddhist *viharas* (monasteries) used for study and worship, but these multistoreyed structures also included cooking, living and sleeping areas. The one exception is Cave 10, which is a *chaitya* (assembly hall). While the earliest caves are simple, Caves 11 and 12 are more ambitious; both comprise three storeys and are on par with the more impressive Hindu temples.

Cave 1, the simplest *vihara*, may have been a granary. **Cave 2** is notable for its ornate pillars and the imposing seated Buddha that faces the setting sun. **Cave 3** and **Cave 4** are unfinished and not well preserved.

Cave 5 is the largest *vihara* in this group, at 18m wide and 36m long; the rows of stone benches hint that it may once have been an assembly hall.

Cave 6 is an ornate *vihara* with wonderful images of Tara, consort of the Bodhisattva Avalokitesvara, and of the Buddhist goddess of learning, Mahamayuri, looking remarkably similar to Saraswati, her Hindu equivalent. **Cave 7** is an unadorned hall. **Cave 8** is the first cave in which the sanctum is detached from the rear wall. **Cave 9**, located above Cave 8, is notable for its wonderfully carved fascia.

Cave 10 is the only *chaitya* in the Buddhist group and one of the finest in India. Its ceiling features ribs carved into the stonework; the grooves were once fitted with wooden panels. The balcony and upper gallery offer a closer view of the ceiling and a frieze depicting amorous couples. A decorative window gently illuminates an enormous figure of the teaching Buddha.

Cave 11, the Do Thal (Two Storey) Cave, is entered through its third basement level, not discovered until 1876. Like Cave 12, it possibly owes its size to competition with Hindu caves of the same period.

Cave 12, the huge Tin Thal (Three Storey) Cave, is entered through a courtyard. The locked shrine on the top floor contains a large Buddha figure flanked by his seven previous incarnations. The walls are carved with relief pictures.

Hindu Caves

Drama and excitement characterise the Hindu group (Caves 13 to 29). In terms of scale, creative vision and skill of execution, these caves are in a league of their own.

All these temples were cut from the top down, so it was never necessary to use scaffolding – the builders began with the roof and moved down to the floor. Highlights include caves 14, 15, 16, 21 and 29.

Cave 13 is a simple cave, most likely a granary. **Cave 14**, the Ravana-ki-Khai, is a Buddhist *vihara* converted to a temple dedicated to Shiva sometime in the 7th century.

Cave 15, the Das Avatara (Ten Incarnations of Vishnu) Cave, is one of the finest at Ellora. The two-storey temple contains a mesmerising Shiva Nataraja and a Shiva emerging from a lingam (phallic image) while Vishnu and Brahma pay homage. Caves 17 to 20 and Caves 22 to 28 are simple monasteries.

Cave 21, known as the Ramesvara Cave, features interesting interpretations of familiar Shaivite scenes depicted in the earlier temples. The figure of the goddess Ganga standing on her Makara (mythical sea creature) is particularly notable.

The large **Cave 29**, the Dumar Lena, is thought to be a transitional model between the simpler hollowed-out caves and the fully developed temples exemplified by the Kailasa. It has views over a nearby waterfall, though the path was inaccessible at time of writing. It's best reached via the MSRTC bus.

Jain Caves

The five Jain caves, the last created at Ellora, may lack the size of the best Hindu temples, but they are exceptionally detailed, with remarkable paintings and carvings.

The Jain caves are 1km north of the last Hindu temple (Cave 29) at the end of the bitumen road.

Cave 30, the Chhota Kailasa (Little Kailasa), is a poor imitation of the great

Temple sculptures

Kailasa Temple and stands by itself some distance from the other Jain temples. It's reached via the unmarked stairway between Caves 31 and 32.

In contrast, **Cave 32**, the Indra Sabha (Assembly Hall of Indra), is the finest of the Jain temples. Its ground-floor plan is similar to that of the Kailasa, but the upstairs area is as ornate and richly decorated as the downstairs is plain.

Cave 31 is really an extension of Cave 32. **Cave 33**, the Jagannath Sabha, is similar in plan to Cave 32 and has some well-preserved sculptures. The final temple, the small **Cave 34**, also has interesting sculptures. On the hilltop over the Jain temples, a 5m-high image of Parasnath looks down on Ellora.

Getting to Ellora

Buses to Ellora leave Aurangabad every half-hour (AC/non-AC ₹251/32, 30 minutes, 5am to 12.30am); the last bus back leaves Ellora at 9pm.

MSRTC buses run frequently from in front of Kailasa Temple (₹20 return; 9.15am to 6pm) to the Jain caves throughout the day.

★ Did You Know?

If you wish to stay close to the caves the **Hotel Kailas** (www.hotelkailas.com; ☎02437-244446; r with/without AC ₹3570/2500) offers attractive air-con stone cottages in leafy surrounds. The restaurant (mains ₹90 to 280) is excellent, but the wi-fi charges are ridiculous.

ALEKSANDRA H. KOSSOWSKA / SHUTTERSTOCK ©

Aurangabad

Aurangabad hit the spotlight when the last Mughal emperor, Aurangzeb, made the city his capital from 1653 to 1707. With the emperor's death came the city's rapid decline, but the brief period of glory saw the building of some fascinating monuments, including Bibi-qa-Maqbara, a Taj Mahal replica, and these continue to draw a steady trickle of visitors.

SIGHTS

Bibi-qa-Maqbara Monument

(Begumpura; Indian/foreigner ₹40/300; 6am-8pm) Built by Aurangzeb's son Azam Khan in 1679 as a mausoleum for his mother Rabia-ud-Daurani, Bibi-qa-Maqbara is widely known as the poor man's Taj. With its four minarets flanking a central onion-domed mausoleum, the white structure certainly does bear a striking resemblance to Agra's Taj Mahal.

It is much less grand, however, and apart from having a few marble adornments, namely the plinth and dome, much of the structure is finished in lime mortar.

Apparently the prince conceived the entire mausoleum in white marble, but was thwarted by his frugal father who opposed his extravagant idea of draining state coffers for the purpose. Despite the use of cheaper material and the obvious weathering, it's a sight far more impressive than the average gravestone.

The Bibi's formal gardens are a delight to explore, with the Deccan hills providing a scenic backdrop. It's located 3km north of the Central Bus Stand – a ₹50 or so Ola rickshaw ride.

Aurangabad Caves Cave

(Grishneswar Temple Rd; Indian/foreigner ₹40/300; 6am-6pm) Architecturally speaking, the Aurangabad Caves aren't a patch on Ellora or Ajanta, but they do shed light on early Buddhist architecture and make for a quiet and peaceful outing. Carved out of the hillside in the 6th or 7th century AD, the 10 caves, comprising two groups 1km apart (retain your ticket for entry into both sets), are all Buddhist.

Bibi-qa-Maqbara

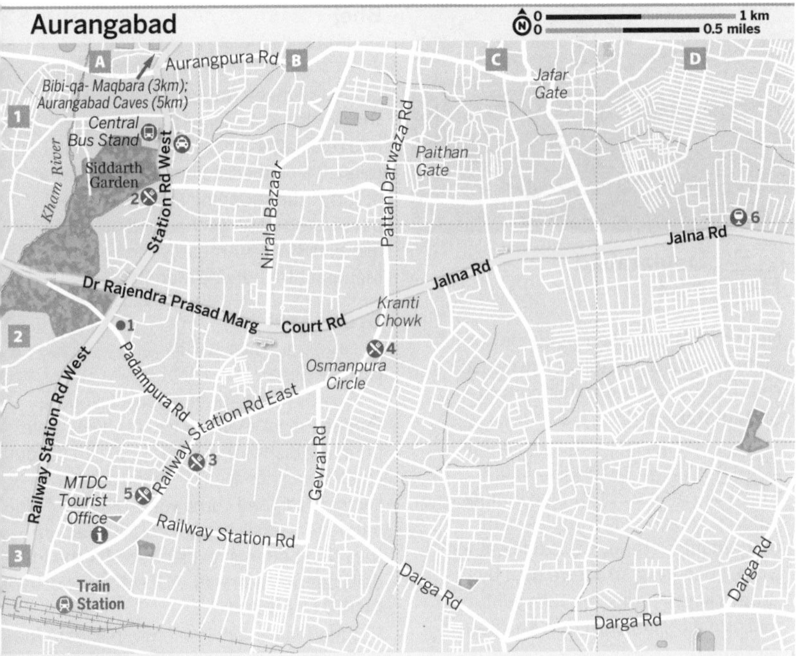

Aurangabad

Aurangabad

Activities, Courses & Tours
1 Ashoka Tours & Travels........A2

Eating
2 Bhoj........A1
3 Kailash........A3
4 Swad Restaurant........B2
5 Tandoor........A3

Drinking & Nightlife
6 KA Lounge........D1

Cave 7, with its sculptures of scantily clad lovers in suggestive positions, is a perennial favourite.

The caves are about 2km north of Bibi-qa-Maqbara. A return autorickshaw from the mausoleum shouldn't cost more than ₹250, including waiting time.

TOURS

Ashoka Tours & Travels Tours

(☎0240-2359102, 9890340816; www.touristaurangabad.com; Hotel Panchavati, Railway Station Rd West; ⏲7am-9pm) The standout Aurangabad agency, with excellent city and regional tours and decent car hire at fair rates. Prices for an air-con car with up to four people are ₹1550 for Ellora and ₹2550 for Ajanta. Run by Ashok T Kadam, a knowledgeable former autorickshaw driver.

EATING

Kailash Indian $

(Railway Station Rd East; mains ₹50-150, thalis ₹110 to ₹160; ⏲8am-11pm; ❄) This bustling, popular pure-veg restaurant looks and feels vaguely like a half-hearted Indian take on an American diner, with big portions of food in familial surrounds. There's lots of Punjabi and South Indian food, as well as rice and noodle dishes, and an extensive list of *pav bhaji* options, a Mumbai street-food staple. Cheap thalis (11am to 4pm), too.

Daulatabad Fort

No trip to Aurangabad would be complete without a pit stop at the ruined (but truly magnificent) hilltop fortress of **Daulatabad** (NH52; Indian/foreigner ₹25/300; ⏲6am-6pm), situated about 15km from town en route to Ellora, which sits atop a 200m-high craggy outcrop known as Devagiri. A 5km battlement surrounds this ancient fort, a most beguiling structure built by the Yadava kings during the 12th century and originally conceived as an impregnable fort.

In 1328, it was renamed Daulatabad, the City of Fortune, by Delhi sultan Mohammed Tughlaq, who decided to shift his kingdom's capital to this citadel from Delhi. Known for his eccentric ways, Mohammed Tughlaq even marched the entire population of Delhi 1100km south to populate it. Ironically, Daulatabad – despite being better positioned strategically than Delhi – soon proved untenable as a capital due to an acute water crisis and Mohammed Tughlaq forced its weary inhabitants to slope all the way back to Delhi, which had by then been reduced to a ghost town.

Ellora-bound bus services departing the **MSRTC bus stand** (Railway Station Rd West) every half-hour (non-AC ₹20, 30 minutes, 5.30am to 8pm) can drop you at the entrance.

4th-century cannon, Daulatabad Fort

JEREMYRICHARDS / SHUTTERSTOCK ©

Bhoj Indian $$

(Railway Station Rd West; thali ₹260; ⏲11am-3pm & 7-11pm) Rightly famous for its delicious, unlimited Rajasthani and Gujarati thalis, Bhoj is a wonderful place to refuel and relax after a hard day on the road (or rails). It's on the 1st floor of a somewhat scruffy little shopping arcade, but the decor, ambience, service and presentation are all first-rate. Arguably the best thali in Maharashtra outside Mumbai.

Green Leaf Indian $$

(www.greenleafpureveg.com; Shop 6-9, Fame Tapadiya Multiplex, Town Centre; mains ₹160-330; ⏲noon-11pm; 📶) Aurangabad's favourite modern vegetarian is loved for delectable pure-veg dishes that really pop with flavour (try the veg handi or off-menu paneer Hyderabadi) and come with spice level indicators (one chilli pepper equals medium – they don't offer an explanation for the four chilli pepper offerings...). It's 400m north of CIDCO Bus Stand.

Tuned-in servers gracefully navigate the clean, contemporary surrounds. So clean, in fact, the kitchen is open for all to see.

Tandoor North Indian $$

(Railway Station Rd East, Shyam Chambers; mains ₹130-470; ⏲11am-11pm) Offers fine tandoori dishes, flavoursome North Indian veg and nonveg options, and an extensive beer list (for Aurangabad) in a weirdly Pharaonic atmosphere. Try the wonderful sizzler kebabs. A few Chinese dishes are also on offer, but patrons clearly prefer the dishes coming out of...well...the tandoor. Fully licensed.

Swad Restaurant Indian $$

(Railway Station Rd East, Kanchan Chamber; thali ₹230-250; ⏲11-3.30pm & 7-11pm) Though prices are similar, always-packed Swad is the simpler, more local and slightly greasier counterpart to some of our other favourite spots in town. Waiters clad in always stylish, seasonally changing uniforms sling spicy *sabzi* (vegetables), dhal and other Gujarati–Rajasthani thali delights – an endless flavour train under the benevolent gaze of patron saint swami Yogiraj Hanstirth.

DRINKING & NIGHTLIFE

KA Lounge Bar

(Satya Dharam Complex, Akashwari Cir, Jalna Rd; 10am-11.30pm;) Aurangabad's one and only trendy bar-restaurant caters to the city's upwardly hip who knock back cocktails (₹350 to ₹450) – like the cool burning basil and green chilli mojito – from cosy lounge seating amid exposed brick walls. You can easily make an evening of it; the modern fusion menu (mains ₹150 to ₹690) features interesting Indian/Asian/continental-hybrid cuisine.

INFORMATION

MTDC Tourist Office (Maharashtra Tourism Development Corporation; 0240-2343169; www.maharashtratourism.gov.in; MTDC Holiday Resort, Railway Station Rd East; 10am-5.30pm Mon-Sat, closed 2nd & 4th Sat) Quite helpful and stocks brochures.

GETTING THERE & AWAY

AIR

Aurangabad Airport (Chikkalthana Airport; Jalna Rd) is 10km east of town. Daily direct flights go to Delhi and Mumbai.

BUS

From the **Central Bus Stand** (0240-2242164; Railway Station Rd West), deluxe overnight buses go to Mumbai (AC sleeper ₹800 to ₹1450, 7½ to 9½ hours). Ordinary buses head to Ellora every half-hour (non-AC/AC ₹37/345, 30 minutes, 5.30am to 8pm) and Fardapur (₹180, three hours), which is the drop-off point for Ajanta.

Bus Day Tours

MSRTC (0240-2242164; www.msrtc.gov.in; Central Bus Stand, Railway Station Rd West) operates Volvo AC bus tours to the Ajanta (₹695) and Ellora (₹345) caves. Be aware that these are tours popular with domestic tourists, designed to cover as much ground as possible in a short time period. Prices include transport only – they don't cover a guide or admission fees. The Ellora tour also includes all the other Aurangabad sites along with Daulatabad Fort, which is a lot in a day. Tours start at the Central Bus Stand.

Ellora

TRAIN

Aurangabad's **train station** (AWB; Railway Station Rd East) is not on a main line, but it has four daily direct trains to/from Mumbai. The Tapovan Express (2nd class/chair ₹235/505, 7½ hours) departs Aurangabad at 2.35pm. The Janshatabdi Express (2nd class/chair ₹170/585, 6½ hours) departs Aurangabad at 6am.

GETTING AROUND

Autorickshaws are common here and are bookable (along with taxis) with Ola Cabs. The **taxi stand** (Railway Station Rd West) is next to the Central Bus Stand; shared 4WDs also depart from here for Ellora and Daulatabad but are usually very packed. Renting a car and driver is a much better option.

GOA

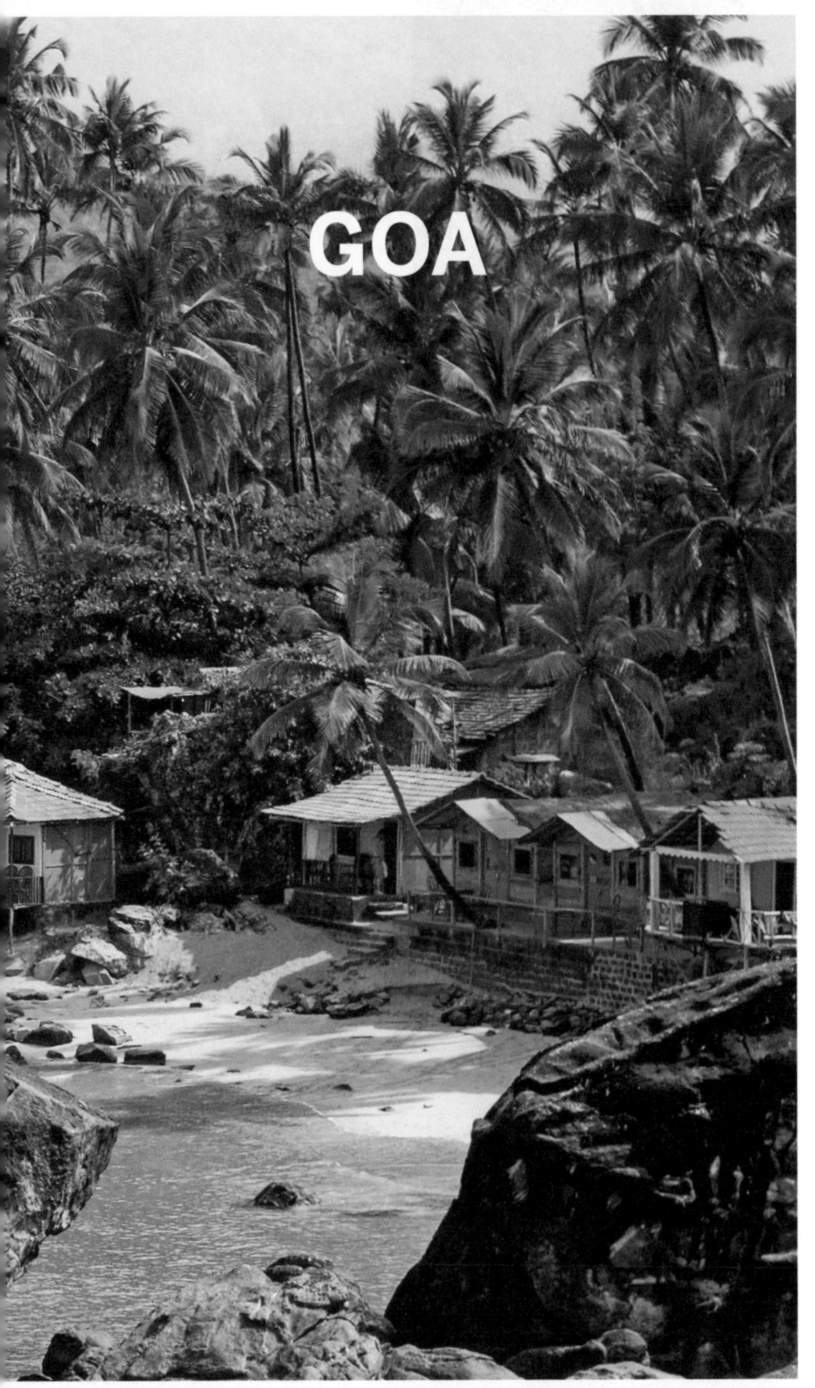

In This Chapter

Old Goa Day Trip 158
Goa's Beaches 160
Yoga by the Sea 164
Panaji (Panjim) 166
Palolem 167
Anjuna 170

Goa at a Glance...

A kaleidoscopic blend of Indian and Portuguese cultures, sweetened with sun, sea, sand and spirituality, Goa is India's pocket-sized paradise. While Goa's biggest draw is undoubtedly its string of golden sands, it also stands out for the charm of its colonial heritage; for the scents, spices and flavours of its tantalising cuisine; and as a spiritual sanctuary where options for yoga, t'ai chi, meditation and healing grow more bountiful each year.

Three Days in Goa

Spend day one in Goa's cultural heartland, **Panaji** (p166) and **Old Goa** (p158), ideally staying in a quaint Panaji heritage hotel.

Then head down to **Palolem** (p167) and spend days two and three enjoying the palm-fringed sands, safe swimming and maybe a spot of yoga, spa pampering, kayaking, a cooking class or a silent headphone party.

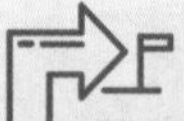

Five Days in Goa

You might be so happy in Palolem you don't want to move on...but if you do, head up to North Goa's all-round best beach base, **Anjuna** (p161), where something of the old hippie vibe lingers but there are also plenty of daytime activities for days four and five; a good **yoga scene** (p164), happening nightclubs and a good range of budget and midrange accommodation.

Previous page: Palolem (p167)
VAL SHEVCHENKO / SHUTTERSTOCK ©

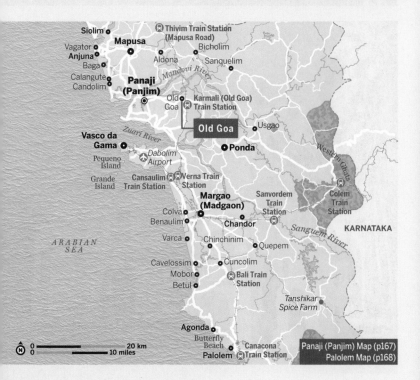

Panaji (Panjim) Map (p167)
Palolem Map (p168)

Arriving in Goa

Dabolim Airport Domestic flights, plus international flights from some Gulf Hubs.

Madgaon Railway Station (Margao) Main stop on Mumbai–Kerala line.

Karmali Railway Station (Old Goa) Closest station to Panaji.

Buses Running from Margao (Madgaon) to Hosapete (for Hampi).

Where to Stay

Goa's accommodation ranges from basic beach huts, hostels and budget guesthouses to charming boutique and heritage havens. Many opulent five-star beachfront resorts are clustered along the southern coast, especially in the Varca–Cavelossim–Mobor stretch.

Sé Cathedral

LEBEDINSKI VLADISLAV / SHUTTERSTOCK ©

Old Goa Day Trip

The 17th-century Portuguese capital of Old Goa once rivalled Lisbon and London in size and importance. Today all that remains is a handful of amazingly well-preserved churches and cathedrals – but what a handful!

Great For...

☑ **Don't Miss**

The 'incorrupt' body of St Francis Xavier in the Basilica de Bom Jesus.

From the 16th to the 18th centuries Goa's former capital was considered the 'Rome of the East'. Old Goa's rise under the Portuguese, from 1510, was meteoric, but cholera and malaria forced its abandonment in the 17th century.

Basilica de Bom Jesus

Famous throughout the Roman Catholic world, the imposing Basilica de Bom Jesus (⏲7.30am-6.30pm) contains the tomb and mortal remains of St Francis Xavier, the so-called Apostle of the Indies. St Francis Xavier's missionary voyages throughout the East became legendary. His 'incorrupt' body is in the mausoleum to the right, in a glass-sided coffin amid a shower of gilt stars.

Basilica de Bom Jesus

DIPAK SHELARE / SHUTTERSTOCK ©

Sé Cathedral

At over 76m long and 55m wide, the cavernous **Sé Cathedral** (8am-6pm, Mass 7am & 6pm Mon-Sat, 7.15am, 10am & 4pm Sun) is the largest church in Asia. Building commenced in 1562, on the orders of King Dom Sebastião of Portugal, and the finishing touches were finally made some 90 years later. The exterior is notable for its plain style, in the Tuscan tradition.

The huge interior of the cathedral is surprisingly plain. To the right as you enter is a small, locked area that contains a font made in 1532, said to have been used by St Francis Xavier. Two small statuettes, inset into the main pillars, depict St Francis Xavier and St Ignatius Loyola. There are four chapels on either side of the nave, two of which have screens across the entrance. Of these, the Chapel of the Blessed Sacrament is outstanding, with every inch of wall and ceiling gorgeously gilded and decorated – a complete contrast to the austerity of the cathedral interior.

Need to Know

Frequent buses to Old Goa (₹10, 20 minutes) leave Panaji's Kadamba bus stand. Return taxi is around ₹400.

Take a Break

A string of little tourist restaurants near the bus stop offers snacks, chai and thalis.

★ Top Tip

Old Goa can get crowded with visitors: consider coming on a weekday morning.

Church of St Francis of Assisi

West of the Sé Cathedral, the **Church of St Francis of Assisi** (9am-5pm) is no longer in use for worship, and consequently exudes a more mournful air than its neighbours. The interior of the church, though now rather ragged and faded, is nevertheless beautiful, in a particularly 'folk art' type style. The walls and ceiling are heavily gilded and decorated with carved wood panels, with large paintings depicting the works of St Francis adorning the walls of the chancel.

Church of St Cajetan

Modelled on the original design of St Peter's in Rome, the **Church of St Cajetan** (9am-5.30pm) was built by Italian friars of the Order of Theatines, who were sent by Pope Urban III to preach Christianity in the kingdom of Golconda (near Hyderabad).

Goa's Beaches

With more than 100km of sand-fringed coastline, Goa's beaches can exude the feel of a tropical island. Each spot has a different character. The question is: which beach is right for you?

Great For...

☑ **Don't Miss**

Goan sunsets – visible from *all* of Goa's beaches!

Deciding which Goan beach to visit is about choosing the community that suits your style of travel and sense of place. The villages vary in character, and accommodation ranges from backpacker-filled beach huts to five-star yoga retreats. Goa is small, so you can easily jump on a scooter or in a taxi and explore.

Arambol (Harmal)

Arambol is the most northerly of Goa's developed beach resorts. It first emerged in the 1960s as a mellow paradise for long-haired long-stayers. Today the main beach is an uninterrupted string of beach shacks, many with accommodation operations stacked behind.

Arambol Beach

Need to Know

Best weather and peak tourist season: November to March. Most tourist businesses close May to September.

Take a Break

Goa's hundreds of winter-season beach shacks are perfect to eat, drink and chill.

★ Top Tip

Take time out from 'your' beach to explore others, plus nearby villages and countryside.

Morjim

Morjim Beach was once very low-key – almost deserted. These days, it's popular with Russian tourists, and consequently there's a bit of a clubbing scene and a growing number of restaurants and beach shacks.

Vagator & Chapora

Dramatic red stone cliffs, thick palm groves and a crumbling 17th-century Portuguese fort give Vagator and its diminutive village neighbour Chapora one of the prettiest settings on the North Goan coast. Once known for wild trance parties, things are considerably calmer these days and upmarket restaurants are more the style.

Anjuna

Anjuna has been a stalwart of the hippie scene since the 1960s and still drags out the sarongs and sandalwood each Wednesday (in season) for its famous flea market (p171). Midrange international and domestic tourists are now making their way here for a dose of hippie-chic.

Anjuna is continuing to evolve, with a heady beach party scene and a constant flowering of new restaurants, bars and backpacker hostels.

Calangute & Baga

This is Goa's party strip, where the raves and hippies have made way for modern thumping nightclubs and wall-to-wall drinking. Everything you could ask for – from a Thai massage to a tattoo – is in close proximity and the beach is now lined with increasingly sophisticated restaurant shacks.

Stretching between the blurred lines of Candolim and Baga, Calangute is centred on the busy market road leading to the beachfront. To the north, Baga Beach consists of jostling shacks, peppered with water sports, and late-night clubs along infamous Tito's Lane, and one very busy road to the Baga River. The north side of the river is an altogether more serene experience.

Candolim

Candolim's long and languid beach, which curves to join smaller Sinquerim Beach to the south, is largely the preserve of charter tourists from the UK, Russia and, more than ever, elsewhere in India.

It's fringed with an unabating line of beach shacks, all offering sunbeds and shade in exchange for your custom. In all it's an upmarket, happy holiday strip with less congestion than Calangute and Baga, but independent travellers may find it a little soulless. The post office, supermarkets, travel agents, pharmacies and plenty of banks with ATMs are all located on the main Fort Aguada Rd, running parallel to the beach.

Agonda

Travellers have been drifting to Agonda for years and seasonal hut villages – some very luxurious – now occupy almost all available beachfront space in season. It's a good choice if you're after some beachy relaxation.

Palolem & Colomb Bay

Palolem is undoubtedly one of Goa's most postcard-perfect beaches: a gentle curve of palm-fringed sand facing a calm bay. But in season the beachfront is transformed into a toy town of colourful and increasingly sophisticated timber and bamboo huts

Palolem Beach

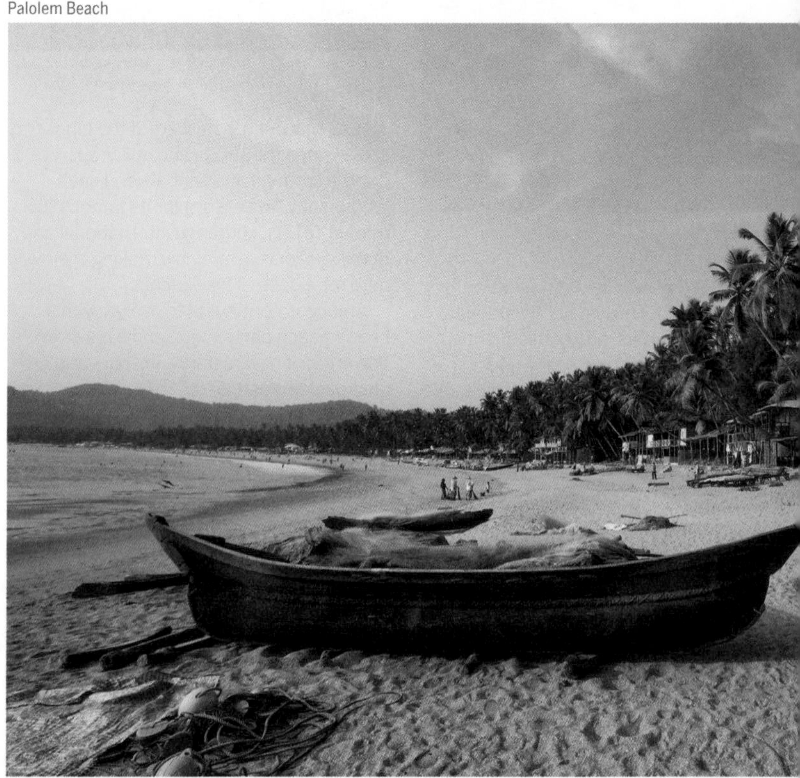

ronted by palm-thatch restaurants. It's still a great place to be and is popular with backpackers, long-stayers and families. The protected bay is one of the safest swimming spots in Goa and you can comfortably kayak and paddleboard for hours here.

Just around the headland at the southern end, Colomb Bay is another little hideaway with several low-key resorts and restaurants.

Safe Swimming

One of the most deceptive dangers in Goa is to be found right in front of you. The Arabian Sea, with its strong currents, often steeply shelving sands and dangerous rips (undertows), claims lives each year. Goa's main beaches are patrolled by lifeguards during 'swimming season' (November to March). Be vigilant with children, avoid swimming after drinking alcohol, and don't even consider swimming during the monsoon.

CINOBY / GETTY IMAGES ©

Luxury Living

Goa has more five-star resorts and boutique hotels per square kilometre than anywhere else in India. Even if you're not staying, you can almost always book a table at a fancy in-house restaurant, an afternoon at a spa, or even pay to use the pool.

Partying & Drinking

Goa loves to party and there's a liberal attitude to drinking, but it's not quite Ibiza on the subcontinent. The all-night trance parties on beaches and in coconut groves are largely consigned to history but EDM parties, raves, dance festivals and nightclubs still happen in season.

Beach Huts

The quintessential Goan accommodation experience is the beach hut – these are also known locally as 'coco-huts' or 'treehouses' (if on stilts). Over time, these huts have moved far beyond their primitive genesis and many are now made of timber or plywood. A variation on the beach huts is the luxury or safari-style tent villages.

Food Shacks

One of the distinguishing features of Goa's beaches is the seasonal restaurant shacks that line the sands on just about every beach. Of the 360-plus shacks erected each year, some 200 are along the mega-busy Candolim–Calangute–Baga beach strip. Other beaches, especially in the south, might have just one or two shacks every few hundred metres.

Yoga by the Sea

India is regarded as the birthplace of yoga and there are few better places than Goa to downward dog or salute the sun.

Great For...

☑ Don't Miss

A meditation class or two, offered by most yoga retreats.

Yoga Season

The best time to visit is mid-November to early April, when all outfits or retreats are open and courses are in full swing. A handful of smaller classes operates year-round, so it's still possible to get your yoga fix, even during the monsoon.

Anjuna This is the closest beach to the retreats at Assagao and there are frequent drop-in classes and courses in Anjuna itself.

Mandrem & Aswem A number of reputable yoga schools and spiritual retreats call Mandrem home in season and there's a good ayurvedic massage centre.

Palolem & Patnem Patnem in particular has become a popular place for beachfront yoga retreats and there are lots of drop-in classes at these perennially popular beaches.

PIKOSO.KZ / SHUTTERSTOCK ©

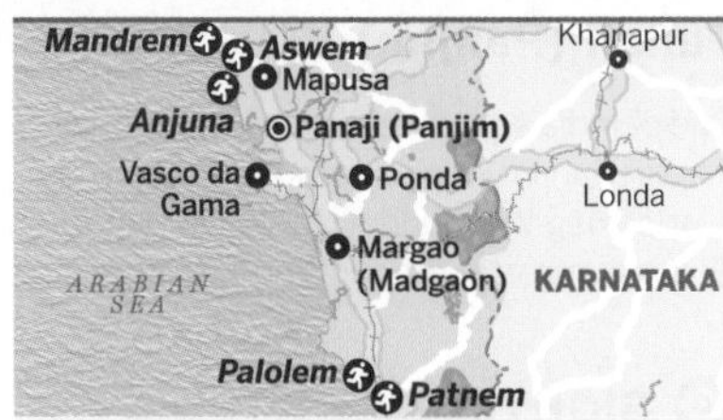

Arambol Popular Iyengar yoga school and numerous drop-in classes and retreats.

Which Kind of Yoga?

Ashtanga Often called 'power yoga', active and physically demanding, good for serious toning.

Bikram Also called 'hot yoga', 26 poses performed at 41°C (105°F) and 40% humidity.

Hatha Yoga focused on breath work (pranayama), and slow, gentle stretching. Good for beginners.

Iyengar Slow and steady, using 'props' in the form of blocks, blankets and straps.

Kundalini Aims to free the base of the spine to unleash hidden energy; involves core, spine and sitting work.

Vinyasa Active, fluid series of changing poses, sometimes called 'flow yoga'.

Need to Know

Good drop-in classes generally cost between ₹300 and ₹700.

Take a Break

Seek out 'pure veg' food if you're looking to extend your yogic balance into vegetarian eating.

★ Top Tip

Check hotel, restaurant or cafe notice boards for current and upcoming courses.

Yoga Centres

Some recommended options:

Anand Yoga Village (7066454773; www.anandyogavillage.com; off Ourem Rd; drop-in classes ₹400, five-pass ₹1500), Palolem

Ashiyana Retreat Centre (9850401714; www.ashiyana-yoga-goa.com; Junas Waddo; drop-in class ₹600), Mandrem

Bamboo Yoga Retreat (9637567730; www.bamboo-yoga-retreat.com; cottages per person €82-92;), Patnem

Brahmani Yoga (p171), Anjuna

Himalayan Iyengar Yoga Centre (www.hiyogacentre.com; Madhlo Vaddo; 5-day yoga course ₹5500; 9am-6pm Nov-Mar), Arambol

Purple Valley Yoga Retreat (0832-2268363; www.yogagoa.com; 142 Bairo Alto; dm/s 1 week £770/850, 2 weeks £1150/1400), Assagao

Panaji (Panjim)

One of India's most relaxed state capitals, Panaji (Panjim) crowds around a peninsula overlooking the Mandovi River. No visit to Goa is complete without time spent here.

SIGHTS

Church of Our Lady of the Immaculate Conception Church

(cnr Emilio Gracia & Jose Falcao Rds; 9am-12.30pm & 3-7.30pm Mon-Sat, 11am-12.30pm & 3.30-5pm Sun, English Mass 8am daily) Panaji's spiritual, as well as geographical, centre is this elevated, pearly white church, built in 1619 over an older, smaller 1540 chapel, and stacked like a fancy white wedding cake. When Panaji was little more than a sleepy fishing village, this church was the first port of call for sailors from Lisbon, who would give thanks for a safe crossing, before continuing to Ela (Old Goa) further east up the river. The church is beautifully illuminated at night.

Panaji's Fontainhas

Fontainhas, said to take its name from local springs, is the larger of Panaji's old districts, comprising pastel-shaded houses towards **Altinho Hill**. The land here was originally reclaimed in the late 18th century by a returning self-made Goan, known as 'the Mosmikar'. Fontainhas' main thoroughfare is 31st January Rd, and it's between here, Ourem Rd, Rue de Natal and further south to Altinho that you'll find many of the colourful mansions, Portuguese homes and bougainvillea blooms that make this district so photogenic. It's also notable for the pretty **Chapel of St Sebastian** (St Sebastian Rd; mass 6.45am daily), built in 1818.

EATING & DRINKING

Viva Panjim Goan $$

(0832-2422405; 31st January Rd; mains ₹160-300; 11.30am-3.30pm & 7-11pm Mon-Sat, 7-11pm Sun) Well-known to tourists, this little side-street eatery, in an old Portuguese house and with a few tables out on the laneway, delivers tasty Goan classics at reasonable prices. There's a whole page devoted to pork dishes, along with tasty *xacuti* (a spicy chicken or meat dish cooked in red coconut sauce) and *cafreal* (a marinated chicken dish) meals.

Black Sheep Bistro European $$$

(0832-2222901; www.blacksheepbistro.in; Swami Vivekanand Rd; tapas ₹250-400, mains ₹350-600; noon-4pm & 7pm-midnight) Among the best of Panaji's burgeoning boutique restaurants, Black Sheep's impressive pale-yellow facade gives way to a sexy dark-wood bar and loungy dining room. The tapas dishes are light, fresh and expertly prepared in keeping with its farm-to-table philosophy. Salads, pasta, seafood and dishes like lamb osso buco grace the menu, while an internationally trained sommelier matches food to wine.

Hotel Venite Goan $$$

(31st January Rd; mains ₹320-440; 9am-10.30pm) With its cute rickety balcony tables overhanging the cobbled street, Venite has long been among the most atmospheric of Panaji's Goan restaurants. The menu is traditional, with spicy sausages, fish curry rice, pepper steak and *bebinca* (Goan 16-layer cake), but Venite is popular with tourists and prices are consequently inflated. Drop in for a beer or shot of feni (Goan liquor) before deciding.

GETTING THERE & AWAY

AIR

Dabolim Airport (Goa International Airport; 0832-2540806; NH566) is around 30km south of Panaji. A new **airport bus** (www.goakadamba.com)

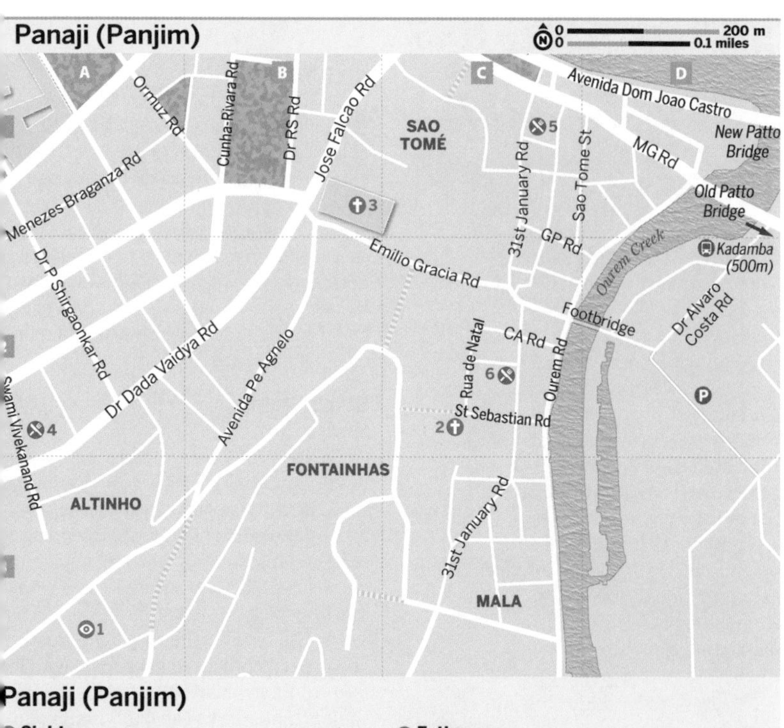

Panaji (Panjim)

Sights

1 Altinho Hill A3
2 Chapel of St Sebastian C2
3 Church of Our Lady of the Immaculate Conception B1

Eating

4 Black Sheep Bistro A2
5 Hotel Venite C1
6 Viva Panjim C2

tween Dabolim and Calangute stops at Panaji request. Some higher-end hotels offer a inibus service.

US

cal buses depart from Panaji's **Kadamba bus and** (interstate 0832-2438035, local 0832-38034; www.goakadamba.com; Patto Centre; reservations 8am-8pm). Major destinations e Mapusa (₹30, 30 minutes) in the north, argao (₹40, one hour) to the south and Ponda 25, one hour) to the east. Most bus services n from 6am to 10pm. There are direct buses to ndolim (₹20, 35 minutes), Calangute (₹25, 25 inutes) and Baga (₹30, 30 minutes).

TRAIN

The closest train station to Panaji is Karmali (Old Goa), 12km to the east near Old Goa. A number of long-distance services stop here, including services to and from Mumbai, and many trains coming from Margao. Panaji's **Konkan Railway Reservation Office** (www.konkanrailway.com; Patto Place; 8am-8pm Mon-Sat) is on the 1st floor of the Kadamba bus stand – not at the train station.

Palolem

In season between November and March, Palolem's beautiful beachfront is transformed into a toy town of colourful and sophisticated timber and bamboo huts

Palolem
0 500 m
0 0.25 miles
A
B
C
D
E
F
1
2
3
4
Leopard Valley (3.5km); Agonda (7km)
6
Bus Stand
PALOLEM
4
3
Palolem Beach
5
1
COLOMB
7
Colomb Bay
Patnem Beach
ARABIAN SEA
Patnem Beach
PATNEM
2
CHAUDI

Palolem

Activities, Courses & Tours

1 Anand Yoga Village B3
2 Bamboo Yoga Retreat C4
3 Rahul's Cooking Class B2

Eating

4 Magic Italy A2
5 Ourem 88 .... B2
6 Space Goa B1

Drinking & Nightlife

7 Neptunes B3

ʼonted by palm-thatch restaurants. The ›rotected bay is one of the safest swim-ning spots in Goa and you can comfortably ayak and paddleboard here.

SIGHTS & ACTIVITIES

ʼutterfly Beach — Beach

ʼire a local boat operator from Palolem ʼeach to ferry you up to Butterfly Beach nd back (₹2000 for the boat), relishing ne views of untouched coastline along he way. The beach can also be reached by oad from Agonda and a walk from the car ›ark.

ʼanshikar ʼpice Farm — Spice Farm

ʼ9421184114, 0832-2608358; www.tanshikar picefarm.com; Netravali; tours incl lunch ₹500; ʼ10am-4pm) Tanshikar Spice Farm is a ʼorking, family-run organic spice farm with rops including vanilla, cashews, pepper, ›utmeg and chillies, as well as beekeeping. ʼhere are no tour buses out here and the miable young owner Chinmay gives a per-ʼonalised tour of the plantation and nearby ›ubble lake. It can also offer cooking lasses and guided jungle treks to nearby ʼaterfalls.

ʼahul's Cooking Class — Cooking

ʼ07875990647; www.rahulcookingclass.com; alolem Beach Rd; per person ₹1500; 11.30am-.30pm & 6-9pm) Rahul's is one of the ›riginal cooking schools, with three-hour norning and afternoon classes each day. ʼrepare five dishes including chapati and oconut curry. Minimum two people; book t least one day in advance.

EATING & DRINKING

Space Goa — Cafe $$

(7066067642; www.thespacegoa.com; 261 Devabag; mains ₹180-350; 8.30am-5.30pm;) On the Agonda road, Space Goa combines an organic whole-food cafe with a deli, craft shop and a wellness centre offering meditation, acupuncture and other treatments. The food is fresh and delicious and the desserts are divine. Drop-in morning yoga classes are ₹500.

Magic Italy — Italian $$

(8805767705; 260 Palolem Beach Rd; mains ₹260-500; 1-11pm;) On the main beach road, Magic Italy has been around since 1999 and the quality of its pizza and pasta remains high, with imported Italian ingredients like ham, salami, cheese and olive oil, imaginative 13-inch wood-fired pizzas and homemade pasta. Sit at tables, or Arabian-style on floor cushions. The atmosphere is busy but chilled.

Ourem 88 — European $$$

(8698827679; mains ₹550-800; 6-10pm Tue-Sun) British-run Ourem 88 is a gastronomic sensation. It has just a handful of tables and a small but masterful menu, with changing specials chalked up on the blackboard. Try baked brie, tender calamari stuffed with Goan sausage, braised lamb shank or fluffy soufflé. English roast dinner on Sunday. Worth a splurge.

Leopard Valley — Club

(www.facebook.com/leopardvalley; Palolem-Agonda Rd; entry from ₹600; 9pm-4am Fri) South Goa's biggest outdoor dance club is a sight (and sound) to behold, with

Silent Discos

Palolem's 'silent parties' are the way to dance the night away without upsetting the neighbours. Turn up around 10pm, don your headphones with a choice of two or three channels featuring Goan and international DJs playing trance, house, hip hop, electro and funk, and then party the night away in inner bliss but outer silence. Try **Neptunes** (www.facebook.com/neptunesgoa; Neptune Point, Colomb Bay; ₹800; ⌚9pm-4am Sat Nov-Apr).

3D laser light shows, pyrotechnics and state-of-the-art sound systems blasting local and international DJs on Friday nights. It's in an isolated but easily reached (by taxi) location between Palolem and Agonda. Check the Facebook page to see what's on.

GETTING THERE & AWAY

Frequent buses run to nearby Chaudi (₹8) from the **bus stand** (Palolem Beach Rd) on the corner of the road down to the beach. Hourly buses to Margao (₹40, one hour) depart from the same place.

An autorickshaw from Palolem to Patnem should cost ₹100, or ₹150 to Chaudi. A taxi to Dabolim Airport is around ₹2500, or ₹2000 to Margao.

Anjuna

Anjuna is continuing to evolve, with a heady beach party scene and a constant flowering of new restaurants, bars and backpacker hostels. Hire a scooter or motorbike and explore the back lanes and southern beach area.

ACTIVITIES

Anjuna's narrow beach runs for almost 2km, from the rocky, low-slung cliffs at the

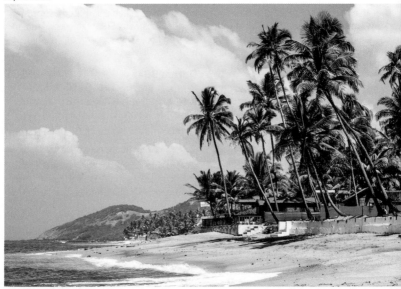

Anjuna Beach

northern village area right down beyond the flea market in the south.

Brahmani Yoga Yoga

(9545620578; www.brahmaniyoga.com; Tito's White House, Aguada-Siolim Rd; class ₹700, 10-class pass ₹5000; classes 9.30am) This friendly drop-in centre offers daily classes from late November to April in ashtanga, vinyasa, hatha and dynamic yoga, as well as pranayama meditation. No need to book: just turn up 15 minutes before the beginning of class.

EATING & DRINKING

Artjuna Cafe Cafe $$

(0832-2274794; www.artjuna.com; Market Rd; mains ₹130-480; 7.30am-10.30pm;) Artjuna is right up there with our favourite cafes in Anjuna. Along with all-day breakfast, outstanding espresso coffee, salads, smoothies, sandwiches and Middle Eastern surprises like baba ganoush, tahini and falafel, this sweet garden cafe has an excellent craft and lifestyle shop, yoga classes, movie nights and a useful noticeboard. Great meeting place.

Baba Au Rhum French $$$

(9657210468; Anjuna-Baga Rd; baguettes ₹210-300, mains ₹480-550) It's tucked away on the back road between Anjuna and Baga but Baba Au Rhum's reputation (it was previously in Arpora) means it's always busy. Part bakery, part French cafe, this is the place for filled baguettes, croissants, crostini or quiche, as well as creamy pastas or a filet mignon. Craft beer on tap and a relaxed, open garden–restaurant vibe.

Curlies Bar

(www.curliesgoa.com; 9am-3am) Holding sway at South Anjuna Beach, Curlies mixes laid-back beach-bar vibe with sophisticated nightspot – the party nights here are notorious, legendary and loud. There's a rooftop lounge bar and an enclosed late-night dance club. Thursday and Saturday are big nights, as are full-moon nights.

Anjuna Flea Market

Anjuna's weekly Wednesday **flea market** (8am-sunset Wed Nov-Apr) is a quintessential Goan experience. More than three decades ago, it was conceived and created by hippies smoking jumbo joints, selling pairs of Levi jeans or handmade jewellery to help fund the rest of their stay. These days it is almost entirely made up of Indian traders selling spices, t-shirts and the like but there's live music in the afternoons and plenty of colour.

Jewellery stall, Anjuna flea market

GETTING THERE & AWAY

Buses to Mapusa (₹15, 30 minutes) depart every half-hour or so from the main **bus stand** at the end of the Anjuna–Mapusa Rd near the beach.

Motorcycle taxis and autorickshaws gather at the main crossroads and you can also easily hire scooters and motorcycles here from ₹250 to ₹400.

KERALA

In This Chapter

Backwater Boat Trips 176
Ayurvedic Resorts 178
Kerala's Beaches 180
Kathakali 182
Thiruvananthapuram (Trivandrum) 184
Kovalam 185
Alappuzha (Alleppey) 187
Kochi (Cochin) 189

Kerala at a Glance...

For many travellers, Kerala is South India's most serenely beautiful state. Behind 600km of glorious Arabian Sea coast extends a languid network of glistening backwaters; behind them rise the spice- and tea-covered hills of the Western Ghats carpeted with lush forests and tea estates. Apart from its idyllic landscapes, the state's signature ayurvedic treatments, taste-bud-tingling cuisine, vibrant traditions such as Kathakali plays, temple festivals and snake-boat races often bring even the smallest villages to life.

Three Days in Kerala

Spend the first day and night enjoying the sights, smells, food, shops and quaint colonial atmosphere of the age-old trading port city of **Kochi** (Cochin; p189). Then start early the next day for **Alappuzha** (Alleppey; p187) and kick back on a two-day houseboat cruise drifting lazily through Kerala's famed backwaters. Wine and dine on board, while visiting remote villages along the way.

Five Days in Kerala

On day four head south, with a stop in the state capital **Thiruvananthapuram** (Trivandrum; p184) for a little sightseeing and shopping en route to **Kovalam** (p185), where you have a night and a day to enjoy the buzzing beach, some fine dining and maybe a spot of surfing or diving.

Previous page: Tea plantations, Kerala

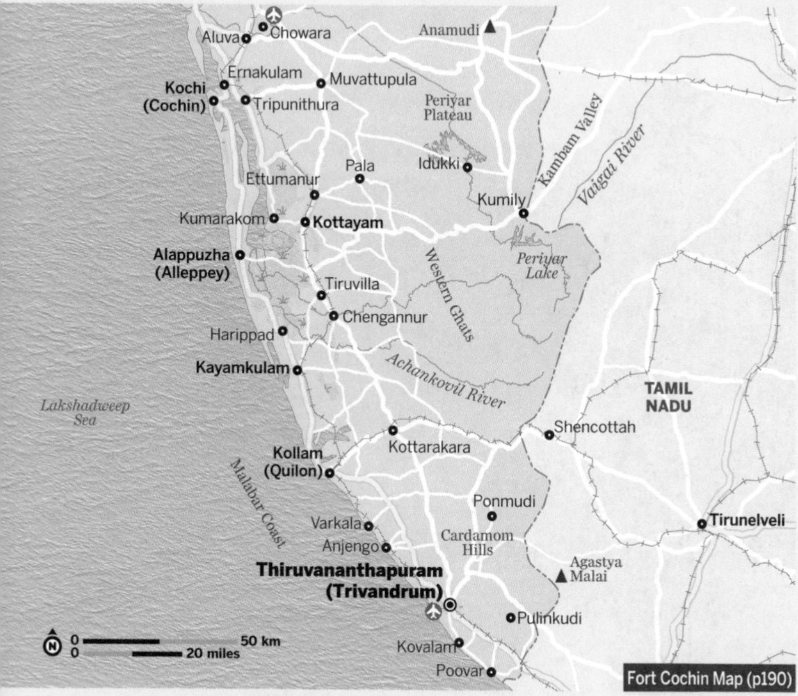

Chowara
Aluva
Anamudi
Ernakulam
Muvattupula
Kochi (Cochin)
Tripunithura
Periyar Plateau
Kambam Valley
Vaigai River
Idukki
Pala
Ettumanur
Kumily
Kumarakom
Kottayam
Alappuzha (Alleppey)
Periyar Lake
Western Ghats
Tiruvilla
Chengannur
Harippad
Kayamkulam
Achankovil River
TAMIL NADU
Lakshadweep Sea
Shencottah
Kottarakara
Kollam (Quilon)
Malabar Coast
Ponmudi
Varkala
Tirunelveli
Cardamom Hills
Anjengo
Agastya Malai
Thiruvananthapuram (Trivandrum)
Pulinkudi
0 50 km
0 20 miles
Kovalam
Poovar

Fort Cochin Map (p190)

Arriving in Kerala

Kerala's three major airports – **Trivandrum**, **Kochi** and **Calicut** – serve international and domestic routes, and were joined in late 2018 by much-anticipated **Kannur International Airport** (with links to the Gulf and across India).

Kerala is well connected to destinations across South India and beyond by trains, particularly along the west coast.

Where to Stay

Kochi, Alleppey, and to a lesser extent Trivandrum, have some of India's most charming accommodation, including heritage guesthouses and family-run homestays. Kovalam is tightly packed with hotels and guesthouses. For the best places you'll usually need to book ahead during the November-to-March high season. At other times, you may get good discounts.

Backwater Boat Trips

Kerala's 900km of waterways spread watery tendrils through a lusciously green landscape, where palm-shaded, winding canals are lined by back-in-time villages. It's an unforgettable South India experience.

To glide along the canals in a punted canoe, or sleep under the stars in a traditional houseboat, is pure enchantment. Backwater trips traverse palm-fringed lakes studded with cantilevered Chinese fishing nets, and wind their way along narrow, shady canals where coir (coconut fibre), copra (dried coconut kernels) and cashews are loaded onto boats.

Great For...

☑ Don't Miss

The experience of sleeping under a firmament of stars on a traditional houseboat.

Houseboats

Houseboats sleep between two to 14 or more people, and vary wildly in luxury and amenities. The hire includes staff, and catering is included, and you'll eat traditional Keralan meals of fish and vegetables cooked in coconut milk. The popularity of these tours can mean that the main waterways get very busy – even gridlocked – in peak season. A one-night houseboat trip

Need to Know

Budget-level boats per 24 hours: ₹6000 to ₹8000 (2 people); ₹10,000 to ₹12,000 (4 people). Larger or air-conditioned boats: ₹15,000 to ₹30,000.

Take a Break

On most backwater trips, you can make chai stops at villages you pass.

★ Top Tip

Avoid peak season (mid-December to mid-January) and domestic holidays when prices and traffic peak.

won't get you far through the backwaters. Plan on spending at least two nights on board.

Choosing a Houseboat

Houseboats can be chartered through private operators in Alleppey, Kollam and Kottayam.

- Try to avoid booking a houseboat until you arrive at the backwaters. Visit the Alleppey houseboat dock (p187), talk to returning travellers or guesthouse owners, and search online to gauge costs and quality.
- Ask to see the operator's certification. Houseboat owners with a 'Green Palm' or 'Gold Star' certificate have met requirements such as solar panels, sanitary tanks and low-emission engines.

Canoes & Kayaks

Canoe tours usually involve small groups of five to six visitors, a knowledegable guide and an open canoe or covered *kettuvallam*. The tours (from Kochi, Kollam or Alleppey) last three to 10 hours and cost around ₹500 to ₹1000 per person. Kochi's **Tourist Desk** (☎9847044688, 0484-2371761; touristdesk1990@gmail.com; Ferry Jetty, Ernakulam; ⏰8am-6pm) organises recommended tours. Kayaking trips, making similar village stops at similar prices, are becoming a popular alternative.

Ferries

The cheapest means of seeing the waterways is to take a public ferry. You can take trips from town to town, though you won't travel much of the smaller canals. Two of the most popular trips are the all-day tourist cruise between Kollam and Alleppey, a scenic but slow eight-hour trip, and the 2½-hour ferry from Alleppey to Kottayam.

DMYTRO GILITUKHA / SHUTTERSTOCK ©

Ayurvedic Resorts

Kerala is regarded as the home of ayurveda – Indian herbal medicine, hich aims to restore balance in the body. Many specialist clinics, resorts and colleges provide ayurvedic treatments or teach ayurvedic techniques.

Great For...

☑ Don't Miss

A revitalising ayurvedic massage under swaying palms near the beach.

Ayurveda sees the world as having intrinsic order and balance. It argues that we possess three *doshas* (humours): *vata* (wind or air); *pitta* (fire); and *kapha* (water/earth). Deficiency or excess in any of them can result in disease.

Treatment aims to restore the balance, principally through two methods: *panchakarma* (internal purification involving five therapies), and herbal massage. The body is first prepared over several days with a special diet, *snehana* (oil massages) and *swedana* (herbal steam baths).

The herbs used in ayurveda grow in abundance in Kerala's humid climate – the monsoon is thought to be the best time of year for treatment, when there is less dust in the air, the pores are open and the body is most receptive to treatment – and every village has its own ayurvedic pharmacy.

Ayurvedic oil treatment

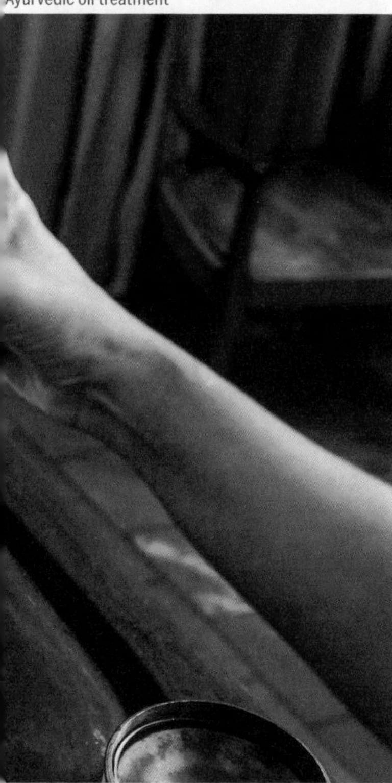

Need to Know

Resorts and centres offer options from single massages to weeks-long treatment programmes.

Take a Break

For a change from the resorts' ayurvedic fare, head to Kovalam's **Waves Restaurant** (www.thebeachhotel-kovalam.com; Beach Hotel, Lighthouse Beach; mains ₹220-550; 7.30am-11pm;).

★ Top Tip

The monsoon is considered the best season for ayurvedic treatment, when the skin's pores are open.

Ayurvedic Centres & Resorts

Pulinkudi & Chowara

Niraamaya Surya Samudra (0471-2267333, 8045104510; www.niraamaya.in; Pulinkudi; r incl breakfast ₹18,990-40,700;) offers A-list-style seclusion. The 33 traditional Keralan homes, in a palm grove above sparkling seas, come with four-poster beds and open-air bathrooms.

Dr Franklin's (0471-2480870; www.dr-franklin.com; Chowara; incl meals & treatments with AC s ₹9620-10,260, d ₹17,230-17,630, without AC s ₹8330-9620, d ₹14,660-17,230;) is a reputable and less-expensive alternative to the flashier resorts, and features tidy, comfortable rooms and cottages, daily yoga, a pool and personalised ayurveda packages.

One of the original resorts, **Somatheeram** (0471-2268101; https://somatheeram.in; Chowara; with AC s ₹17,900-20,550, d ₹19,900-22,950, without AC s ₹6820-15,330, d ₹7540-17,000;) offers a full range of ayurvedic and *panchakarma* treatments, ayurvedic food, yoga and a high-standard of accommodation, overlooking Chowara Beach.

Kochi

Run by third-generation ayurvedic practitioner Dr Subhash, the delightful waterside **Ayurdara** (9447721041; https://ayurdara.com; Murikkumpadam, Vypeen Island; per day ₹1650; 9am-5.30pm) centre specialises in personalised treatments of one to three weeks (₹1650 per day). It also offers yoga (₹200). It's on Vypeen Island, 3km north of the Fort Cochin ferry jetty. By appointment only.

DMITRY RUKHLENKO / SHUTTERSTOCK ©

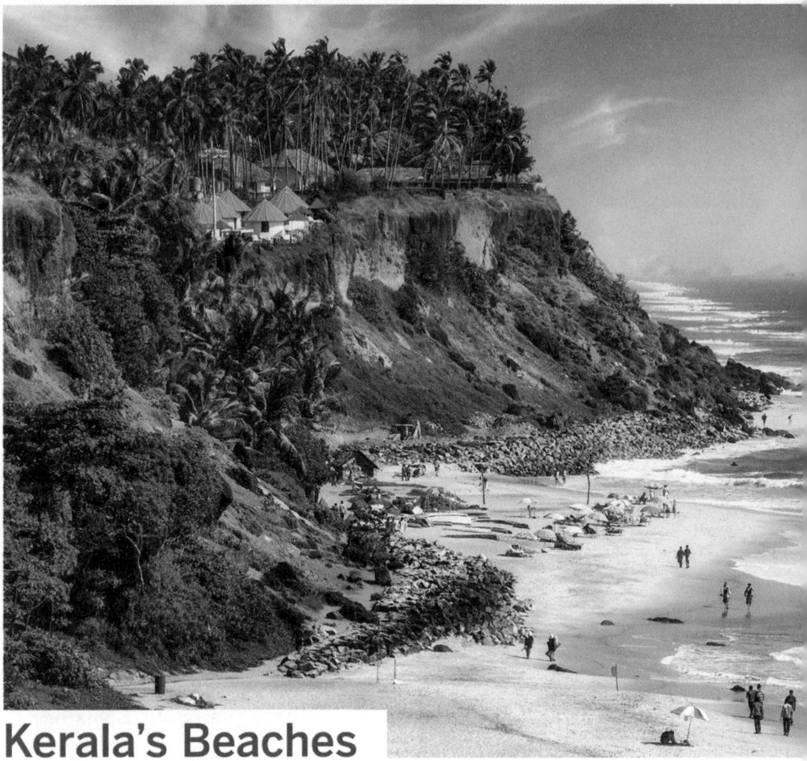

Kerala's Beaches

Goa might pull in the beach-holiday crowds, but Kerala's coastline – almost 600km of it – boasts a stunning string of golden-sand beaches, fringed by palms and washed by the Arabian Sea.

Great For...

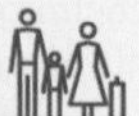

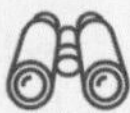

☑ **Don't Miss**

The fresh, inexpensive seafood in the beach shacks on the sands.

Kerala's southern beaches are the most popular, while wilder, less-discovered choices await in the north.

Best Beach Towns

Varkala The beautiful cliff-edged coastline of Varkala is an important Hindu holy place as well as a lively backpacker-focused beach hang-out. Great base for yoga, surfing and traveller vibes.

Kovalam (p185) Kerala's most commercial beach resort, but still fun and easily accessible with good waves, yoga and surfing. Resorts here and further southeast have a strong ayurvedic focus.

Kannur While Kannur itself is not particularly exciting for visitors, head 8km southeast to Thottada for gorgeous beaches and family-owned homestays.

Varkala Beach

Need to Know

Some tourists wear bikinis on tourist beaches, but if you do, expect stares.

Take a Break

On Kovalam's **Lighthouse Beach**, pick your seafood dinner from the day's catch displayed by restaurants.

★ Top Tip

Take great care with the currents at Varkala and Kovalam. Swimmers are carried away every year.

Southern Beaches

The most established of the resorts along Kerala's southern coast is **Kovalam**, just a short hop from the capital Trivandrum. Once a quiet fishing village, Kovalam has two sheltered crescents of beach. It's perfect for paddling or novice surfing, overlooked by low-rise hotels, ayurvedic centres and restaurants. Some lovely beaches and ayurvedic resorts cluster southeast of Kovalam in less-busy Pulinkudi and Chowara.

North of Trivandrum is **Varkala**, which straggles along dramatic, russet-and-gold-streaked cliffs. Although a holy town popular with Hindu pilgrims, Varkala has also developed into Kerala's favourite backpacker bolthole and the cliffs are lined with guesthouses, open-front cafes and bars all moving to a reggae, rock and trance soundtrack. Travellers looking for a quieter scene are drifting north to **Odayam Beach**.

Even further north, **Alleppey** (p187) is best known for its backwaters but also has a pretty coastline stretching up to increasingly popular **Marari**, with is golden sands and intimate resorts. Just north of Kochi on Vypeen Island lies **Cherai Beach**, a lovely stretch of dusty-blonde sand, with kilometres of lazy lagoons and backwaters only a few hundred metres inland.

Northern Beaches

Fewer travellers make it to Kerala's far north, where there are some beautifully deserted pockets of powdery beach and traditional village life. Among the best are the peaceful sands south of Kannur, or a little further north around the Valiyaparamba backwaters, **Nileshwar** and Bekal.

Kathakali

Kerala has an intensely rich culture of performing arts, and the most celebrated Keralan art form is Kathakali, a colourful dance-drama usually based on stories from the great Hindu epics.

Great For...

☑ **Don't Miss**

Kochi's Kerala Kathakali Centre is a great choice for an introductory Kathakali performance.

Kathakali crystallised at around the same time that Shakespeare was writing his plays. The Kathakali performance is the dramatised presentation of a play, usually based on the Hindu epics the Ramayana, the Mahabharata and the Puranas. All the great themes are covered – righteousness and evil, frailty and courage, poverty and prosperity, war and peace, love, lust and power struggles. Traditionally, all Kathakali performers are men, taking on both male and female roles (though there's now the odd woman Kathakali artist, too).

Drummers and singers accompany the actors, who tell the story through their precise movements, particularly mudras (hand gestures) and facial expressions. Preparation for the performance is lengthy. Paint, fantastic costumes, ornamental headpieces and meditation transform the

Need to Know

Abbreviated introductory shows for tourists usually last about two hours, including make-up and costume sessions.

Take a Break

Kochi's **Teapot** (Peter Celli St, Fort Cochin; dishes ₹180-300; 8.30am-9pm) is perfect for 'high tea' before a Kathakali Centre performance.

★ Top Tip

Some Kathakali centres in Kochi and Kumily also give demonstrations of the Keralan ritual martial art *kalarippayat*.

actors physically and mentally into the gods, heroes and demons they are about to play. Dancers even stain their eyes red with seeds from the chundanga plant to maximise the drama.

Where to See Kathakali

The easiest places for travellers to see performances are at cultural centres such as **Kerala Kathakali Centre** (9895534939, 0484-2217552; www.kathakalicentre.com; KB Jacob Rd, Fort Cochin; shows ₹300-350; shows from 4pm) and **Greenix Village** (0484-2217000, 9349372050; www.greenix.in; Calvathy Rd, Fort Cochin; shows ₹350-650; 8am-7.30pm, shows from 4pm) in Kochi. In Kovalam there are often short versions of Kathakali shows in season.

Standard programs start with the intricate make-up application and costume-fitting, followed by a demonstration and commentary on the dance and then the performance – usually two hours in all.

If you're interested in learning more about the art of Kathakali, **Kerala Kalamandalam** (0488-4262418; www.kalamandalam.org; Cheruthuruthy; courses per month ₹600; Jun-Mar) near Thrissur and **Margi Kathakali School** (0471-2478806; www.margitheatre.org; Fort; admission by donation) in Trivandrum offer courses for serious students, or you can attend these schools to see performances and practise sessions. Kochi's Kerala Kathakali Centre also runs classes.

Thiruvananthapuram (Trivandrum)

Thiruvananthapuram, Kerala's capital – still usually referred to by its colonial-era name, Trivandrum – is an easygoing introduction to urban life down south. Most travellers merely springboard from here to the nearby beaches of Kovalam and Varkala

SIGHTS

Museum of History & Heritage Museum

(www.museumkeralam.org; Park View, Museum Rd; adult/child Indian ₹20/10, foreigner ₹200/50, camera ₹25; ⏲10am-5.30pm Tue-Sun) Occupying a handsome 120-year-old heritage building located within the Kerala Tourism complex, this intelligently presented museum traces Kerala's history and culture through superb static and multimedia displays. Exhibits range from Iron Age implements to bronze, wood and terracotta sculptures, murals, *dhulichitra* (floor paintings), Roman-era coins, re-creations of traditional Keralite homes and replicas of engravings at Wayanad's **Edakkal Caves** (adult/child ₹30/20, camera/video ₹50/200; ⏲8am-4pm Tue-Sun).

Napier Museum Museum

(Art Museum; off Museum Rd; adult/child Indian ₹20/10, foreigner ₹200/100; ⏲10am-4.45pm Tue & Thu-Sun, 1-4.45pm Wed) Housed in an 1880 wooden building designed by Robert Chisholm (a British architect whose Fair Isle–style version of the Keralite vernacular shows his enthusiasm for local craft), this museum holds an eclectic display of bronzes, Buddhist sculptures, temple carts, ivory carvings and a wood-carved model of Kerala's famous Guruvayur temple. The architectural style fuses neo-Gothic and Keralan elements, and the carnivalesque interior is worth a look in its own right.

SHOPPING

Connemara Market Market

(MG Rd; ⏲6am-9pm) At the busy Connemara Market (named after a British Madras Presidency governor) vendors sell vegeta-

Napier Museum

bles, fish, goats, fabric, clothes, spices and much more.

EATING

Ariya Nivaas South Indian $

(Manorama Rd; mains ₹40-150, thalis ₹120; 7am-10pm) Trivandrum's best all-you-can-eat South Indian veg thalis mean long-running Ariya Nivaas is always busy (especially at lunchtime), but service is snappy and the food fresh. There's an air-con dining room upstairs.

Padmavilasom Palace Keralan $$$

(8086080286, 7902203111; http://padmavilasompalace.com; TC29/1769 Perumthanni, Airport Rd, Injakkal; breakfast ₹370, lunch ₹530; 7.30-10.30am & 12.30-3pm;) At elegant, history-rich Padmavilasom Palace, Kerala's traditional vegetarian *sadya* (banquet) is delivered in all its banana-leaf sumptuousness within the courtyards of an exquisitely restored 19th-century *ammaveedu* (royal residence for consorts of the Travancore maharajas). Freshly prepared curries, rice, chutneys, pappadams and more are laid out for lunch, while breakfasts revolve around gourmet South Indian thalis.

GETTING THERE & AWAY

AIR

Trivandrum International Airport (www.trivandrumairport.com), 4km west of the city centre, serves international destinations with direct flights to/from Colombo in Sri Lanka, Malé in the Maldives, and Gulf destinations such as Dubai, Doha, Sharjah, Muscat, Bahrain and Kuwait.

TRAIN

Trains are often heavily booked; reserve ahead online or visit the upstairs **reservation office** (1st fl, Trivandrum Central; 8am-2pm & 2.15-5.30pm) just north of Platform 1 at Trivandrum Central train station. Most major trains arrive at Trivandrum Central, but some express services terminate at Kochuveli train station, 7km northwest of the centre.

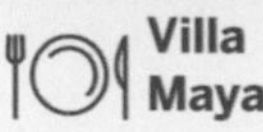

Villa Maya

Villa Maya (0471-2578901; www.villamaya.in; 120 Airport Rd, Injakkal; mains ₹600-1600; noon-11pm;) is more an experience than a mere restaurant. Dining is either in the magnificent 18th-century Dutch-built mansion or in private curtained niches in the tranquil courtyard garden. The Keralan cuisine is expertly crafted, delicately spiced and beautifully presented. Seafood is a speciality, with dishes like stuffed crab with lobster butter, though there are some tantalising vegetarian offerings, too.

Fine dining at Villa Maya

GARY COOK / ALAMY STOCK PHOTO ©

GETTING AROUND

Taxi apps Ola Cabs and Uber are the easiest way to get around town. Autorickshaw drivers will *sometimes* use their meters; short hops cost ₹20 to ₹50. There are prepaid autorickshaw stands outside the **bus** (Central Station Rd) and **train** (Thampanoor Junction) stations.

Kovalam

Once a calm fishing village, Kovalam now competes with Varkala as Kerala's most-developed resort. The touristed main stretch, **Lighthouse Beach**, is flanked by hotels and restaurants stretching back into the hillside from the shore; just north, **Hawa Beach** is usually crowded with day trippers heading straight from the taxi and bus stands to the sand. About 2km further north, more peaceful **Samudra Beach** hosts several upmarket resorts.

Fresh Seafood

Each evening the restaurants along the Lighthouse Beach promenade display the catch of the day – settle on a price and decide how you'd like your seafood prepared (grilled? fried? steamed Keralan-style in a banana leaf?). Market prices vary enormously, but at research time costs were around ₹90 per 100g of snapper and ₹180 per 100g of tiger prawns.

Keralan fish in banana leaf
SANTHOSH VARGESE / SHUTTERSTOCK ©

SIGHTS & ACTIVITIES

Vizhinjam Lighthouse Lighthouse

(Lighthouse Rd; Indian/foreigner ₹20/50, camera ₹10; ⏲10am-1pm & 2-6pm Tue-Sun) Kovalam's most distinguishing feature is the working candy-striped lighthouse at the southern end of Lighthouse Beach. Climb the spiral staircase – or zip up in the lift – for vertigo-inducing, palm-drenched views sweeping up and down the coast.

Cool Divers & Bond Safari Diving

(☎9946550073, 7560906575; www.bondsafarikovalam.com; Suseela Tower, Kovalam Beach Rd; introductory dive ₹6000; ⏲8.30am-5.30pm) An efficient dive outfit providing state-of-the-art equipment, PADI courses (four-day Open Water Diver ₹25,000) and guided trips to local dive sites. It also has nifty Bond submarine scooters, where your head is enclosed in a helmet with an airhose to the surface – no diving experience required! (Sadly, these scooters were out of action at research time.)

EATING & DRINKING

For a romantic splurge, try the top-class restaurants at the **Leela** (☎0471-3051234; www.theleela.com; Samudra Beach; r from ₹13,800, ste from ₹40,880; ❄@🛜≋) and **Taj Green Cove** (☎0471-6613000; https://taj.tajhotels.com; GV Raja Vattapara Rd, Samudra Beach; r/ste incl breakfast from ₹14,200/21,890; ❄🛜≋) resorts. Just about all of Kovalam's restaurants serve beer and wine discreetly.

Varsha South Indian $$

(☎9995100301; dishes ₹150-225; ⏲8am-10pm; 🛜) In the lanes behind southern Lighthouse Beach, this little restaurant plates up some of Kovalam's best vegetarian food at reasonable prices, in a simple garden-like space with sandy floors, plastic chairs and a few potted plants. Dishes are fresh and carefully prepared, including spicy masala dosa and a deliciously light off-menu pumpkin-and-spinach curry.

Bait Seafood $$$

(☎0471-6613000; https://taj.tajhotels.com; Taj Green Cove, GV Raja Vattapara Rd, Samudra Beach; mains ₹360-990; ⏲12.30-10.30pm) Designed as an upmarket alfresco beach shack, the fabulous seafood restaurant at the Taj Green Cove fronts the sea, with waves and palms on one side and chefs in a semi-open kitchen on the other. Seafood and spicy preparations are as glorious as the blazing sunsets, including delicious fresh fish or tofu steak soaked in 'Kerala coast' spices, with Maharashtrian Sula wines.

INFORMATION

Tourist Office (☎0471-2480085; Kovalam Beach Rd; ⏲9.30am-5pm Mon-Sat) This helpful office is at the main entrance to the Leela resort near the bus stand.

GETTING THERE & AROUND

Taxis running between Trivandrum and Kovalam cost ₹500 (including prepaid taxis from Trivandrum airport); autorickshaws charge

Houseboat, Alappuzha

₹350. Taxis to Kanyakumari are ₹4000 and to Varkala ₹2800.

The main **autorickshaw and taxi stand** is located at Hawa Beach; there's another **autorickshaw stand** (Lighthouse Rd) at the southern end of Lighthouse Beach. From the bus stand to the north end of Lighthouse Beach costs ₹50.

Alappuzha (Alleppey)

Alappuzha – most still call it Alleppey – is the hub of Kerala's backwaters, home to a vast network of waterways and over 1000 houseboats. The city centre is small and chaotic, but head out towards the backwaters and Alleppey becomes graceful and greenery-fringed, disappearing into a watery world of villages, punted canoes, toddy shops and, of course, houseboats. Kerala's main backwaters stretch north, east and south of Alleppey, while Vembanad Lake, Kerala's largest, reaches all the way north to Kochi.

SIGHTS & ACTIVITIES

Alleppey Lighthouse Lighthouse
(Indian/foreigner ₹20/50, camera ₹10; 9-11.45am & 2-5.30pm Tue-Sun) A few blocks back from the beach, the candy-striped 1862 lighthouse contains a small museum with an original oil lamp, but is best visited for the 360-degree views of a green Alleppey from the top of its spiralling staircase.

Houseboat Dock Boating
(9400051796; dtpcalpy@yahoo.com; off Punnamada Rd; prepaid counter 9.30am-4.30pm) Dozens of houseboats gather at Alleppey's main dock. There's a government-run prepaid counter with 'official' posted prices, starting at ₹7000 for two people and up to ₹34,000 for a seven-berth boat (reduced rates June to October), though even these fluctuate with demand. Note that some houseboats dock elsewhere and the most reputable ones often get booked up in advance.

Kayaking, Kerala

Kerala Kayaking Kayaking

(☎9846585674, 8547487701; www.keralakayaking.com; Vazhicherry Bridge, VCNB Rd; per person 4/7/10hr ₹1500/3000/4500) Alleppey's original and best kayaking outfit. The young crew offers excellent guided kayaking trips through narrow backwater canals. Paddles in single or double kayaks include a support boat and motorboat transport to your starting point. There are four-hour morning and afternoon trips and seven- or 10-hour day trips, as well as multiday village tours (from ₹13,000 per two people).

EATING

Mushroom Arabic, Indian $

(☎9633085702; www.facebook.com/MushroomRestaurant; CCSB Rd; mains ₹90-170; ⏱noon-midnight) A breezy open-air town-centre restaurant embellished with fairy lights and greenery, specialising in cheap, spicy halal meals like chicken *kali mirch,* fish tandoori and chilli mushrooms, plus peppery noodle and rice stir-fries. Lots of locals and travellers give it a fun, relaxed vibe. Also does takeaway.

Chakara Multicuisine $$$

(☎0477-2239767; www.raheemresidency.com; Beach Rd; mains ₹350-550; ⏱7.30-10am, 12.30-3pm & 7-10pm) Opposite the beach, this elegant restaurant at the 1860s heritage-style **Raheem Residency** (s ₹9220-11,980, d ₹10,240-13,310; ❄📶🏊) is Alleppey's finest. It has seating on a bijou open-sided terrace reached via a spiral staircase (though the sea views are now mostly blocked by a flyover). The menu creatively combines Keralan and European cuisine, specialising in local seafood; try the Alleppey fish curry or paneer-cashew curry.

INFORMATION

DTPC Tourist Office (☎9400051796, 0477-2251796; www.dtpcalappuzha.com; Boat Jetty Rd; ⏱9.30am-5.30pm) Close to the bus stand and boat jetty, with helpful staff who provide maps and book full-day canoe tours (₹700).

GETTING THERE & AWAY

BOAT

From Alleppey's **boat jetty** (VCSB Rd), State Water Transport (www.swtd.gov.in) ferries are *scheduled* for Kottayam (₹15, 2½ hours) at 7.30am, 9.30am, 11.30am, 2.30pm and 5.15pm, returning at 6.45am, 11.30am, 1pm, 3.30pm and 5.15pm; at the time of writing, ongoing renovation works meant only the 11.30am ferry (returning at 1pm) was operating. Ferries leave for Kollam (₹400, eight hours) daily at 10.30am (every other day April to June).

TAXI

Taxis cost around ₹1700 to Kochi, ₹2200 to Kollam and ₹3800 to Munnar.

TRAIN

Alleppey's train station is 4km southwest of the town centre, with numerous daily trains to Ernakulam (2nd class/sleeper/3AC ₹50/140/495, 1½ hours) and Trivandrum (₹80/140/495, three to four hours) via Kollam (₹60/140/495, 1½ to 2½ hours). Six daily trains go to Varkala (2nd class/AC chair ₹65/315, two to three hours).

GETTING AROUND

Autorickshaws from the town centre or bus stand to the beach cost around ₹60. Guesthouses hire out scooters for ₹300 to ₹400 per day, including reliable **Nanni Tours & Travel** (9895039767; www.nannitours.com; Cullan Rd; 8am-9pm).

Kochi (Cochin)

Serene Kochi has been drawing traders, explorers and travellers to its shores for over 600 years. Nowhere else in India could you find such an intriguing mix: giant Chinese fishing nets, a 450-year-old synagogue, ancient mosques, Portuguese- and Dutch-era houses, and the crumbling remains of the British Raj. It's a delightful place to explore, laze in arty cafes and relax at some of India's finest homestays and heritage hotels. It's also an important centre for Keralan arts (traditional and contemporary) and a standout place to see Kathakali and the Keralan martial art *kalarippayat*.

Mainland Ernakulam is Kochi's hectic transport and cosmopolitan hub, while the historical towns of Fort Cochin and Mattancherry, though well-touristed, remain wonderfully atmospheric.

SIGHTS

Fort Cochin

The historical European part of the city, Fort Cochin has a couple of small, sandy beaches, which are only really good for people-watching in the evening and gazing out at the incoming tankers. A popular promenade meanders from west-coast Mahatma Gandhi Beach to the Chinese fishing nets (p192) and **fish market** (River Rd, Fort Cochin; restaurants 8am-9pm).

Keep an eye out along the shore for the scant remains of **Fort Immanuel**, the 16th-century Portuguese fort from which the area takes its name.

Indo-Portuguese Museum Museum
(0484-2215400; Bishop Kureethara Rd, Fort Cochin; adult/child ₹40/20; 9am-1pm & 2-6pm Tue-Sun) The heritage of one of India's earliest Catholic communities – including vestments, silver processional crosses, altarpieces from the Kochi diocese and 19th-century sketches of Santa Cruz Basilica – is on show at this thoughtfully presented museum hidden in the tranquil garden of the Bishop's House. The basement contains remnants of the 16th-century Portuguese-built Fort Immanuel.

Mattancherry & Jew Town

About 32.5km southeast of Fort Cochin, Mattancherry is the old bazaar district and centre of the spice trade. These days it's packed with spice shops and pricey Kashmiri-run emporiums that autorickshaw drivers will fall over backwards to take you to for a healthy commission – any offer of a cheap tour of the district will inevitably lead to a few shops. In the midst of this, Jew

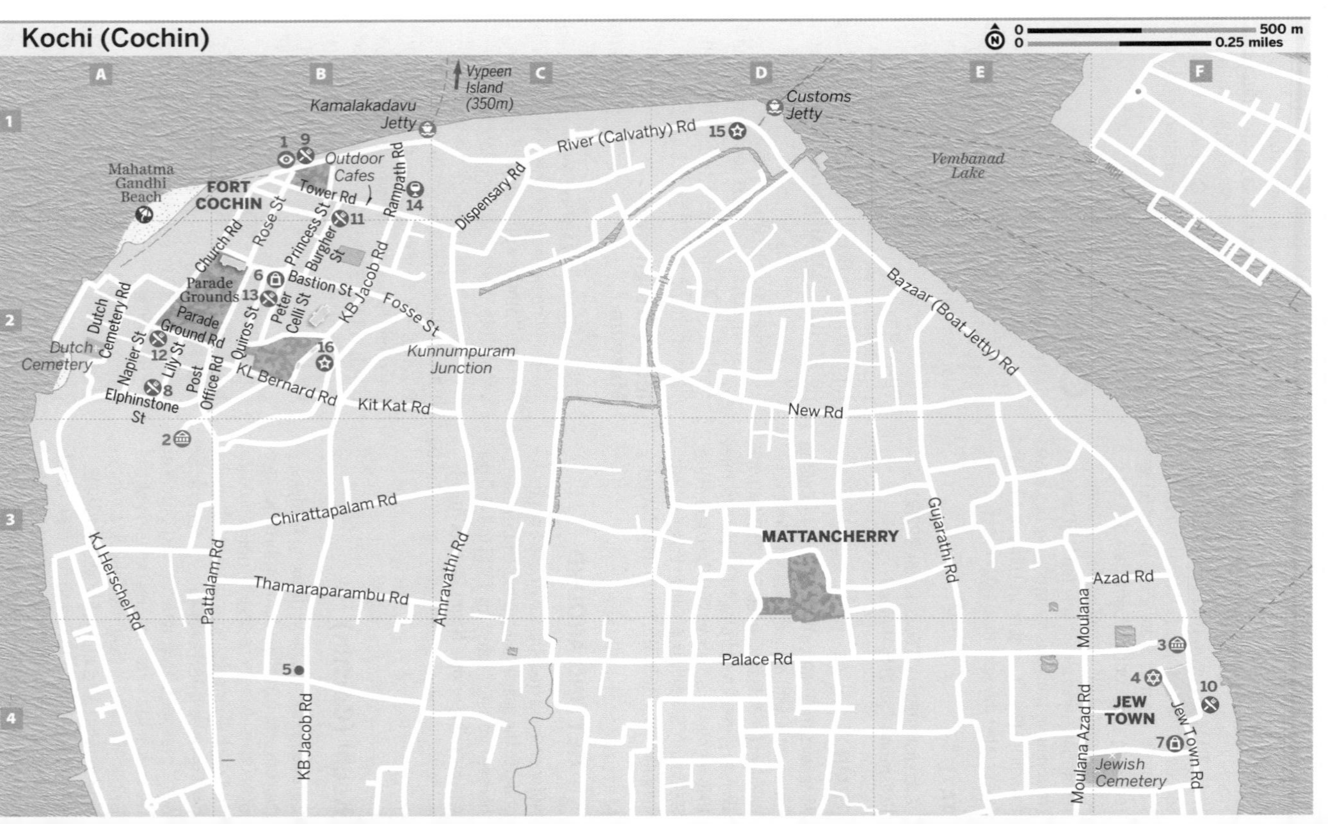
Kochi (Cochin)
0 500 m
0 0.25 miles
A
B
C
D
E
F
1
2
3
4
Vypeen Island (350m)
Kamalakadavu Jetty
Customs Jetty
Vembanad Lake
Mahatma Gandhi Beach
FORT COCHIN
Outdoor Cafes
Tower Rd
Rampath Rd
River (Calvathy) Rd
Dispensary Rd
Church Rd
Rose St
Princess St
Burgher St
KB Jacob Rd
Bastion St
Parade Grounds
Parade Ground Rd
Peter Celli St
Fosse St
Quiros St
Dutch Cemetery Rd
Dutch Cemetery
Napier St
Lily St
Post Office Rd
KL Bernard Rd
Kunnumpuram Junction
Elphinstone St
Kit Kat Rd
Bazaar (Boat Jetty) Rd
New Rd
Chirattapalam Rd
Gujarathi Rd
MATTANCHERRY
KJ Herschel Rd
Pattalam Rd
Thamaraparambu Rd
Amravathi Rd
Azad Rd
Moulana
Palace Rd
KB Jacob Rd
Moulana Azad Rd
JEW TOWN
Jew Town Rd
Jewish Cemetery
1
2
3
4
5
6
7
8
9
10
11
12
13
14
15
16

Kochi (Cochin)

Sights
1 Chinese Fishing Nets....B1
2 Indo-Portuguese Museum....A3
3 Mattancherry Palace....F4
4 Pardesi Synagogue....F4

Activities, Courses & Tours
5 Art of Bicycle Trips....B4

Shopping
6 Niraamaya....B2
7 Niraamaya....F4

Eating
8 Dal Roti....A2
9 Fishmongers....B1
10 Ginger House....F4
11 Kashi Art Cafe....B1
12 Malabar Junction....A2
13 Teapot....B2

Drinking & Nightlife
14 Clubb18....B1
DiVine....(see 12)

Entertainment
15 Greenix Village....D1
16 Kerala Kathakali Centre....B2

Town is a bustling port area with a fine synagogue. Scores of small firms huddle together in dilapidated old buildings and the air is filled with the biting aromas of ginger, cardamom, cumin, turmeric and cloves, though the lanes around Mattancherry Palace and the synagogue are packed with antique and tourist-curio shops rather than spices. Just south is Kochi's old Muslim quarter.

Mattancherry Palace Museum
(Dutch Palace; Palace Rd, Mattancherry; adult/child ₹5/free; ⊙9am-5pm Sat-Thu) Mattancherry Palace was a generous gift presented to the Raja of Kochi, Veera Kerala Varma (1537–65), as a gesture of goodwill by the Portuguese in 1555. The Dutch renovated it in 1663, hence the alternative name, the Dutch Palace. The building combines European and Keralan styles, but the star attractions are the royal bedchamber's preserved Hindu murals from the 17th to 19th centuries, which depict scenes from the Ramayana, Mahabharata and Puranic legends in intricate, colourful detail.

Pardesi Synagogue Synagogue
(Synagogue Lane, Mattancherry; ₹5; ⊙10am-1pm & 3-5pm Sun-Thu, 10am-1pm Fri, closed Sat & Jewish holidays) Originally built in 1568, Mattancherry's synagogue was partially destroyed by the Portuguese in 1662, and rebuilt two years later when the Dutch took Kochi. It features an ornate brass *bimah* (pulpit), elegant wooden benches, and elaborate hand-painted, willow-pattern floor tiles from Canton, China, added in 1762 during major remodelling under Ezekial Rahabi. It's magnificently illuminated by Belgian chandeliers and coloured-glass lamps. The graceful clock tower dates from 1760, with inscriptions in Malayalam, Hebrew, Roman and Arabic script.

TOURS

Art of Bicycle Trips Cycling, Walking
(☎8129945707; https://artofbicycletrips.com; KB Jacob Rd; 3hr/half-day tours ₹2250/4200; ⊙9am-6pm Mon-Sat) Guided bicycle tours on quality mountain bikes with this India-wide operator include the three-hour Vasco Safari morning tour of the historic Fort area and a half-day ride around the backwaters. There are also evening walking food tours of Fort Cochin and Mattancherry (₹950).

SHOPPING

There are some elegant boutiques scattered around Fort Cochin, though most shops here are identikit Kashmiri-run stores selling North Indian crafts. On Jew Town Rd in Mattancherry you'll find Gujarati-run shops selling genuine antiques mingled with knock-offs. Broadway in Ernakulam is good for local shopping, spice

Chinese Fishing Nets

The unofficial emblems of Kerala's backwaters, and perhaps the most photographed, are the half-dozen giant cantilevered Chinese fishing nets on Fort Cochin's northeastern shore, known locally as *cheena vala*. A legacy of traders from the AD 1400 court of Kublai Khan, these spiderlike, 10m-tall contraptions rest on teak or bamboo poles and require five or six people to operate their counterweights at high tide.

Modern fishing techniques are making these labour-intensive methods less and less profitable, with nets slowly disappearing from Kerala's coastline. Smaller fishing nets are dotted around the shores of Vembanad and Ashtamudi lakes; some of the best are just east of Cherai Beach on Vypeen Island.

Fort Cochin's Chinese fishing nets

shops and clothing; Kochi's major shopping malls are also in Ernakulam.

Niraamaya Fashion & Accessories
(0484-2217778; https://niraamaya.org; 1/605 Peter Celli St, Fort Cochin; 10am-5.30pm Mon-Sat) A world of soothing pinks, greys and oranges, Niraamaya sells 'ayurvedic' clothing, accessories, homewares and yoga mats – all made of organic cotton, coloured with natural herb dyes, or infused with ayurvedic oils, based on the ancient concept of *ayurvastra* (healthy fabrics). There's another **branch** (0484-2217778; https://niraamaya.org; 6/217 AB Salem Rd, Mattancherry; 10am-5.30pm) in Mattancherry.

EATING & DRINKING

Dal Roti Indian $$
(9746459244; 1/293 Lily St, Fort Cochin; mains ₹170-350; noon-3pm & 6.30-10pm Wed-Mon) Always-busy Dal Roti is one of Fort Cochin's most-loved restaurants. Knowledgeable owner Ramesh will guide you through his expansive North Indian menu and help you dive into a delicious world of vegetarian, eggetarian and nonvegetarian options. From *kati* rolls (filled *paratha* fried with a coating of egg) and stuffed *paratha* to seven thali types, you won't go hungry.

Kashi Art Cafe Cafe $$
(Burgher St, Fort Cochin; dishes ₹150-350; 8.30am-10pm;) Fort Cochin's original (and best) art cafe, this fashionable, natural-light-filled space has a Zen vibe, a creeping vertical garden and stylish wood tables spreading out into a courtyard dotted with contemporary artwork. The coffee is strong, organic ingredients are used wherever possible, and the luscious breakfasts and lunches are excellent (French toast, home-baked cakes, creative salads).

Malabar Junction International $$$
(0484-2216666; www.malabarhouse.com; Parade Ground Rd, Fort Cochin; mains ₹450-800, tasting menus ₹2500; 7am-11pm) Set in an open-sided pavilion or at candlelit poolside tables, this outstanding restaurant at **Malabar House** (r incl breakfast €220-360;) is (almost) Bollywood-star glam. The ambitious East-meets-West menu creatively fuses local and European flavours – the signature dish is the seafood platter (₹3200), or try an elegant 'trilogy' of Indian curries. An impressive choice of Indian wines (Sula, Fratelli, Grover Zampa) accompanies meals.

Ginger House Indian $$$
(0484-2213400; http://museumhotel.in; Jew Town Rd, Mattancherry; mains ₹230-800; 8am-8pm May-Oct, to midnight Nov-Apr) Hidden behind a massive antique-filled godown (warehouse) is this wonderful waterfront restaurant, where you can relax over fresh juices and punchy Indian dishes

South Indian thali, Malabar Junction

and snacks. Walk through the priceless Heritage Arts showroom to reach it.

DRINKING & ENTERTAINMENT

Fort Cochin has a handful of beer parlours and new late-night spot **Clubb18** (www.no18.co.in; No 18 Hotel, Rampath Rd, Fort Cochin; 11.30am-midnight) is a favourite hang-out. A couple of top-end Fort Cochin hotels have bars, including **DiVine** (0484-2216666; www.malabarouse.com; Parade Ground Rd, Fort Cochin; 11am-11pm) at Malabar House.

Greenix Village (p183) is a good place to watch Kathakali performances.

GETTING THERE & AWAY

AIR

Cochin International Airport (0484-2610115; http://cial.aero; Nedumbassery), 30km northeast of Ernakulam, is a popular hub, with international flights to/from the Gulf States, Sri Lanka, the Maldives, Malaysia, Bangkok and Singapore. Domestic connections include Mumbai, Bengaluru (Bangalore), Delhi, Goa and Trivandrum.

TRAIN

Ernakulam has two train stations, Ernakulam Junction and Ernakulam Town. There's a **reservations office** (8am-8pm Mon-Sat, to 1pm Sun) at Ernakulam Junction. There are frequent local and express trains to Trivandrum (2nd class/sleeper/3AC ₹95/165/490, four to five hours), via Alleppey (₹50/140/495, 1½ hours).

GETTING AROUND

Bright-orange AC buses run between the airport and Fort Cochin (₹88, 1¾ hours, at least 16 daily) via Ernakulam. There are 24-hour prepaid taxi stands at the domestic and international terminals. Uber and Ola taxis charge around ₹700 and ₹1000, respectively.

Ferries are the fastest and most enjoyable form of transport between Fort Cochin and the mainland. The main stop at Fort Cochin is **Customs Jetty** (Bazaar Rd); some ferries also use Fort Cochin's **Kamalakadavu Jetty** (River Rd).

MYSURU

In This Chapter

Mysuru City Tour 198
Mysuru 202
Kodagu (Coorg) 205
Bengaluru 206

Mysuru at a Glance...

The historic settlement of Mysuru (which changed its name from Mysore in 2014) is one of South India's most enchanting cities, famed for its glittering royal heritage and magnificent monuments and buildings. Its World Heritage–listed palace brings most travellers here, but Mysuru is also rich in tradition, with a deeply atmospheric bazaar district replete with spice stores and incense stalls. Ashtanga yoga is another drawcard and there are several acclaimed schools that attract visitors from across the globe.

Two Days in Mysuru

On day one, explore the splendid **Mysuru Palace** (p198) and **Chamundi Hill** (p199), dive into **Devaraja Market** (p199) and bite into a classic Mysuru dosa at **Vinayaka Mylari** (p204). On day two, go on a day trip to the serene plantation-draped hills of the **Kodagu** (p205) region.

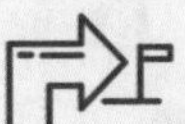

Four Days in Mysuru

After your return from Kodagu (Coorg), on day three perhaps gift yourself a lavish Ayurvedic spa session at **Indus Valley Ayurvedic Centre** (p202). Finally, head to Bengaluru on day four, explore **Krishnarajendra Market** (p207) and sip on some fine craft beers at **Biere Club** (p209).

Previous page: Namdroling Monastery (p205), Kodagu

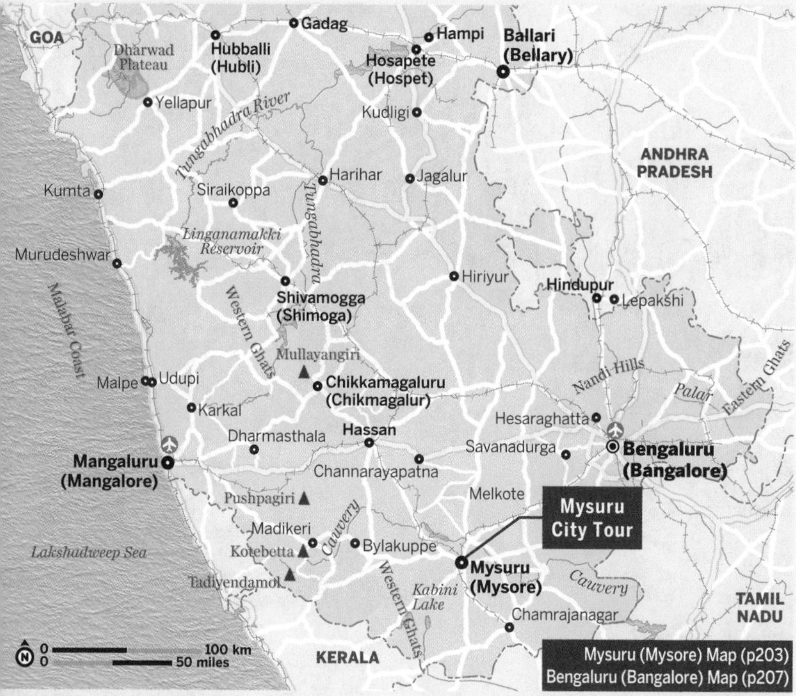

Mysuru (Mysore) Map (p203)
Bengaluru (Bangalore) Map (p207)

Arriving in Mysuru

Kempegowda International Airport, Bengaluru for international and domestic flights.

Bus Frequent connections between Mysuru and Bengaluru.

Train Bengaluru City is Bengaluru's main station; Yeshvantpur station is the starting point for trains to Goa.

Where to Stay

Mysuru has a decent selection of hotels and guesthouses. The city attracts tourists throughout the year and can fill up very quickly during the Dussehra festival (when booking early is highly recommended).

Devaraja Market

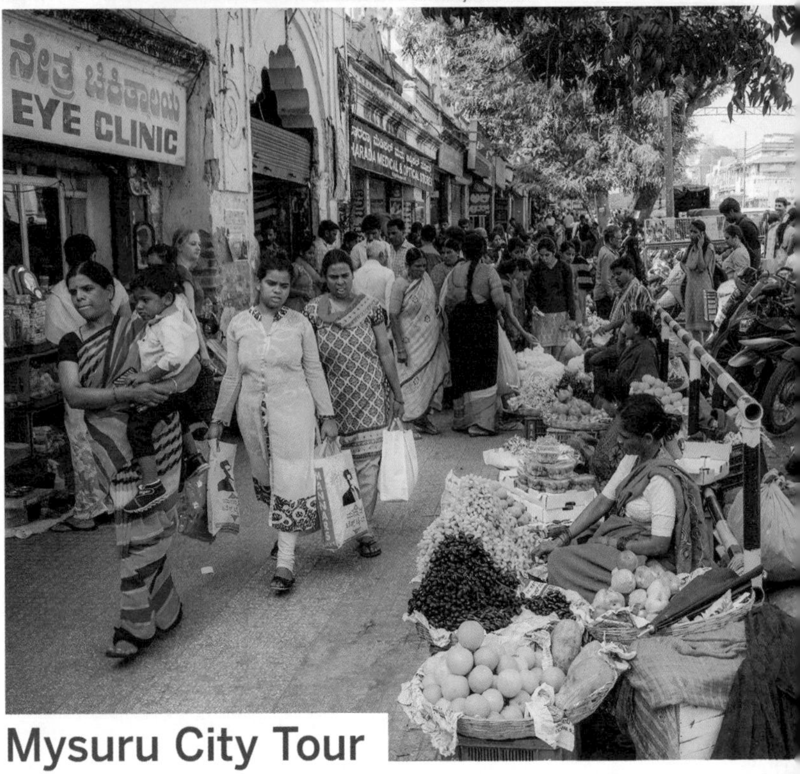

CHRISTIAN OUELLET / SHUTTERSTOCK ©

Mysuru City Tour

Mysuru isn't known as the City of Palaces for nothing – it's home to a total of seven, plus an abundance of majestic architecture from the Wodeyar dynasty and British rule.

Great For...

☑ Don't Miss

Seeing how silk is made at the Government Silk Weaving Factory (p202).

Mysuru Palace

The second-most-visited sight in India (after the Taj Mahal), this **palace** (Maharaja's Palace; http://mysorepalace.gov.in; Purandara Dasa Rd; adult/child ₹50/free; ⏲10am-5.30pm) is among the very grandest of India's royal buildings and was the seat of the Wodeyar maharajas. The original palace was gutted by fire in 1897; today's structure was completed in 1912. The lavish Indo-Saracenic interior – a kaleidoscope of stained glass, mirrors and gaudy colours – is undoubtedly over the top. It's further embellished by carved wooden doors, mosaic floors and a series of paintings depicting life here during the Raj. On the way in you'll pass a fine collection of sculptures and artefacts. Don't forget to check out the armoury, with an intriguing collection of 700-plus weapons. Entrance to the grounds is at the South

Sri Chamundeswari Temple

DENIS.VOSTRIKOV / SHUTTERSTOCK ©

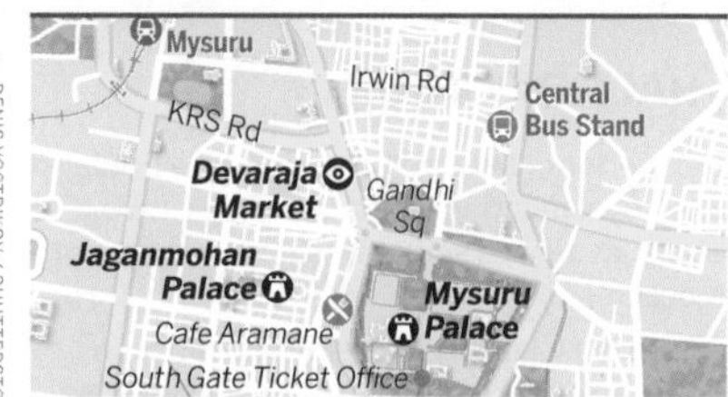

Need to Know

Visit www.karnatakatourism.org/mysore for a list of Mysuru's most notable buildings.

Take a Break

Cafe Aramane (p204), between the Mysuru and Jaganmohan Palaces, is great for dosas and thalis.

★ Top Tip

Visit Mysuru during the colourful Dussehra (p202) festival in September/October.

Gate ticket office on Purandara Dasa Rd. See p200 for a suggested half-day tour.

Devaraja Market

Dating from Tipu Sultan's reign in the 18th century, this lively **bazaar** (Sayyaji Rao Rd; 6am-8.30pm) has local traders selling traditional items such as flower garlands, spices and conical piles of *kumkum* (coloured powder used for bindi dots), all of which make for some great photo ops. There's a large fruit and veg section on the western side, too. Gully Tours (p202) offers good guided walks here.

Jaganmohan Palace

Built in 1861 as the royal auditorium, this stunning **palace** (Jaganmohan Palace Rd) just west of the Mysuru Palace now houses the **Jayachamarajendra Art Gallery**, including works by noted artist Raja Ravi Varma, traditional Japanese art and some rare musical instruments.

Chamundi Hill

This 1062m **hill** offers spectacular views of the city below, and is crowned with the striking **Sri Chamundeswari Temple** (7am-2pm, 3.30-6pm & 7.30-9pm). Queues are long at weekends, so visit during the week. From Central bus stand (p204) take bus 201 (₹28, AC); a return autorickshaw/Uber is around ₹450/700.

Alternatively, you can take the foot trail comprising 1000-plus steps that Hindu pilgrims use to visit the temple. One-third of the way up is a 5m-high statue of Nandi (Shiva's bull) that was carved out of solid rock in 1659. The path starts by the Sri Ayyappa Swamy Temple, 800m south of Mysuru racecourse.

Mysuru Palace

A HALF-DAY TOUR

The interior of Mysuru Palace houses opulent halls, royal paintings, intricate decorative details, as well as sculptures and ceremonial objects.

There is a lot of hidden detail and much to take in, so be sure to allow yourself at least a few hours for the experience. A guide can also be invaluable.

After entering the palace the first exhibit is the **1 Dolls' Pavilion**, which showcases the maharaja's fine collection of traditional dolls and sculptures acquired from around the worl Opposite the **2 Elephant Gate** you'll see the seven cannons that were used for special occa sions, such as the birthdays of the maharajas. Today the cannons are still fired as part of Dussehra festivities.

At the end of the Dolls' Pavilion you'll find the **3 Golden Howdah**. Note the fly whisks on

ROBERT WYATT/ALAMY STOCK PHOTO ©

Private Durbar Hall
Rosewood doors lead into this hall, which is richly decorated with stained-glass ceilings, steel grill work and chandeliers. It houses the Golden Throne, only on display to the public during Dussehra.

PJHPIX/SHUTTERSTOCK ©

Public Durbar Hall
The open-air hall contains a priceless collection of paintin by Raja Ravi Varma and opens onto an expansive balcony supported by massi pillars with an ornat painted ceiling of 10 incarnations of Vis

ither side; the bristles are made from fine ory.

Make sure you check out the paintings epicting the Dussehra procession in the alls on your way to the **4 Marriage Pavilion** nd look into the courtyard to see what was nce the wrestling arena. It's now used during ussehra only. In the Marriage Pavilion, take few minutes to scan the entire space. You an see the influence of three religions in the esign of the hall: the glass ceiling represents Christianity, stone carvings along the hallway ceilings are Hindu design and the top-floor balcony roof (the traditional women's gallery) has Islamic-style arches.

When you move through to the **5 Private Durbar Hall**, take note of the intricate ivory-inlay motifs depicting Krishna in the rosewood doors. The **6 Public Durbar Hall** is usually the last stop, where you can admire the panoramic views of the gardens through the Islamic arches.

Dolls' Pavilion

The first exhibit, the Dolls' Pavilion, displays the gift collection of 19th- and early-20th-century dolls, statues and Hindu idols that were given to the maharaja by dignitaries from around the world.

Elephant Gate

Next to the Dolls' Pavilion, this brass gate has four bronze elephants inlaid at the bottom, an intricate double-headed eagle up the top and a hybrid lion-elephant creature (the state emblem of Karnataka) in the centre.

Golden Howdah

At the far end of the Dolls' Pavilion, a wooden elephant howdah decorated with 80kg of gold was used to carry the maharaja in the Dussehra festival. It now carries an idol of goddess Chamundeshwari.

arriage Pavilion

is lavish hall used for royal weddings features themes of Christianity, nduism and Islam in its design. The highlights are the octagonal painted-ass ceiling featuring peacock motifs, the bronze chandelier and the lonnaded turquoise pillars.

Keshava Temple

Small in scale but masterly in detail, the astonishingly beautiful **Keshava Temple** (Somnathpur; Indian/foreigner ₹25/300; ⌚8.30am-5.30pm) is one of the finest examples of Hoysala architecture, on par with the masterpieces of Belur and Halebid. Built in 1268, this star-shaped temple, located some 33km from Mysuru, is adorned with superb stone sculptures depicting various scenes from the Ramayana, Mahabharata and Bhagavad Gita, and the life and times of the Hoysala kings.

Ancient stone carvings, Keshava Temple
TATHAART / SHUTTERSTOCK ©

Mysuru

SIGHTS

Rail Museum Museum

(KRS Rd; Indian adult/child ₹20/10, foreigner adult/child ₹80/40, camera/video ₹20/30; ⌚9.30am-6pm Thu-Tue) This open-air museum's main exhibit is the Mysuru maharani's saloon, an 1899 wood-panelled beauty with gilded ceilings and chandeliers that provides an insight into the stylish way the royals once rode the rails. There are also steam engines, locomotives and carriages to investigate, many of which were manufactured in the UK. A toy train rides the track around the museum 16 times daily.

ACTIVITIES

Gully Tours Walking

(☎9632044188; https://gully.tours; walks from ₹1100) Formerly Royal Mysore Walks, these excellent guided tours are the perfect way to familiarise yourself with Mysuru's epic history and heritage. Offers a range of walks (themes include royal history and food) as well as cycle and jeep tours.

Indus Valley Ayurvedic Centre Ayurveda

(☎0821-2473263; www.ayurindus.com; Lalithadripura) Set in 10 hectares of gardens and 6km from the city centre, this classy retreat derives its therapies from ancient scriptures and prescriptions. Aromatherapy, *basti* detox treatments and all manner of ayurvedic treats are offered. The overnight package including full board, ayurveda treatment, yoga session and beauty therapy starts at US$212.

SHOPPING

Government Silk-Weaving Factory Clothing

(☎8025586550; www.ksicsilk.com; Mananthody Rd, Ashokapuram; ⌚8.30am-4pm Mon-Sat, outlet 10.30am-7pm daily) Given that Mysuru's prized silk is made under its very sheds, this government-run outlet, set up in 1912, is the best and cheapest place to shop for the exclusive textile. Behind the showroom is the factory, where you can drop by to see how the fabric is made. It's around 2km south of town.

Mysuru (Mysore)

Sights
1 Devaraja Market C2
2 Jaganmohan Palace B3
3 Mysuru Palace C4
4 Rail Museum A1
5 South Gate Ticket Office D4

Eating
6 Cafe Aramane C4
7 Vinayaka Mylari F3

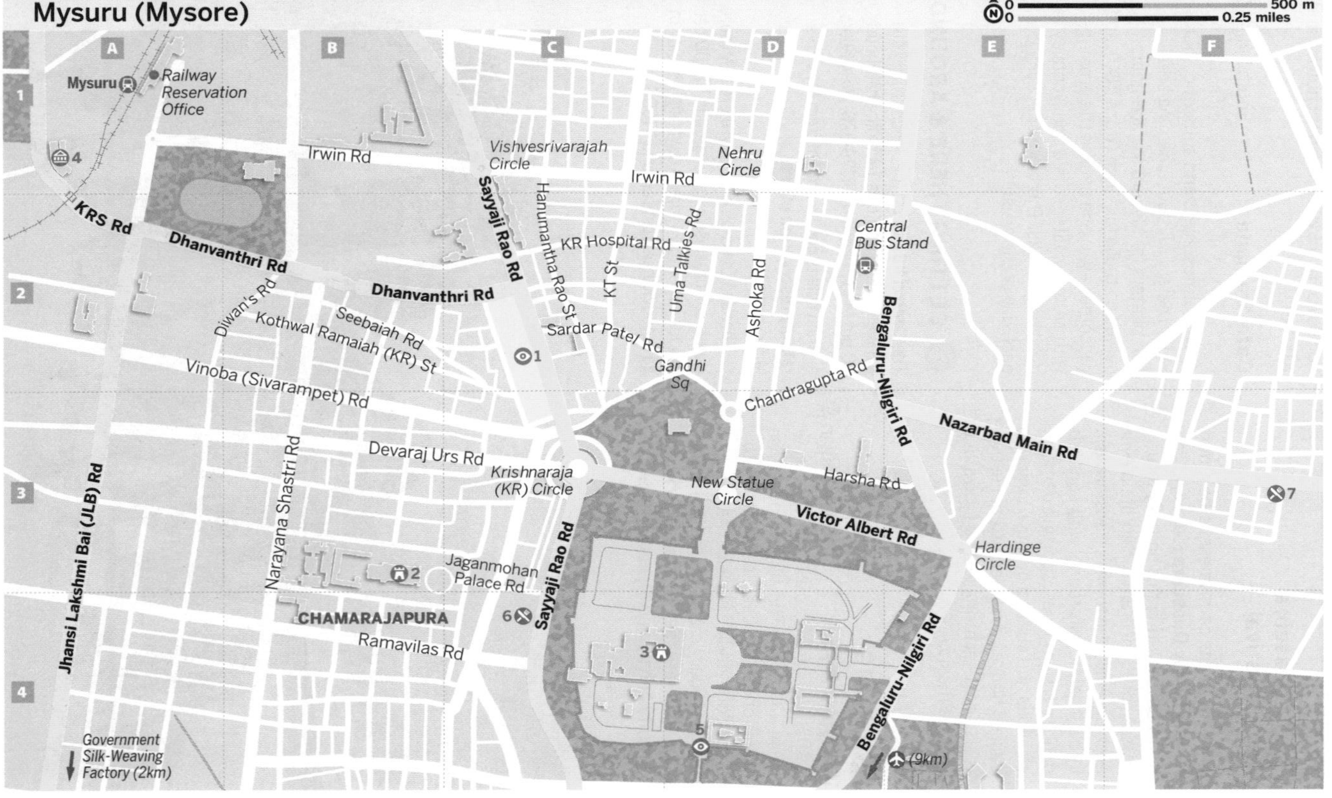
Mysuru (Mysore)
0 500 m
0 0.25 miles
A
B
C
D
E
F
1
2
3
4
Mysuru
Railway Reservation Office
4
Irwin Rd
Vishvesrivarajah Circle
Nehru Circle
KRS Rd
Dhanvanthri Rd
Sayyaji Rao Rd
Hanumantha Rao St
KR Hospital Rd
KT St
Uma Talkies Rd
Ashoka Rd
Central Bus Stand
Diwan's Rd
Kothwal Ramaiah (KR) St
Seebaiah Rd
Sardar Patel Rd
1
Gandhi Sq
Chandragupta Rd
Bengaluru-Nilgiri Rd
Vinoba (Sivarampet) Rd
Nazarbad Main Rd
Devaraj Urs Rd
Krishnaraja (KR) Circle
New Statue Circle
Harsha Rd
7
Narayana Shastri Rd
Victor Albert Rd
Hardinge Circle
Jhansi Lakshmi Bai (JLB) Rd
2
Jaganmohan Palace Rd
6
CHAMARAJAPURA
Ramavilas Rd
3
5
Government Silk-Weaving Factory (2km)
(9km)

Dussehra Festival

Mysuru is at its carnivalesque best during the 10-day **Dussehra** (Dasara; Sep/Oct) festival. During this time Mysuru Palace (p198) is dramatically lit up every evening, while the town is transformed into a gigantic fairground, with concerts, dance performances, sporting demonstrations and cultural events running to packed houses. An Open Street Festival is also held, featuring festive food stalls and live music.

EATING

Vinayaka Mylari South Indian $

(769 Nazarbad Main Rd; dosa ₹30-50; 6am-1.30pm & 3-8.30pm) This tiny, no-nonsense place is one of the best spots in town to try the South Indian classic masala dosa (a large savoury crepe stuffed with spiced potatoes). Here they're beautifully light and fluffy and served on banana leaves. Locals eat them with coconut chutney and a coffee.

Cafe Aramane South Indian $

(Sayyaji Rao Rd; mains ₹90-120; 8am-10pm) This atmospheric and authentic South Indian eatery rolls out steaming breakfast platters for Mysuru's office-goers, serves up thalis for lunch (from ₹80), and welcomes everyone back in the evenings with aromatic filter coffee and a convoy of delicious snacks. There are speciality dosa each day of the week.

GETTING THERE & AROUND

The **Central bus stand** (Bengaluru-Nilgiri Rd) handles all KSRTC buses, including half-hourly AC buses to Bengaluru (₹129-326, 2½-4 hours).

Train tickets can be bought from Mysuru's **railway reservation office** (131; 8am-8pm Mon-Sat, to 2pm Sun).

Uber and Ola cabs are everywhere in Mysuru. Hotels can organise cars for around ₹2500 per day for out-of-town trips. A day's sightseeing in an autorickshaw costs around ₹1000.

Dussehra Festival

Kodagu (Coorg)

Nestled amid evergreen hills that line the southernmost edge of Karnataka is the luscious Kodagu (Coorg) region, gifted with emerald landscapes and hectares of plantations. A major centre for coffee and spice production, its uneven terrain and cool climate make it a fantastic area for trekking, birdwatching or lazily ambling down little-trodden paths winding around carpeted hills.

SIGHTS

Madikeri

Madikeri Fort Historic Site

There are good views from this hilltop fort, built by Tipu Sultan in the 16th century, though today it's the less glamorous site of the municipal headquarters. You can walk a short section of ramparts, and within the fort's walls are the hexagonal palace (now the dusty district-commissioner's office) and a colonial-era church, which houses a quirky **museum** (free entry; ⊙10am-5.30pm Sun-Fri).

Bylakuppe

Namdroling Monastery Monastery

(www.namdroling.org; ⊙7am-6pm) The striking Namdroling Monastery is a large Tibetan Buddhist compound home to the striking **Golden Temple** (Padmasambhava Buddhist Vihara; ⊙7am-6pm) and impressive **Zangdogpalri Temple** (⊙7am-6pm). Around 5000 monks and nuns live within the complex, and there's a small bookstore and cafe, too.

ACTIVITIES

Jiva Spa Spa

(☎08272-265900; jivaspa.coorg@tajhotels.com; 1st Monnangeri, Galibeedu Post; treatments from ₹2700; ⊙9am-9pm) Based at the stunning **Taj Madikeri Resort & Spa** (Vivanta; ☎08272-265900; www.tajhotels.com; r from ₹19,200; @📶🏊), this is an excellent place to indulge in a rejuvenating ayurvedic treatment. With soak tubs, a relaxation lounge, a beauty salon and a yoga-and-meditation zone, it's one of the best spas in South India. Appointments essential.

SHOPPING

Pick up local spices and natural produce from Madikeri's main market, which has coffee beans, vanilla, nutmeg, lemongrass, pepper and cardamom from the region's plantations. Sickly-sweet 'wines' are widely available. Several chocolatiers make handmade truffles using cardamom, pepper and coffee. Try the betel-nut chocolate at **Choci Coorg** (www.facebook.com/chocicoorgmadikeri; Bus Stand Rd; ⊙9am-9pm).

Trekking in Kodagu (Coorg)

Treks in Kodagu are part cultural experience, part nature encounter, involving hill climbs, plantation visits, forest walks and homestays. The best season for trekking is October to March. Popular peaks to trek to include Tadiyendamol (1745m), Pushpagiri (1712m) and Kotebetta (1620m). Plenty of day hikes are possible; **Rainforest Retreat** (☎08272-265639, 08272-265638; www.rainforestours.com; Galibeedu; s/d tent ₹1500/2000, cottages from ₹2000/3000; 📶) 🌿 organises several. Guides are essential.

Trekking, Kodagu region

EATING & DRINKING

Coorg Cuisine Indian $

(Main Rd, Madikeri; mains ₹100-195; ⏰noon-4pm & 7-10pm) Specialising in Kodagu specialities such as *pandhi barthadh* (pork dry fry), *kadambuttu* (rice dumplings) and *koli nallamolu barthad* (chicken-pepper fry), this restaurant is well worth trying. It's not exactly atmospheric, located above a shop on the main road, but the seating is comfy and prices reasonable.

Raintree Indian $$

(www.raintree.in; 13-14 Pension Lane, Madikeri; meals ₹160-300; ⏰11.30am-10pm) This cute converted bungalow makes a cosy place for a delicious meal, with solid wooden furniture and tribal art. The food doesn't disappoint, either, with local specialities and dishes from the coast. It also sells wine and great Kodagu coffee. Located just behind Madikeri Town Hall.

GETTING THERE & AWAY

Very regular buses depart from the KSRTC bus stand in Madikeri for Bengaluru (Bangalore; fan/AC ₹365/550, 5½ to seven hours), stopping in Mysuru (Mysore; ₹165/260, 2½ to four hours) en route.

Bengaluru

Cosmopolitan Bengaluru (formerly Bangalore) is one of India's most progressive and developed cities, blessed with a benevolent climate, a modern metro system, and a burgeoning drinking, dining and shopping scene.

SIGHTS

National Gallery of Modern Art Gallery

(NGMA; ☎080-22342338; www.ngmaindia.gov.in/ngma_bangaluru.asp; 49 Palace Rd; Indian/foreigner ₹20/500; ⏰11am-6.30pm Tue-Sun) Housed in a century-old mansion – the former vacation home of the raja of Mysuru – this world-class art museum showcases an impressive permanent collection (and exhibitions). The Old Wing exhibits works from pre-Independence, including

Idli (fermented rice cakes)

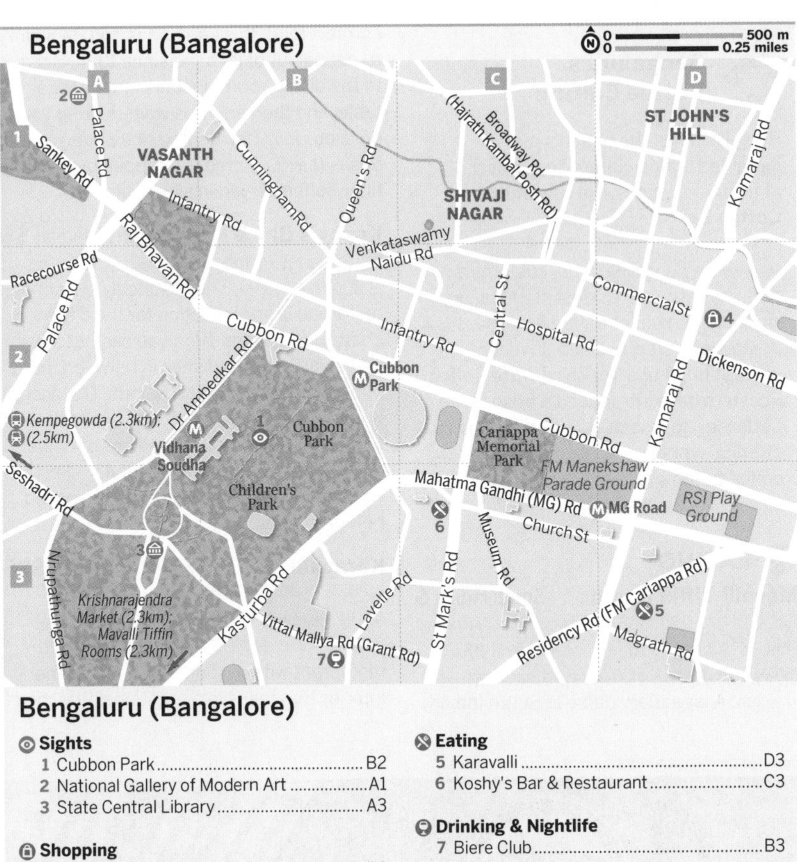

paintings by Raja Ravi Varma and Abanindranath Tagore. Connected by a pedestrian bridge, the sleek New Wing focuses on contemporary post-Independence works by artists including Sudhir Patwardhan and Vivan Sundaram. Guided walks (11.30am Wednesday, 3pm Saturday) are a great way to learn about the museum's highlights.

Krishnarajendra Market Market

(City Market; Silver Jubilee Park Rd; 6am-10pm; M Chickpet) For a taste of traditional urban India, dive into the bustling, gritty Krishnarajendra Market and the dense grid of commercial streets that surrounds it. Weave your way around the lively, colourful stalls, past fresh produce, piles of vibrant dyes, spices and copper ware. The vibrant **flower market** in the centre is the highlight.

SHOPPING

Mysore Saree Udyog Clothing

(www.mysoresareeudyog.com; 1st fl, 316 Kamaraj Rd; 10.30am-8.30pm) A great choice for top-quality silk saris, blouses, fabrics and men's shirts, this fine store has been in business for more than 70 years and has something to suit all budgets. Most garments are made with Mysuru silk. Also stocks 100% *pashmina* (fine cashmere) shawls.

Bengaluru's Coffee Culture

Bengaluru has the nation's most-ingrained coffee culture. In the best of traditional cafes, like **Brahmin's Coffee Bar** (Ranga Rao Rd, Basavanagudi; snacks ₹16-22; 6am-noon & 3-7pm Mon-Sat; M National College), customers often have their breakfast standing up, while slugging filter coffee from glass or stainless-steel beakers. In recent years young guns like Third Wave Coffee Roasters have introduced a fresh (even boffinish) approach to coffee making by offering syphon, chemex and cold-brew coffee to the city.

EATING

Mavalli Tiffin Rooms South Indian $

(MTR; 080-22220022; www.mavallitiffinrooms.com; 14 Lalbagh Rd, Mavalli; snacks from ₹52, meals from ₹90; 6.30-11am & 12.30-9pm Tue-Sun) A legendary name in South Indian comfort food, this eatery has had Bengaluru eating out of its hand since 1924. Head to the dining room upstairs, queue for a table, and then enjoy as waiters bring you delicious *idlis* (fermented rice cakes) and dosas (savoury crepes), capped by frothing filter coffee served in silverware.

Koshy's Bar & Restaurant Indian $$

(39 St Mark's Rd; mains ₹95-400; 9am-11.30pm; M MG Rd) This decidedly old-school resto-pub is an institution for the city's chattering classes: here you can put away tasty North Indian dishes in between mugs of beer and fervent discussions. The decor is all creaky ceiling fans, dusty wooden shuttered windows and lashings of nostalgia. Between lunch and dinner it's 'short eats' only (British-style snacks like baked beans on toast).

Karavalli Seafood $$$

(080-66604545; Gateway Hotel, 66 Residency Rd; mains ₹525-1575; 12.30-3pm & 6.30-11.30pm; M MG Rd) Superior seafood restaurant with a wonderfully atmospheric interior that takes in a traditional thatched

South Indian breakfast dosas (lentil-flour pancakes)

roof, vintage woodwork and beaten brassware – though the garden seating is equally appealing. Choose from fiery Mangalorean fish dishes, prawns cooked with coriander and saffron (₹1100) or crab Milagu in a pepper masala (₹1575). Meat and veg dishes are also available.

DRINKING & NIGHTLIFE

Biere Club Pub

(www.facebook.com/thebiereclub; 20/2 Vittal Mallya Rd; 11am-11pm Sun-Thu, to midnight Fri & Sat;) There's a continual buzz about this multistorey temple to craft beer, which always has a guest beer or two on the blackboard. You'll find plenty on the menu (platters, burgers) to nibble while you sup.

Third Wave Coffee Roasters Cafe

(https://thirdwavecoffee.in; 984, 80 Feet Rd, Koramangala; 9am-11pm;) A mecca for hardcore java heads, this temple to the arabica bean has a multitude of gourmet-coffee combos, including espresso classics, quirky cold brews like coffee colada (with coconut water and the sweetener jaggery) and seasonal specials. Coffee culture is a serious business here. The Third Wave scene is young freelancers on Macbooks, polished-concrete floors and acoustic tunes on the stereo.

GETTING THERE & AWAY

International and domestic flights arrive at and depart from Bengaluru's **Kempegowda International Airport** (1800 4254425; www.bengaluruairport.com), about 35km north of the MG Rd area.

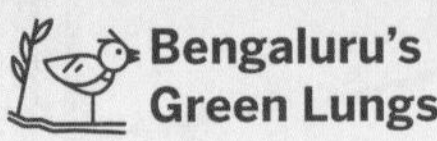

Bengaluru's Green Lungs

In the heart of Bengaluru's business district is **Cubbon Park** (www.horticulture.kar.nic.in/cubbon.htm; Kasturba Rd; M Cubbon Park), a well-maintained 120-hectare garden where Bengaluru's residents converge to steal a moment from the rat race that rages outside. The gardens encompass the red-painted Gothic-style **State Central Library** (Cubbon Park; M Cubbon Park). Unfortunately, Cubbon is not completely closed to traffic, except on Sundays, when there are concerts, fun runs, yoga and even a small farmers market.

Cubbon Park

Bengaluru's huge, well-organised **Kempegowda bus stand** (Majestic; Gubbi Thotadappa Rd; M Kempegowda), has bus connections to Mysuru and Hosapete (for Hampi).

Bengaluru's **City train station** (Gubbi Thotadappa Rd; M Kempegowda) is the main train hub, and has a computerised **reservation office** (139; City Train Station; 8am-8pm Mon-Sat, to 2pm Sun; M Kempegowda). **Yeshvantpur train station** (Rahman Khan Rd), 8km northwest of downtown, is the starting point for trains to Goa.

SOUVIK BHATTACHARYA / GETTY IMAGES ©

Hampi

The magnificent ruins of Hampi, capital of the Hindu Vijayanagar empire, dot an unearthly landscape where giant, rusty-hued boulders perch between jade-green palm groves, banana plantations and paddy fields.

Great For...

☑ Don't Miss

The ornate stone chariot, Vishnu's vehicle, in the Vittala Temple courtyard.

In 1336, the local prince Harihararaya chose Hampi as the site for his new capital Vijayanagar, which – over the next couple of centuries – grew into one of the largest Hindu empires in Indian history. By the 16th century it was a thriving metropolis of about 500,000 people, its busy bazaars dabbling in international commerce and brimming with precious stones and merchants from faraway lands. All this, however, ended at a stroke in 1565, when a confederacy of Deccan sultanates razed Vijayanagar to the ground, striking it a blow from which it never recovered.

The Ruins

The 36-sq-km ruins have two main focal areas: the **Sacred Centre**, around Hampi Bazaar, and the **Royal Centre**, 2km south, where the Vijayanagar royalty lived and

Vittala Temple

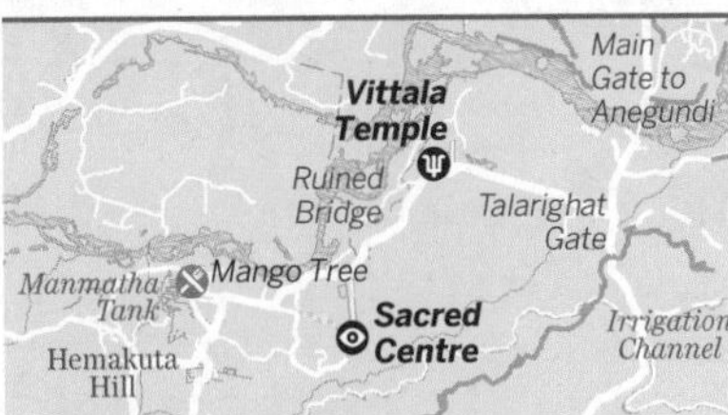

Need to Know

The ₹500 ticket for Vittala Temple gives same-day admission to most of the paid sites here.

Take a Break

The legendary **Mango Tree** (mains ₹130-310; 7.30am-9.30pm) in Hampi Bazaar serves delicious Indian fare.

★ Top Tip

It's possible to see Hampi in a day or two, but it's a fine place to linger longer.

governed. You can rent bicycles (₹30 to ₹50 per day), mopeds (₹250 to ₹500) or an autorickshaw for the day (around ₹750) in Hampi Bazaar.

When visiting the Sacred Centre, don't miss the Virupaksha Temple, the Sule Bazaar, the Achyutaraya Temple and Lakshimi Narasmiha. Highlights of the Royal Centre include the Mahanavami-diiba, the Hazarama Temple, the Zenana Enclosure, Elephant Stables and Queen's Bath.

The undisputed highlight of the Hampi ruins, the 16th-century **Vittala Temple** (Indian/foreigner/child under 15yr ₹40/500/free; 8.30am-5.30pm) stands amid the boulders 2km northeast of Hampi Bazaar. Work possibly started on the temple during the reign of Krishnadevaraya (r 1509–29). It was never finished or consecrated, yet its incredible sculptural work remains the pinnacle of Vijayanagar art.

Hampi Demolitions

A long-time favourite for budget travellers, Hampi has become the scene of a bizarre struggle between local villagers and authorities bent on protecting Hampi's architectural heritage. In 2011 shops, hotels and homes in Hampi Bazaar were bulldozed overnight, with 1500 villagers evicted. Virupapur Gaddi village across the river became a new popular hangout, only for many buildings there to be demolished in 2016. As of 2018, Hampi Bazaar still exists as an enclave of guesthouses and restaurants, but the future for both areas remains uncertain.

Getting There & Away

The town of Hosapete is the gateway to Hampi, with daily trains and overnight sleeper bus services to/from Goa, Bengaluru and Mysuru. Buses run between Hosapete's bus stand and Hampi (₹18, 30 minutes) every half-hour between about 6am and 7pm.

DARJEELING

In This Chapter

Tea Experience....216
Singalila Ridge Trek....218
Sights....222
Shopping....225
Eating....225
Drinking & Nightlife....226
Information....226
Getting There & Away....227
Getting Around....227

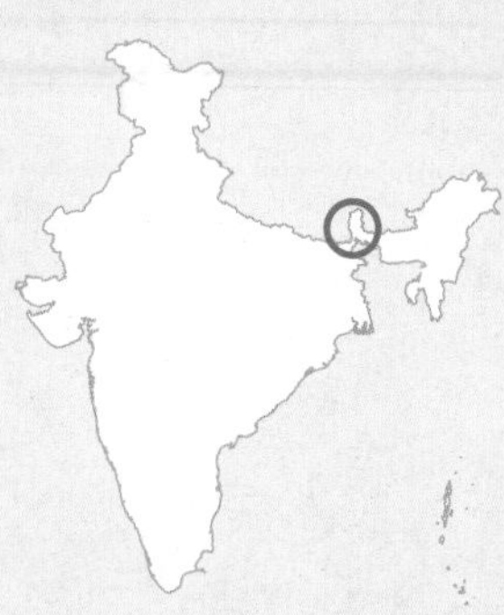

Darjeeling at a Glance...

Spread in ribbons over a steep mountain ridge, surrounded by emerald-green tea plantations and towered over by majestic Khangchendzonga (8598m), Darjeeling is the definitive Indian hill station. Visit Buddhist monasteries, explore the winding bazaars teeming with Himalayan products, take an adventurous trek on Singalila Ridge or hire a mountain bike for a guided ride around the hilltops. And if your energy starts to flag, a steaming Darjeeling brew is never far away.

Darjeeling in Three Days

Your first day, see town sights like the **zoo** (p222), **Himalayan Mountaineering Institute** (p222) and **Lloyd Botanic Garden** (p222). Start day two with the sunrise from **Tiger Hill** (p223), visit **Ghum** (p223) and be back in time for tea at the **Windamere** (p223). On day three visit **Makaibari tea estate** (p217) and take a joy ride on the **toy train** (p226).

Darjeeling in One Week

Try the challenging five-day **Singalila Ridge Trek** (p218) from Mane Bhanjhang to Phalut, through the scenic Singalia National Park (or there's a four-day version if you prefer more time sipping tea in Darjeeling).

Previous page: Tea plantations, Darjeeling

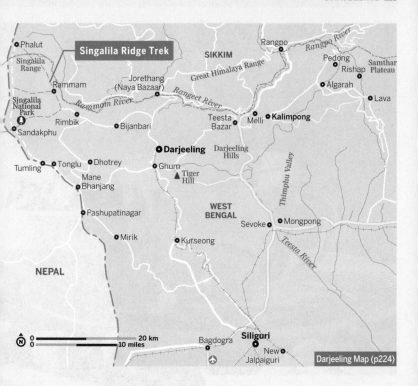

Darjeeling Map (p224)

Arriving in Darjeeling

Bagdogra Airport Near Siliguri, 90km south of Darjeeling.

New Jalpaiguri (NJP) train station 6km from Siliguri, connected to big cities along the main Indian railway corridor.

Where to Stay

Darjeeling has several hundred hotels. The main backpacker enclave is Dr Zakir Hussain Rd, following the highest ridge in Darjeeling, so be prepared for a hike to the best budget places.

Book ahead in the high-season months (October to early December; mid-March to mid-May). At other times prices can drop by 50%.

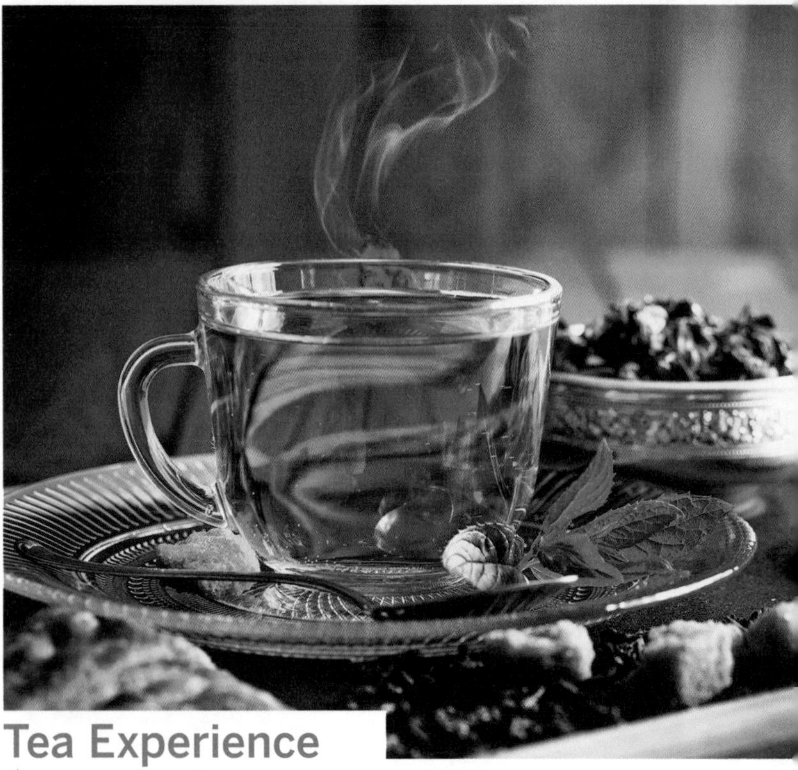

Tea Experience

There's no better place to enjoy the brew that has carried Darjeeling's name around the world. While you're here, you can learn all about tea by visiting or staying at tea estates.

Great For...

☑ Don't Miss

The genuine afternoon-tea experience at the Windamere Hotel (p223).

Darjeeling's aromatic muscatel tea is known for its amber colour, tannic astringency and a musky, spicy flavour, considered by many to be the world's best. These days, other teas including green, oolong and premium white varieties are produced alongside the traditional black tea. Most of the local produce is now organic.

Tea Facts

The Darjeeling tea region stretches south to Kurseong and Mirik and has 195 sq km o tea bushes on 87 tea estates ('gardens'). It produces less than 1% of Indian tea, but the best grades fetch hundreds of dollars per kilogram at auctions. Darjeeling tea is 'orthodox', meaning it goes through a labour-intensive manual production process that results in long-leaf tea.

Tea plantation

SURIYADESATIT / GETTY IMAGES ©

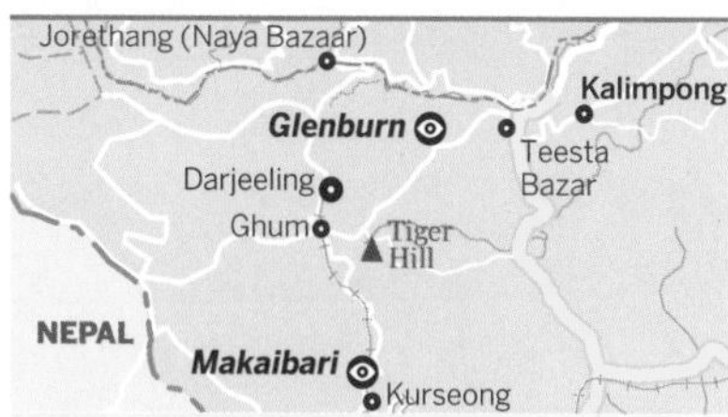

Need to Know

Purists say Darjeeling teas are best taken alone or with lemon – never with milk!

Take a Break

It's hard to beat Sunset Lounge (p226) for fine teas with a view.

★ Top Tip

Read Jeff Koehler's *Darjeeling: A History of the World's Greatest Tea* (2015).

Visiting Tea Estates

For an absorbing and enlightening experience, several tea estates welcome visitors. The easiest places to learn about tea production are **Makaibari** (☎033-22489091; www.makaibari.com; Pankhabari Rd; factory visit ₹50, day tour ₹800; ⊙5am-5pm Mon-Sat mid-Mar–mid-Nov) in Kurseong and **Happy Valley** (☎8017700700; Lebong Cart Rd; tour ₹100; ⊙9am-4.30pm) at Darjeeling. Spring, monsoon and autumn are the busiest times, when the three respective 'flushes' are harvested. There's no plucking on Sunday, which means most of the machinery isn't working on Monday.

Staying Over

If you wish to spend a night amid the plantations, try a tea pickers' family at a **homestay** (☎9832447774; www.makaibari.com; Makaibari tea estate, Pankhabari Rd; per person full board ₹1000) at Makaibari. If you're in the mood for splurging, accommodation doesn't get any more exclusive than top-end **Glenburn** (☎9830070213; www.glenburnteaestate.com; s/d full board ₹25,850/43,710; ᯤ), a tea estate between Darjeeling and Kalimpong.

How Darjeeling Got Started

In 1828 two British officers stumbled across the Dorje Ling monastery, on a forested ridge, and passed word to Kolkata that it would be a perfect site for a sanatorium. The chogyal (king) of Sikkim agreed to give the sparsely inhabited land to the East India Company, receiving an annual allowance of ₹3000 in return. In 1837 the hill station of Darjeeling was born and the first tea bushes were planted four years later. By 1857, the population of Darjeeling had reached 10,000, mainly because of a massive influx of Nepali tea labourers (known as Gorkhas).

Trekking the Singalila Ridge

Singalila Ridge Trek

The most popular multiday walk in the Darjeeling area is the five-day Singalila Ridge Trek from Mane Bhanjhang to Phalut, through the scenic Singalila National Park. The highlights are the great views of the Himalayan chain stretching from Nepal to Sikkim and Bhutan. The usual trekking itinerary is 84km over five days.

Great For...

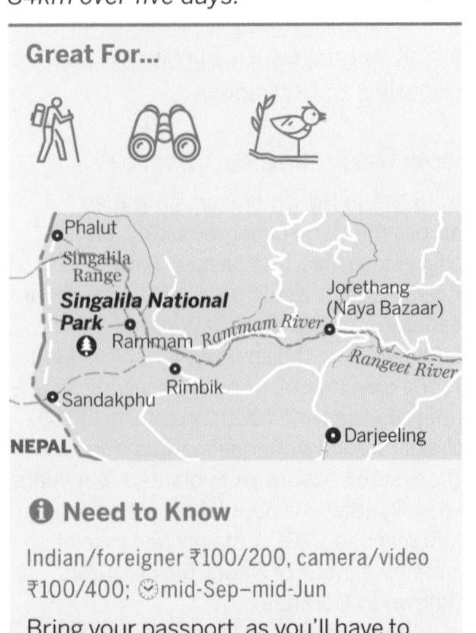

Need to Know

Indian/foreigner ₹100/200, camera/video ₹100/400; mid-Sep–mid-Jun

Bring your passport, as you'll have to register at army checkpoints en route.

★ **Top Tip**

Many lodges can now be booked ahead on the internet.

The classic trek heads north along the ridge from **Mane Bhanjhang** (25km west of Darjeeling) to Sandakphu and Phalut (hopping back and forth between India and Nepal), then southeast down via Gorkhey and Rammam to **Srikhola** or **Rimbik**. A typical itinerary is 84km over five days. A shorter four-day option is possible by descending from Sandakhphu to Srikhola on day three.

Darjeeling trekking agencies offer all-inclusive guided trips for between ₹3000 and ₹4500 per person per day, including transfers, accommodation and meals. Recommended agencies include **Himalayan Travels** (☎0354-2256956; www.himalayantravel.co.in; 18 Gandhi Rd; ⏲9am-6pm) and **Adventures Unlimited** (☎9933070013; www.adventuresunlimited.in; 142/1 Dr Zakir Hussain Rd; ⏲9am-8.30pm); however it's easy enough to arrange a DIY trek for less.

Trek Stages

Day 1 (13km) Mane Bhanjhang (1950m) to Tumling (2980m) via Chitre and Meghma

Day 2 (17km) Tumling to Sandakphu (3636m) via Ghairibas and Kalipokhri

Day 3 (19km) Sandakphu to Phalut (3600m) via Sabarkum

Day 4 (16km) Phalut to Rammam (2530m) via Gorkhey

Day 5 (19km) Rammam to Rimbik (2290m) via Srikhola

Accommodation

Mane Bhanjhang, the starting point, has several guesthouses – **Hawk's Nest** (☎9733081184; Chitre; dm ₹300, s/d ₹850/1700, half board ₹1000/2000), 2.5km up the hill, is quite pleasant. There are also lodges in end-point Rimbik – the

Sacred symbols, Mane Bhanjhang

best are **Hotel Sherpa** (☎9609790491; Rimbik; s/d incl breakfast ₹800/1000) and **Green Hill** (☎9733069143; Rimbik; s/d/tr ₹1000/1100/1500).

Accommodation en route ranges from state-run trekkers' huts with dorm beds (₹220) to simple lodges with private bathroom (hot water by bucket) for ₹1500 to ₹2500. All lodgings offer meals, and bottled and boiled water is available along the route. The better lodges can fill up quickly during peak seasons of April–May and October–November. All have clean bedding and blankets, but a sleeping bag liner is nice to have. Trekkers' huts can be booked at Darjeeling's GTA Tourist Information Centre (p226).

These are the main lodges for overnight stops, in ascending order of price and quality:

Tumling Mountain Lodge, Siddharta Lodge, Shikhar Lodge

Sandakphu Trekkers' Huts, View Point Homestay, Sunrise Hotel

Phalut Trekkers' Hut, Forest Rest House

Rammam Dhurba Rai Homestay, Namobuddha Lodge, Sherpa Lodge

☑ Don't Miss

Views of four eight-thousander peaks: Everest, Khangchendzonga, Lhotse and Makalu.

ROBERTO MOIOLA SYSAWORLD / GETTY IMAGES ©

When to Trek

October and November's clear skies and warm daytime temperatures make it an ideal time to trek, as do the long days and incredible rhododendron blooms of late April and May.

Guides

Local guides (per day ₹1300) are mandatory within the park. They must be arranged at the office of the **Highlander Trekking Guides Association** (☎9734056944; ⏱6am-6pm mid-Sep–mid-Jun) at Mane Bhanjhang, along with porters per day (₹1000) if required.

Getting To/From the Trek

The cheapest way to get to the trailhead is by shared jeep from Darjeeling's Motor Stand (p227) to Mane Bhanjang. From Rimbik, there are shared jeeps back to Darjeeling (₹220, five hours) from 6am to 1pm.

Take A Break

All lodgings on the trail offer meals. Bottled and boiled water is also available.

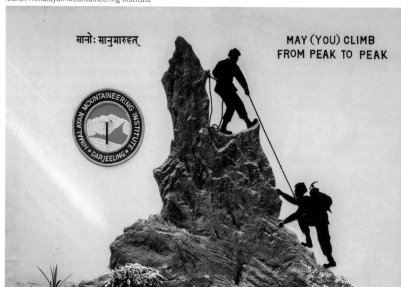

SIGHTS

Himalayan Mountaineering Institute
Museum

(HMI; ☎0354-2254087; www.hmidarjeeling.com; Jawahar Parvat; Indian/foreigner incl zoo ₹60/100; ⏰8.30am-4pm Fri-Wed) Within the zoo precinct, the prestigious HMI was founded in 1954 and has provided training for some of India's leading mountaineers. Its fascinating **Mountaineering Museum** exhibits evocative memorabilia from the 1922 and 1924 Everest expeditions, which set off from Darjeeling, as well as more-recent summit attempts – including the successful 1953 climb. Just outside the museum are **Tenzing Norgay's samadhi** (cremation spot) and a Tenzing statue. The intrepid Everest summiteer was a director and adviser at the institute for many years.

Padmaja Naidu Himalayan Zoological Park
Zoo

(☎0354-2253709; www.pnhzp.gov.in; Jawahar Parvat; Indian/foreigner incl Himalayan Mountaineering Institute ₹60/100, camera ₹10; ⏰8.30am-4pm Fri-Wed) This zoo, one of India's better ones, was established in 1958 to study, conserve and preserve Himalayan fauna. Housed within its rocky and forested environment are species such as Asiatic black bear, clouded leopard, red panda and Himalayan wolf. The zoo and its snow-leopard breeding centre (closed to the public) are home to the world's largest captive population of snow leopards (currently 11). It's a reasonably pleasant 2km walk, mostly downhill, northwest from Chowrasta.

Lloyd Botanic Garden
Gardens

(☎0354-2252358; ⏰7am-4.30pm) FREE These half-hidden gardens contain an impressive collection of Himalayan plants, most famously orchids and rhododendrons. Follow the signs down Loch Nagar near the Motor Stand, until the hum of cicadas replaces the honking of jeeps at the entrance.

Tibetan Refugee Self-Help Centre
Community

(☎0354-2252552; www.tibetancentredarjeeling.com; Lebong Cart Rd; ⏰8am-5pm Mon-Sat) Established in 1959, this refugee centre includes a Tibetan Buddhist temple,

Mural, Himalayan Mountaineering Institute

workshops producing carpets, woodcarvings, wool and woollen items, plus a home for the aged, a kindergarten and a clinic. Visitors are welcome to wander through the workshops. There's also an interesting, politically charged **photographic exhibition** on Tibetan history. The handicrafts are for sale in the **showroom** (8am-5pm Mon-Sat). A quick walking approach is to take the lane down beside Hotel Dolphin on The Mall and zigzag downhill about 1.2km (asking directions a few times).

Bhutia Busty Gompa Buddhist Monastery

This temple originally stood on Observatory Hill, but was rebuilt in its present location in the 19th century. It houses fine murals depicting the life of Buddha, and Khangchendzonga provides a spectacular northern backdrop. Prayers are held at 3pm; the temple is often locked at other times. The monastery is about a 1.2km walk down from Chowrasta: start down CR Das Rd, fork right 200m after the Central Nirvana Resort, and keep asking directions.

Yiga Choeling Gompa Buddhist Monastery

(Old Monastery; www.yigachoeling.com; Ghum; camera ₹100; dawn-dusk) Yiga Choeling Gompa, the Darjeeling area's most famous monastery, founded in 1850, houses up to 40 monks of the Gelugpa school. The serene temple has wonderful old murals and enshrines a 5m-high statue of Jampa (Maitreya; 'Future Buddha') and 300 beautifully bound Tibetan texts. It's on the western edge of Ghum, 6km south of Darjeeling: from Ghum station, walk 100m west along the main road towards Darjeeling, turn left at the sign for the monastery and go 600m.

Tiger Hill Viewpoint

To watch the dawn light break over a spectacular 250km stretch of Himalayan horizon, including Everest (8848m), Khangchendzonga (8598m) and two more of the world's five highest peaks, rise very early and take a jeep out to Tiger Hill (2590m), 11km south of Darjeeling, above Ghum. This daily morning spectacle (views are best in autumn and spring) is a major tourist attraction, however, so if you prefer your Himalayan views in peace you might want to try somewhere else.

Hundreds of jeeps leave Darjeeling for Tiger Hill every morning at 4am – traffic snarls en route are quite common. Sunrise trips (usually with stops at Batasia Loop and a Buddhist monastery in Ghum on the way back) can be booked through a travel agency or directly with jeep drivers at the Clubside taxi stand. Return trips cost ₹1200 for a three/four passenger car, ₹1800 for a bigger, comfier Innova, or ₹200 per seat.

Observatory Hill Religious Site

The hill rising above Chowrasta is home to several much-visited temples, approached through a flurry of colourful prayer flags and hanging bells. The main summit temple

High Tea at Windamere

The authentic afternoon-tea experience at **Windamere Hotel** (0354-2254041; www.windamerehotel.com; Observatory Hill; afternoon tea ₹900; 4-6pm) is a joy for aficionados of things colonial, with crustless cucumber and tuna sandwiches, shortcake, scones with jam and (albeit synthetic) cream, and brews from the well-reputed Castleton estate, all enjoyed while seated on chintz sofas. You need to book in advance and will probably be required to provide a cash advance or bank card details.

Windamere Hotel

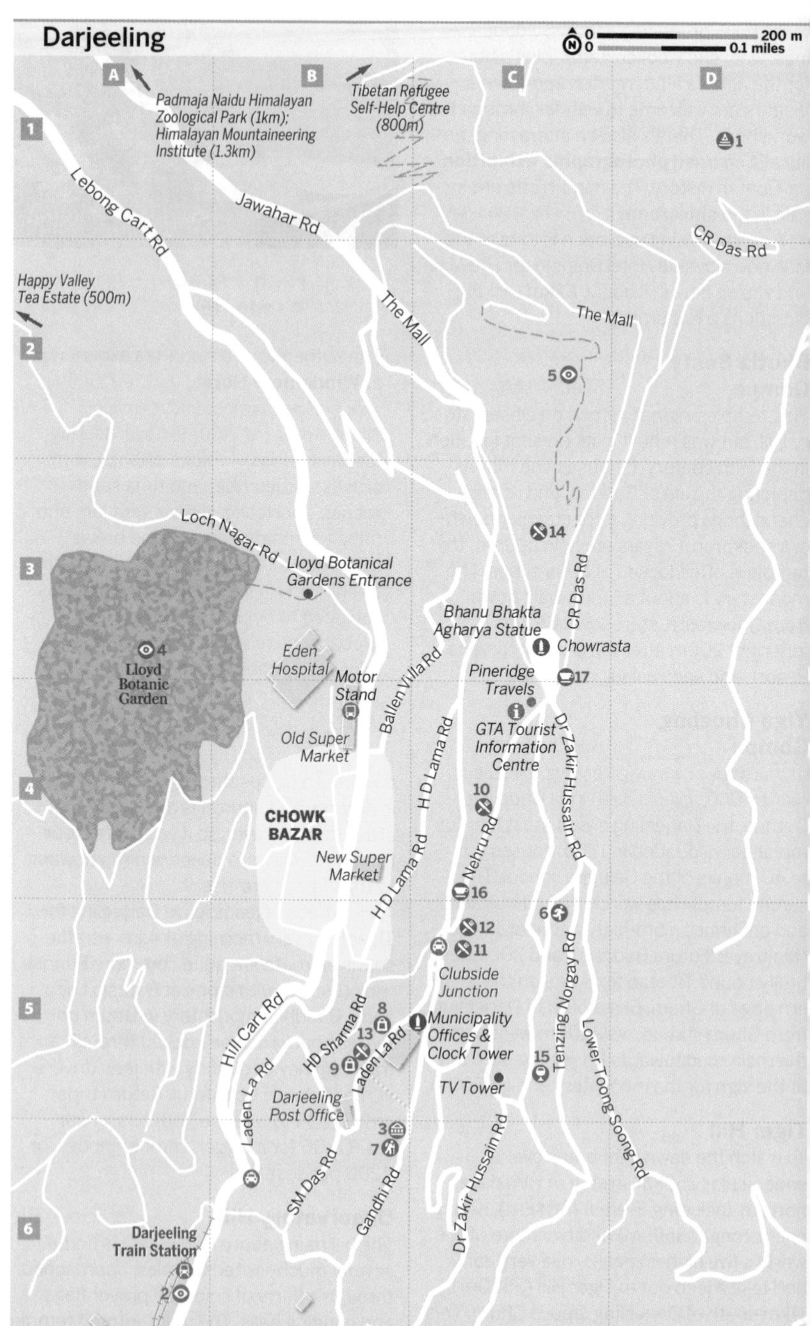
Darjeeling
0 200 m
0 0.1 miles
A
B
C
D
1
2
3
4
5
6
Padmaja Naidu Himalayan Zoological Park (1km); Himalayan Mountaineering Institute (1.3km)
Tibetan Refugee Self-Help Centre (800m)
Happy Valley Tea Estate (500m)
Lebong Cart Rd
Jawahar Rd
CR Das Rd
The Mall
The Mall
Loch Nagar Rd
Lloyd Botanical Gardens Entrance
Bhanu Bhakta Agharya Statue
Chowrasta
CR Das Rd
4
Lloyd Botanic Garden
Eden Hospital
Motor Stand
Ballen Villa Rd
Pineridge Travels
17
GTA Tourist Information Centre
Old Super Market
H D Lama Rd
H D Lama Rd
Dr Zakir Hussain Rd
10
CHOWK BAZAR
Nehru Rd
New Super Market
16
6
12
11
Clubside Junction
Hill Cart Rd
HD Sharma Rd
8
13
Laden La Rd
Municipality Offices & Clock Tower
9
Laden La Rd
15
Tenzing Norgay Rd
Lower Toong Soong Rd
TV Tower
Darjeeling Post Office
3
7
SM Das Rd
Gandhi Rd
Dr Zakir Hussain Rd
Darjeeling Train Station
2
1
5
14

Darjeeling

Sights
1 Bhutia Busty Gompa D1
2 Darjeeling Himalayan Railway A6
3 Himalayan Tibet Museum B6
4 Lloyd Botanic Garden A3
5 Observatory Hill C2

Activities, Courses & Tours
6 Adventures Unlimited C5
7 Himalayan Travels B6

Shopping
8 Hayden Hall B5
9 Nathmulls Tea Room B5

Eating
10 Glenary's C4
11 Kunga C5
12 Lunar Restaurant C5
13 Park B5
14 Windamere Hotel C3

Drinking & Nightlife
15 Gatty's C5
16 House of Tea C4
17 Sunset Lounge C3

is sacred to Mahakala, a Buddhist protector deity also worshipped as a wrathful avatar of Shiva. It is staffed by a Hindu priest and Buddhist lama sitting side by side in an admirable display of religious coexistence. A 300m path up to the summit starts about 100m along the eastern Mall road from Chowrasta.

Himalayan Tibet Museum Museum

(☎0354-2252977; 12 Gandhi Rd; ₹50; ⊙10am-5pm Thu-Tue, to 6pm Apr-Oct) This well-thought-out museum (one large room) is a good, colourful introduction to Tibet and its culture. The attractive displays introduce the Dalai Lama, stupas, and Tibetan religion, script, medicine, history and geography with just the right amount of information to avoid overload. Exhibits include fine *thangkas* (Tibetan cloth paintings), a 3D map of Tibet and a sand mandala (a visual meditation aid symbolising the universe).

SHOPPING

Nathmulls Tea Room Tea

(www.nathmulltea.com; Laden La Rd; ⊙9am-8pm daily 15 Apr-14 Jun & 15 Sep-14 Nov, Mon-Sat rest of year) The Darjeeling area produces arguably the world's finest teas and Nathmulls is one of the best retailers, with more than 50 varieties. Expect to pay ₹200 to ₹400 per 100g for a decent tea, and up to ₹2500 for the finest flushes. There are also attractive teapots, strainers and cosies as souvenirs. To taste Nathmulls teas, head to Sunset Lounge (p226).

Hayden Hall Handicrafts

(www.haydenhall.org; 42 Laden La Rd; ⊙10am-5pm Mon-Sat, 10am-12.30pm Sun) Sells Tibetan-style yak-wool carpets (₹10,800 for a 6ft by 3ft carpet) as part of its charitable work with mothers from poor Darjeeling-area families, and offers shipping. You can see the carpets being made out the back. There are also good scarves, tea cosies, bags and other items made by the women.

EATING

Glenary's Multicuisine $$

(Nehru Rd; mains ₹200-375; ⊙noon-9.30pm; 📶) Popular Glenary's sits above the famous bakery-cafe of the same name and is a classy Darjeeling staple. Of note are the continental and Chinese dishes and the tandoori specials; try the beef steak or roast pork or the tasty baked-cheese macaroni. Linen tablecloths, white-and-gold decor and plenty of tables with a view enhance the elegant experience.

Kunga Tibetan $$

(51 Gandhi Rd; mains ₹150-220; ⊙7.30am-8.30pm) Kunga is a cosy little wood-panelled place run by a friendly Tibetan family, strong on noodles and *momos* (Tibetan dumplings), and with excellent *shabhaley* (Tibetan pies), juice, and fruit and muesli with curd. It's always busy and

Riding the Toy Train

The **Darjeeling Himalayan Railway** (DHR; www.dhr.in.net; joy ride ₹805-1405, Darjeeling–Kurseong 2nd-/1st-class ₹60/685, Darjeeling–Siliguri 1st-class ₹1105), known affectionately as the toy train, made its first journey along its precipice-topping, 2ft-wide tracks in 1881 and is one of the few hill railways still operating in India. It has had Unesco World Heritage listing since 1999. Two-hour 'joy rides' from Darjeeling to Ghum and back satisfy most people's toy-train urges. There are normally around six of these pulled by antique steam locomotives daily, and three or so with diesel engines.

Just one (diesel-powered) train in each direction daily makes the whole 88km (seven-hour!) trip between New Jalpaiguri and Darjeeling; another runs just from Kurseong to Darjeeling and back.

Darjeeling Himalayan Railway

BEIBAOKE / SHUTTERSTOCK ©

the clientele includes locals, a mark of its culinary authenticity.

Lunar Restaurant Indian $$

(1st fl, 51 Gandhi Rd; mains ₹150-225; 8am-9.30pm) This bright and clean space is perhaps the best vegetarian Indian restaurant in town, with good service and great views from the large windows. The Lunar special masala dosas come with delicious dried fruits, peanuts and cheese. Access is via the same staircase as Hotel Dekeling.

Park Indian, Thai $$

(0354-2255270; 41 Laden La Rd; mains ₹160-400; 11am-9pm) The Park is deservedly very popular for its North Indian curries (great chicken-tikka kebab) and authentic Thai dishes, including coconut-chicken soup, spicy green-papaya salad and Thai street noodles. Everything we've had here is good. You can pick from four separate dining rooms, and it has alcoholic drinks, too. Look for the ornate Thai-style entrance.

DRINKING & NIGHTLIFE

Gatty's Bar

(Dr Zakir Hussain Rd; beer/shots from ₹240/100; 6-11pm;) Backpacker-friendly Gatty's is the only place in town that has a pulse after 9pm, with live music at weekends. The food (dishes ₹80 to ₹280) includes house-made lasagne, and pita with hummus or falafel. It brews good espresso and there's cold Kingfisher and Tuborg, too.

Sunset Lounge Teahouse

(CR Das Rd, Chowrasta; cup of tea ₹25-400; 9.30am-8.30pm;) This two-floor tearoom run by the Nathmulls tea company offers aficionados a range of quality white, green and black teas by the cup or pot, with in-house baked treats, fine valley views and wi-fi. Ask for the six-cup tasting sample for two people (it's not on the menu).

House of Tea Teahouse

(Nehru Rd; 2-cup pot of tea ₹100-200; 10am-1pm & 2.30-8.30pm) Sit and sip a variety of teas from several local Goodricke estates before purchasing a package of your favourite leaves.

INFORMATION

GTA Tourist Information Centre (www.tourism-darjeeling.com; Nehru Rd; 9am-6pm Mon-Sat, to 1pm every other Sat) The staff are friendly, well organised and the best source of information on Darjeeling. You can book government-run trekkers' huts on the Singalila Ridge here.

Tandoori *momos* (dumplings)

GETTING THERE & AWAY

AIR

The nearest airport is 70km south at Bagdogra, 14km from Siliguri, with flights to Delhi and Kolkata. **Wizzride** (www.wizzride.com) runs several daily shuttle trips for ₹500 to ₹600 per person. **Pineridge Travels** (☎0354-2253912; pineridge travels@gmail.com; Nehru Rd; ⊙10.30am-5.30pm Mon-Sat) sells domestic and international flight tickets.

JEEP & TAXI

Numerous shared jeeps leave the south end of the crowded **Motor Stand** (Old Super Market, Hill Cart Rd) for Siliguri (₹150, three hours, 6am to 6pm), Kurseong (₹80, 1½ hours, 6am to 4pm or 5pm) and Mane Bhanjang (₹60, 1½ hours, 7am to 5pm). Jeeps for Rimbik (₹220, five hours) leave from the northern end.

To New Jalpaiguri or Bagdogra, get a connection in Siliguri, or charter a jeep or taxi from Darjeeling for ₹2200. A chartered jeep to Kalimpong is ₹2000; a taxi to Mane Bhanjang is ₹1500.

TRAIN

The nearest major train stations are Siliguri Junction, 65km from Darjeeling, and New Jalpaiguri (NJP), 6km further. Tickets for major services from these stations can be bought at **Darjeeling train station** (☎0354-2252555; Hill Cart Rd; ⊙8am-5pm Mon-Sat, 8am-2pm Sun).

GETTING AROUND

Darjeeling is quite an enjoyable town to walk around. There are several taxi stands, including at **Clubside** and on **Hill Cart Road** near the train station, but rates are absurdly high for short hops.

VARANASI

In This Chapter

The Ghats 232
Sights 236
Tours 237
Shopping 237
Eating.. 239
Drinking & Nightlife.......................... 240
Information....................................... 241
Getting There & Away 242
Getting Around 242

Varanasi at a Glance...

Varanasi is the India of your imagination. It's one of the world's oldest continually inhabited cities, where pilgrims come to wash away their sins in the sacred waters of the Ganges, and to cremate their loved ones, hoping for their liberation from the cycle of rebirth. Confronting the reality and ritual of death can be a powerful experience, and the frenzy of the maze-like old town can be intense. But strolling the ghats or watching sunrise from a boat on the Ganges are bound to enthral.

Varanasi in Two Days

Rise early on day one to explore the ghats, preferably starting at sunrise. In the evening witness the *ganga aarti* (river worship ceremony) at **Dashashwamedh Ghat** (p234). On day two enjoy a sunrise boat trip on the Ganges, browse some shops and cafes, visit the **Vishwanath Temple** (p236) and treat yourself to dinner at **Darbangha** (p239).

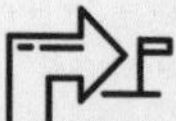

Varanasi in Four Days

On day three dig deeper into Varanasi life (and death) on a **Varanasi Walks** (p237) tour. Enjoy a great meal and some Indian classical music at **Brown Bread Bakery** (p239). On day four revisit the ghats, make a trip to **Banares Hindu University** (p237), and don't miss India's best lassi at **Blue Lassi** (p240).

Previous page: Ganges River

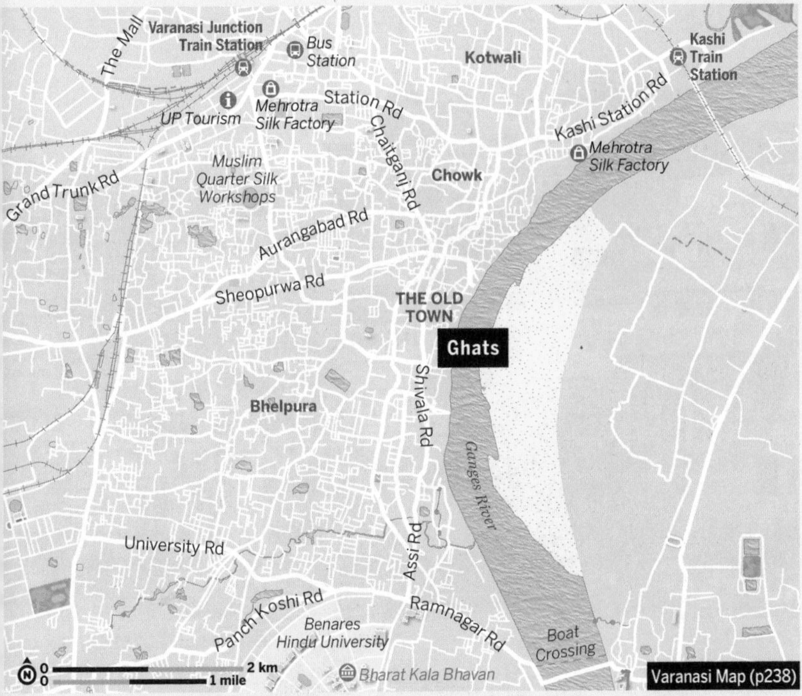

Varanasi Map (p238)

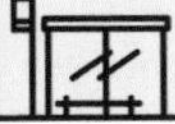

Arriving in Varanasi

Lal Bahadur Shashtri Airport In Babatpur, 24km northwest of Varanasi, with connections across India.

Varanasi Junction station Trains from Delhi, Agra and Kolkata (Calcutta).

Mughal Sarai Junction station (Deen Dayal Upadhyaya station) 18km south-east of Varanasi: more Agra trains.

Bus stand AC buses to/from Delhi.

Where to Stay

Most of Varanasi's budget hotels are tucked among the narrow streets off the ghats. Assi, Scindhia and Meer are three ghats with multiple pickings. There's a concentration of midrange places around Assi Ghat; others are clustered between Scindha and Meer Ghat. If you want a local experience, the **UP Tourism** (p241) office at the train station has a list of homestays (₹500 to ₹900 per night).

The Ghats

Spiritually enlightening and fantastically photogenic, Varanasi is at its brilliant best by the ghats, the long stretch of steps leading down to the water on the western bank of the Ganges.

Great For...

☑ **Don't Miss**

The 7pm *ganga aarti* (river worship ceremony), with prayers, fire and dance, at Dashashwamedh Ghat.

The best time to visit the ghats is at dawn, when the river is bathed in a mellow light as pilgrims come to perform *puja* (prayers) to the rising sun, and at sunset when the popular *ganga aarti* takes place at Dashashwamedh Ghat and others.

About 80 ghats border the river, but the main group extends from Assi Ghat, near the university, northwards to Raj Ghat, near the road and rail bridge. Most ghats in Varanasi are used for bathing, but there are also several 'burning ghats' where bodies are cremated in public. The main burning ghat is Manikarnika (p234): you'll often see funeral processions threading their way through the backstreets to this ghat.

A boat trip along the river provides the perfect introduction, but you can also walk along the whole length of the ghats. It's a world-class people-watching stroll as

Manikarnika Ghat (p234)

you mingle with the fascinating mixture of people who come to the river to bathe, wash clothes, do yoga, sell flowers, get a massage, play cricket, wash buffaloes, give alms to beggars or simply stare at the Ganges.

Major Ghats

Listed below from south to north.

Assi Ghat

The furthest south of the main ghats and one of the biggest, Assi Ghat is particularly important as the River Assi meets the Ganges near here and pilgrims come to worship a Shiva lingam (phallic image of Shiva) beneath a peepul tree. Evenings are particularly lively, as the ghat's vast concreted area fills up with hawkers and entertainers.

Manikarnika Ghat
Scindhia Ghat
Man Mandir Ghat
Dashashwamedh Ghat
Munshi Ghat
Pandhey Ghat
Kedar Ghat
Harishchandra Ghat
Hanuman Ghat
Ganges River
Assi Ghat

Need to Know

Tourists can, respectfully, watch cremations at the 'burning' ghats, but don't take photos.

Take a Break

Brown Bread Bakery (p239) is a fabulous stop any time from the breakfast buffet onwards.

★ Top Tip

Resist offers of 'follow me for a better view': you'll be pressured for money.

There's also music and yoga at sunrise. It's a popular starting point for boat trips.

Hanuman Ghat

Hanuman Ghat is popular with Rama devotees: Hanuman was Rama's stalwart ally in his quest to rescue Sita from the demon Ravana.

Harishchandra Ghat

Harishchandra Ghat is a cremation ghat – smaller and secondary in importance to Manikarnika, but one of the oldest in Varanasi.

Kedar Ghat

A colourful ghat with many steps and a small pool, where a fire *aarti* is held every evening at 6.30pm.

Pandhey Ghat

Lots of laundry is spread to dry at this ghat along the Ganges.

Munshi Ghat

Munshi Ghat (Darbhanga Ghat) is one of the more-photogenic ghats along the Old City stretch of the Ganges.

Dashashwamedh Ghat

Varanasi's liveliest and most-colourful ghat. The name indicates that Brahma *medh* (sacrificed) *das* (10) *aswa* (horses) here. In spite of the oppressive boat owners, flower sellers, massage practitioners and touts trying to drag you off to a silk shop, it's a wonderful place to linger and people-watch while soaking up the atmosphere. Every evening at 7pm an elaborate *ganga aarti* ceremony with *puja*, fire and dance is staged here.

Man Mandir Ghat

Man Mandir Ghat was built in 1600 by Raja Man Singh, but was poorly restored in the 19th century. Its northern corner has a fine stone balcony.

Manikarnika Ghat

Manikarnika Ghat, the main burning ghat, is the most auspicious place for a Hindu to be cremated. Dead bodies are handled by outcasts known as *doms*, and are carried to the piers on a bamboo stretcher, swathed in cloth. The corpse is doused in the Ganges prior to cremation.

Huge piles of firewood are stacked along the top of the ghat; every log is carefully weighed on giant scales so that the price of cremation can be calculated. Each type of wood has its own price, sandalwood being the most expensive.

Pilgrims bathing in the Ganges River

You can watch cremations but always show reverence by behaving respectfully. Photography is strictly prohibited. You'll likely be led by a priest or guide to the upper floor of a nearby building from where you can watch the piers below, and then asked for a donation (in dollars). Don't follow them if you wish to be on your own.

Above the steps here is a tank known as the **Manikarnika Well**. The **Charanpaduka**, a slab of stone between the well and the ghat, bears footprints made by Vishnu. Privileged VIPs are cremated at the Charanpaduka, which also has a temple dedicated to Ganesh.

Scindhia Ghat

Scindhia Ghat was originally built in 1830, but was so huge and magnificent that it collapsed into the river and had to be rebuilt.

Trilochan Ghat

At Trilochan, two turrets emerge from the river, and the water between them is especially holy.

Touts & Guides

- The attention from touts in Varanasi, particularly around the ghats and the Old City, is incredible: you will have to put up with persistent offers from touts and rickshaw drivers for 'cheapest and best' boat trips, guides, tour operators, travel agents, silk shops and money changers (to name a few). Take it all in good humour but politely refuse.
- If you want a guide, go through UP Tourism (p241) to avoid most of the hassles above.

Vehicle Access

Taxis and autorickshaws cannot access the Dashashwamedh Ghat area between 9am and 9pm due to high pedestrian traffic. You'll be dropped off at Godaulia Crossing and will need to walk the remaining 400m to the entrance to the Old City, or 700m all the way to Dashashwamedh Ghat.

★ Did You Know?

Varanasi is a particularly auspicious place to die, as dying here is believed to bring moksha (liberation from the cycle of rebirth).

MAZZZUR / GETTY IMAGES ©

SIGHTS

The 'old town' of Varanasi is situated along the western bank of the Ganges and extends back from the riverbank ghats in a labyrinth of alleys called *galis* that are too narrow for anything bigger than a motorbike and the occasional cow.

While the alleys and bazaars can be disorienting, they are fascinating to explore, and the popular hotels and restaurants are well signposted. However lost you may become, you will eventually end up at a ghat and get your bearings.

Vishwanath Temple — Hindu Temple

(Golden Temple; ⌚3-11am, 12.30-8pm & 9-11pm)
There are temples at almost every turn in Varanasi, but this is the most famous of the lot. It is dedicated to Vishveswara – Shiva as lord of the universe. The current temple was built in 1776 by Ahalya Bai of Indore; the 800kg of gold plating on the tower and dome was supplied by Maharaja Ranjit Singh of Lahore 50 years later.

The area is full of soldiers because of security issues and communal tensions. Bags, cameras, mobile phones, pens and any electronic device must be deposited in lockers (₹20) before you enter the alleyway it's in – or just leave your stuff at your hotel. If you are a foreigner, head to **Gate 2**, where security will instruct you to walk past the long lines of Indians waiting in the queue, then go through a metal detector and security check. Walk past another line of Indians until you are pointed to a desk, where you must show your passport (not a copy) and leave your shoes. Then enter the temple through a door across the alley.

Once inside, things can be quite intense, with people pushing and tripping over each other for a chance to give an offering and touch the lingam, which absolves one of all sins. Hindus routinely wait in lines for 48 hours to enter on holy days. If you are not fussed about Hindu temples, it's probably not worth the hassle required to visit.

On the northern side of Vishwanath Temple is the **Gyan Kupor Well**. The faithful believe drinking its water leads to a higher spiritual plane, though they are prevented from doing so by a strong security screen. Non-Hindus are not allowed to enter.

Vishwanath Temple

Banares Hindu University University, Historic Site

(BHU; www.bhu.ac.in) Long regarded as a centre of learning, Varanasi's tradition of top-quality education continues today at Banares Hindu University, established in 1916. The wide, tree-lined streets and parkland of the 5-sq-km campus offer a peaceful atmosphere a world away from the city outside. On campus is **Bharat Kala Bhavan** (Indian/foreigner ₹20/250; 10.30am-4.30pm Mon-Sat), a roomy museum with a wonderful collection of miniature paintings, as well as 12th-century palm-leaf manuscripts, sculptures and local history displays.

TOURS

If time is short, UP Tourism (p241) can arrange guided tours by taxi of the major sites, including a 5.30am boat ride and an afternoon trip to the nearby Buddhist centre of **Sarnath**.

Varanasi Walks Walking

(7081070222; www.varanasiwalks.com; Assi Ghat; tours ₹1200-2000) The cultural walks on offer from this agency explore beyond the most popular ghats and temples, giving eye-opening insight into this holy city. The American founder has lived in Varanasi for years, and most of the guides were born and raised here. Walks are available by reservation; book online or by phone.

SHOPPING

Varanasi is justifiably famous for silk brocades and beautiful Benares saris, but don't believe much of what the silk sales people tell you about the relative quality of products, even in government emporiums. Instead, shop around and judge for yourself.

Baba Blacksheep Fashion & Accessories

(B12/120 A-9, Bhelpura; 9.30am-8pm) If the deluge of traveller enthusiasm is anything to go by, this is one of the most trustworthy, nonpushy shops in India. Indeed it is one of the best places you'll find for silks (scarves/saris from ₹500/4000) and *pashmina* (shawls from ₹1700).

Prices are fixed (though unmarked) and the friendly owner refuses to play the commission game, so autorickshaws and taxis don't like to come here (ignore anyone who says you cannot drive here, and make sure you're in the right place, not an imposter venue). It's located at Bhelpura crossing under the mosque. It's not the cheapest, but it's a pleasant experience.

Mehrotra Silk Factory Fashion & Accessories

(www.mehrotrasilk.in; 4/8A Lal Ghat; 10am-8pm) Located in a labyrinth of alleys behind Lal Ghat, this fixed-price shop, its floor cushioned for seating, offers fine silks for fair prices. Products are as small as a scarf or as big as a bedcover. There's another

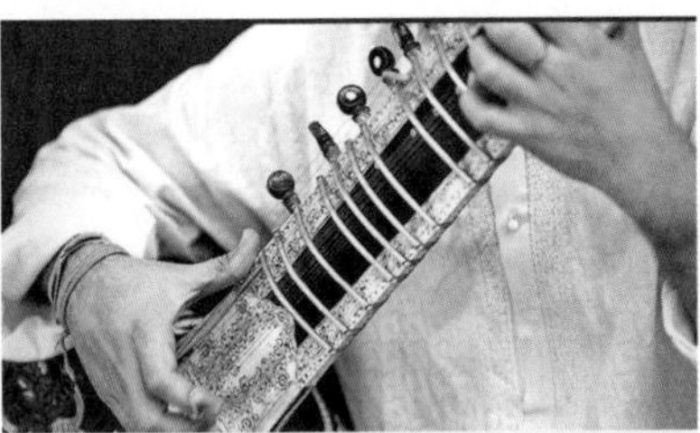

Musical Buys

The musical instrument shops along Bengali Tola are good places to shop for sitars (ranging from ₹6000 to ₹60,000) and tablas (from ₹5000 to ₹15,000). The cost depends primarily on the type of wood used. Mango is cheapest (and cracks or warps correspondingly), while black *shisham* (rosewood) or mahogany are of the highest quality. Serious buyers should be sure to double-check that their chosen wood isn't banned for export.

Musician playing the sitar

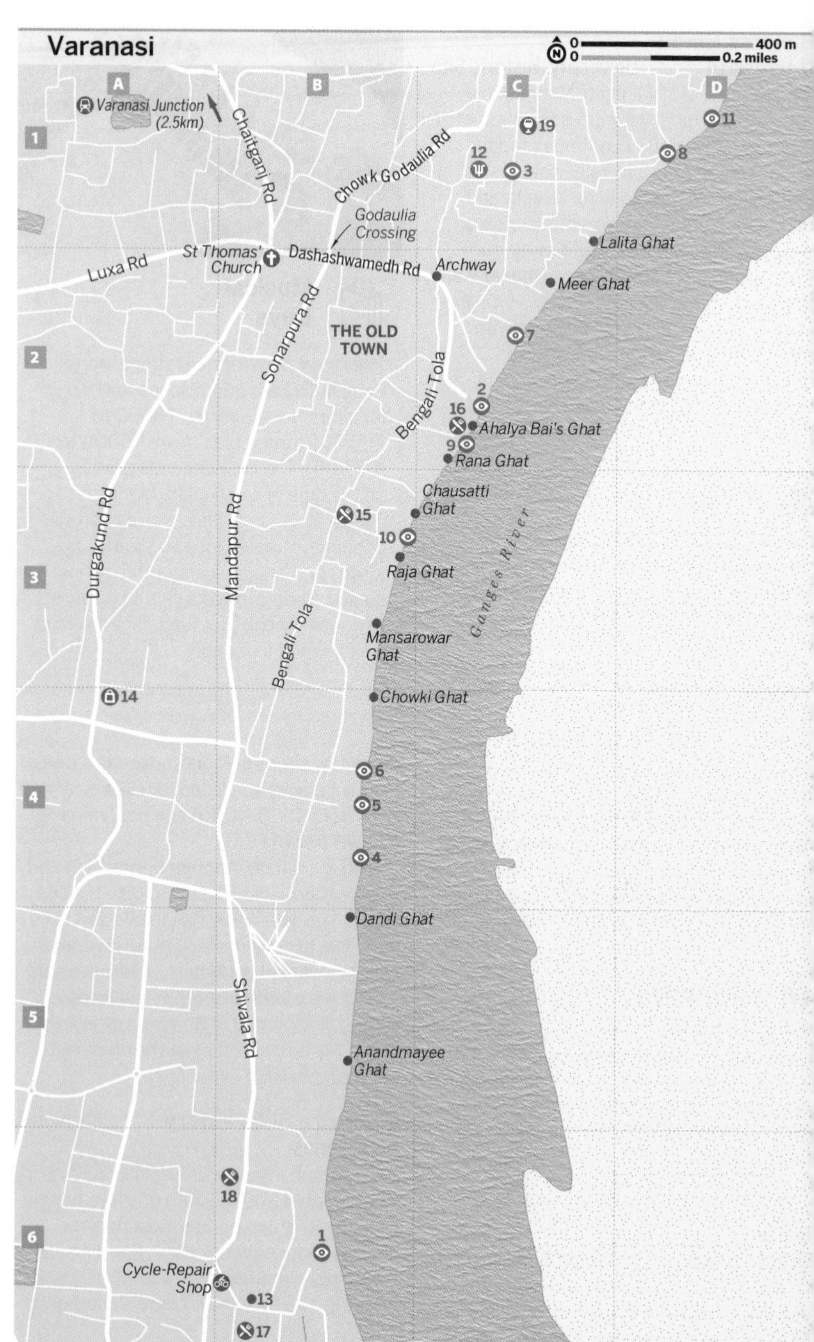

Varanasi
0
400 m
0
0.2 miles
A
B
C
D
1
2
3
4
5
6
Varanasi Junction (2.5km)
Chaitganj Rd
Chowk Godaulia Rd
Godaulia Crossing
St Thomas' Church
Luxa Rd
Dashashwamedh Rd
Archway
Sonarpura Rd
THE OLD TOWN
Bengali Tola
Lalita Ghat
Meer Ghat
Ahalya Bai's Ghat
Rana Ghat
Chausatti Ghat
Raja Ghat
Mansarowar Ghat
Chowki Ghat
Dandi Ghat
Anandmayee Ghat
Ganges River
Durgakund Rd
Mandapur Rd
Shivala Rd
Cycle-Repair Shop
1
2
3
4
5
6
7
8
9
10
11
12
13
14
15
16
17
18
19

Varanasi

Sights

1 Assi Ghat B6
2 Dashashwamedh Ghat C2
3 Gate 2 .... C1
4 Hanuman Ghat B4
5 Harishchandra Ghat B4
6 Kedar Ghat B4
7 Man Mandir Ghat C2
8 Manikarnika Ghat D1
9 Munshi Ghat C2
10 Pandhey Ghat B3
11 Scindhia Ghat D1
12 Vishwanath Temple C1

Activities, Courses & Tours

Learn for Life Society .... (see 15)
13 Varanasi Walks B6

Shopping

14 Baba Blacksheep A4

Eating

15 Brown Bread Bakery B3
16 Darbhanga C2
17 Open Hand B6
18 Vegan & Raw B6

Drinking & Nightlife

19 Blue Lassi C1

branch (21/72 Englishia Line; 10am-8pm) near the railway station.

EATING

Many eateries in the old town shut in summer due to unbearable humidity and water levels that often flood the ghats and the surrounding area.

Brown Bread Bakery — Multicuisine $$

(9792420450; www.brownbreadbakery.com; Bengali Tola, near Pandhey Ghat; mains ₹125-400; 7am-10pm;) This restaurant's fabulous menu includes more than 40 varieties of European-quality cheese and more than 30 types of bread, cookies and cakes – along with excellent pastas, sandwiches and breakfasts. Sit downstairs at street level or upstairs at the casual rooftop cafe, with seating on cushions around low tables and glimpses of the Ganges.

Pop in for the European breakfast buffet (7am to noon; ₹350) or the free, nightly classical-music performances (7.30pm). Part of the profits goes to the **Learn for Life** (0542-2390040; www.learn-for-life.net; D55/147 Aurangabad) school. Warning: don't be fooled by impostors who pretend to be the BBB, and remember: the real BBB will never accept cash donations for Learn for Life.

Open Hand — Cafe $$

(www.openhand.in; 1/128-3 Dumraub Bagh; mains ₹160-280; 7am-9pm;) This shoes-off cafe/gift shop serves real espresso and French-press coffee alongside breakfast platters featuring pancakes, omelettes and muesli. There's also a range of salads, sandwiches, pastas and baked goods, which are excellent. Sit on the narrow balcony or lounge around the former home, a short walk from Assi Ghat.

There's also a large selection of gorgeous handicrafts (pillows, bags, clothing) made in the local community.

Vegan & Raw — Vegan $$

(B-2/224 D1 Shivala Rd; mains ₹170-220; 9am-9.30pm;) This casual courtyard restaurant near Tulsi Ghat is an offshoot of Brown Bread Bakery, featuring xcellent vegan dishes, including a full page of salads from spinach-radish-walnut to

Fruity Delights

Look for locally grown *langda aam* (mangoes) in summer or *sitafal* (custard apples) in autumn. *Singharas* are water chestnuts that are sold raw (green) or cooked (black) – there's a risk of intestinal parasites with the raw ones.

No 1 Lassi in All Varanasi

Your long, thirsty search for the best lassi in India is over. Look no further than **Blue Lassi** (lassi ₹80; 9am-10pm), a tiny, hole-in-the-wall yoghurt shop that has been churning out the freshest, creamiest, fruit-filled lassis since 1925. The grandson of the original owner still works here, sitting by his lassi-mixing cauldron in front of a small room with walls plastered with the passport photos of happy drinkers.

There are more than 80 delicious flavour combos, divided by section – plain, banana, apple, pomegranate, mango, papaya, strawberry, blueberry, coconut and saffron. We think banana and apple, the latter flecked with fresh apple shreds, just about top the long list.

The whole scene here is surreal: the lassi takes ages to arrive while a group of thirsty nationalities chats away in a dozen languages; when it does arrive, the lassi is handed off to you in an earthenware pot with the care of a priceless work of art, as the occasional dead body passes by the front of the shop at eye level en route to the Burning Ghat (Manikarnika). It's a classic Varanasi moment, best slotted in between visits to Vishwanath Temple and Manikarnika Ghat.

Lassi topped with pomegranate seeds

SHIGEMITSU / GETTY IMAGES ©

papaya-pomegranate-linseed. Entrees lean towards pizza from the separate **Pizzeria Nicoletta** kitchen, but it also offers tofu, *momo* (Tibetan dumplings) and couscous. Friday is DJ night and Saturday brings swing dance classes.

Canton Royale Indian $$$
(www.hotelsuryavns.com; S-20/51A-5 The Mall Rd; mains ₹350-450; 11am-11pm;) Housed in a nearly 200-year-old heritage building, the excellent main restaurant at **Hotel Surya** (0542-2508465; s/d incl breakfast ₹3540/4010, luxury ₹4490/4960;) has colonial elegance; on warm evenings eat on the large lawn. It's one of Varanasi's best top-end choices, offering a great-value, global hodgepodge, from Mexican and Thai to Chinese and continental. But really, it's the Indian that's excellent, including a wonderful thali (₹500 to ₹750).

Darbhanga Indian, Multicuisine $$$
(9129414141; Brijrama Palace Hotel, Munshi/Darbhanga Ghat; mains ₹750-1100, thalis ₹1750; noon-3pm & 7.30-10.30pm;) Seriously some of the best Indian food we've ever had. The *palak chaman* (paneer in spinach and spices) is heaven in your mouth and the *aloo chaat* (fried pieces of parboiled potato mixed with chickpeas and chopped onions, and garnished with spices and chutney) is a gourmet-street-food revelation. There's also a good list of Continental and Thai options. For nonguests there's a minimum charge of ₹1000 per person. It's a classy night out that's worth it.

DRINKING & NIGHTLIFE

Wine and beer shops are dotted discreetly around the city, but away from the holy river. Liquor laws regarding the proximity of temples ensure nobody is licensed, but rooftop restaurants can usually discreetly serve up a beer, disguised in a teapot. For bars, head to midrange and top-end hotels away from the ghats.

Mangi Ferra Cafe
(www.hotelsuryavns.com; S-20/51A-5 The Mall Rd; cocktail ₹310-550; 11am-11pm) This colourful, laid-back lounge in the garden at Hotel Surya is a relaxing place where you can sip an espresso (₹90), a cold one or a

cocktail in the large garden, or on waves of couches and armchairs. It's also called Sol Bar. Get 30% off a cocktail between 4pm and 7pm.

Prinsep Bar Bar

(www.tajhotels.com; Gateway Hotel Ganges, Raja Bazaar Rd; beer/cocktail ₹375/650; ⏲noon-11pm Mon-Sat, to midnight Sun) For a quiet drink with a dash of history, try this tiny bar named after James Prinsep, who drew wonderful illustrations of Varanasi's ghats and temples (look for an 1830 copy of his *Benares Illustrated* in a glass case here). Stick to beer as the 25ml cocktail pour is weak.

INFORMATION

TOURIST INFORMATION

UP Tourism (☎0542-2506670; www.uptourism.gov.in; Varanasi Junction train station; ⏲10am-6pm) Get the heads-up on autorickshaw prices, the best trains for your travels, details on Varanasi's paying-guesthouse program or arrange a guided tour.

SAFETY & SCAMS

- Don't take photos at the 'burning' ghats and resist offers to 'follow me for a better view', where you'll be pressured for money and possibly be placed in an uncomfortable situation.
- Do not go to any shop with a guide or autorickshaw driver. Be firm and don't do it. Ever. You will pay 40% to 60% more for your item due to insane commissions, and you'll also be passively encouraging this practice. Do yourself a favour and walk there, or have your ride drop you a block away.
- Imposter stores are rampant in Varanasi, usually spelled one letter off or sometimes exactly the same as the original. The shops we have recommended are the real deal. Ask for a visiting card (ie business card) – if the info doesn't match, you have been had.
- When negotiating with boaters, confirm the price and currency before setting out. Many just love to say '100!' and then at the end claim they meant dollars or euros.
- Do not book guides through your guesthouse, as most of the time the guides will be

Banares Hindu University (p237)

Ganges River Rides

A dawn rowing boat ride along the Ganges is a quintessential Varanasi experience. The early-morning light is particularly inspiring, and all the colour and clamour of pilgrims bathing and performing *puja* (prayers) unfolds before you. An hour-long trip south from Dashashwamedh Ghat to Harishchandra Ghat and back is popular – be prepared to see a burning corpse at Harishchandra.

Early evening is also a good time to be on the river, when you can light a lotus-flower candle (₹10) and set it adrift on the water before watching the nightly *ganga aarti* (7pm) at Dashashwamedh Ghat directly from the boat.

The official government price of boats is ₹250 per hour for two to four people, but you'll have to haggle hard to get near that. It's best to organise a boat the day before. Many guesthouses offer boat trips, and most are good value. **Brown Bread Bakery** (p239) arranges rides in its own boats (₹150/250 per hour for one/two people).

Evening boat ride, Ganges River
DE VISU / SHUTTERSTOCK ©

unofficial. Instead go through UP Tourism (p241) to avoid most of the hassles above.

- Be wary of *bhang lassis* – these are made with hashish (degraded cannabis) and can be very strong if that's not what you're looking for (we've heard reports of robberies of intoxicated people).
- Beware of fake 'yoga teachers' as many are interested in hands-on lessons with young women.

GETTING THERE & AWAY

AIR

Varanasi's **Lal Bahadur Shashtri Airport** has nonstop flights to several cities in India, including Delhi, Mumbai, Benguluru (Bangalore) and Hyderabad. Air India has three flights a week to Agra.

Thai Airways flies directly to Bangkok daily. Nepal's Buddha Air has irregular flights to Kathmandu twice a week.

BUS

The main **bus stand** is opposite Varanasi Junction train station. Get timings and prices for AC buses at www.upsrtconline.co.in. There's an AC bus to Delhi at 1pm (₹1988, 16 hours).

TRAIN

Varanasi Junction train station is the main station, though many connections only go through Mughal Sarai junction (renamed Deen Dayal Upadyaya in 2017), located 18km southeast of the city.

Some daily trains leave for Delhi and Kolkata/Howrah and there is a daily overnight train to Agra Fort. It's easier to get a ticket on trains departing from Varanasi, and they are generally more punctual than long-distance trains.

Book tourist-quota tickets from the comfortable **foreigners' ticket office** (8am-8pm Mon-Sat, to 2pm Sun) and waiting room in the main station lobby.

Luggage theft has been reported on trains to and from Varanasi, so you should take extra care. Reports of drugged food and drink aren't unheard of, so it's probably best to politely decline any offers from strangers.

GETTING AROUND

BICYCLE & CYCLE RICKSHAW

You can hire bikes from a small **cycle-repair shop** (7237045565; 1/105 Assi-Dham; bike hire per day ₹50; 9am-7pm) near Assi Ghat.

A short cycle-rickshaw ride – up to 2km – costs ₹50, but be prepared for hard bargaining.

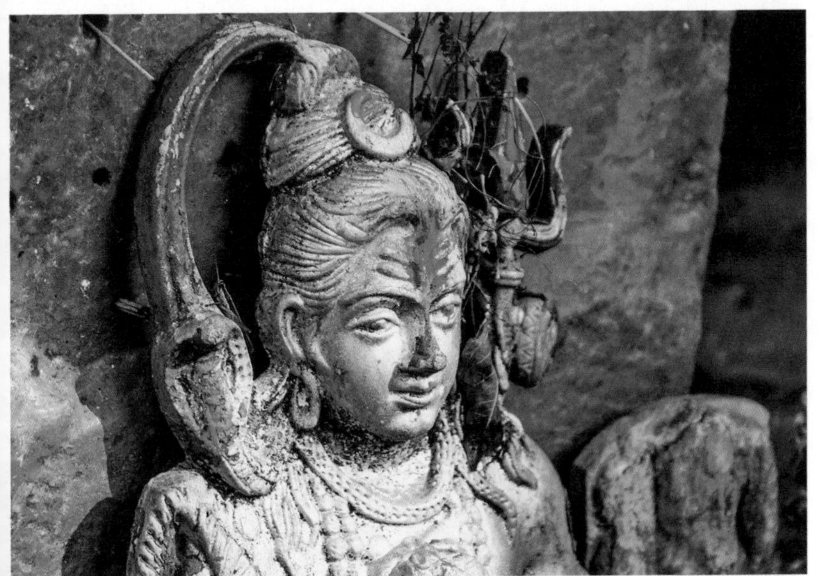

Shiva statue, Assi Ghat (p233)

TAXI & AUTORICKSHAW

Prepaid booths for autorickshaws and taxis are directly outside Varanasi Junction train station. There are usually no officials policing them, so you may have to haggle here, too.

Autorickshaws cannot enter the backstreets of the old town, so you'll have to carry your luggage from Mandapur Rd.

Sample fares from the train station:

Assi Ghat auto/taxi ₹150/300

Godaulia Crossing auto/taxi ₹100/250

Sarnath auto/taxi ₹180/400

Mughal Serai auto/taxi ₹400/750

Shared autorickshaws to Assi Ghat and Lanka Crossing for Banares University leave from Godaulia Crossing and travel down Mandapur/Shivala Rd.

Taxis offer half-/full-day city tours (four/eight hours) for ₹500/1000.

An autorickshaw to the airport in Babatpur, 24km northwest of the city, costs ₹400. A taxi is about ₹850.

MANALI

In This Chapter

Manali Adventure Activities............ 248
Sights 252
Shopping 253
Eating.. 253
Drinking & Nightlife......................... 256
Information 257
Getting There & Away 257
Getting Around 257

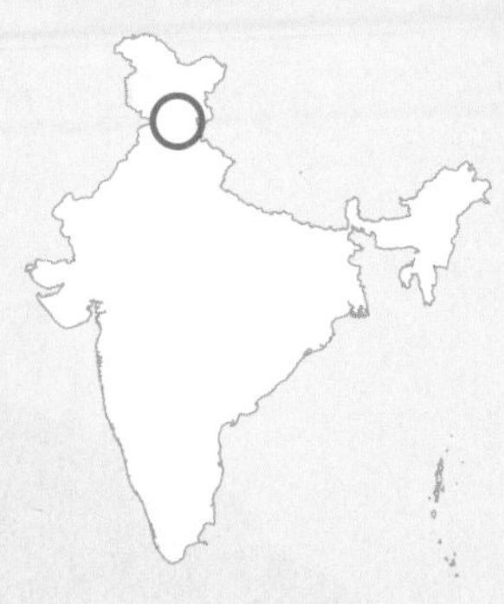

Manali at a Glance...

With mountain adventures beckoning from all directions, Manali is a year-round magnet. In parts of Vashisht and Old Manali, numerous agents offer trekking, climbing, rafting and skiing according to season. While the whole area gets jam-packed from mid-April to mid-July, and again from October to November, it doesn't take much effort to get off the main tourist trail. From December to February (barring the New Year holidays), slashed prices make Manali a bargain – if you can handle the cold and the closure of some restaurants.

Three Days in Manali

Visit **Hadimba Mandir** (p252), **Himalayan Nyinmapa Buddhist Temple** (p252) and **Von Ngari Institute** (p252) on day one, and dine at **Johnson's Cafe** (p253). On day two, go to nearby **Solang Nullah** for adventure-sport action. Reserve day three for some quality relaxation in **Old Manali**.

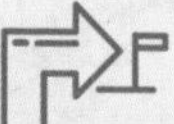

One Week in Manali

Spend days four and five on a local Himalayan **trek** (p248) of your choice. Then try some rafting, mountain-biking, paragliding or fishing.

Previous page: Bridge near Vashisht village

Manali Adventure Activities

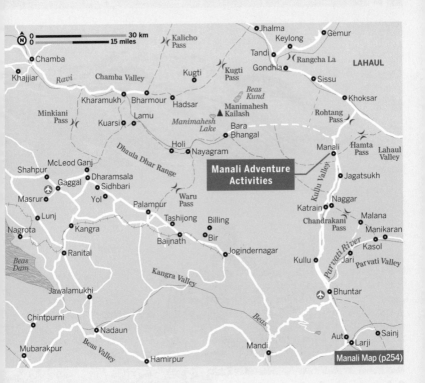

0 30 km
0 15 miles
Jhalma
Gemur
Keylong
Kalicho Pass
Tandi
Rangcha La
LAHAUL
Chamba
Gondhla
Khajjiar
Ravi
Chamba Valley
Kugti
Kugti Pass
Sissu
Beas Kund
Kharamukh
Bharmour
Hadsar
Khoksar
Manimahesh Kailash
Minkiani Pass
Lamu
Rohtang Pass
Kuarsi
Manimahesh Lake
Bara Bhangal
Holi
Nayagram
Manali
Hamta Pass
Lahaul Valley
Dhaula Dhar Range
McLeod Ganj
Shahpur
Dharamsala
Jagatsukh
Gaggal
Sidhbari
Kullu Valley
Masrur
Yol
Waru Pass
Naggar
Palampur
Katrain
Lunj
Tashijong
Billing
Malana
Chandrakani Pass
Nagrota
Kangra
Manikaran
Bir
Baijnath
Kasol
Parvati River
Ranital
Jogindernagar
Jari
Kullu
Parvati Valley
Beas Dam
Kangra Valley
Jawalamukhi
Bhuntar
Chintpurni
Beas
Nadaun
Aut
Sainj
Larji
Mandi
Beas Valley
Mubarakpur
Hamirpur
Manali Map (p254)

Arriving in Manali

Air Bhuntar Airport is located 50km from Manali.

Bus Frequent bus services connect Manali to Delhi, as well as to Dharamsala (for McLeod Ganj).

Where to Stay

Manali has well over 1000 accommodation choices and counting. The best budget places are a couple of kilometres north in Old Manali (and across the river in **Vashisht**), with good upmarket choices in between.

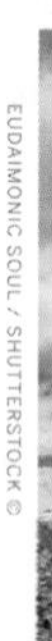

Manali Adventure Activities

Manali is the adventure-sports capital of Himachal Pradesh, and all kinds of activities can be organised through operators here.

Great For...

☑ **Don't Miss**

Getting up into the hills outside Manali – the scenery is magnificent!

Walking & Trekking

Manali is a popular jumping-off point for organised mountain treks. June, September and October are overall the best months. Popular short trekking options include:

Hamta Pass (four days) crossing into Lahaul Valley

Beas Kund lake (three days, with the option of extra days hiking up surrounding mountains)

Bhrigu Lake 4250m high (three days through lovely upland meadows)

Prices vary incredibly widely by season, group size and facilities offered. A typical range is ₹1600 to ₹3000 per person per day including guides, transport, pack animals, food and camping equipment.

Plenty of shorter walks are possible from Manali. From Old Manali a very pleasant forest stroll towards **Goshal** (around an

Need to Know

Different activities have different seasons; June, September and October are best overall.

Take a Break

Drifters' Inn (p255) in Old Manali is great for food and all manner of drinks.

★ Top Tip

Best avoid the monsoon (essentially July and August) for any outdoor activities.

hour, three possible routes) winds through woodlands, with occasional views across the valley to the Jogini Waterfalls. A fuller day hike (about five hours up, four hours back) is to **Lama Dugh meadow** at 3380m: the way starts along the uphill cobbled path from behind the upper of two water tanks above Hotel Delfryn in the Log Huts Area of town. Don't take the mud path that runs almost parallel at first.

Hamta Pass Trek

Easily accessible from Manali, this utterly beautiful and very varied camping trek crosses from the Kullu Valley to Chatru, located on the Keylong–Spiti road in Lahaul's Chandra Valley. Bring spare shoes for a knee-deep stream crossing and be aware that there are two (non-technical) glacier traverses. Starting from Jobri, where the Hamta and Jobri streams meet, the first two days have a combined ascent of around 800m and are fairly easygoing, helping with acclimatisation. Continuing up and over the 4270m Hamta Pass from the Balu Ka Gera campsite is contrastingly long, steep and tiring, but there are sublime snow-peak views from the top. The best time for this trek is after the monsoon, ie late September and October. Snow on the pass generally lasts until May.

Day 1 Jobri to Chika (5km, two hours).

Day 2 Chika to Balu Ka Gera (9km, four hours).

Day 3 Balu Ka Gera to Shiagouru via Hamta Pass (15km, eight hours).

Day 4 Shiagouru to Chatru (10km, four hours).

Mountain Biking

Many agents offer bike hire for ₹400 to ₹800 per day and can give current info on routes. Some will take you on guided rides – ranging from day outings to two-week trips to Ladakh or Spiti with vehicle support. Central Manali's **Himalayan Bike Bar**

(9418612482; www.facebook.com/himalayanbikebar; The Mall at Mission Rd; 10am-8pm Mon-Sat) is an MTB specialist renting and selling bikes, as well as a good source of information on extreme off-road events.

Rafting

The region's main rafting takes place near **Kullu**, 40km from Manali, but Manali agencies can prove helpful in getting together a group of travellers and organising shared transport. There is 14km of Grade II and III white water between Pirdi, on the Beas River 43km south of Manali, and the take-out point at Jhiri. May, June, late September and October are the best times.

Skiing & Snowboarding

Solang Nullah, 13km frm Manali, is viewed as Manali's main ski resort. It has the region's only cable car, but there's only one piste (around 1.5km) whose lower end is at a mere 2450m. Climate change keeps shortening the season, which is basically just January and February (or less). A plan has been mooted for a much-more-ambitious gondola to be built at far-higher Sethan village; currently skiers have to climb the slopes on foot. Others come to Solang Nullah for snowshoeing. Further ski options are available in the upper Solang Valley and around Gulaba. For ski packages, contact Himalayan Caravan, Himalayan Extreme Centre or the very-experienced family team at Solang Nullah's **Hotel Iceland** (9418016008, 9816066508; www.hotelicelandsolang.com; r old block ₹1000-1500, new block ₹2500-3800;). Heli-skiing packages to high-altitude powder in February and March can be arranged

Rafting, Kullu

through **Himalayan Heli Adventures** (☎9816025899; www.himachal.com; ⏲9am-6pm).

Rock Climbing

Cliffs at Solang, Aleo and Vashisht have a good range of bolted and traditional routes, ranging from British 4a to 6b (French 5a to 7b). A day's climbing for beginners or experienced climbers costs ₹1500 to ₹2000 with Manali agencies, including transport. Longer courses are also offered. Solang and the Chatru area in Lahaul are tops for bouldering. Sunny, dry November is a good month.

★ Top Tip

Himalayan Extreme Centre charges ₹1700 to ₹2000 per person for a day of descending four different waterfalls above Vashisht.

ANAND PUROHIT / GETTY IMAGES ©

Paragliding

Paragliding is popular at Solang Nullah, Gulaba and Marhi (below Rohtang La), from April to November – weather permitting. Paragliding is rare during the monsoon. September and October generally have the best thermals, though May and June can be good, too. Tandem flights at Solang Nullah cost around ₹1000 for a one-minute flight above the beginners' ski slope, though that's basically just take-off and land. For ₹3200 you get around 10 minutes (includes the cable-car fare).

Fishing

The rivers around Manali are rich in brown and rainbow trout. The angling season runs March to June and October to November. Himalayan Extreme Centre rents rods for ₹400 a day, and can set you up with a fishing permit and other equipment for a day's fishing on Manalsu Nala, which flows through Old Manali.

Agencies

Himalayan Extreme Centre (☎9816174164; www.himalayan-extreme-centre.com; Old Manali; ⏲9.30am-10pm high season, 10.30am-7pm off season) Long-running, professional and friendly, HEC is one of just a few tour agencies to open year-round. It can arrange almost any activity you fancy: drop in for informed, unpressured advice and browse a catalogue of options with accompanying videos.

Himalayan Trails (☎9816365557, 9816828583; www.himalayantrails.in; Dragon Market, Old Manali; ⏲9.30am-10pm Apr–mid-Oct) Trekking, day hikes, mountain biking, rock climbing and more.

Himalayan Caravan (☎9816316348; www.himalayancaravan.com; Manu Temple Rd, Old Manali; ⏲mid-Mar–mid-Dec) Professional operator for rock climbing, mountaineering and trekking plus winter sports.

SIGHTS

About 2km northwest of The Mall, Old Manali is the hub of the backpacker scene. Relatively little is actually old, but a few remarkable antiquated houses and barns made of wood and stone do still survive in small areas. Explore down Tiger Alley and around the path between there and the 1991-built, towered Manu Rishi Temple.

Hadimba Mandir — Hindu Temple

This much-revered wood-and-stone temple, constructed in 1553, has a three-tier pagoda-style roof plus conical top. The wooden doorway is richly carved with figures of gods, animals and dancers, and the outside walls are adorned with antlers and ibex horns. The setting, amid towering deodar cedar trees around 2km northwest of central Manali, would be magical were it not for hordes of selfie-takers. They seek a nearby range of 'attractions', including photo-with-yak opportunities, a funfair and a trinket market.

Despite the tourism overload, the site is still deeply holy and pilgrims come from across India to honour Hadimba, the demon wife of the Pandava Bhima from the Mahabharata. Inside is a large sacrificial stone where animal slaughters used to take place. Over several days in mid-May, the **Dhungri Mela festival** sees a gathering of *devtas* (village deities) carried here on palanquins. Gatothkach, the warrior son of Hadimba and Bhima, is worshipped in the form of a **sacred tree** (Gatothkach 'temple') growing behind the tourist market.

Himalayan Nyinmapa Buddhist Temple — Buddhist Temple

(⌚6am-6pm) This temple, containing a two-storey statue of the historical Buddha, was built in 1957. The land was donated to commemorate the death of the Wazir of Lahaul's son, who died while serving with the UN in Laos.

Von Ngari Institute — Buddhist Monastery

(⌚6am-7pm) This small Tibetan monastery has an atmospheric prayer room crammed with statues of bodhisattvas (enlightened beings) and revered lamas.

Himalayan Nyinmapa Buddhist Temple

SHOPPING

Manali is crammed with shops selling souvenirs from Himachal, Tibet and Ladakh, including turquoise jewellery and lots of brass Buddhas. The local speciality is Kullu shawls, known for their vibrant colours and geometric patterns.

Bhuttico Clothing

(The Mall; 9am-7pm Mon-Sat) Shawls are sold all over Manali, but multibranch co-operative Bhuttico offers fixed prices that make it a good place to start looking.

EATING

Manali has some fine Indian and international restaurants, and, in season, lots of traveller-oriented cafes (mostly in Old Manali). Many restaurants serve trout from local farms for around ₹500.

Johnson's Cafe International $$$

(www.johnsonshotel.com; Circuit House Rd; meals ₹400-650, trout ₹550-700, pizza ₹280-1100; 8.30am-10.30pm or later;) The relaxed yet stylish garden-fronted restaurant at **Johnson's Hotel** (8626814404, 01902-253764; r/cottage ₹6000/12,000;) frames a mountain view through foldaway windows, and its wood-fired pizza oven is cleverly positioned to warm the bar area in winter. Excellent European food includes lamb with mint gravy and plum-sauce spare ribs, but the standout is majestic Manali trout-fillet curry served with rice, salad and delicious *madra-palak* (a spinach-cheese dish).

Follow with apple crumble and a quality coffee (espresso ₹70, Irish coffee ₹450). Wines by the glass/bottle from ₹500/1200, beers from ₹350.

Cafe 1947 Italian $$$

(Manu Temple Rd; 10-inch pizza ₹270-530, trout ₹530; noon-11pm Thu-Tue, from 7pm Wed) This mood-lit bar-restaurant with a willow-shaded riverside terrace is popular for smoking sheesha pipes (₹460) to an insistently upbeat soundtrack. It also serves good lasagne, thin-crust pizza and superb fresh-trout platters: perfectly grilled fish with garlic-coriander sauce, orange and lemon garnish, and a whole array of crunchy fresh veggies. Hard to beat.

Drinkswise, a beer/mojito costs ₹350/400 and single/double espressos ₹70/95. Acoustic music on Saturday nights, even off season.

La Plage French $$$

(9805340977; www.facebook.com/la.plage.manali; Shanag Lane; mains ₹400-700; noon-11pm mid-May–late Aug, closed Mon in Aug) This decadent summer-only outpost of a chic Goan eatery serves French standards, like onion soup or mushroom quiche. You can also try specialities like overnight-cooked lamb, smoked trout, broccoli-and-courgette lasagne and an indulgent chocolate thali as dessert. Decent Indian and international wines, too.

Manu Rishi Temple

The towered **Manu Rishi Temple** (Old Manali) is built on the legendary landing site of an ark bearing Manu, creator of civilisation, after a great flood, in a tale that closely parallels that of Biblical Noah. Manu Rishi himself 'lives' with his sister Hadimba in the **Madhar** (Upper Old Manali), currently a gloriously unspoiled striped tower-house that is scheduled to be rebuilt. Nine silver masks with golden moustaches represent the co-deities. These are taken for outings by palanquin among much musical fanfare, for festivals or when called upon to bless a new house or business.

Manu Rishi Temple, Manali

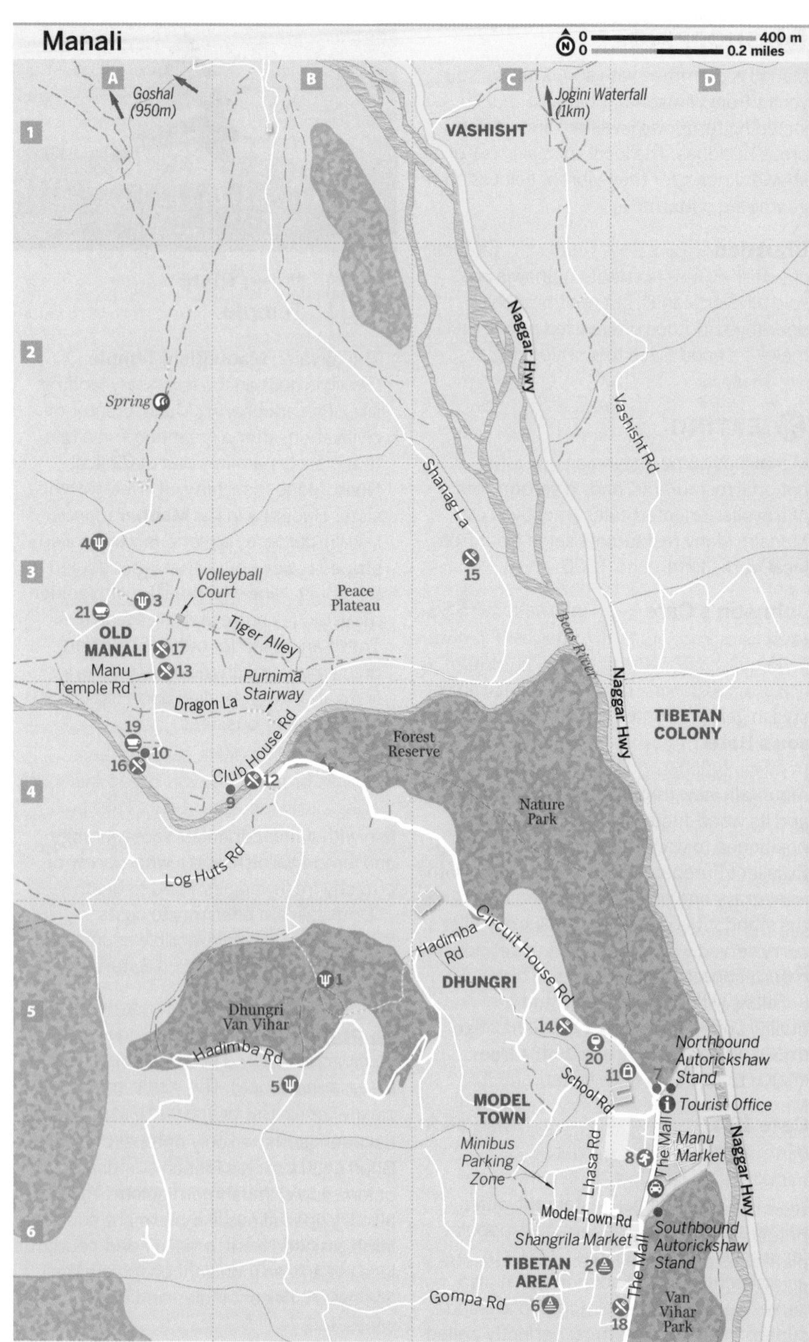
Manali
0
400 m
0
0.2 miles
A
B
C
D
1
2
3
4
5
6
Goshal (950m)
Jogini Waterfall (1km)
VASHISHT
Naggar Hwy
Vashisht Rd
Spring
Shanag La
15
4
Volleyball Court
Peace Plateau
21
3
Tiger Alley
OLD MANALI
17
Manu Temple Rd
13
Purnima Stairway
Dragon La
Beas River
Naggar Hwy
TIBETAN COLONY
19
Club House Rd
Forest Reserve
10
16
12
9
Nature Park
Log Huts Rd
Hadimba Rd
Circuit House Rd
1
DHUNGRI
Dhungri Van Vihar
14
Hadimba Rd
20
Northbound Autorickshaw Stand
5
11
7
School Rd
Tourist Office
MODEL TOWN
Minibus Parking Zone
Lhasa Rd
8
The Mall
Manu Market
Naggar Hwy
Model Town Rd
Southbound Autorickshaw Stand
Shangrila Market
TIBETAN AREA
2
The Mall
Gompa Rd
6
18
Van Vihar Park

Manali

Sights

1 Hadimba Mandir B5
2 Himalayan Nyinmapa Buddhist Temple C6
3 Madhar A3
4 Manu Rishi Temple A3
5 Sacred Tree B5
6 Von Ngari Institute C6

Activities, Courses & Tours

7 Antrek Tours & Travels D5
8 Himalayan Bike Bar D6
9 Himalayan Caravan B4
10 Himalayan Extreme Centre A4

Shopping

11 Bhuttico D5

Eating

12 Cafe 1947 .... B4
13 Drifters' Inn A3
14 Johnson's Cafe C5
15 La Plage C3
16 Lazy Dog Lounge A4
17 Renaissance A3
18 Vibes D6

Drinking & Nightlife

19 Backstreet Cafe A4
20 Johnson Lodge Bar C5
21 Shiva Tea Stall A3

It's in a peaceful spot, 1km from Old Manali bridge, surrounded by apple orchards.

Drifters' Inn Multicuisine $$

(9810978051, 9816005950; www.driftersinn-cafe.com; Manu Temple Rd; meals ₹230-410, trout ₹440-490; 9.30am-10.30pm Wed-Mon, closed early Jan–mid-Feb;) This restaurant-cafe with a mellow, jazzy soundtrack is good for hearty breakfasts, strong coffee and international dishes, from eggs Florentine to remarkably good Thai green curries.

Prices usually include rice, potato or garlic bread. Beer/shots cost from ₹230/90 but you have to buy at least two. The **guest rooms** (₹1100 to ₹2500) are spotless, if rather less stylish, sharing outdoor-terrace seating areas on each of three floors.

Renaissance International $$

(9816096835; Manu Temple Rd; mains ₹150-290) Twinkling fairy lights and strings of plastic flowers give a sweetly naïve charm to this cosy cafe-restaurant. Its Mexican meals are worth trying, while the beers/mocktails are great value (from ₹180/100).

Despite the signs, its food isn't pure vegan, but the on-display kitchen does produce an excellent stir-fried veggie plate with garlic bread and tomato-rosette garnish.

Vibes Himachali $$

(9816245280; www.facebook.com/vibeshimachalicuisine; mains ₹150-200, thali ₹250-430; 11am-11pm) Upstairs, 250m south of the bus station, Vibes is a great place to try authentic, beautifully presented Himachali food that's rarely available outside local family weddings.

The menu offers helpful explanations, but do note that several dishes, like the *lingdi* (fiddlehead fern-leaves) and *patrodu* (stuffed taro-root), are seasonal and need pre-ordering. There's also a menu of specialist Himalayan teas (₹100 per pot) including first flush with lavender or authentic Tibetan-butter tea.

Lazy Dog Lounge Multicuisine $$$

(Manu Temple Rd; mains ₹220-532, trout ₹706; 11am-1am, off season to 10.30pm;) This slick restaurant-bar produces flavoursome international food – from roast-pumpkin soup to peri-peri chicken, quinoa salad to semideconstructed pad Thai (Thai noodles in tamarind sauce). The inside space is classy yet earthy, or you can relax in the riverside garden with its weeping willow fronds and Buddha rocks.

There's an extensive drinks list (beer/shots from ₹280/190), sheesha water-pipes to puff (₹480), and a trancey soundtrack with varied live-music sessions in season.

Backpacker Cuisine

Countless half-open-air restaurants serve a wide range of backpacker-town suspects – *momos* (Tibetan dumplings), omelettes, banana pancakes, apple pie and the three Is (Italian/Israeli/Indian dishes) – plus increasing hints of Thai. The main selection is found by simply turning left at Old Manali bridge and climbing the hook of Manu Temple Rd. Many of these places close November to March.

DRINKING & NIGHTLIFE

A well-chosen range of excellent Himachali teas are elegantly served in glass teapots at Vibes. In Old Manali, Backstreet Cafe is also a tea specialist. If you just want a cheap but superb masala chai, it's hard to beat ramshackle Shiva Tea Stall.

Restaurants doubling as bars provide the bulk of Manali's nightlife, mostly in Old Manali. Their live-music nights offer diverse musical genres and equally diverse quality, but they are often the liveliest around.

Backstreet Cafe Cafe

(www.instagram.com/backstreetcafemanali; Old Manali; ⌚closed Sep-Mar) Off the main Manu Temple Rd, climb the stairway marked Rock Top Guesthouse to discover this oasis. It's a cafe amid apple trees, featuring a range of sitting spaces: shaded, sunny, fireside and indoors within a pine-clad main room with big windows.

Johnson Lodge Bar Cocktail Bar

(Circuit House Rd; ⌚noon-11pm) Capacious settees around the fireplace, backed barstools, and garden seating complement a fine cocktail list and four happy hours (ntil8pm). Welcome to one of Manali's most effortlessly stylish drinking spots.

Small/large beers cost from ₹230/450, cocktails ₹300 to ₹820. Great food, too, taking a world tour that includes Vietnamese and Korean options plus a range of gourmet burgers.

Masala chai

Shiva Tea Stall Teahouse
(Upper Old Manali; ⏲7am-9pm) Manali's best ₹10 masala chai. The tea comes richly suffused with ginger and cinnamon at this ultrabasic shack-shop, where just a handful of plastic chairs are plonked around a single outdoor table.

 INFORMATION

Tourist Office (☎01902-252175; The Mall; ⏲10am-5pm Mon-Sat, closed 2nd Sat of the month) Answers questions and has a few glossy, giveaway pamphlets.

 GETTING THERE & AWAY

AIR

Manali's closest airport is 50km south at Bhuntar. There are daily flights to Delhi, weather permitting.

BUS

Delhi Government-run HPTDC's comfortable AC Volvo coaches (₹1300, 14 hours) go to Delhi at 5.30pm and, in busy seasons, 5pm and/or 6pm. Private bus companies run similar overnight services for ₹900 to ₹1800, depending on season. State-operated HRTC also runs five AC Volvos (₹1412) each afternoon, plus an AC deluxe (₹1122) at 5.50pm, and seven 'semi-deluxe' services daily.

Dharamsala In addition to HRTC buses (one of which is a Volvo AC), there are usually a couple of private evening buses for Dharamsala (for McLeod Ganj), for around ₹550.

Fruity Alcoholic Drinks

Apples and pears from Himachal's bounteous orchards are made into cider and perry (pear cider). Plums, apricots, peaches, kiwi fruit and even rhododendron flowers yield a range of strong, inexpensive and quite drinkable wines (typically ₹300 a bottle) sold from several specialist shops.

TAXI & JEEP

The **Him-aanchal Taxi Operators Union** (☎01902-252205, 01902-252120; The Mall; ⏲8am-10pm May-Oct, to 8pm Nov-Apr) offers fixed-price rides and charters. You can also organise charters through almost any travel agency.

 GETTING AROUND

For trips to Old Manali bridge, autorickshaws from **outside the tourist office** should cost around ₹70 after bargaining. Those from the **southbound autorickshaw stand** (☎01902-253366; The Mall) near the bus station will charge more.

Several motorbike renters also offer mopeds ('Scooties'), which are good for pottering around the main valley villages. **Antrek** (☎9816022292; www.antrek.co.in; 1 Rambagh, The Mall; ⏲9am-7pm) charges ₹500/600 per day for older/newer vehicles.

Kalachakra Temple

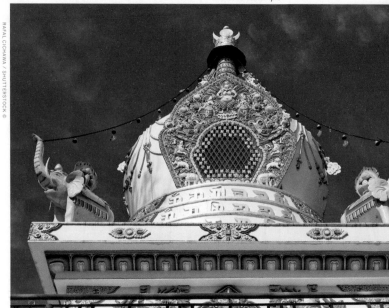

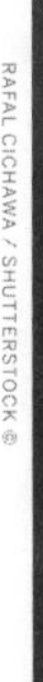

Tibetan Culture in McLeod Ganj

The residence of His Holiness the 14th Dalai Lama and home to a large Tibetan population, the small mountain town of McLeod Ganj has a strong spiritual/ alternative vibe and attracts thousands of international visitors each year.

Great For...

☑ Don't Miss

The monks' lively debating sessions in the Tsuglagkhang courtyard (2pm to 3pm, except Sunday).

Some visitors come to McLeod for courses in Buddhism, meditation or yoga, or to volunteer with the Tibetan community, or to trek in the Dhauladhar mountains. On a short visit, there's plenty to absorb and fascinate in the main Tibetan religious and cultural centres, as well as good shopping and eating.

McLeod's Tibetan community took off when the Dalai Lama established his base here in 1960. China had invaded Tibet, then a de facto independent state, in 1950. The Dalai Lama fled to India in 1959. Many other Tibetans have risked similar dangerous crossings, and today there are 85,000 or more of them in India. Many new arrivals come first to the McLeod Ganj area, where they find support from their community (over 10,000 strong) and a legion of NGOs.

Gilded Buddha statue, Tsuglagkhang

HRTC Ticket Office
Branch Security Office
Tibetan Handicraft Centre
Tibet Museum
Kalachakra Temple
Tsuglagkhang Complex
Men-Tsee-Khang
Central Tibetan Secretariat

Need to Know

The monsoon (late June to early September) is exceptionally heavy here, and best avoided.

Take a Break

Moonpeak (www.moonpeak.org; Temple Rd; mains ₹150-300; 7.30am-8.30pm; wi-fi) is a great cafe, just uphill from the complex.

★ Top Tip

For the Dalai Lama's schedules and just about everything you need to know about His Holiness, visit www.dalailama.com.

Tsuglagkhang Complex

The main focus of visiting pilgrims, monks and many tourists, the **Tsuglagkhang Complex** (Temple Rd; 5am-8pm Apr-Oct, 6am-6pm Nov-Mar) includes the main Tibetan temple and other dependencies.

Tsuglagkhang

The revered **Tsuglagkhang**, built in 1969, is the Tibetan exiles' concrete equivalent of the Jokhang Temple in Lhasa. Its central image is a gilded statue of the Sakyamuni Buddha (the name refers to the Buddha's birthplace Sakya). To its left is a gilded replica of the 7th-century statue of Avalokitesvara (the bodhisattva of compassion, Tibet's patron deity), containing relics smuggled out of Tibet. Beside the Avalokitesvara is a gilded statue of Padmasambhava, the Indian sage believed to have helped spread Buddhism in 8th-century Tibet.

Kalachakra Temple

Before visiting the Tsuglagkhang itself, pilgrims first visit the **Kalachakra Temple** on its west side. Mesmerising murals here depict the Kalachakra (Wheel of Time) mandala, specifically linked to Avalokitesvara, of whom the Dalai Lama is believed to be a manifestation.

Tibet Museum

This absorbing **museum** (www.tibetmuseum.org; 9am-1pm & 2-5pm Tue-Sun, closed some Sat) FREE tells the story of Tibetan history, the Chinese occupation and the Tibetan resistance and exodus, through photographs, video and clear English-language display panels. It also covers the Dalai Lama and his life's work.

Meeting the Dalai Lama

Put simply, the Dalai Lama is too busy with spiritual duties to give private audiences to everyone who comes to McLeod Ganj. Tibetan refugees are automatically guaranteed an audience, but travellers must make do with the occasional public teachings held at the Tsuglagkhang. These are typically given in September or October and after Losar (Tibetan New Year) in February or March, and on other occasions depending on his schedule.

To attend a teaching, register with your passport at the **Branch Security Office** (☎01892-221560; Bhagsu Rd, McLeod Ganj; ⌚9am-1pm & 2-5pm Mon-Fri & 1st Sat of the month) in the days leading up to the teaching (registration is also usually possible at the temple in the early morning before the teaching starts). Bring a cushion and an FM radio with headset (around ₹600 in local shops) for simultaneous translation.

Central Tibetan Secretariat

Inside the government-in-exile compound at Gangchen Kyishong, 2km downhill from the Tsuglagkhang, the **Library of Tibetan Works & Archives** (☎9218422467; www.tibetanlibrary.org; Gangchen Kyishong; ⌚9am-1pm & 2-5pm Mon-Sat, closed 2nd & 4th Sat of the month) began life as a collection of sacred manuscripts saved from the Cultural Revolution. Today it has over 120,000 manuscripts and books in Tibetan, and over 15,000 books on Tibet, Buddhism and the Himalayan region in English and other languages.

Upstairs is a fascinating **cultural museum** (₹20; ⌚9am-1pm & 2-5pm Mon-Sat, closed 2nd & 4th Sat of the month) with statues, old

Prayers at Tsuglagkhang (p259)

Tibetan artefacts and books, and some astonishing three-dimensional mandalas in wood and sand.

Also worth a visit is the colourful **Nechung Gompa** below the library building, seat of the Tibetan state oracle.

Tibetan Handicraft Center

This women's cooperative employs refugees for the hand weaving of Tibetan wool carpets, a process that you're welcome to watch in action.

There's also a more general gift shop selling souvenirs, quality *thangkas* (Tibetan cloth paintings) and bronze meditation gong-bowls. A tailoring section across the road can make you a Tibetan costume in around five days from ₹1000/2500 cotton/silk. Plastic is accepted and international shipping can be arranged.

ALEX EROFEENKOV / SHUTTERSTOCK ©

Men-Tsee Khang

Established to preserve the traditional arts of Tibetan medicine and astrology, **Men-Tsee-Khang** (Tibetan Medical & Astrological Institute; ☎01892-223113; www.men-tsee-khang.org; Gangchen Kyishong; ⊙9am-1pm & 2-5pm Mon-Sat, closed 2nd & 4th Sat of the month) is a college, clinic, museum, research centre and astrological institute rolled into one. The astrological folk can do you a 45-minute oral consultation (₹2000; register in person half a day ahead with your birth date, time and place), or a detailed life-horoscope online (US$85 plus US$20 taxes).

The **Men-Tsee-Khang Museum** (Gangchen Kyishong; ₹20; ⊙9am-1pm & 2-5pm Mon-Sat, closed 2nd & 4th Sat of the month) has three floors of fascinating displays on the sophisticated sciences of Tibetan astrology and medicine, told via illustrative *thangkas* as well as samples of medicines, their plant and mineral sources, and instruments that have been used for treatments – such as the brass hammer for treating tumours, insanity and body-ache.

Up in McLeod Ganj, the **Men-Tsee-Khang Therapy Centre** (☎01892-221484; www.men-tsee-khang.org; TIPA Rd; ⊙9am-1pm & 2-5pm Mon-Sat, closed 2nd & 4th Sat of the month) offers traditional Tibetan medical treatments including massages, compresses, herbal baths and steam therapies.

Tibetan Institute of Performing Arts

This flourishing **arts school** (Tibetan Institute of Performing Arts; ☎9418087998; www.tipa.asia; TIPA Rd; ⊙9am-5pm Mon-Sat, closed 2nd & 4th Sat of the month) keeps traditional Tibetan dance, music and *lhamo* (colourful folk opera) very much alive among the exile community. You can visit its folk museum and ask at the office for a tour (donations welcome for both).

TIPA stages irregular Tibetan cultural performances including a 1½-hour show of folk and ritual dance and song, Dances from the Roof of the World. Check the websites for upcoming events.

Delhi (p35)

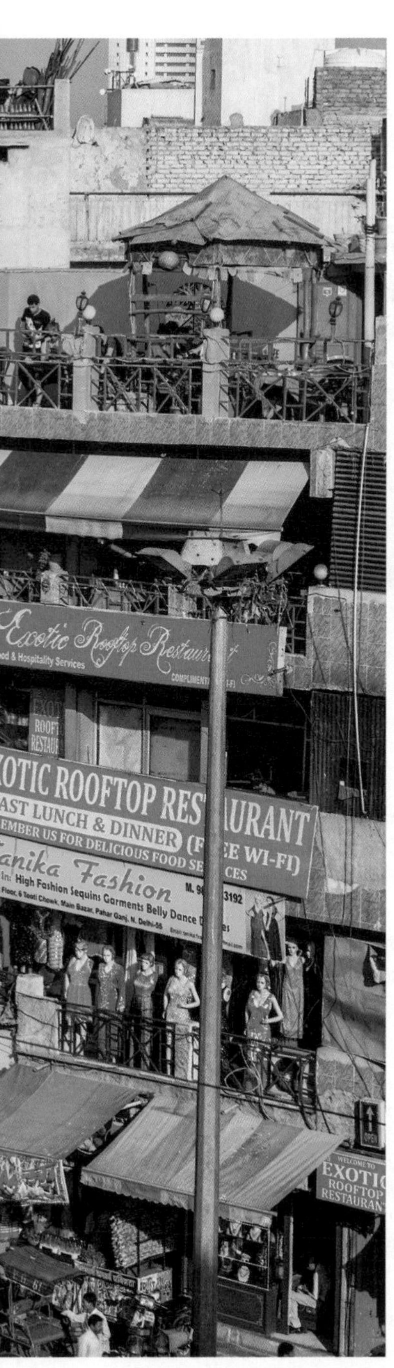

In Focus

India Today 264

India struggles with poverty, population and gender issues, while emerging as a superpower.

History 266

Mughal majesty, the British Raj, the world's biggest democracy – it's all here.

The Way of Life 277

The threads that bind the multicoloured fabric of Indian society.

Understanding Hinduism 280

The deities and beliefs of the country's major religion.

Delicious India 282

Delectable, delightful and downright irresistible, Indian cuisine will set your tastebuds dancing with joy.

Architecture & the Arts 285

Indian creativity is everywhere, from sitar strains to sculpted temples to Bollywood dances.

Landscape & Wildlife 288

Vast and varied landscapes are home to a fabulous family of creatures large and small.

Jama Masjid (p48), Delhi

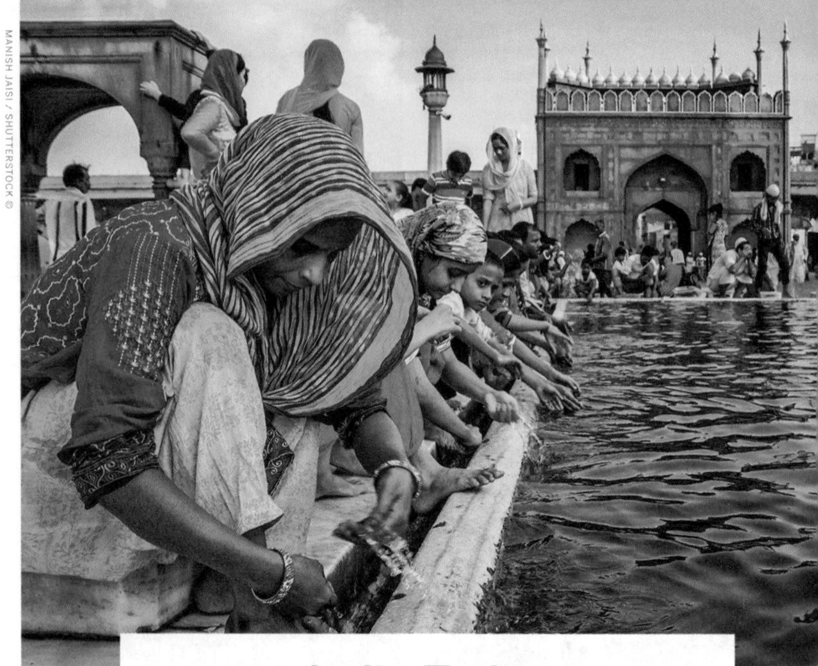

India Today

Given its diverse array of traditions, languages, religions and political views, it's amazing how well things work in India. Despite the hurdles and differences that arise, and the challenges ranging from social welfare and caste politics to religious tensions and military tiffs with neighbours, India thrives as the most successful South Asian nation and the world's largest democracy.

The Political Landscape

After the Bharatiya Janata Party (BJP) surged to power in the 2014 general elections, Prime Minister Narendra Modi vowed to boost the economy with reforms and campaigns such as 'Make in India', which set out to encourage foreign companies to manufacture and invest in the country. This appears to have yielded some positive results. One of Modi's most daring fiscal moves, however – the demonetisation of ₹500 and ₹1000 banknotes in 2016 to flush out black money – failed to achieve its objective, according to most analysts. It also dampened economic growth following its announcement. Modi was re-elected in May 2019.

Modi's government has come under criticism for failing to adequately curb communal tension, and for failing to control sporadic mob attacks affecting Muslims or liberal

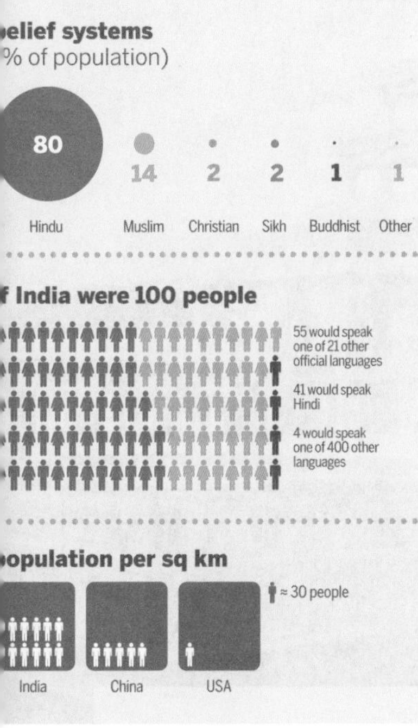

individuals. It has also been criticised for not doing enough to alleviate the nation's agrarian crisis, which has seen numerous farmers commit suicide due to chronic financial stress.

Plentiful People & Problem Neighbours

India is emerging as a global superpower, but its greatest resource – its 1.35 billion people – is also perhaps its greatest challenge. The country regularly ranks as the world's fastest-growing economy, but almost a quarter of its vast population live below the official poverty line, surviving on less than the equivalent of US$1.90 a day.

India's growing power has also placed it in conflict with its neighbours. The traditional divide between China and India – the impregnable line of the Himalaya – is becoming increasingly porous as China expands its influence in Nepal and Pakistan to check Indian power in the region. China's continued supply of military equipment as well as infrastructural support to Pakistan is a further bone of contention.

India–China relations have been further complicated by the Dalai Lama, the spiritual leader of Tibetan Buddhism, who lives in exile in Himachal Pradesh, along with members of the pre-1959 Tibetan government. Following the 1950 invasion by the Chinese People's Liberation Army, China claims all territory formerly administered by Tibet, and its government continues to dispute Indian ownership of parts of Arunachal Pradesh and Aksai Chin in Kashmir.

Chinese and Indian troops recently entered brief but tense standoffs along the border in 2013, 2016 and 2017. On each occasion, India and China agreed to withdraw troops, but tension and distrust remain high.

The Kashmir Impasse

Decades of border skirmishes between India and Pakistan over the disputed territory of Kashmir show no signs of letting up. The dispute has plagued India–Pakistan relations ever since Partition in 1947, and the predominantly Muslim Kashmir Valley is still claimed in its entirety by both countries.

The dispute has led to three India-Pakistan Wars (in 1947, 1965 and 1971) and a major conflict in 1999. Routine incursions and firing incidents across the Line of Control over the years has killed tens of thousands of soldiers and civilians on both sides of the divide.

Fatehpur Sikri (p74)

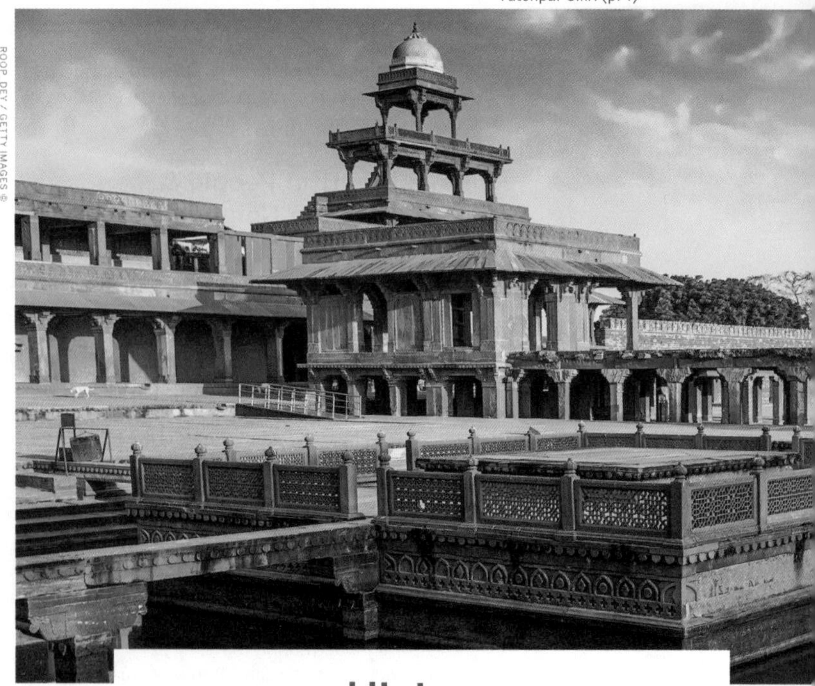

History

Through invasions and empires, birth of religions and collapse of civilisations, bold leaps forward and countless cataclysms, India has proved to be, in the words of its first prime minister Jawaharlal Nehru, 'a bundle of contradictions held together by strong but invisible threads'. India's history is that of a legion of communities and cultures who found greater strength bonded together than apart.

1500 BC

Indo-Aryan civilisation takes root in the fertile Indo-Gangetic basin, speaking early Sanskrit, from which Hindi later evolves.

563–483 BC

The life of Siddhartha Gautama, who attains enlightenment in Bodhgaya, transforming into the Buddha (Awakened One).

321–185 BC

Rule of the Maurya kings. This pan-Indian empire briefly adopts Buddhism during the reign of emperor Ashoka.

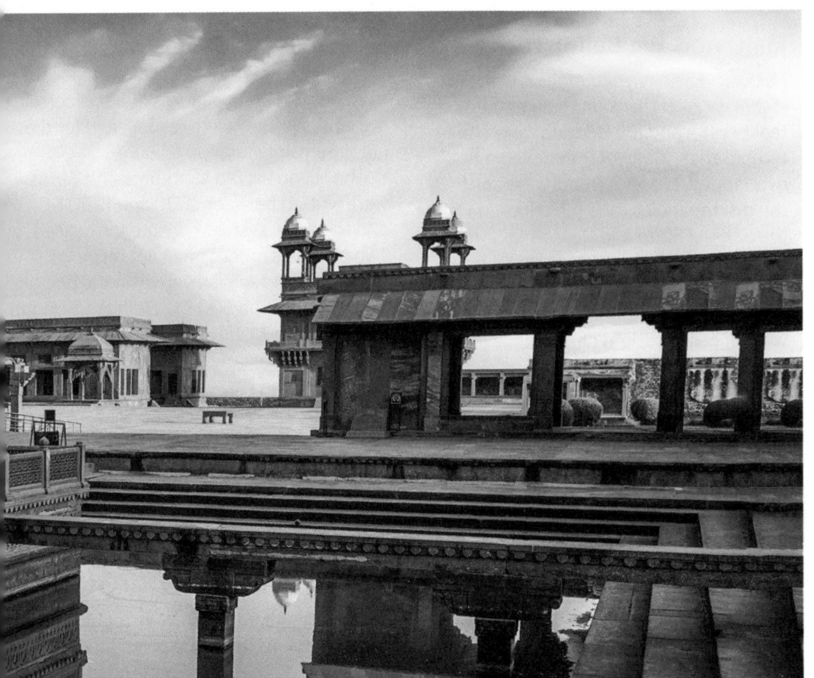

Indus Valley Civilisation

Urban culture on the subcontinent first emerged in the Indus Valley, across the modern India–Pakistan border, where the Harappan culture flourished for over 1000 years from around 2500 BC. Its greatest cities were Mohenjodaro and Harappa in Pakistan; Lothal near Ahmedabad is a major site in India. Many elements of Harappan culture would later become assimilated into Hinduism: Harappan clay figurines suggest worship of a mother goddess (later personified as Kali) and a male three-faced god in yogi pose (believed to bethe historic Shiva).

The Aryans & the Rise of Religions

A traditional explanation for the decline of Harappan civilisation is that from around 1500 BC, Aryan tribes from Afghanistan and Central Asia began to filter into northwest India, with many of the original inhabitants, the Dravidians, being pushed south. A rival theory claims that the Aryans (from a Sanskrit word for 'noble') were the original inhabitants of

c 300 BC
Buddhism spreads across the subcontinent, to Sri Lanka and Southeast Asia via Ashoka's monastic ambassadors.

500–600
Emergence of the Rajputs in Rajasthan: 36 clans spread across the region to secure their own kingdoms.

1192
Forces of the Muslim Mohammed of Ghur (from present-day Afghanistan) take Delhi, ending Hindu supremacy in North India.

Mahavir & the Buddha

Mahavir – Jainism's founder and the last of its 24 *tirthankars* (enlightened teachers) – and the Buddha were contemporaries. Many of their teachings overlapped, too. The Buddha lays out the discrepancies (and his critiques) in the *Sankha Sutta* and *Devadaha Sutta*, referring to Mahavir as Nigantha ('free from bonds') Nataputta. Read them at the Theravada Buddhism resource, www.accesstoinsight.com.

India. It's questionable whether the Aryans were a distinct race, so any 'invasion' could simply have been an arrival of new ideas from neighbouring cultures. What is certain is that the Aryans were responsible for the great Sanskrit literary tradition.

The Hindu sacred scriptures, the Vedas, were written between 1500 and 1200 BC, and the caste system became formalised. Two of India's most significant religions, Buddhism and Jainism, arose in the northern plains around 500 BC. Both the Buddha and Jainism's Mahavir questioned the Vedas and were critical of the caste system, attracting many lower-caste followers.

The Mauryan Empire

Chandragupta Maurya, who came to power in 321 BC, was the founder of the first great Indian empire. With its capital at Pataliputra (modern-day Patna), the Mauryan empire eventually stretched from Bengal to Afghanistan and south into modern-day Karnataka. It reached its peak under emperor Ashoka, who converted to Buddhism in 262 BC and spread the faith across the subcontinent.

Ashoka's rule was characterised by flourishing art and sculpture, while his reputation as a philosopher-king was enhanced by the expressive rock-hewn 'Ashokan edicts' that he used to instruct his people, express remorse at the suffering resulting from his battles, and delineate his enormous territory. Most of these mention and define the concept of dharma, variously as good behaviour, obedience, generosity and goodness.

But after Ashoka's death in 232 BC, the disparate Mauryan empire rapidly disintegrated, collapsing altogether in 185 BC. One of his many legacies is the Indian national flag: its central design is the Ashoka Chakra, a wheel with 24 spokes.

The Golden Age of the Guptas

North India's next major empire didn't arise until the 4th century AD, when Chandragupta I, king of a minor tribe called the Guptas, came to prominence by marrying a princess of one of the most powerful tribes, the Liccavis. The Gupta empire grew rapidly and under Chandragupta II (r 375–413) achieved its greatest extent. The Chinese pilgrim Faxian, visiting India at the time, described a people 'rich and contented', ruled over by enlightened and just kings.

1206
Mohammed of Ghur is murdered; in the absence of an heir, his kingdom is usurped by his generals. The Delhi Sultanate is born.

1325–51
Mohammed bin Tughlaq expands the Delhi Sultanate southwards but has to abandon the new capital at Daulatabad.

1336
Foundation of the mighty Hindu Vijayanagar empire, the ruins of whose capital can be seen today around Hampi (Karnataka).

Astronomy, medicine and the arts flourished, with some of the finest work done at Ajanta, Ellora, Sanchi and Sarnath. The Guptas were tolerant of Buddhism but towards the end of their period, Hinduism became the dominant religious force, eclipsing Jainism and Buddhism.

The invasions of the Huns at the beginning of the 6th century signalled the end of Gupta power, and power in North India again devolved to a number of separate Hindu kingdoms.

The Persian Language

Persian was the official language of several Indian empires, from Mahmud of Ghazni to the Delhi Sultanate to the Mughals. Urdu, which combines Persian, Arabic and indigenous languages, evolved over hundreds of years and came into its own during Mughal times.

The Hindu South

Southern India has always laid claim to its own unique history, insulated by distance from the political developments in the north. It was from the fertile coastal plains that the greatest southern empires – the Cholas, Pandyas, Chalukyas, Cheras and Pallavas – came into their own.

The Chalukyas ruled mainly over the Deccan region of south-central India. In the far south, the Pallavas ruled from the 4th to 9th centuries and pioneered Dravidian architecture, with its exuberant, almost baroque, style.

The south's prosperity was based on trading links with other civilisations, among them Egypt and Rome. In return for spices, pearls, ivory and silk, the Indians received Roman gold. Indian merchants also extended their influence to Southeast Asia. The Cholas, based in modern-day Tamil Nadu, set about turning trade influence into territorial conquest. Under Rajaraja Chola I (985–1014) they controlled almost the whole of South India, the Deccan plateau, Sri Lanka, parts of the Malay peninsula and the Sumatran-based Srivijaya kingdom. Throughout this period, Hinduism remained the bedrock of South Indian culture.

The Muslim North

From 1001 to 1025, Mahmud of Ghazni – hailing from the then-Afghan megacity of Ghazni – conducted 17 raids into India, most notably on the famous Shiva temple at Somnath in Gujarat. A Hindu force of 70,000 died trying to defend this temple, which fell in early 1026. Mahmud transported a massive haul of gold and other booty back to his capital. These raids shattered the balance of power in North India, allowing subsequent invaders to claim territory for themselves.

In 1191, Mohammed of Ghur advanced into India in brutal fashion, before being defeated in a major battle against a confederacy of Hindu rulers. He returned the following year and routed his enemies. One of his generals, Qutb ud-din Aibak, captured Delhi and was

1398
Timur (Tamerlane) mercilessly sacks Delhi, on the pretext that the sultans are too tolerant with their Hindu subjects.

1469
Guru Nanak, founder of the Sikh faith, is born in a village near Lahore (in modern-day Pakistan).

1510
Portuguese forces capture Goa under the command of Alfonso de Albuquerque.

★ History Reads

A Traveller's History of India, SinhaRaja Tammita-Delgoda

Empires of the Indus, Alice Albinia

India: A History, John Keay

Indian Summer: The Secret History of the End of an Empire, Alex von Tunzelmann

Gateway of India (p128), Mumbai

appointed governor; he eventually went on to become the city's first sultan. It was during his reign that the great Delhi landmark, the Qutab Minar, along with India's first mosque, was built. Within a short time almost all of North India was under Muslim control.

North Meets South

Mohammed bin Tughlaq ascended the Delhi throne in 1324. With dreams of controlling South India directly as part of his empire, Tughlaq decided to move his capital 1100km south to Daulatabad, near Aurangabad in Maharashtra. He forcefully marched the entire population of Delhi south to his new city – but soon realised this left the north undefended, so the entire capital was moved north again.

After Tughlaq's withdrawal from the south, several splinter kingdoms arose. The two most significant were the Islamic Bahmani sultanate, which emerged in 1345 with its capital at Gulbarga, and later Bidar, and the Hindu Vijayanagar empire, founded in 1336 with its capital at Hampi. The battles between the two were among the bloodiest communal violence in Indian history and ultimately resolved nothing in the two centuries before the Mughals ushered in a more enlightened age.

The last great sultan of Delhi, Firoz Shah, died in 1388, and the sultanate's fate was sealed when Timur (Tamerlane) made a devastating raid from Samarkand in 1398. Timur's sacking of Delhi was truly merciless; some accounts say his soldiers slaughtered every Hindu inhabitant.

The Mughals

At its height the Mughal empire covered almost the entire subcontinent. Its significance, however, lay not only in its size. Mughal emperors presided over an artistic golden age and had a passion for building that resulted in some of the finest architecture in India, including Shah Jahan's sublime Taj Mahal.

1526
Babur becomes the first Mughal emperor after conquering Delhi, and stuns Rajasthan by routing its confederate force.

1601
Sir James Lancaster commands the maiden trading voyage of the British East India Company.

1631
Construction of the Taj Mahal begins after Shah Jahan vows to build the world's most beautiful mausoleum for wife Mumtaz Mahal.

The founder of the Mughal line, Babur, marched into Punjab from his capital at Kabul in 1525. With technological superiority brought by firearms, Babur defeated the larger armies of the sultan of Delhi at the Battle of Panipat in 1526.

Babur's son, Humayun (r 1530–56) was defeated by a powerful ruler of eastern India, Sher Shah, in 1539 and forced to withdraw to Iran. Humayun eventually conquered Delhi in 1555, dying the following year to be succeeded by his son Akbar (r 1556–1605), who managed to extend the empire over a mammoth area.

Akbar, whose name means 'great' in Arabic, was indeed probably the greatest of the Mughals: he not only had military ability but was also a man of culture and a wise leader, skilfully integrating Hindus into his empire, using them as advisers, generals and administrators.

Akbar's son Jehangir (r 1605–27) kept his father's empire intact, despite challenges to his authority. His son Shah Jahan (r 1627–58) secured his position by executing all male relatives who stood in his way. He also built the Taj Mahal (the mausoleum of his wife Mumtaz Mahal), as well as constructing the mighty Red Fort in Delhi and converting Agra Fort into a palace that would later become his own prison.

The last of the great Mughals, Aurangzeb (r 1658–1707), imprisoned his father (Shah Jahan) and gained the throne after a two-year struggle against his brothers. He faced serious challenges from the Hindu Marathas under their great leader Shivaji, in central India, and from the British in Bengal. After Aurangzeb's death, Delhi was sacked by Persia's Nadir Shah in 1739. Mughal 'emperors' continued to rule until the First War of Independence (Indian Uprising) in 1857, but they were emperors without an empire.

Arrival of European Traders

During the 15th century, the Portuguese sought a sea route to the Far East so they could trade directly in spices. En route, they found lucrative trading opportunities on the Indian coast, when Vasco da Gama arrived on the Kerala coast in 1498, having sailed around Africa. In 1510, the Portuguese captured Goa and in its heyday, the trade flowing through 'Golden Goa' was said to rival that passing through Lisbon. The Portuguese enjoyed a century-long monopoly over Indian and Far Eastern trade with Europe.

In 1600, Queen Elizabeth I granted a London trading company the monopoly on British trade with India. In 1613, the East India Company established its first trading post at Surat in Gujarat. Further posts governed by the company were established at Madras (Chennai) in 1639, Bombay (Mumbai) in 1661 and Calcutta (Kolkata) in 1690.

The French, who established themselves at Pondicherry (Puducherry) by 1672, vied with the British for control of Indian trade. At one stage, they appeared to hold the upper hand, even taking Madras in 1746. But they were outmanoeuvred by the British, and by the 1750s were no longer a serious influence on the subcontinent.

1707
The death of Aurangzeb, the last great Mughal emperor, triggers the gradual collapse of the Mughal empire into rebellion and anarchy.

1757
Battle of Plassey: Robert Clive defeats nawab of Bengal in East India Company's first military victory in India.

1857
The First War of Independence (Indian Uprising) against the British.

★ Mughal Marvels

Taj Mahal (p66)
Red Fort (p38)
Agra Fort (p78)
Fatehpur Sikri (p74)
Humayun's Tomb (p48)

Humayun's Tomb (p48), Delhi

Britain's Surge to Power

Following the establishment of the British trading post at Calcutta in 1690, business expanded rapidly. Under the apprehensive gaze of the nawab (local ruler) Siraj-ud-daula, the 'factories' took on an increasingly permanent (and fortified) appearance. In June 1756, the nawab attacked Calcutta and locked his British prisoners in a tiny cell. The space was so cramped and airless that many were dead by the following morning.

Six months later, Robert Clive, an employee in the military service of the East India Company, led an expedition to retake Calcutta and made an agreement with one of the nawab's generals to overthrow the nawab himself. He did this in June 1757, at the Battle of Plassey (now called Palashi). The company's agents embarked on a period of unbridled profiteering, and when a subsequent nawab was defeated at the Battle of Baksar in 1764, the British were confirmed as the paramount power in east India.

In 1771, Warren Hastings was made governor in Bengal. During his tenure, the company greatly expanded its control, concluding a series of treaties with local rulers in the power vacuum following the disintegration of the Mughal empire.

In the south, a local ruler, Hyder Ali, and his son Tipu Sultan, waged a brave and determined campaign against the British. But in the Fourth Mysore War (1789–99), Tipu Sultan was killed at Srirangapatnam, and British power took another step forward. The long-running struggle with the Marathas in central India was concluded a few years later.

By the early-19th century, India was effectively under British control, although there remained a patchwork of nominally independent 'princely states' governed by maharajas (or similarly titled princes) and nawabs. Trade and profit remained the main focus of British rule in India: iron and coal mining were developed, tea, coffee and cotton became key crops, and a start was made on the vast rail network that's still in use today. The Mughal-era zamindar (landowner) system was encouraged, further entrenching the growth of an impoverished, landless peasantry.

1858
Power is officially transferred from the East India Company to the British Crown, beginning the period known as the British Raj.

1885
The Indian National Congress, a key player in the future freedom struggle, is set up.

1919
Protesters massacred by British troops at Jallianwala Bagh, Amritsar. Gandhi responds with programme of civil disobedience.

The First War of Independence (Indian Uprising)

In 1857, half a century after establishing firm control of India, the British suffered a serious setback. To this day, the causes of the Indian Uprising are the subject of debate. The key factors included the influx of cheap goods from Britain, such as textiles, that destroyed many livelihoods; the dispossession of territories from many rulers; and taxes on landowners.

The incident popularly held to have sparked the uprising took place at an army barracks in Meerut in Uttar Pradesh on 10 May 1857. A rumour leaked out that a new type of bullet was greased with what Hindus claimed was cow fat, while Muslims maintained that it came from pigs; pigs are considered unclean to Muslims, and cows are sacred to Hindus.

In Meerut, the commanding officer lined up his soldiers and ordered them to bite off the ends of their bullets. Those who refused were immediately marched off to prison. The following morning, the soldiers of the garrison rebelled, shot their officers and marched to Delhi. Of the 74 Indian battalions of the Bengal army, 47 rebelled. The soldiers and peasants rallied around the ageing Mughal emperor in Delhi. They held Delhi for some months and besieged the British residency in Lucknow for five months before they were finally suppressed.

Almost immediately, the East India Company was wound up and direct control of India was assumed by the British government.

The Rajputs

Throughout the Mughal period, there remained strong Hindu powers, most notably the Rajputs, a proud warrior caste with a passionate belief in the dictates of chivalry, both in battle and state affairs. Hereditary rulers of many princedoms in Rajasthan, the Rajputs opposed every foreign incursion into their territory, but they were never united. When they weren't battling outside oppressors, they squandered their energies fighting one another. This eventually led to their territories becoming vassal states of the Mughal empire. Their prowess in battle, however, was acknowledged, and some of the best military men in the Mughal armies were Rajputs – among them Maharaja Man Singh, founder of the mighty Amber Fort near Jaipur, who was a leading general of emperor Akbar.

The Road to Independence

Opposition to the British increased at the turn of the 20th century, spearheaded by the Indian National Congress, the country's oldest political party, which first met in 1885 and soon began to push for participation in government.

India contributed hugely to Britain's WWI war effort, with more than one million Indian volunteers enlisted and sent overseas, suffering more than 100,000 casualties. The

1940
The Muslim League adopts its Lahore Resolution, championing greater Muslim autonomy.

1942
Mahatma Gandhi launches the Quit India campaign, demanding that the British leave India without delay.

1947
India gains independence on 15 August, a day after Pakistan. Mass cross-border migration of Hindus and Muslims follows Partition.

Hindi Words

The British brought many things to India but also took many things home with them, including dozens of words. Pyjamas, shampoo, bandanas, dinghies, bangles and bungalows all have their origins in Hindi or Urdu.

contribution was sanctioned by Congress leaders, but no rewards for it resulted after the war, and disillusion followed. Disturbances were particularly persistent in Punjab, and in April 1919 a British army contingent was sent to quell the unrest in Amritsar, where it ruthlessly fired into a crowd of unarmed protesters at Jallianwala Bagh. News of the massacre quickly turned huge numbers of otherwise apolitical Indians into Congress supporters.

Mahatma Gandhi

One of the great figures of the 20th century, Mohandas Karamchand Gandhi was born in 1869 in Porbandar, Gujarat. After studying in London (1888–91), he worked as a barrister in South Africa, where he became politicised, railing against the discrimination he encountered.

Gandhi returned to India in 1915 with the doctrine of *ahimsa* – nonviolence – central to his political plans, and committed to a simple and disciplined lifestyle. Within a year, Gandhi had won his first victory, defending farmers in Bihar from exploitation. This was when it's said he first received the title 'Mahatma' (Great Soul).

Gandhi came to the forefront in the Congress movement after the Jallianwala Bagh massacre, coordinating a national campaign of *satyagraha* (nonviolent protest) against British rule. Not everyone involved in the struggle agreed with Gandhi's policy of nonviolence, yet the Congress Party and Gandhi remained at the forefront of the push for independence.

In early 1930, Gandhi captured the imagination of the country by leading a march of several thousand followers to Dandi on the Gujarat coast, where he ceremoniously made salt by evaporating sea water, thus publicly defying the much-hated salt tax. Released from jail in 1931 to represent the Indian National Congress at the second Round Table Conference in London, he won the hearts of many British people but failed to gain any real concessions from the government.

As political power-sharing began to look more likely, India's large Muslim minority realised that an independent India would be dominated by Hindus and that, while Gandhi's approach was fair-minded, others in the Congress Party might not be so willing to share power. By the 1930s Muslims were raising the possibility of a separate state.

Disillusioned with politics, Gandhi resigned his parliamentary seat in 1934. He returned spectacularly to the fray in 1942 with the Quit India campaign, urging the British to leave India immediately. His actions were deemed subversive, and he and most of the Congress leadership were imprisoned.

1947–48
First India-Pakistan War, after the maharaja of Kashmir signs the Instrument of Accession ceding his state to India.

1948
Mahatma Gandhi is assassinated in New Delhi by Nathuram Godse, who is later convicted and hanged.

1965
Skirmishes in Kashmir and the Rann of Kutch flare into the Second India-Pakistan War, with the biggest tank battles since WWII.

In the frantic independence bargaining that followed the end of WWII, Gandhi stood almost alone in urging the preservation of a single India, and his work on behalf of all communities drew resentment from some Hindu hardliners. He was assassinated in Delhi on 30 January 1948 by a Hindu zealot, Nathuram Godse.

Indian Rupee

Prime Minister Modi's demonetisation of ₹500 and ₹1000 banknotes in 2016 is just the latest twist in the long history of the rupee. The name rupee comes from the struck silver coins known as *rupa*, first mentioned in Sanskrit texts in the 6th century BC.

Independence & Partition

The Labour Party victory in the British elections in July 1945 dramatically altered the political landscape. For the first time, Indian independence was accepted as a legitimate goal. The two major Indian parties, however, had deeply divergent ideas of what form independence would take. Mohammed Ali Jinnah, the leader of the Muslim League, championed a separate Islamic state, while the Congress Party, led by Jawaharlal Nehru, campaigned for an independent greater India.

In early 1946, a British mission failed to bring the two sides together and the country slid closer towards civil war. In February 1947, the nervous British government made the momentous decision that Independence would come by June 1948. A new viceroy, Lord Louis Mountbatten, encouraged the rival factions to agree upon a united India, but to no avail. A decision was made to divide the country and, faced with increasing civil violence, Mountbatten made the precipitous decision to bring forward Independence to 15 August 1947.

Dividing the country into separate Hindu and Muslim territories was immensely tricky; some areas were clearly Hindu or Muslim, but others were evenly mixed, and there were 'islands' of communities in areas predominantly settled by other religions. The problem was worst in Punjab, one of the most fertile and affluent regions of the country, which had large Muslim, Hindu and Sikh communities, with antagonisms already running at fever pitch. The Sikhs saw their homeland divided down the middle.

Huge population exchanges took place and the resulting bloodshed was even worse than anticipated. Trains full of Muslims, fleeing westward, were held up and slaughtered by Hindu and Sikh mobs. Hindus and Sikhs fleeing to the east suffered the same fate at Muslim hands. By the time the Punjab chaos had run its course, more than 10 million people had changed sides and at least 500,000 had been killed.

India and Pakistan became sovereign nations in August 1947 as planned, but the violence and migrations continued and the integration of a few states, especially Kashmir, was yet to be completed. The Constitution of India went into effect on 26 January 1950, and, after untold struggles, independent India officially became a republic.

1971
Third India-Pakistan War: India gets involved in East Pakistan's (now Bangladesh) campaign for independence from West Pakistan.

1984
Indira Gandhi orders assault on Sikh separatists occupying Amritsar's Golden Temple; four months later, she is assassinated.

2014
After a landslide election victory by the BJP, Gujarat-born Narendra Modi becomes prime minister.

Independent India

Jawaharlal Nehru tried to steer India towards a policy of nonalignment, balancing cordial relations with Britain with moves towards the USSR.

The 1960s and 1970s were tumultuous times for India. A border war with China resulted in the loss of parts of Aksai Chin (Ladakh) and smaller areas in the northeast. Wars with Pakistan in 1965 (over Kashmir) and 1971 (over Bangladesh) also contributed to a sense among many Indians of having enemies on all sides.

The hugely popular Nehru died in 1964 and his daughter Indira Gandhi (no relation to Mahatma Gandhi) was elected prime minister in 1966. Unlike Nehru, however, Indira Gandhi was always a profoundly controversial figure whose historical legacy remains hotly disputed.

In 1975, facing serious opposition and unrest, she declared a state of emergency (later known as 'the Emergency'). Freed of parliamentary constraints, Gandhi was able to boost the economy, control inflation remarkably well and decisively increase efficiency. On the negative side, political opponents often found themselves in prison, India's judicial system was turned into a puppet theatre and the press was fettered.

Gandhi was bundled out of office in the 1977 elections, but the 1980 election brought her back to power with a larger majority than ever before, firmly laying the foundation for a family dynasty that continues to dominate Indian politics to this day. Indira Gandhi was assassinated in 1984 by one of her Sikh bodyguards after her decision to attack the Golden Temple in Amritsar, which was being occupied by a fundamentalist Sikh preacher. Her son Rajiv took over and was subsequently killed in a suicide bomb attack in 1991. His widow, Sonia, later became president of the Congress party. However, the party lost popularity as the economy slowed, and has been accused of cronyism and corruption.

The 2014 federal elections saw the Congress party suffer a humiliating defeat under the shaky leadership of Rahul Gandhi, Indira's grandson. The Bharatiya Janata Party (BJP), headed by Narendra Modi, swept to power in a landslide victory, promising to shake up Indian politics and usher in a new era of neoliberal economics. Some continue to ask questions about Modi's role in riots in Gujarat in 2002 (when he was the state's chief minister), which killed nearly 1000 people, mostly Muslims. But an official inquiry in 2014 cleared him of any wrong-doing. His forceful, charismatic style has made him hugely popular with business leaders and the BJP's Hindu-nationalist traditionalists, as well as with the ordinary person on the street. Modi was re-elected in May 2019.

2016
Modi's government demonetises ₹500 and ₹1000 banknotes to stamp out tax evasion and corruption. Economic growth is dampened.

2017
The Indian Space Research Organisation (ISRO) makes world history by launching a record 104 satellites into orbit in a single mission.

2018
India's Supreme Court votes to decriminalise homosexuality, removing colonial-era criminal penalties for gay sex from the penal code.

Bridal attire

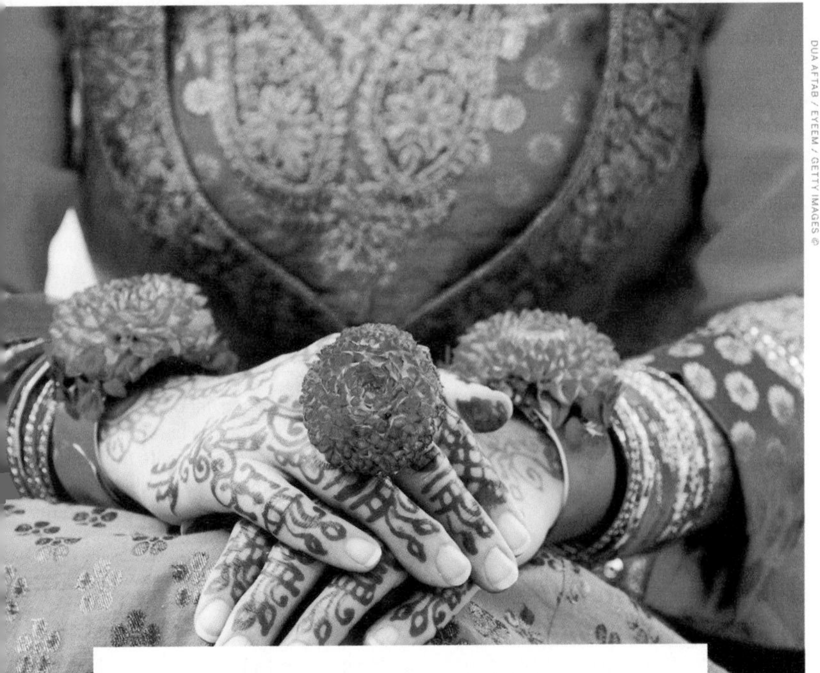

The Way of Life

Spirituality and family are central to Indian society, often intertwined in various ceremonies to celebrate auspicious occasions and life's milestones. Despite the growing number of nuclear families – primarily in the more cosmopolitan cities – the extended family remains a cornerstone of both urban and rural India, with males generally considered the head of the household.

Marriage, Birth & Death

For all Indian communities, marriage, birth and death are important and marked with ceremonies according to religion. Hindus are in the majority in India (around 80% of the population), while around 15% of the population is Muslim.

Marriage is an exceptionally auspicious event for Indians – for most, the idea of being unmarried by their mid-30s is unpalatable. Although 'love marriages' have spiralled upwards in recent times (mainly in urban hubs), most Indian marriages are still arranged, be the family Hindu, Muslim, Sikh, Jain or Buddhist.

Dowry, although illegal, is still a key issue in many arranged marriages, mostly in conservative communities. Some families plunge into debt to raise the required cash and merchandise, from cars and computers to refrigerators and televisions. Health workers claim

Traditional Indian Attire

The elegant sari comes in a single piece (between 5m and 9m long and 1m wide) and is ingeniously tucked and pleated into place without pins or buttons. Worn with the sari are the choli (tight-fitting blouse) and a drawstring petticoat. Also common is the *salwar kameez*, a tunic-and-trouser combination accompanied by a *dupatta* (long scarf).

Traditional men's attire includes the dhoti (a long loincloth pulled up between the legs) and in the south, the sarong-like *lungi* and *mundu*. A kurta is a long, usually collarless, tunic or shirt; *churidar* are close-fitting trousers often worn under a kurta.

that India's high rate of abortion of female foetuses is predominantly due to the financial burden of providing a daughter's dowry. (Sex identification tests are banned in India, but they still occur in some clinics.)

Divorce and remarriage is becoming more common, primarily in bigger cities, but courts still don't grant divorce as a matter of routine and it is not looked upon very favourably by society.

The birth of a child is another momentous occasion, with its own set of special ceremonies at various auspicious times during early childhood. For Hindus these include the casting of the child's first horoscope, name-giving, feeding the child its first solid food, and the first hair cut.

Hindus and Sikhs cremate their dead, and funeral ceremonies are designed to purify and console both the living and the deceased. Muslims bury their dead.

The Caste System

Although the Indian constitution does not recognise the caste system, caste still wields considerable influence. Especially in rural India, the caste you are born into largely determines your social standing in the community. It can also influence your vocational and marriage prospects.

Traditionally, caste is the basic social structure of Hindu society. Living a righteous life and fulfilling your dharma (moral duty) raises your chances of being reborn into a higher caste and thus into better circumstances. Hindus are born into one of four varnas (castes): Brahmin (priests and scholars), Kshatriya (soldiers and administrators), Vaishya (merchants) and Shudra (labourers). Castes are further divided into thousands of *jati*, groups of 'families' or social communities, which are sometimes but not always linked to occupation.

Beneath the four main castes are the Dalits (formerly known as Untouchables), who hold menial jobs such as sweepers and latrine cleaners. To improve the Dalits' position, the government reserves a number of parliamentary seats and almost 25% of government jobs and university student places for them.

Women in India

According to the most recent census (2011), India's 586 million women accounted for some 48.5% of the total population, with an estimated 68% of those working (mostly as labourers) in the agricultural sector.

Women in India are entitled to vote and own property. Although the professions are male dominated, women are steadily making inroads. Still, they account for less than 12% of national parliamentary members.

In low-income families, especially, girls can be regarded as a serious financial liability because a dowry might be demanded at marriage. Urban middle-class women are far more likely to receive a tertiary education, but once married they are still often expected to 'fit in' with their in-laws and be a homemaker above all else.

India remains a conservative society, and many traditionally minded people still consider that a woman is somehow wanton if she goes out after dark or does not dress modestly.

Following the highly publicised gang-rape and murder of a 23-year-old student in Delhi in 2012, tens of thousands of people protested in the capital and beyond. It took a year before laws were amended to address the problem of sexual assault, including harsher punishments such as life imprisonment and the death penalty. Despite this, sexual violence against women is still a major problem. According to the latest National Crime Records Bureau report, Delhi has the highest number of crimes against women – 13,803 out of a total of 41,761 cases registered in 19 major Indian cities. A considerable number of foreign female travellers to India have reported some form of sexual harassment.

Hijras

India's most visible nonheterosexual group is the *hijras*, a caste of transvestites and eunuchs who dress in women's clothing. Some are gay, some are hermaphrodites and some were unfortunate enough to be kidnapped and castrated. *Hijras* have long had a place in Indian culture, and in 2014 the Indian Supreme Court recognised *hijras* as a third gender and as a class entitled to reserved places in education and jobs. *Hijras* work mainly as uninvited entertainers at weddings and celebrations of the birth of male children. In 2014, Padmini Prakash became India's first transgender daily TV news-show anchor, indicating a new level of acceptance.

Adivasis

India's Adivasis (tribal communities) have origins that precede the Vedic Aryans and the Dravidians of the south. The word *adivasi* translates to 'original inhabitant' in Sanskrit. These groups range from the Gondi of the central plains to the animist tribes of the Northeast States. Today, they constitute less than 10% of India's population and comprise more than 300 different tribal groups. The literacy rate for Adivasis is significantly below the national average.

In recent decades, an increasing number of Adivasis have been dispossessed of their ancestral land and turned into impoverished labourers. Although they still have political representation thanks to a parliamentary quota system, the dispossession and exploitation of Adivasis has reportedly sometimes occurred with the connivance of officialdom.

Sport

Cricket has long been engraved on the nation's heart. The first recorded match was held in 1721, and India's first test match victory was in 1952, in Chennai against England. It's not only a national sporting obsession, but a matter of enormous patriotism, especially evident whenever India plays against Pakistan. Cricket – especially the Twenty20 format (www.cricket20.com) – is big business in India, attracting lucrative sponsorship deals and celebrity status for its players. International games are played at various centres; check Indian newspapers or online (www.espncricinfo.com is excellent) for details about upcoming matches.

Meantime, the launch of the Indian Super League (ISL; www.indiansuperleague.com) in 2013 has achieved its aim of promoting football/soccer as a big-time, big-money sport.

Temple art depicting Krishna and Radha

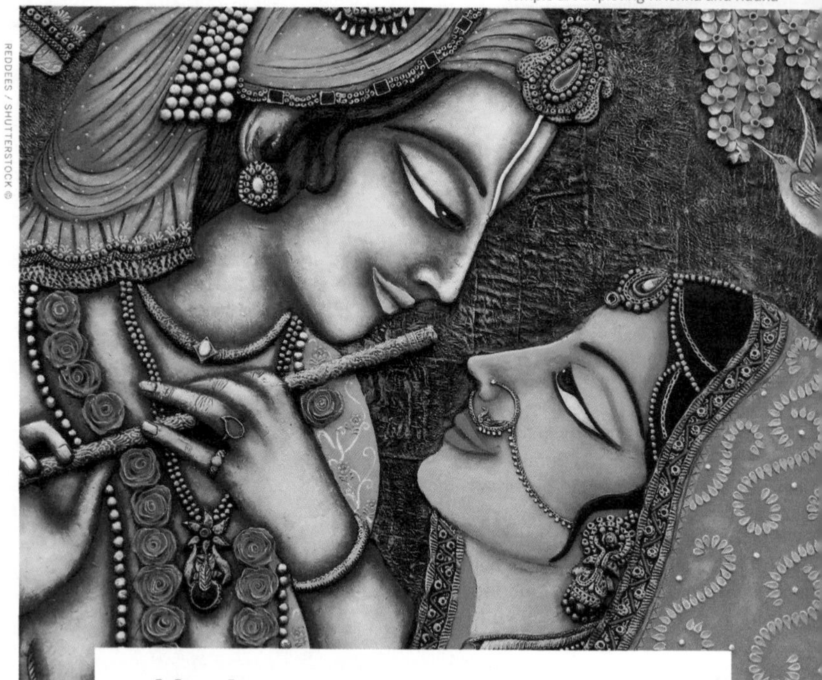

Understanding Hinduism

Hinduism, India's major faith, is practised by around 80% of the population. It has no central authority and is not a proselytising religion. Essentially, Hindus believe in Brahman, who is eternal, uncreated and infinite. Everything that exists emanates from, and ultimately returns to, Brahman. The multitude of gods and goddesses worshipped across India are merely manifestations of this formless phenomenon.

Brahman

The One; the ultimate reality. Brahman is formless, eternal and the source of all existence. Brahman is *nirguna* (without attributes), as opposed to all the other gods and goddesses, who are manifestations of Brahman and therefore *saguna* (with attributes).

Brahma

Only during the creation of the universe does Brahma play an active role. At other times he is in meditation. India has few Brahma temples today. His consort is **Saraswati**, the goddess of learning, and his vehicle is a swan. Brahma is generally depicted with four crowned and bearded heads.

Vishnu

The preserver or sustainer, Vishnu is associated with 'right action'. He protects and sustains all that is good in the world. He is usually depicted with four arms, holding a lotus, a conch shell (which can be blown like a trumpet, symbolising the cosmic vibration from which existence emanates), a discus and a mace. His consort is **Lakshmi**, the goddess of wealth, and his vehicle is **Garuda**, the man-bird creature. The Ganges is said to flow from his feet.

Fascinating Hindu Temples

Vittala Temple (p211), Hampi
Kailasa Temple (p146), Ellora
Vishwanath Temple (p236), Varanasi
Hadimba Temple (p252), Manali

Shiva

Shiva is the destroyer – to deliver salvation – without whom creation couldn't occur. Shiva's generative role is symbolised as the frequently worshipped lingam (phallus). With 1008 names, Shiva takes many forms, including Nataraja, lord of the *tandava* (cosmic victory dance), who paces out the creation and destruction of the cosmos.

Sometimes Shiva has snakes draped around his neck and is shown holding a trident (representing the Trimurti) while riding **Nandi**, his bull. Nandi symbolises power and potency, justice and moral order. Shiva's consort, **Parvati**, is also capable of taking many forms.

Other Prominent Deities

The Hindu pantheon is said to have a staggering 330 million deities. Elephant-headed **Ganesh**, son of Parvati and Shiva, is the god of good fortune, remover of obstacles, and patron of scribes (the broken tusk he holds was used to write sections of the Mahabharata). His animal vehicle is the ratlike **Mooshak**.

Krishna is an incarnation of Vishnu sent to earth to fight for good and combat evil. His dalliances with the *gopis* (milkmaids) and his love for **Radha** have inspired countless paintings and songs. Hero of the Mahabharata epic, Krishna is depicted with blue skin, and is often seen playing the flute.

Hanuman, king of the monkeys, is a hero of the Ramayana epic and loyal ally of its protagonist **Rama**. He embodies the concept of *bhakti* (devotion).

Among Shaivites (followers of the Shiva movement), *shakti,* the divine creative power of women, is worshipped as a force in its own right. It is embodied in the ancient goddess **Devi** (divine mother), who is also manifested as **Durga** and, in a fiercer evil-destroying incarnation, **Kali**.

Reincarnation

Hindus believe that earthly life is cyclical: you are born again and again (a process known as samsara). Living a righteous life and fulfilling your dharma (moral code of behaviour; social duty) will enhance your chances of being reborn into a higher caste and better circumstances. Alternatively, if enough bad karma has accumulated, rebirth may take animal form. But it's only as a human that you can gain sufficient self-knowledge to escape the cycle of reincarnation and achieve moksha (liberation).

Vegetarian thali

Delicious India

India's culinary terrain is deliciously diverse. The country has a particularly impressive array of vegetarian food, but carnivores won't be disappointed either, with plenty on offer from hearty curries to succulent kebabs. Adding flair to the national smorgasbord is the sheer variety of regional ingredients, spices and herbs.

Land of Spices

Christopher Columbus was actually searching for the black pepper of Kerala's Malabar Coast when he stumbled upon the Americas. The Kerala region still grows the finest quality of the world's favourite spice, and it's integral to most savoury Indian dishes.

Indian 'wet' dishes – commonly known as curries in the West – usually begin with the crackle of cumin, coriander or mustard seeds in hot oil and have turmeric as an essential spice. The green cardamom of Kerala's Western Ghats is commonly regarded as the world's best. Saffron, the dried stigmas of crocus flowers grown in Kashmir, is so light it takes more than 1500 hand-plucked flowers to yield just one gram.

Rice Paradise

Rice is a staple, especially in South and East India. Long-grain white rice varieties are the most popular, served hot with just about any 'wet' cooked dish. You'll find countless regional varieties that locals will claim to be the best in India, though this honour is usually conceded to basmati, a fragrant long-grain variety that's widely exported around the world. In South India, rice is often accompanied by curd to enrich the mix, and is usually served after you have finished with your meal.

Flippin' Fantastic Bread

While rice is paramount in the south, wheat is the mainstay in the north. Roti is the generic term for Indian-style bread, and is also used interchangeably with chapati to describe the most common variety, an unleavened round bread made with whole-wheat flour and cooked on a *tawa* (hotplate). *Paratha* is a layered pan-fried flat bread, that may be stuffed, and makes for a hearty breakfast. *Puri* – puffy fried bread pillows – are another popular sauce soaker-upper. Naan is a larger, thicker bread, baked in a tandoor and usually eaten with meaty sauces or kebabs.

Street Food

Tucking into street eats is a highlight of travelling in India. Whatever the time of day, vendors are frying, boiling, roasting, peeling, simmering or baking different foods to lure peckish passers-by. The fare can be as simple as peanuts roasted in hot sand, or a cavalcade of taste like *chhole bhature* (puffed bread served with spicy chickpeas and dipped in fragrant sauce).

To avoid tummy troubles:

- Avoid dirty-looking stalls or ones that locals are avoiding (places popular with families are probably your safest bets).
- Unless a place is reputable (and busy), it's best to avoid eating meat from the street.
- Don't be tempted by glistening pre-sliced fruit, whose luscious veneer comes from regular dousing of (often dubious) water.

Dhal-icious!

The whole of India is united in its love for dhal (curried lentils or pulses). You may encounter up to 60 different pulses: the most common are *channa* (chickpeas); tiny yellow or green ovals called *moong* (mung beans); salmon-coloured *masoor* (red lentils); the ochre-coloured southern favourite, *tuvar* (yellow lentils; also known as *arhar*); *rajma* (kidney beans); *urad* (black gram or lentils); and *lobhia* (black-eyed peas).

Meaty Matters

Although India probably has more vegetarians than the rest of the world combined, it still has an extensive repertoire of carnivorous fare. Chicken, lamb and mutton (which is sometimes actually goat) are the mainstays; religious taboos forbid beef to devout Hindus and pork to Muslims.

In northern India, you'll come across meat-dominated, spicy Mughlai cuisine, which includes rich curries, kebabs, koftas (meatballs) and biryanis, and traces its history back to the Mughal empire. Tandoori meat dishes are another North Indian favourite. The name is derived from the clay oven, or tandoor, in which the marinated meat is cooked.

Deep-Sea Delights

Seafood is particularly prominent on the west coast, from Mumbai south to Kerala, which is the biggest fishing state. Goa has particularly succulent prawns and fiery fish curries, and the fishing communities of the Konkan Coast – between Goa and Mumbai – are renowned for their seafood recipes. Fish is also king in West Bengal, a state puddled with ponds and lakes.

Fruit & Veg

Sabzi (vegetables) is a word recognised in every Indian vernacular. They're generally cooked *sukhi* (dry) or *tari* (in a sauce).

Potatoes are ubiquitous and popularly cooked with various masalas (spice mixes) or other vegetables, or mashed and fried for the street snack *aloo tikki* (mashed-potato patties), or cooked with cauliflower to make *aloo gobi* (potato-and-cauliflower curry). Fresh green peas turn up stir-fried with other vegetables in pilaus and biryanis and in one of North India's signature dishes, *mattar paneer* (unfermented-cheese-and-pea curry). Also popular is *saag* (a generic term for leafy greens), which can include mustard, spinach and fenugreek.

India's fruit basket is bountiful. Luscious tropical fruits such as pineapples and papayas abound along the southern coast. Peak mango season is April and May, with India offering more than 500 juicy varieties.

Dear Dairy

Milk and milk products make a huge contribution to Indian cuisine: *dahi* (curd/yoghurt) is commonly served with meals and is great for subduing heat; paneer is a godsend for the vegetarian majority; lassi is one in a host of nourishing sweet and savoury beverages; ghee is the traditional and pure cooking medium; and some of the finest *mithai* (Indian sweets) are made with milk.

Vegan Basics

India excels when it comes to vegetarian fare. There's little understanding of veganism (the term 'pure vegetarian' means without eggs), and animal products such as milk, butter, ghee and curd are included in most Indian dishes. If you are vegan, your first problem is likely to be getting the cook to understand your requirements, though big hotels and larger cities are getting better at catering for vegans.

For further information, try Vegan India (www.veganindia.net).

Sweet at Heart

India has a colourful kaleidoscope of *mithai* (Indian sweets), often sticky and sinfully sugary. The main categories are *barfi* (a fudgelike milk-based sweet), soft *halwa* (made with vegetables, cereals, lentils, nuts or fruit), *ladoos* (sweet balls made with gram flour and semolina), and sweets made from *chhana* (unpressed paneer), such as *rasgulla*. An equally scrumptious offering is crunchy *jalebi* (coils of deep-fried batter dunked in sugar syrup; served hot).

Dancers, Rajasthan

Architecture & the Arts

India's magnificent artistic heritage is a reflection of its richly diverse ethnic groups and traditions. From the exquisite body art of mehndi (henna) to soulful chants in ancient temples, the wealth of creative expression is a highlight of India travel. Many artists today fuse ancient and modern techniques to create work that is edgy and evocative.

Religious Architecture

For Hindus, a temple essentially represents a map of the universe. At the centre is an unadorned space, the *garbhagriha* (inner sanctum), providing a residence for the temple's deity and symbolising the 'womb-cave' of the universe's origin. Above a Hindu temple's shrine rises a tower – a stepped *vimana* in South India, a curvilinear *sikhara* in North India.

Jain temples can resemble Hindu ones from the outside, but inside they're often a riot of sculptural ornamentation, the very opposite of ascetic austerity.

Buddhist shrines have their own unique features. Stupas, composed of a solid hemisphere topped by a spire, essentially evolved from burial mounds. They served as repositories for relics of the Buddha and, later, other venerated souls. Some have a *chaitya* (assembly hall) leading up to the stupa itself.

★ Magnificent Megastructures

Taj Mahal, Agra (p66)

Humayun's Tomb, Delhi (p48)

Kailasa Temple, Ellora (p146)

Basilica of Bom Jesus, Goa (p158)

Vittala Temple, Hampi (p211)

Basilica de Bom Jesus, Goa (p158)

India has a wealth of Islamic sacred sites. The Mughals uniquely melded Persian, Indian and provincial styles. Renowned examples include Humayun's Tomb (p48) in Delhi, Agra Fort (p78), and the ancient fortified city of Fatehpur Sikri. Emperor Shah Jahan was responsible for some of India's most spectacular architectural creations, most notably the Taj Mahal (p66).

Music

Indian classical music traces its roots back to Vedic times, when religious poems chanted by priests were first collated in an anthology called the Rig-Veda. Over the millennia classical music has been shaped by many influences, and the legacy today divides into Carnatic (characteristic of South India) and Hindustani (the classical style of North India, influenced by Persian conventions from Mughal times) music. With common origins, they share a number of features. Both use the raga (the melodic shape of the music) and *tala* (the rhythmic meter characterised by the number of beats) as a basis for composition and improvisation; *tintal,* for example, has a *tala* of 16 beats. The audience follows the *tala* by clapping at the appropriate beat, which in *tintal* is at beats one, five and 13. There's no clap at the beat of nine; that's the *khali* (empty section), which is indicated by a wave of the hand.

Carnatic and Hindustani music are performed by small ensembles, generally of three to six musicians, and have many instruments in common. The most striking difference, at least for those unfamiliar with them, is Carnatic music's greater use of voice.

Dance

The ancient Indian art of dance is traditionally linked to mythology and classical literature.

Classical dance is based on well-defined traditional disciplines. Some major classical styles:

Bharatanatyam Originated in Tamil Nadu, and has been embraced throughout India.

Kathak With Hindu and Islamic influences, Kathak suffered a period of notoriety when it moved from the courts into houses where nautch (dancing) girls tantalised audiences with renditions of the Krishna-and-Radha love story. It was restored as a serious art form in the 20th century.

Kathakali Has its roots in Kerala; it's essentially a kind of drama based on mythological subjects.

India folk dance ranges from the high-spirited bhangra of Punjab to the theatrical dummy-horse dances of Karnataka and Tamil Nadu.

Cinema

India's film industry is the biggest in the world – twice as big as Hollywood – with around 2000 feature films produced in the country annually. Mumbai (Bombay), the Hindi-language film capital, aka Bollywood, is the biggest, but India's other major film-producing cities – Chennai (Kollywood), Hyderabad (Tollywood) and Bengaluru (Sandalwood) – also have considerable output.

Mainstream 'masala' movies – named for their 'spice mix' of elements – are designed to have something for everyone, blending romance, action, slapstick humour and moral themes. They are often tear-jerkers, packed with dramatic twists and interspersed with numerous song-and-dance performances. Indian films made for the local market eschew explicit sex, and admit very little kissing, but lack of overt eroticism is often compensated for by heroines dressed in skimpy attire, and plenty of intense flirting and innuendo.

Some Indian art house films, usually more socially and politically relevant than their commercial cousins, and made on infinitely smaller budgets, win kudos at global film festivals. In 2013, *Lunchbox*, a non-Bollywood romantic comedy written and directed by Ritesh Batra, won the Critics' Week Viewers' Choice Award (Grand Rail) at Cannes.

Painting

The Indo-Persian style – characterised by geometric design coupled with flowing form – arose in Islamic royal courts, with the Persian influence blossoming after artisans fled to India following the 1507 Uzbek attack on Herat (in present-day Afghanistan).

The development of the characteristic Mughal style of painting is generally credited to the third Mughal emperor, Akbar (r 1556–1605), who recruited artists from far and wide. Often in colourful miniature form, Mughal painting depicts court life, architecture, nature and battle and hunting scenes, and also embraced detailed portraits. As Mughal power and wealth declined, many artists moved to Rajasthan where the Rajasthani school of miniature painting developed from the late 17th century.

In the 21st century, paintings by modern Indian artists have been selling at record numbers (and prices) around the world. One very successful online art auction house is Saffronart (www.saffronart.com). The larger cities, especially Delhi and Mumbai, are India's contemporary art centres, with a range of galleries.

Literature

India has a long tradition of literature in Sanskrit (today used mainly as a ceremonial language in religious contexts) such as the Vedas, scriptures that began to be compiled over 3000 years ago, and the epic tales of the Ramayana, Mahabharata and the Puranas.

The writer mostly credited with first propelling India's cultural richness onto the world stage is the Nobel Prize winner, Bengali Rabindranath Tagore (1861–1941), with works such as *Gitanjali* (Song Offerings), *Gora* (Fair-Faced) and *Ghare-Baire* (The Home and the World).

India has an ever-growing list of internationally acclaimed contemporary authors. Several India-born authors have won the prestigious Man Booker Prize, the most recent being Aravind Adiga, who won in 2008 for his debut novel, *The White Tiger*. The prize went to Kiran Desai in 2006 for *The Inheritance of Loss;* Kiran's mother, novelist Anita Desai, has thrice been a Booker Prize nominee. Arundhati Roy won the 1997 Booker for *The God of Small Things*, while Salman Rushdie took this coveted award in 1981 for *Midnight's Children*.

Giant Malabar squirrel, Nagarhole National Park

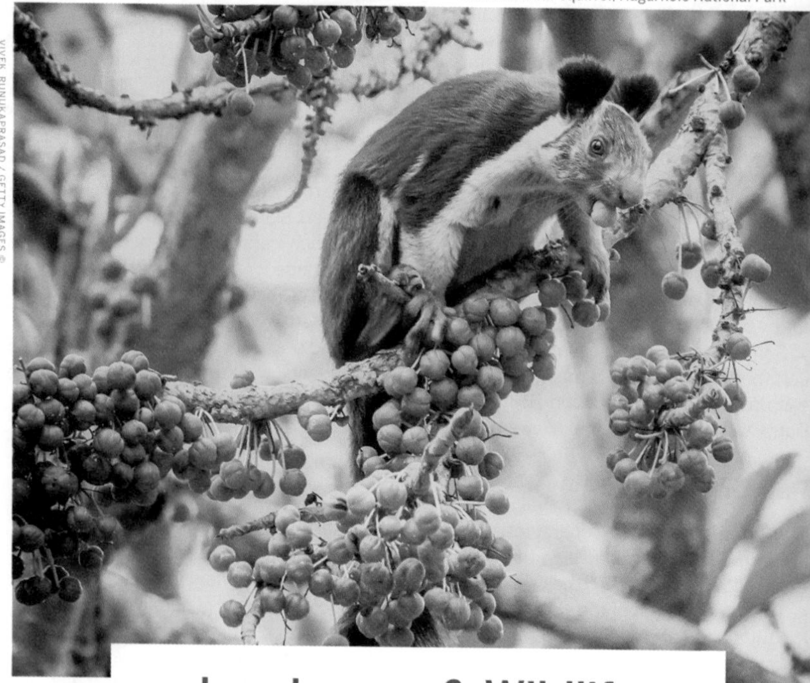

Landscape & Wildlife

India is the world's seventh-largest country, with everything from tropical jungles to arid deserts to icy mountain peaks. It is known for its big, bold species – tigers, elephants, rhinos, leopards and bears. But there's also a collection of colourful birds, and some endangered wildlife, such as the Ganges river dolphin and the Asiatic lion.

The Land

Three major features shape India's topography: the Himalaya, along the northern borders; the alluvial plains of the sacred River Ganges across the north of the country; and the Deccan, an elevated plateau that forms the core of India's triangular southern peninsula.

The Big Beasts

Asian elephants are revered in Hindu custom, and were once domesticated and put to work. Many still survive in the wild. Because they migrate long distances in search of food, these 3000kg animals require huge parks; some of the best for elephant viewing are **Corbett Tiger Reserve** in Uttarakhand and **Nagarhole National Park** in Karnataka.

There are far fewer one-horned rhinos left, and two-thirds of the world's total population can be found in **Kaziranga National Park** in Assam, where over 2000 wander the lush grasslands.

Then there's the tiger. This awesome, iconic animal is critically endangered but can be seen, if you're lucky, at tiger reserves around the country – your best chances are in Ranthambhore National Park (p114) and some tiger reserves in Madhya Pradesh.

Project Tiger

When naturalist Jim Corbett first raised the alarm in the 1930s, no one reckoned that tigers would ever be threatened. It was believed there were once 40,000 tigers in India. Then came Independence, which put guns into the hands of villagers, who then pushed into formerly off-limits hunting reserves seeking highly profitable tiger skins. When an official count was made in 1972, there were only 1800 tigers left, prompting Indira Gandhi to set up Project Tiger (National Tiger Conservation Authority; http://projecttiger.nic.in). It has since established 50 tiger reserves to protect the predator and other animals sharing its habitat. Due to relentless poaching, however, tiger numbers dipped to a low of 1706 in 2011, but the most-recent tiger census from January 2015 shows an encouraging rise to 2226.

Other Mammals

Tigers apart, India is home to 14 other cat species. Several thousand leopards are scattered among forests throughout the country. Up to 600 highly elusive snow leopards (a separate species) inhabit Himalayan regions. The Asiatic lion, on the brink of extinction a century ago, now seems to be doing quite well in Gujarat's Sasan Gir National Park, with a population of over 600.

The most abundant animals you'll see in India are deer, antelope and primates. India's primates range from the extremely rare hoolock gibbons and golden langur of Northeast India to species that are so common as to be pests – most notably the stocky and aggressive rhesus macaque and the grey langur.

Endangered Species

Wildlife is severely threatened by poaching and habitat loss. One report suggested India had over 500 threatened species, including 53 species of mammals, 78 birds, 22 reptiles, 68 amphibians, 35 fish, 22 invertebrates and 247 plants.

All of India's wild cats face extinction from habitat loss and poaching for the lucrative trade in skins and body parts for Chinese medicine (a tiger carcass can fetch upwards of UK£32,000). Even highly protected rhinos are poached for the medicine trade – rhino horn is highly valued as an aphrodisiac in China and for making dagger handles in the Gulf.

Ivory poaching has reportedly been responsible for between 45% and 70% of all male elephant deaths in three Indian provinces; we implore you not to support this trade by buying ivory souvenirs.

Birds

With well over 1200 bird species, India is a birdwatcher's dream. Wherever critical habitat has been preserved in the midst of human activity, you might see phenomenal numbers of birds in one location. Winter can be a particularly good time, as wetlands throughout the country host northern migrants arriving for the lush subtropical warmth of the Indian peninsula. Throughout the year, wherever you're travelling, look for colourful kingfishers, barbets, sunbirds, parakeets and magpies, or the blue flash of an Indian roller.

★ Parks & Reserves

Ranthambhore National Park, Rajasthan

Kaziranga National Park, Assam

Corbett Tiger Reserve, Uttarakhand

Bandhavgarh Tiger Reserve, Madhya Pradesh

Nagarhole National Park, Karnataka

Water buffalo, Kaziranga National Park

Plants

India was once almost entirely covered in forest; now its forest cover is estimated to be around 22%. The country still has nearly 50,000 plant species. Those on the southern peninsula show Malaysian ancestry, while desert plants in Rajasthan are more clearly allied with the Middle East, and the Himalayan conifer forests have European and Siberian origins.

Nearly all the lowland forests are types of tropical forest, with native sal forests forming the mainstay of the timber industry. Some tropical forests are true rainforest, staying green year-round, but most forests lose their canopies during the hot, dry months of April and May (often the best time to spot wildlife).

National Parks & Wildlife Sanctuaries

India has 104 national parks and 543 wildlife sanctuaries, comprising around 5% of its territory. There are also 18 biosphere reserves, overlapping many of the national parks and sanctuaries, providing safe migration channels for wildlife and allowing scientists to monitor biodiversity.

Visiting a national park or sanctuary is an experience that can stay with you for a lifetime, especially if you come face-to-face with a wild elephant, rhino or tiger. Your visits also add momentum to efforts to protect India's natural environment. Wildlife reserves tend to be off the beaten track and infrastructure can be limited – book transport and accommodation in advance, and check opening times, permit requirements and entry fees before you visit.

Facing the Future

India is grappling with a growing dilemma: how to modernise and expand economically without destroying what's left of its environment or adding to the global climate problem.

Prime Minister Modi has made it his personal mission to clean up the heavily polluted River Ganges. He has launched the much-publicised Swachh Bharat campaign to reduce rubbish pollution, and supports large-scale solar-power generation. His government aims to increase renewable energy capacity to 175 gigawatts by around 2022. But it faces challenges when it comes to domestic coal mining (a major source of greenhouse gases).

Ganges River, Varanasi (p229)

ZENOBILLIS / GETTY IMAGES ©

Survival Guide

DIRECTORY A–Z 292

Accessible Travel 292
Accommodation 292
Climate 293
Customs Regulations 293
Electricity 294
Food 294
Health 294
Insurance 297
Internet Access 298
Legal Matters 298
LGBT+ Travellers 299
Money 299
Opening Hours 300
Photography 301
Public Holidays 301
Safe Travel 301
Solo Travellers 303
Taxes & Refunds 303
Telephone 303
Time 304
Toilets 304
Visas 304
Weights & Measures 305
Women Travellers 305

TRANSPORT 308

Getting There & Away 308
Getting Around 308

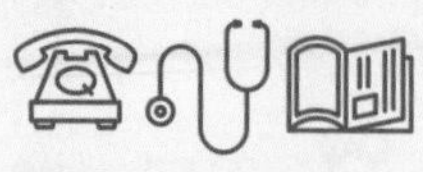

Directory A–Z

Accessible Travel

If you have a physical disability or are vision impaired, the difficulties of travel in India can be exacerbated. If your mobility is considerably restricted, you may like to ease the stress by travelling with an able-bodied companion. One way that India makes it easier to travel with a disability is the access to employed assistance – you could hire an assistant, or a car and driver to get around, for example.

Accessibility Some restaurants and offices have ramps, but most tend to have at least one step. Staircases are often steep; lifts frequently stop at mezzanines between floors.

Accommodation Wheelchair-friendly hotels are almost exclusively top end. Make enquiries before travelling and book ground-floor rooms at hotels that lack adequate facilities.

Footpaths Where footpaths exist, they can be riddled with holes, littered with debris and crowded. If using crutches, bring along spare rubber caps.

Transport Hiring a car with driver will make moving around a lot easier; if you use a wheelchair, make sure the car-hire company can provide an appropriate vehicle.

The following organisations may provide further information:

Accessible Journeys (www.accessiblejourneys.com)

Disabled Holidays (www.disabledholidays.com)

Travel Eyes (www.traveleyes-international.com)

Enable Holidays (www.enableholidays.com)

Mobility International USA (www.miusa.org)

Download Lonely Planet's free Accessible Travel guide from http://lptravel.to/AccessibleTravel.

Book Your Stay Online

For more accommodation reviews by Lonely Planet authors, check out http://hotels.lonelyplanet.com/india. You'll find independent reviews, as well as recommendations on the best places to stay. Best of all, you can book online.

Accommodation

Accommodation in India ranges from new-style hostels, with charging stations and soft pillows, to opulent palaces with private plunge pools, and from dodgy dives with bucket showers to guesthouses with superlative home cooking.

Prices are highest in large cities (eg Delhi, Mumbai), and lowest in rural areas. Costs are also seasonal – hotel prices can drop by 20% to 50% outside peak season.

Reservations

Except during peak seasons in particular places, reservations are seldom essential. It's very rare to arrive in a town and not be able to find somewhere to stay; also, you usually get the cheapest price as a walk-in guest, particularly for budget accommodation.

Seasons

- High season usually coincides with the best weather for the area's sights and activities – normally spring and autumn (March to May and September to November) in the mountains, and the cooler months (around November to mid-February) in the plains.
- In areas popular with foreign tourists, there's an additional peak period over Christmas and New Year; reserve well ahead at this time.
- Many temple towns have additional peak seasons around major festivals and pilgrimages.
- At other times significant discounts may be available; it's worth asking for one if your hotel seems quiet.

- Some hotels in places like Goa close during the monsoon period; hill stations such as Manali close in winter.

Budget & Midrange Hotels

- Shared bathrooms (often with squat toilets) are usually only found at the cheapest lodgings.
- If you're staying in budget places, bring your own sheet or sleeping-bag liner, towel and soap.
- Insect repellent, a torch (flashlight) and padlock are essential accessories in many budget hotels.
- Sound pollution can be irksome (especially in urban hubs); pack earplugs and request a room that doesn't face a busy road.

Hostels

There is an ever-increasing array of excellent backpacker hostels across India, notably in Delhi, Varanasi, Goa and Kerala, all high quality, with air-con dorms, cafe/bar, lockers, and free wi-fi. They're hugely popular with travellers wanting to connect with like-minded folk. They'll usually have mixed dorms, plus a female-only option. Impressive chains with branches dotted over India include **Stops** (www.gostops.com), **Backpacker Panda** (www.backpackerpanda.com), **Moustache** (www.moustachehostel.com) and **Zostel** (www.zostel.com).

Top-End & Heritage Hotels

India's top-end properties are stupendously fabulous, creating a cushioning bubble from the outside world, and ranging from wow-factor five-star chain hotels to historic palaces.

In states such as Gujarat and Odisha (Orissa) there are increasing numbers of converted heritage properties.

Customs Regulations

You're supposed to declare Indian rupees in excess of ₹10,000, any amount of cash over US$5000, or a total amount of currency over US$10,000 on arrival. You're also prohibited from importing more than one laptop, more than 2L of alcohol, more than 100 cigarettes or equivalent, or gifts and souvenirs worth over ₹8000.

Climate

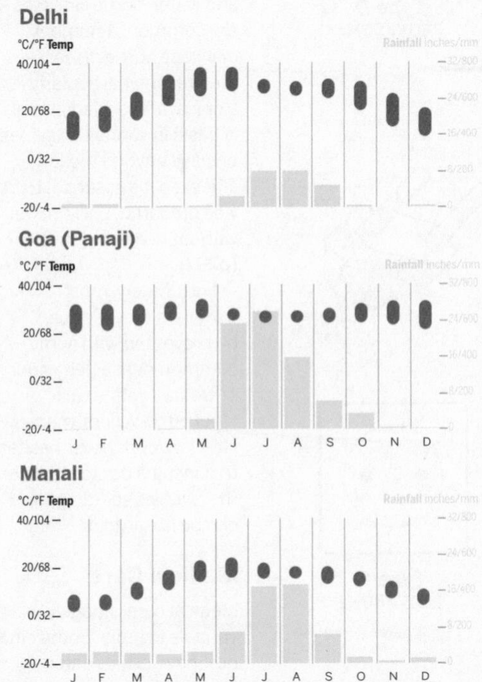

Electricity

Type D
220V/50Hz

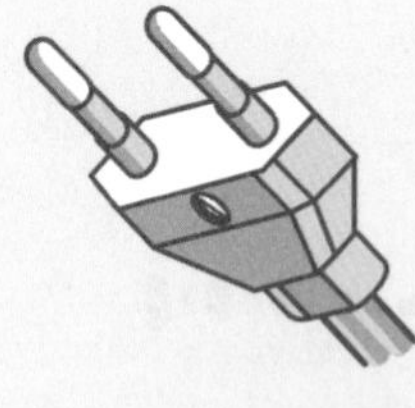

Type C
220V/50Hz

Food

Prices refer to the cost of a main course.

$ less than ₹150

$$ ₹150–₹300

$$$ more than ₹300

Health

There is huge geographical variation in India, so in different areas, heat, cold and altitude can cause health problems. Hygiene is poor in most regions so food and water-borne illnesses are common. A number of insect-borne diseases are present, particularly in tropical areas. Medical care is basic in various areas (especially beyond the larger cities) so it's essential to be well prepared. Don't travel without health insurance (p297).

Fortunately, most travellers' illnesses can be prevented with some common-sense behaviour or treated with a well-stocked travellers' medical kit – however, never hesitate to consult a doctor while on the road, as self-diagnosis can be hazardous.

Medical Care

Medical care is hugely variable in India. Some cities now have clinics catering specifically to travellers and expatriates; these clinics are usually more expensive than local medical facilities, and offer a higher standard of care. Additionally, the staff members know the local system, including reputable hospitals and specialists. They may also liaise with insurance companies should you require evacuation. It's usually difficult to find reliable medical care in rural areas.

Self-treatment may be appropriate if your problem is minor (eg traveller's diarrhoea), you are carrying the relevant medication, and you cannot attend a recommended clinic. If you suspect a serious disease, especially malaria, travel to the nearest quality facility.

Before buying medication over the counter, check the use-by date, and ensure that the packet is sealed and properly stored (eg not exposed to the sunshine).

Drinking Water

- Never drink tap water.
- Bottled water is generally safe – check the seal is intact at purchase.
- Avoid ice unless you know it has been made hygienically.
- Boiling water (a full rolling boil for one minute) is usually the most efficient method of purifying it.

Infectious Diseases

Malaria

This is a serious and potentially deadly disease. Before you travel, seek

Vaccinations

The only vaccine required by international regulations is **yellow fever**. Proof of vaccination will only be required if you have visited a country in the yellow-fever zone within the six days prior to entering India.

The World Health Organization (WHO) recommends the following vaccinations for travellers going to India (as well as being up to date with measles, mumps and rubella vaccinations):

Adult diphtheria & tetanus Single booster recommended if none in the previous 10 years.

Hepatitis A Provides almost 100% protection for up to a year; a booster after 12 months provides at least another 20 years' protection.

Hepatitis B Now considered routine for most travellers. Given as three shots over six months. A rapid schedule is also available, as is a combined vaccination with Hepatitis A. In 95% of people lifetime protection results.

Polio Only one booster is required as an adult for lifetime protection. Inactivated polio vaccine is safe during pregnancy.

Typhoid Recommended for all travellers to India, even those only visiting urban areas. The vaccine offers around 70% protection, lasts for two to three years and comes as a single shot. Tablets are also available.

Varicella If you haven't had chickenpox, discuss this vaccination with your doctor.

Immunisations recommended for long-term travellers (more than one month) or those at special risk include **rabies** (three injections in all; a booster after one year will then provide 10 years' protection). Seek further advice from your doctor.

expert advice according to your itinerary (rural areas are especially risky) and on medication and side effects.

Malaria is caused by a parasite transmitted by the bite of an infected mosquito. The most important symptom of malaria is fever, but general symptoms, such as headache, diarrhoea, cough or chills, may also occur. Diagnosis can only be properly made by taking a blood sample.

Two strategies should be combined to prevent malaria: mosquito avoidance and antimalarial medications. Most people who catch malaria are taking inadequate or no antimalarial medication.

Travellers are advised to prevent mosquito bites by taking these steps:

- Use a DEET-based insect repellent on exposed skin. Wash this off at night – as long as you are sleeping under a mosquito net. Natural repellents such as citronella can be effective, but must be applied more frequently than products containing DEET.
- Choose accommodation with proper screens and fans (if not air-conditioned).
- Wear long sleeves and trousers in light colours.
- Use mosquito coils.

Other Diseases

Dengue Fever This mosquito-borne disease is becomingly increasingly problematic, especially in the cities. As there is no vaccine available it can only be prevented by avoiding mosquito bites at all times. Symptoms include high fever, severe headache and body ache and sometimes a rash and diarrhoea. Treatment is rest and paracetamol – do not take aspirin or ibuprofen as it increases the likelihood of haemorrhaging. Make sure you see a doctor to be diagnosed and monitored.

Hepatitis A This food- and water-borne virus infects the liver, causing jaundice (yellow skin and eyes), nausea and lethargy. There is no specific

Government Travel Advice

The following government websites offer travel advice and information on current hotspots.

Australian Department of Foreign Affairs (www.smartraveller.gov.au)

British Foreign Office (www.gov.uk/foreign-travel-advice)

Canadian Department of Foreign Affairs (www.voyage.gc.ca)

Dutch Ministry of Foreign Affairs (www.government.nl)

German Foreign Office (www.auswaertiges-amt.de)

Japanese Ministry of Foreign Affairs (www.mofa.go.jp)

New Zealand Ministry of Foreign Affairs & Trade (https://safetravel.govt.nz/health-and-travel)

Swiss Department of Foreign Affairs (www.eda.admin.ch)

US State Department (http://travel.state.gov)

treatment for hepatitis A, you just need to allow time for the liver to heal. All travellers to India should be vaccinated against hepatitis A.

Hepatitis B This sexually transmitted disease is spread by body fluids and can be prevented by vaccination. The long-term consequences can include liver cancer and cirrhosis.

HIV Spread via contaminated body fluids. Avoid unsafe sex, unsterile needles (including in medical facilities) and procedures such as tattoos. The growth rate of HIV in India is one of the highest in the world.

Rabies This fatal disease is spread by the bite or possibly even the lick of an infected animal – most commonly a dog or monkey. You should seek medical advice immediately after any animal bite and commence postexposure treatment. If an animal bites you, gently wash the wound with soap and water, and apply iodine-based antiseptic. If you are not prevaccinated you will need to receive rabies immunoglobulin as soon as possible; this is very difficult to obtain in much of India.

Typhoid Serious bacterial infection spread via food and water. It gives a high and slowly progressive fever and headache, and may be accompanied by a dry cough and stomach pain. It is diagnosed by blood tests and treated with antibiotics. Vaccination is not 100% effective, so you must still be careful with what you eat and drink.

Travellers' Diarrhoea

This is by far the most common problem affecting travellers in India – between 30% and 70% of people will suffer from it within two weeks of starting their trip. It's usually caused by bacteria, and thus responds promptly to treatment with antibiotics.

Traveller's diarrhoea is defined as the passage of more than three watery bowel actions within 24 hours, plus at least one other symptom, such as fever, cramps, nausea, vomiting or feeling generally unwell.

Treatment consists of staying well hydrated; rehydration solutions like Gastrolyte are the best for this. Antibiotics such as ciprofloxacin or azithromycin should kill the bacteria quickly. Seek medical attention quickly if you do not respond to an appropriate antibiotic.

Loperamide is just a 'stopper' and doesn't get to the cause of the problem. It can be helpful, though (eg if you have to go on a long bus ride). Don't take loperamide if you have a fever or blood in your stools.

Amoebic dysentery Amoebic dysentery is very rare in travellers but is quite often misdiagnosed by poor-quality labs. Symptoms are similar to bacterial diarrhoea: fever, bloody diarrhoea and generally feeling unwell. You should always seek reliable medical care if you have blood in your diarrhoea. Treatment involves two drugs: tinidazole or metronidazole to kill the parasite in your gut and then a second drug to kill the cysts. If left untreated, complications such as liver or gut abscesses can occur.

Giardiasis Giardia is a parasite that is relatively common in travellers. Symptoms include nausea, bloating, excess gas, fatigue and intermittent diarrhoea. The parasite will eventually go away if left untreated, but this can take months; the best advice is to seek medical treatment. The treatment of choice is tinidazole, with metronidazole a second-line option.

Environmental Hazards

Food

Dining out brings with it the possibility of contracting diarrhoea. Ways to help avoid food-related illness:

- avoid tap water, and food rinsed in it
- eat only freshly cooked food
- avoid shellfish and buffets
- peel fruit
- cook vegetables
- soak salads in iodine water for at least 20 minutes
- eat in busy restaurants with a high turnover of customers.

Heat

Many parts of India, especially down south, are hot and humid throughout the year. For most visitors it takes around two weeks to comfortably adapt to the hot climate. Swelling of the feet and ankles is common, as are muscle cramps caused by excessive sweating. Prevent these by avoiding dehydration and excessive activity in the heat. Don't eat salt tablets (they aggravate the gut); drinking rehydration solution or eating salty food helps. Treat cramps by resting, rehydrating with double-strength rehydration solution and gently stretching.

Dehydration is the main contributor to heat exhaustion. Recovery is usually rapid and it is common to feel weak for some days afterwards. Symptoms include:

- feeling weak
- headache
- irritability
- nausea or vomiting
- sweaty skin
- a fast, weak pulse
- normal or slightly elevated body temperature.

Treatment:

- get out of the heat
- fan the sufferer
- apply cool, wet cloths to the skin
- lay the sufferer flat with their legs raised
- rehydrate with water containing one quarter-teaspoon of salt per litre.

Heatstroke is a serious medical emergency requiring urgent attention. Symptoms include:

- weakness
- nausea
- a hot, dry body
- temperature of over 41°C
- dizziness
- confusion
- loss of coordination
- seizures
- eventual collapse.

Treatment:

- get out of the heat
- fan the sufferer
- apply cool, wet cloths to the skin or ice to the body, especially to the groin and armpits.

Prickly heat is a common skin rash in the tropics, caused by sweat trapped under the skin. Treat it by moving out of the heat for a few hours and by having cool showers. Creams and ointments clog the skin so they should be avoided. Locally bought prickly-heat powder can be helpful.

Insurance

- Comprehensive travel insurance to cover theft, loss and medical problems (as well as air evacuation) is strongly recommended.
- Some policies exclude potentially dangerous activities such as scuba diving, skiing, motorcycling, paragliding and even trekking; read the fine print.
- Some trekking agents may only accept customers who have cover for emergency helicopter evacuation.
- If you plan to hire a motorcycle in India, make sure that the rental policy includes at least third-party insurance.

- Check in advance whether your insurance policy will pay doctors and hospitals directly or reimburse you later (keep all documentation for your claim).
- It's crucial to get a police report in India if you've had anything stolen; insurance companies may refuse to reimburse you without one.
- Worldwide travel insurance is available at www.lonelyplanet.com/bookings. You can buy, extend and claim online anytime – even if you're already on the road.

Internet Access

Wi-fi/3G/4G access is widely available; wi-fi is usually free but some places charge. Many restaurants and cafes offer wi-fi, including Cafe Coffee Day branches.

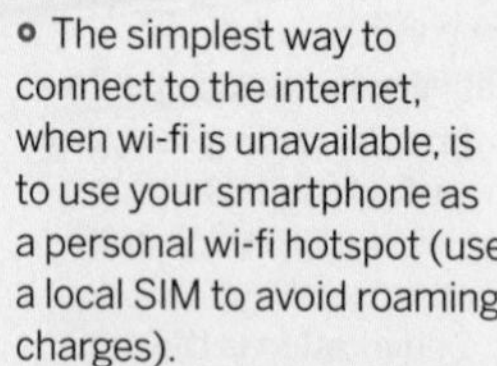

- The simplest way to connect to the internet, when wi-fi is unavailable, is to use your smartphone as a personal wi-fi hotspot (use a local SIM to avoid roaming charges).
- Alternatively, companies that offer prepaid wireless 3G/4G modem sticks (dongles) include Reliance, Airtel and Vodafone. To connect you have to submit your proof of identity and address in India; activation can take up to 24 hours.
- Make sure your destinations are covered by your service provider.

Legal Matters

If you're in a sticky legal situation, contact your embassy immediately. However, be aware that all your embassy may be able to do is monitor

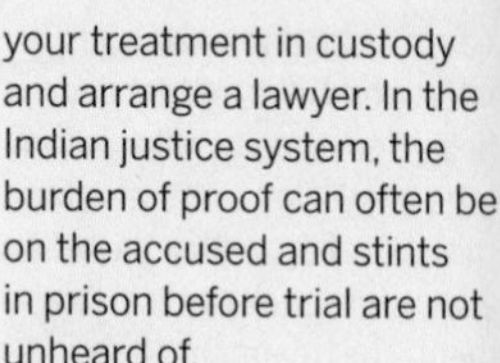

your treatment in custody and arrange a lawyer. In the Indian justice system, the burden of proof can often be on the accused and stints in prison before trial are not unheard of.

Drugs

Possession of any illegal drug is regarded as a criminal offence, which will result in a custodial sentence. This may be up to 10 years for possession, even for personal use, or up to 20 years if it's deemed the purpose was for sale or distribution. There's also usually a hefty fine on top.

Police

You should always carry your passport; police are entitled to ask you for identification at any time.

If you're arrested for an alleged offence and asked for a bribe, be aware that it is illegal to pay a bribe in India. Many people deal with an on-the-spot fine by just paying it, to avoid trumped-up charges. Corruption is rife, so the less you have to do with local police the better; try to avoid all potentially risky situations.

Smoking

- Smoking in public places is illegal, but this is rarely enforced; if caught you may be fined ₹200, which could rise to ₹500.
- People can smoke inside their homes and in most open spaces such as streets

Prohibited Exports

To protect India's cultural heritage, the export of certain antiques is prohibited, especially those that are verifiably more than 100 years old. Reputable antique dealers know the laws and can make arrangements for an export-clearance certificate for old items that are OK to export. Detailed information on prohibited items can be found on the Archaeological Survey of India (ASI) website (http://asi.nic.in).

The Indian Wildlife Protection Act bans any form of wildlife trade. Don't buy any product that endangers threatened species and habitats – doing so can result in heavy fines and even imprisonment. This includes ivory, shahtoosh shawls (made from the down of chirus or rare Tibetan antelopes) and anything made from the fur, skin, horns or shell of any endangered species. Products made from certain rare plants are also banned.

(heed any signs stating otherwise).

- Vaping (smoking e-cigarettes) is banned in Jammu, Kashmir, Karnataka, Punjab, Maharashtra and Kerala, and this is quite strongly enforced.

LGBT+ Travellers

In a landmark decision in 2018, India's Supreme Court legalised gay sex in India, scrapping a colonial-era law under which gay sex was categorised an 'unnatural offence'. The court also ruled that discrimination on the basis of sexual orientation is a fundamental violation of rights.

A 2014 ruling provided legal recognition of a third gender in India, a step towards increased acceptance of the large yet marginalised *hijra* (transgender) population.

Despite these rulings, India's LGBT+ scene remains relatively discreet, though less so in cities such as Delhi. The capital hosts the annual Queer Pride event in November and also has a men-only gay guesthouse, Mister & Art House (www.misterandarthouse.com), in South Delhi. It's run by Delhi-based gay travel agency Indjapink (www.indjapink.co.in), which offers tailor-made tours. Serene Journeys (www.serenejourneys.co) is also recommended as a gay-friendly travel agency.

Nevertheless, LGBT+ visitors should be discreet in this conservative country. Public displays of affection are frowned upon for both homosexual and heterosexual couples.

Websites & Support Groups

Bombay Dost (http://bombaydost.co.in) Annual LGBTQ India magazine that's been running since 1990.

Gay Bombay (www.gaybombay.org) Lists gay events and offers support and advice.

Gaysi Zine (http://gaysifamily.com) Thoughtful monthly magazine and website featuring gay writing and issues.

Indian Dost (www.indiandost.com/gay.php) News and information, including contact groups in India.

Orinam (orinam.net) Has helpful, up-to-date info on LGBT+ support, events and pride marches in Chennai and Tamil Nadu.

Queer Azaadi Mumbai (http://queerazaadi.wordpress.com) Mumbai's queer-pride blog, with news.

Queer Ink (www.queer-ink.com) Online bookstore and multimedia platform for India's LGBT+ community.

Salvation Star (https://en-gb.facebook.com/SalvationStar) An LGBT+ Facebook community in Mumbai that organises and promotes gay events and parties.

Money

ATMs widely available; carry cash as backup, especially in remote regions. Don't accept damaged banknotes: they won't be accepted by others.

ATMs

- Visa, MasterCard, Cirrus and Maestro are the most commonly accepted cards.
- ATMs at Axis Bank, Citibank, HDFC, HSBC, ICICI and State Bank of India recognise foreign cards. Other banks may accept major cards (Visa, MasterCard etc).
- The limit you may withdraw in one transaction can be as low as ₹2000, up to a maximum of usually ₹10,000. The higher the amount you withdraw, the less charges you will incur. Citibank ATMs are often the best for withdrawing a large amount of cash in one transaction.
- Notify your bank that you'll be using your card in India to avoid having it blocked; take along your bank's phone number in case.

Bargaining

Bargaining is a way of life in many contexts in India, including at markets and most shops. Keep things in perspective: haggle hard but not without a sense of humour. There are also plenty of more-upmarket shops and government emporiums where haggling is inappropriate, as prices are fixed. You'll usually have to agree to a price before hiring a taxi or autorickshaw, or a car and driver for longer trips.

Cash

- Major currencies such as US dollars, pounds sterling and euros are easy to change throughout India.
- Some banks also accept other currencies such as Australian and Canadian dollars and Swiss francs.
- Private money-changers deal with a wider range of currencies.
- When travelling off the beaten track, always carry an adequate stock of cash (including rupees).
- It can be tough getting change, so a stock of smaller currency (₹10, ₹20 and ₹50 notes) is invaluable.
- You can change leftover rupees into foreign currency most easily at the airport. You may have to present encashment certificates or credit-card/ATM receipts, and show your passport and airline ticket.

Credit Cards

- Credit cards are accepted at a growing number of shops, upmarket restaurants, and midrange and top-end hotels, and they can usually be used to pay for flights and train tickets.
- Cash advances on major credit cards are possible at some banks.
- MasterCard and Visa are the most widely accepted cards.

Currency

The Indian rupee (₹) is notionally divided into 100 paise. Coins usually come in denominations of ₹1, ₹2, ₹5 and ₹10 (the 1s and 2s look almost identical), while notes come in denominations of ₹5, ₹10, ₹20, ₹50, ₹100, ₹200, ₹500 and ₹2000.

The rupee is linked to a basket of currencies and has been subject to wide fluctuation in recent years. Check going rates online before your trip.

Exchange Rates

Australia	A$1	₹49
Canada	C$1	₹51
Euro zone	€1	₹80
Japan	¥100	₹64
New Zealand	NZ$1	₹47
UK	UK£1	₹89
USA	US$1	₹70

For current exchange rates, see www.xe.com

Money-changers

Private money-changers are usually open for longer hours than banks and are found almost everywhere (many also double as travel agents).

Hotels may also change money, but their rates are usually not as competitive.

Tipping

Restaurants & hotels Service fees are sometimes added to bills automatically; otherwise, 10% is reasonable.

Bellboys & train/airport porters ₹10 to ₹20.

Taxis & rickshaws Not expected, but it's good to tip drivers/riders who are honest about the fare.

Private drivers ₹200 per day for good service.

Trekking Per day: guides ₹350 to ₹500, porters ₹200 to ₹350.

Tour guides ₹200 to ₹350 per day is fair.

Opening Hours

The following are guidelines and may vary:

Banks (nationalised) 10am to 2pm/4pm Monday to Friday, to noon/1pm/4pm Saturday; closed second and fourth Saturday

Bars and clubs noon to 12.30am

Markets 10am to 7pm in major cities, with one closed day; rural markets once weekly, early morning to lunchtime

Post offices 9.30am to 5pm Monday to Saturday

Restaurants 8am to 10pm, or lunch (noon to 3pm) and dinner (7pm to 10/11pm)

Shops 10am to 7pm or 8pm, some closed Sunday

Museums/Sights Often closed Monday

Photography

Memory cards for digital cameras are available in most large cities and towns. However, quality is variable – some don't carry the advertised amount of data.

To be safe, regularly back up your memory card. If your camera isn't wi-fi–enabled, take a memory-card reader or USB stick with you.

- India is touchy about anyone taking photographs of military installations – this can include train stations, bridges, airports, military sites and sensitive border regions.
- Photography from the air is mostly OK, unless you're taking off from (or landing in) airports actively shared by defence forces.
- Many places of worship – such as monasteries, temples and mosques – also prohibit photography. Taking photos inside a shrine, at a funeral, at a religious ceremony or of people publicly bathing (including in rivers) can also be offensive – ask first.
- Flash photography may be prohibited in certain areas of a shrine or historical monument, or may not be permitted at all.
- It's not uncommon for people in touristy areas to ask for a posing fee in return for being photographed. Exercise your discretion in these situations. Ask first to avoid misunderstandings later.

Public Holidays

There are three official national public holidays – Republic Day, Independence Day and Gandhi's birthday (Gandhi Jayanti). Also celebrated are numerous other national or local holidays, many of them marking important days in various religions and falling on variable dates. The most important are the 'gazetted holidays' (listed) which are observed by central-government offices throughout India. On these days most businesses (offices, shops etc), banks and tourist sites close, but transport is usually unaffected. It's wise to make transport and hotel reservations well in advance if you intend visiting during major festivals.

Republic Day 26 January

Holi February/March

Ram Navami March/April

Mahavir Jayanti March/April

Good Friday March/April

Dr BL Ambedkar's Birthday 14 April

Buddha Purnima May

Eid al-Fitr May/June

Eid al-Adha July/August

Independence Day 15 August

Janmastami August/September

Muharram August/September

Dussehra September/October

Gandhi Jayanti 2 October

Diwali October/November

Guru Nanak Jayanti November

Eid-Milad-un-Nabi November/December

Christmas Day 25 December

Major Religious Festivals

Holi (Hindu) February/March

Easter Sunday (Christian) 12 April 2020, 4 April 2021

Mahavir Jayanti (Jain) March/April

Buddha Purnima (Buddhist) April/May

Eid al-Fitr (Muslim) May/June

Dussehra (Hindu) September/October

Diwali (Hindu) October/November

Guru Nanak Jayanti (Sikh) November

Christmas Day (Christian) 25 December

Safe Travel

- Travellers to India's major cities may fall prey to opportunistic crime, but many problems can be avoided with a bit of common sense and an appropriate amount of caution.

- Reports of sexual assaults have increased in recent years, so women should take care to avoid potentially risky situations.
- Have a look at the India branch of Lonely Planet's Thorn Tree forum (www.lonelyplanet.com/thorntree), where travellers often post timely warnings about problems hat they have encountered while on the road.
- Always check your government's travel-advisory warnings.

Keeping Safe

- A good travel-insurance policy is essential.
- Email copies of your passport identity page, visa and airline tickets to yourself, and keep copies on you.
- Keep your money and passport in a concealed money belt or a secure place under your shirt.
- Store at least US$100 separately from your main stash.
- Don't publicly display large wads of cash when paying for services or checking into hotels.
- Consider using your own padlock at cheaper hotels.
- If you can't lock your hotel room securely from the inside, think about staying somewhere else.

Scams

Credit Card Con

Be careful when paying for souvenirs with a credit card. While government shops are usually legitimate, private souvenir shops have been known to surreptitiously run off extra copies of the credit-card imprint slip and use them for phoney transactions later.

Ask the trader to process the sales transaction in front of you. Memorising the CVV/CVC2 number and scratching it off the card is also a good idea, to avoid misuse.

In some restaurants, waiters will ask you for your PIN with the intention of taking your credit card to the machine – never give your PIN to anyone, and ask to use the payment machine in person.

Druggings

Be extremely wary of accepting food or drink from strangers, even if you feel you're being rude. Women should be particularly circumspect.

Occasionally, tourists (especially those who are travelling solo) have been drugged and robbed or even attacked. A spiked drink is the most commonly used method for sending victims off to sleep – chocolates, chai from a co-conspiring vendor, 'homemade' Indian food and even bottled water have also been used.

Touts & Commission Agents

- Cabbies and autorickshaw drivers will often try to coerce you to stay at a hotel of their choice, to collect a commission (included in your room tariff) afterwards.
- Wherever possible, prearrange hotel bookings (if only for the first night), and request a hotel pickup. You'll often hear stories about hotels of your choice being 'full' or 'closed' – check things out yourself.
- Avoid friendly people and 'officials' in train and bus stations who offer unsolicited help, then guide you to a commission-paying travel agent. Look confident, and if anyone asks if this is your first trip to India, say you've been here several times.

Transport Scams

- Upon arriving at train stations and airports, if you haven't prearranged a pickup, call an Uber or go to the radio cab, prepaid taxi or airport shuttle bus counters. Never choose a loitering cabbie who offers you a cheap ride into town, especially at night.
- When buying a bus, train or plane ticket anywhere other than the registered office of the transport company, make sure you're getting the ticket class you paid for. Use official online-booking facilities where possible.

- Train station touts (even in uniform or with 'official' badges) may tell you that your intended train is cancelled/flooded/broken down or that your ticket is invalid or that you must pay to have your e-ticket validated on the platform. Do not respond to any approaches at train stations.

Theft

- Keep luggage locked and chained on buses and trains. Remember that snatchings often occur when a train is pulling out of the station, as it's too late for you to give chase.
- Remember to lock your door at night; it is not unknown for thieves to take things from hotel rooms while occupants are sleeping.

Solo Travellers

Travelling solo in India may be great, because local people are often so friendly, helpful and interested. You're more likely to be 'adopted' by families, especially if you're commuting together on a long rail journey. It's a great opportunity to make friends and get a deeper understanding of local culture. If you're keen to hook up with fellow travellers, tourist hubs such as Delhi, Goa, Rajasthan, Kerala, Manali, McLeod Ganj, Leh, Agra and Varanasi are some popular places to do so. You may also be able to find travel companions on Lonely Planet's Thorn Tree forum (www.lonelyplanet.com/thorntree).

The most significant issue facing solo travellers is cost: single-room accommodation rates are sometimes not much lower than double rates, and some midrange and top-end places don't offer a single tariff at all. You'll save money if you find others to share taxis and autorickshaws, as well as when hiring a car for longer trips.

Safety

- Some less honourable souls (locals and travellers alike) view lone tourists as an easy target for theft and sexual assault.
- Single men wandering around isolated areas have been mugged, even during the day.

Etiquette

Dress Avoid offence by eschewing tight, sheer or skimpy clothes.

Shoes It's polite to remove your shoes before entering homes and places of worship.

Photos It's best to ask before snapping people, sacred sites or ceremonies.

Feet Avoid pointing the soles of your feet towards people or deities, or touching anyone with your feet.

Greetings Saying *'namaste'* with your hands together in a prayer gesture is a respectful Hindu greeting; for Muslims, say *'salaam alaikum'* ('peace be with you'; the response is *'alaikum salaam'*).

Hands The right hand is for eating and shaking hands; the left is the 'toilet' hand.

Taxes & Refunds

India has a tiered goods-and-services tax (GST), applicable to restaurant prices and hotel rates, that ranges from 12% to 28%. A service charge of 10% is added to bills at many restaurants in addition to GST.

There are plans to introduce a system for tourists to claim GST refunds at Indian airports on goods taken out of the country.

Telephone

There are few pay phones in India (apart from in airports). Private STD/ISD/PCO booths offer inexpensive local, interstate and international calls, though

Emergency & Important Numbers

From outside India, dial your international access code, India's country code (☎91), then the number (minus the initial '0').

Country code	☎91
International access code	☎00
Emergency (ambulance/fire/police)	☎112

they aren't as widespread as in the past. A meter displays how much the call is costing and usually provides a receipt when the call is finished.

Mobile Phones

Roaming connections are excellent in urban areas, but poor in the countryside. To avoid expensive roaming costs (often highest for incoming calls), get hooked up to the local mobile-phone network by applying for a local prepaid SIM card at a phone shop. India operates on the GSM network at 900MHz, the world's most common; mobile phones from most countries will work here.

The leading service providers are Jio (part of Reliance), Airtel, Vodafone-Idea and BSNL. Mobile phone coverage varies from region to region. It's best to check your SIM has been properly activated before you leave the area where you bought it.

Indian mobile phone numbers usually have 10 digits, mostly beginning with a 9 (but sometimes with a 6, 7 or 8).

Charges

- Calls within India are often included in prepaid packages along with the local SIM.
- International calls start at around ₹1 a minute. International outgoing messages cost ₹5. Incoming calls and messages are less than ₹1 and free, respectively.
- Unreliable signals and problems with international texting (messages or replies not coming through or being delayed) are not uncommon.
- A SIM card or ISD (international subscriber dialling) package is usually only valid for a particular region, and once you leave it, it may function but you'll pay roaming charges, however, these are not particularly steep (eg ₹1 per minute within India rather than ₹0.10). There are no roaming charges for internet-data packs.

Time

The subcontinent uses Indian Standard Time (GMT/UTC plus 5½ hours). India does not follow a daylight-saving system.

Toilets

Public toilets are most easily found in major cities and tourist sites; the cleanest (usually with sit-down and squat choices) are often at modern restaurants, shopping complexes and cinemas.

Beyond urban centres, toilets are of the squat variety and locals may use the 'hand-and-water' technique, which involves carrying out ablutions with a small jug of water and the left hand. It's always a good idea to carry your own toilet paper and hand sanitiser, just in case.

Visas

To enter India you need a valid passport, an onward/return ticket and a visa. Your passport needs to be valid for at least six months beyond your intended stay in India, with at least two blank pages.

Apart from citizens of Maldives, Bhutan and Nepal (unless arriving from mainland China), and citizens of Japan and South Korea (who can obtain a visa on arrival), everyone needs to apply for a visa before arriving in India. More than 150 nationalities can obtain the wonderfully hassle-free

60-day e-Visa. There's also a six-month tourist visa, valid from the date of issue, not the date of arrival.

Visas are available at Indian missions worldwide, though in many countries applications are processed by a private company.

- Student and business visas have strict conditions (consult the Indian embassy).
- A standard 180-day tourist visa permits multiple entry for most nationalities.
- The 60-day e-Visa is usually a double-entry visa.
- Five- and 10-year tourist visas are available to US citizens *only* under a bilateral arrangement. But you can still only stay in India for up to 180 days continuously.
- Currently you are required to submit two digital photographs with your visa application (format jpeg 10-300kb), though only one for the e-Visa.
- Visas are priced in the local currency and may have an added service fee.
- Extended visas are possible for those of Indian origin (excluding those in Pakistan and Bangladesh) who hold a non-Indian passport and live abroad.
- Check with the Indian embassy in your home country for any special conditions that may exist for your nationality.

E-Visa

- Citizens from more than 150 countries can apply for an e-Visa (www.indianvisaonline.gov.in/evisa). Upload a photograph and a copy of your passport; have at least 180 days' validity in your passport and at least two blank pages.
- Apply a minimum of four days and a maximum of 120 days before your visit. The visa will be valid from your date of arrival in India. It's a double-entry visa that lasts for 60 days from your first date of entry.
- If your application is approved, you will receive an attachment to an email within 72 hours (though normally much sooner), which you'll need to print out and take with you to the airport. You'll then have the e-Visa stamped into your passport on arrival.
- Note that the e-Visa is also sometimes referred to as a 'visa on arrival', though you need to apply for it before you arrive.
- E-Visas are only valid for entry through 26 designated airports and five designated seaports (check the website for details). E-Visa holders can, however, leave India from any authorised immigration checkpoint.

Weights & Measures

India uses the metric system. Additional units of measure you're likely to come across are lakh (one lakh equals 100,000) and crore (one crore equals 10 million).

Women Travellers

Reports of sexual assaults against women and girls are on the increase in India, despite tougher punishments being established following the notorious gang rape and murder of a local woman in Delhi in 2012. There have been several instances of sexual attacks on tourists over the last few years, though it's worth bearing in mind that the vast majority of visits are trouble free.

Clothing

In upper-middle-class districts of Delhi, Mumbai and Chennai, you'll see local women dressing as they might in New York or London, but elsewhere women are dressed traditionally. For travellers, culturally appropriate clothing will help reduce undesirable attention.

- Steer clear of sleeveless tops, shorts, short skirts (ankle-length skirts are recommended) and anything else that's skimpy, see-through, tight-fitting or reveals too much skin.
- Wearing Indian-style clothes is viewed favourably.
- Draping a dupatta (long scarf) over t-shirts is another good way to avoid stares.

It's also handy if you visit a shrine that requires your head to be covered.

- Wearing a *salwar kameez* (traditional dress-like tunic and trousers) will help you blend in; a smart alternative is a kurta (long shirt) worn over jeans or trousers.
- Avoid going out in public wearing a choli (sari blouse) or a sari petticoat (which some foreign women mistake for a skirt); it's like being half-dressed.
- Aside from at pools, many Indian women wear long shorts and a T-shirt when swimming in public view; it's wise to wear a sarong from the beach to your hotel.

Health & Hygiene

Sanitary pads are widely available, but tampons are usually restricted to pharmacies in some big cities and tourist towns. Carry additional stock for travel off the beaten track.

Sexual Harassment

Many female travellers have reported sexual harassment while in India, most commonly lewd comments and groping.

- Women travellers have experienced provocative gestures, jeering, getting 'accidentally' bumped into on the street and being followed.
- Incidents are particularly common at exuberant (and crowded) public events such as the Holi festival. If a crowd is gathering, make yourself scarce or find a safer place overlooking the event so that you're away from wandering hands.
- Women travelling with a male partner will receive less hassle; however, be aware that travelling as a couple/with a friend is not a guarantee of safety. Still be careful to avoid crowds or lonely places, even during daylight hours.

Staying Safe

The following tips will help you avoid uncomfortable or dangerous situations during your journey:

- Always be aware of your surroundings. If it feels wrong, trust your instincts. Tread with care. Don't be scared, but don't be reckless either.
- Don't accept any drinks, even bottled water, from strangers. Don't drink or eat with local men that you don't know: there have been several cases where tourist guides or hotel employees have allegedly drugged foreign women by offering them a drink or food.
- After you've been in the country for a while, you may start to feel safer and relax your guard. Don't stress, but maintain your vigilance.
- Keep conversations with unknown men short – getting involved in an inane conversation with someone you barely know can be misinterpreted.
- If you feel that a guy is encroaching on your space, he probably is. A firm request to keep away may well do the trick, especially if your tone is loud and curt enough to draw the attention of passers-by.
- The silent treatment can also be effective.
- Follow local women's cues and instead of shaking hands say *namaste* – the traditional, respectful Hindu greeting.
- Avoid wearing expensive-looking jewellery and carrying flashy accessories.
- Only go for massage or other treatments with female therapists.
- Female movie-goers will lessen the chances of harassment by going to the cinema with a companion.
- At hotels, keep your door locked, as staff (particularly at budget and midrange places) could knock and walk in without waiting for your permission.
- Don't let anyone you don't know or have just met into your hotel room, even if they work for the tourist company with whom you're travelling and claim it's to discuss an aspect of your trip.
- Avoid wandering alone in isolated areas, even during daylight hours. Steer clear of *galis* (narrow lanes), deserted roads, beaches, ruins and forests.

- Use your smartphone's GPS maps to keep track of where you are – this way it's easier to avoid getting lost and you can tell if a taxi/rickshaw is taking the wrong road.
- Act confidently in public and try always to have a plan of where you're going and what's next. If you haven't a clue, look as if you do. Consult maps at your hotel (or at a restaurant) rather than on the street.

Transport

Women can usually queue-jump for buses and trains without consequence and on trains there are special ladies-only carriages. There are also women-only waiting rooms at some stations.

Taxi & Autorickshaw

- Prearrange an airport pickup from your hotel. This is particularly important if your flight is scheduled to arrive after dark.
- If travelling after dark, use a recommended, registered taxi service.
- Never hail a taxi in the street or accept a lift from a stranger.
- Avoid taking taxis alone late at night and never agree to have more than one man (the driver) in the car – ignore claims that this is 'just my brother' etc.
- App-based taxi services like Uber (www.uber.com) and Ola Cabs (www.olacabs.com) are useful. The rates are fixed and you get the driver's licence plate in advance, so you can check it's definitely the right taxi and pass the details on to someone else if you want to be on the safe side.
- When taking rickshaws alone, call/text someone, or pretend to, to indicate that someone knows where you are.

Bus & Train

- Don't organise your travel in such a way that it means you're hanging out at bus/train stations or arriving late at night, or even after dark.
- Avoid empty rail carriages.
- Solo women have reported less hassle by opting for the more-expensive classes on trains.
- If you're travelling overnight by train, the best option is the upper outer berth in 2AC; you're out of the way of wandering hands but surrounded by plenty of other people and not locked in a four-person 1AC room (which might only have one other person in it).
- If you're feeling uncomfortable on public transport, don't hesitate to return any errant limbs, put an item of luggage between you and others, be vocal (attracting public attention) or simply find a new spot.

Unwanted Attention

Unwanted attention from men is a common problem.

- Be prepared to be stared at; it's something you'll simply have to live with, so don't allow it to get the better of you.
- Increased use of smartphones means more and more people taking surreptitious photos of you – again, try not to let it get to you.
- Refrain from returning male stares; this will be taken as encouragement.
- Dark glasses, phones, books or electronic tablets are useful props for averting unwanted conversations.
- Wearing a wedding ring, and saying you're married and due to meet your husband shortly, is another way to ward off unwanted interest.

Websites

Peruse personal experiences proffered by female travellers at www.journeywoman.com and www.wanderlustandlipstick.com. Blogs such as Breathe, Dream, Go (https://breathedreamgo.com) and Hippie in Heels (https://hippie-inheels.com) are also full of tips.

Transport

Getting There & Away

Air

India has four main gateways for international flights: **Delhi** (01243376000; www.newdelhiairport.in; M IGI Airport), **Mumbai** (022-66851010; www.csia.in; Santa Cruz/E), **Chennai** (044-22560551; Tirusulam) and **Bengaluru** (1800 4254425; www.bengaluruairport.com).

However, a number of other cities, such as **Hyderabad** (040-66546370; http://hyderabad.aero; Shamshabad), **Kochi** (0484-2610115; http://cial.aero; Nedumbassery) in Kerala, **Kolkata** (NSCBIA/CCU; www.calcuttaairport.com), Lucknow, Amritsar, Thiruvananthapuram (Trivandrum) and Kunnar, also service international carriers.

India's national carrier is **Air India** (1860-2331407, 011-24667473; www.airindia.com), which operates international and domestic flights. Air travel in India has had a decent safety record in recent years.

Land

Although most visitors fly into India, it is possible to travel overland between India and Bangladesh, Bhutan, Nepal, Pakistan and Myanmar (Burma). The overland route from Nepal is the most popular. For more on these routes, check for up-to-date information on Lonely Planet's Thorn Tree forum (www.lonelyplanet.com/thorntree) or see the 'Europe to India overland' section on www.seat61.com/India.htm.

Climate Change & Travel

Every form of transport that relies on carbon-based fuel generates CO_2, the main cause of human-induced climate change. Modern travel is dependent on aeroplanes, which might use less fuel per kilometre per person than most cars but travel much greater distances. The altitude at which aircraft emit gases (including CO_2) and particles also contributes to their climate change impact. Many websites offer 'carbon calculators' that allow people to estimate the carbon emissions generated by their journey and, for those who wish to do so, to offset the impact of the greenhouse gases emitted with contributions to portfolios of climate-friendly initiatives throughout the world. Lonely Planet offsets the carbon footprint of all staff and author travel.

Getting Around

Transport in India is frequent and inexpensive, though prone to overcrowding and delays. Trains, buses and shared jeeps run almost everywhere. To save time, consider domestic flights over long-distance buses and trains. Urban transport is cheap and frequent, and you'll never struggle to find a taxi or autorickshaw.

Air

Transporting vast numbers of passengers annually, India's domestic airline industry is very competitive. Major carriers include Air India, **IndiGo** (011-43513200; www.goindigo.in), **SpiceJet** (0987-1803333; www.spicejet.com) and **Jet Airways** (91-39893333; www.jetairways.com), **AirAsia** (Delhi office 011-26303939, customer care 80-46662222; www.airasia.com), **GoAir** (18602-100999; www.goair.in) and **Vistara** (9289-228888; www.airvistara.com).

Apart from airline sites, bookings can be made through portals such as **Cleartrip** (www.cleartrip.com), **Make My Trip** (www.makemytrip.com) and **Yatra** (www.yatra.com).

Security norms require you to produce your ticket and passport when you enter an airport; a digital ticket on your smartphone is usually sufficient. Keeping peak-hour congestion in mind, the recommended check-in time for domestic flights is two hours before departure, even though check-in actually closes 45 minutes before departure. The usual baggage allowance is 15kg (10kg for smaller aircraft) in economy class, though Air India allows 25kg.

Bus

Buses go almost everywhere in India and are the only way to get around many mountainous areas. They tend to be the cheapest way to travel. Services are fast and frequent.

Roads in mountainous or curvy terrain can be perilous; buses are often driven with wilful abandon, and accidents are always a risk. Avoid night buses unless there's no alternative: driving conditions are more hazardous and drivers may be inebriated or overtired.

Car

Few people bother with self-drive car hire – not only because of the hair-raising driving conditions but also because hiring a car with driver is comparatively affordable in India, particularly if several people share the cost. **Hertz** (www.hertz.com) is one of the few international companies with representatives in India.

Hiring a Car & Driver

Most towns have taxi stands or car-hire companies where you can arrange short or long tours.

Not all hire cars are licensed to travel beyond their home state. Those that are will pay extra state taxes, which are added to the hire charge.

Ask for a driver who speaks some English and knows the region you intend to visit. Try to see the car and meet the driver before paying anything.

A wide range of cars now operate as taxis. From a proletarian Tata Indica hatchback to a comfy Toyota Innova SUV, there's a model to suit every budget.

Hire charges for multiday trips cover the driver's meals and accommodation – drivers should make their own sleeping and eating arrangements. Many hotels have inexpensive rooms specifically set aside for drivers.

It's essential to set the ground rules from day one: to avoid difficulties later, politely but firmly let the driver know that you're in charge.

Costs

Car-hire costs depend on the distance and the terrain (driving on mountain roads uses more petrol, hence the higher cost).

One-way trips usually cost the same as return ones (to cover the petrol and driver charges for getting back).

Hire charges vary from state to state. Some taxi unions set a maximum time limit or a maximum kilometre distance for day trips – if you go over, you'll have to pay extra. Prices also vary according to the make and model of the taxi.

To avoid misunderstandings, get *in writing* what you've been promised (quotes should include petrol, sightseeing stops, all your chosen destinations, and meals and accommodation for the driver). If drivers ask you for money for petrol en route because they are short of cash, get receipts for reimbursement later. If you're travelling by the kilometre, check the odometer reading before you set out so as to avoid confusion later.

For sightseeing day trips around a single city, expect to pay upwards of ₹1400/1800 for a non-AC/AC car with an eight-hour, 80km limit per day (extra charges apply for longer trips). For multiday trips, operators usually peg a 250km minimum running distance per day and charge around ₹8/10 per kilometre for a non-AC/AC car for anything over this.

A tip is customary at the end of your journey; around ₹200 per day is fair.

Local Transport

For any transport without a fixed fare, agree on the price *before* you start your journey and make sure that it covers your luggage and every passenger. Even where meters exist, drivers may refuse to use them, demanding an elevated 'fixed' fare; bargain hard. Fares usually increase at night (by up to 100%) and some drivers charge a few rupees extra for luggage.

Carry plenty of small bills for taxi and rickshaw fares, as drivers rarely have change.

Apps such as **Uber** and **Ola** have transformed local transport: if you have a smartphone you can call a taxi or autorickshaw and the fare is electronically calculated.

Autorickshaw

Similar to the tuk-tuks of Southeast Asia, the Indian autorickshaw is a three-wheeled motorised contraption with a tin or canvas roof and sides, usually with room for two passengers (although you'll often see many more squeezed in) and limited luggage.

They are also referred to as autos, scooters and riks.

You can call autos via the Ola app, which electronically calculates your fare when you finish the journey – no more haggling! Flagfall is around ₹25, then it's ₹8 to ₹14 per kilometre.

Travelling by auto is great fun but, thanks to the open windows, can be noisy and hot (or severely cold!).

Cycle-Rickshaw

A cycle-rickshaw is a pedal cycle with two rear wheels, supporting a bench seat for passengers. Fares must be agreed in advance – speak to locals to get an idea of a fair price for the distance you intend to travel.

Taxi

To avoid fare-setting shenanigans, use prepaid taxis where possible. Apps such as **Uber** and **Ola** are the most efficient option in larger cities.

Prepaid Taxis

Major Indian airports and train stations have prepaid-taxi and radio-cab booths. Here you can book a taxi, even long distance, for a fixed price (which will include baggage) and thus avoid commission scams. Hold onto your receipt until you're sure you've reached your destination, then give it to your driver. The driver won't get paid without it.

Radio cabs cost marginally more than prepaid taxis but are air-conditioned and staffed by the company's chauffeurs. Cabs have electronic, receipt-generating fare meters and are fitted with GPS units, so the company can monitor the vehicle's movements around town. This minimises the chances of errant driving or unreasonable demands for extra cash by the driver afterwards.

Smaller airports and stations may have prepaid-autorickshaw booths instead of or as well as prepaid-taxi booths.

Railway Razzle Dazzle

You can live like a maharaja on one of India's luxury train tours. Accommodation on board, tours, admission fees and meals are included in the ticket price. As well as the following, consider the **Golden Chariot**, a luxurious round-trip journey from Bengaluru highlighting the romance of Karnataka. See www.goldenchariottrain.com for the latest developments.

Palace on Wheels (www.palaceonwheels.net) Eight- to 10-day tours of Rajasthan, departing from Delhi. Trains run on fixed dates from September to April; the fare per person for seven nights in a single/double cabin starts at US$4550/3500. Try to book 10 months in advance.

Royal Rajasthan on Wheels (www.royal-rajasthan-on-wheels.com) Modelled on the Palace on Wheels and running along similar routes through Rajasthan. Lavish one-week trips take place from September to April, starting and finishing in Delhi. The fare per single/double cabin for seven nights starts at US$6055/9100, plus taxes.

Deccan Odyssey (www.deccan-odyssey-india.com) Seven-night whirls around Maharashtra, Goa and beyond cost from US$6100/8750 per single/double.

Motorcycle

Long-distance motorcycle touring is hugely popular in India. However, it can be quite an undertaking; there are some popular motorcycle tours for those who don't want the rigmarole of going it alone. Popular starting points are Delhi and Manali; popular destinations include Rajasthan, South India, Himachal Pradesh and Ladakh.

Organised Tours

Dozens of companies offer motorcycle tours around India with support vehicle, mechanic and guide. Here are a few well-established companies:

Blazing Trails (www.blazingtrailstours.com)

H-C Travel (www.hctravel.com)

Himalayan Roadrunners (www.ridehigh.com)

Indian Motorcycle Adventures (www.indianmotorcycleadventures.com)

Lalli Singh Adventures (☎09811 140161, 011-47652551; www.lallisinghadventures.com; 1266/4 Naiwala St, Payarelal Rd, New Delhi; ⏲10am-7pm Tue-Sun; Ⓜ Karol Bagh)

Moto Discovery (www.motodiscovery.com)

World on Wheels (www.worldonwheels.tours)

Train

Travelling by train is a quintessential Indian experience. Trains offer a smoother ride than buses and are especially recommended for long journeys that include overnight travel. India's rail network is one of the largest and busiest in the world and Indian Railways is the largest utility employer on earth, with roughly 1.3 million workers. There are almost 7000 stations scattered across the country.

The best way of sourcing updated train information is from websites such as **Indian Railways** (http://enquiry.indianrail.gov.in) and the excellent **India Rail Info** (http://indiarailinfo.com), with added offline browsing support, as well as the user-friendly **Erail** (https://erail.in).

Booking Tickets

You can book through a travel agency or hotel (for a commission), in person at the train station or online. Refunds are available on any ticket, even after departure, with a penalty (rules are complicated, so check when you book).

You must make a reservation for chair-car, executive-chair-car, sleeper, 1AC, 2AC and 3AC carriages. Book well ahead for overnight journeys or travel during holidays and festivals. Reserved tickets show your seat/berth and carriage number. Many stations have signs marking the approximate spot where each carriage stops (ask station staff for assistance).

Online Booking

Start by visiting http://erail.in – the search engine will bring up a list of all trains running between your chosen stations, with their numbers, times and information on classes and fares.

Step two is to register for an account with **IRCTC** (www.irctc.co.in), the government-run ticket-booking service. This is required even if you plan to use a private ticket agency. Registration is a complex process, involving passwords, emails, scans of your passport and texts to your mobile phone. You'll usually need an Indian mobile number, though a possible workaround is to enter a random number then use email to communicate. The ever-helpful **Man in Seat 61** (www.seat61.com/India.htm) has a detailed guide to all the steps.

Once registered, you can use a credit card to book travel on specific trains, either directly with IRCTC, or with private agencies. You'll be issued with an e-ticket, which you must print out ready to present alongside your passport and booking reference once you board the train.

The following websites are useful for online bookings, all accepting MasterCard and Visa.

Cleartrip (www.cleartrip.com) A reliable private agency and the easiest way to book.

IRCTC (www.irctc.co.in) The e-ticketing division of Indian Railways.

Make My Trip (www.makemytrip.com) Reputable private agency.

Yatra (www.yatra.com) Books flights and trains.

Express Train Fares in Rupees

Distance (km)	1AC*	2AC*	3AC*	Chair Car (CC)**	Sleeper**	2nd Class (II)**
100	₹1203	₹706	₹498	₹205	₹77	₹47
200	₹1203	₹706	₹498	₹282	₹136	₹73
300	₹1356	₹798	₹561	₹378	₹181	₹103
400	₹1678	₹978	₹687	₹467	₹222	₹128
500	₹2054	₹1209	₹846	₹577	₹276	₹151
1000	₹3362	₹1949	₹1352	₹931	₹446	₹258
1500	₹4320	₹2498	₹1708	₹1189	₹573	₹334
2000	₹5272	₹3025	₹2057	₹1443	₹698	₹412

* Rajdhani/Duronto Trains
** Mail/Express Trains

At the Station

Get a reservation slip from the information window, fill in the name of the departure station, destination station, the class you want to travel and the name and number of the train. Join the long queue for the ticket window where your ticket will be printed. Women should take advantage of the separate women's queue – if there isn't one, go to the front of the regular queue.

Tourist Quota

A special (albeit small) tourist quota is set aside for foreign tourists travelling between popular stations. These seats can only be booked at dedicated reservation offices in major cities, and you need to show your passport and visa as ID.

Classes

Express and mail trains form the mainstay of Indian rail travel. Most long-distance trains have 'general' compartments with unreserved seating, and more comfortable reserved compartments, usually with the option of sleeper berths for overnight journeys.

Reserved classes are:

Air-Conditioned 1st Class (1AC) Most expensive, with two- or four-berth compartments with locking doors and meals included.

Air-Conditioned 2-Tier (2AC) Two-tier berths arranged in groups of four and two in an open-plan carriage. Bunks convert to seats by day and there are curtains, offering some privacy.

Air-Conditioned 3-Tier (3AC) Three-tier berths arranged in groups of six in an open-plan carriage with no curtains; popular with Indian families.

AC Executive Chair (EC) Comfortable, reclining chairs and plenty of space; usually on Shatabdi express trains.

AC Chair (CC) Similar to the Executive Chair carriage but with less-fancy seating.

Sleeper Class (SL) Open-plan carriages with three-tier bunks and no AC; the open windows afford great views.

Costs

- Fares are calculated by distance and class of travel; Rajdhani and Shatabdi trains are slightly more expensive, but the price includes meals. Most air-conditioned carriages have a catering service (meals are brought to your seat).
- Children under the age of five travel free, while those aged between five and 12 are charged half-price if they do not have their own berth (but full price if they do).
- Senior discounts (40% and 50% off for men over 60 and women over 58, respectively) only apply to Indian citizens.

Language

Hindi

Hindi has about 180 million speakers in India, and it has official status along with English and 21 other languages.

If you read our pronunciation guides as if they were English, you'll be understood. The length of vowels is important (eg 'a' and 'aa'), and 'ng' after a vowel indicates nasalisation (ie the vowel is pronounced 'through the nose'). The stressed syllables are marked with italics. The abbreviations 'm' and 'f' indicate the options for male and female speakers respectively.

Basics

Hello./Goodbye.
नमस्ते। — na·ma·*ste*

Yes.
जी हाँ। — jee haang

No.
जी नहीश्व। — jee na·*heeng*

Excuse me.
सुनिये। — su·ni·*ye*

Sorry.
माफ़ कीजिये। — maaf *kee*·ji·ye

Please …
कृपया … — kri·pa·*yaa* …

Thank you.
थैश्वक्यू। — *thayn*·kyoo

How are you?
आप कैसे/कैसी हैश्व? — aap *kay*·se/*kay*·see hayng (m/f)

Fine. And you?
मैश्व ठीक हूँ। — mayng teek hoong
आप सुनाइये। — aap su·*naa*·i·ye

Do you speak English?
क्या आपको अश्वग्रेज़ी आती है? — kyaa aap ko an·*gre*·zee *aa*·tee hay

How much is this?
कितने का है? — *kit*·ne kaa hay

I don't understand.
मैश्व नहीश्व समझा/समझी। — mayng na·*heeng sam*·jaa/*sam*·jee (m/f)

Accommodation

Do you have a single/double room?
क्या सिश्वगल/डबल कमरा है? — kyaa *sin*·gal/da·*bal kam*·raa hay

How much is it (per night/per person)?
(एक रात/हर व्यक्ति) के लिय कितने पैसे लगते हैश्व? — (ek raat/har *vyak*·ti) ke li·*ye kit*·ne *pay*·se *lag*·te hayng

Eating & Drinking

I'd like …, please.
मुझे … दीजिये। — mu·*je* … *dee*·ji·ye

That was delicious.
बहुत मज़ेदार हुआ। — ba·*hut* ma·ze·*daar* hu·*aa*

Please bring the menu/bill.
मेन्यू/बिल लाइये। — *men*·yoo/bil *laa*·i·ye

I don't eat …
मैश्व … नहीश्व खाता/खाती। — mayng … na·*heeng kaa*·taa/*kaa*·tee (m/f)

fish	मछली	*mach*·lee
meat	गोश्त	gosht
poultry	मुर्ग़ी	*mur*·gee

Emergencies

I'm ill.
मैश्व बीमार हूँ। — mayng *bee*·maar hoong

Help!
मदद कीजिये! — ma·*dad kee*·ji·ye

Call the doctor/police!
डॉक्टर/पुलिस को बुलाओ! — *daak*·tar/pu·*lis* ko bu·*laa*·o

Directions

Where's a/the …?
… कहाँ है? — … ka·*haang* hay

bank
बैश्वक — baynk

market
बाज़ार — *baa*·zaar

post office
डाक ख़ाना — daak *kaa*·naa

restaurant
रेस्टोरेश्वट — *res*·to·rent

toilet
टॉइलेट — *taa*·i·let

tourist office
पर्यटन ऑफ़िस — *par*·ya·tan *aa*·fis

Tamil

Tamil is the official language in the state of Tamil Nadu and one of the major languages of South India, with about 62 million speakers. Note that in our pronunciation guides, the symbol 'aw' is pronounced as in 'law' while 'ow' is pronounced as in 'how'.

Basics

Hello.
வணக்கம். — va·*nak*·kam

Goodbye.
போய் வருகிறேன். — *po*·i va·*ru*·ki·reyn

Yes./No.
ஆமாம்./இல்லை. — *aa*·maam/*il*·lai

Excuse me.
தயவு செய்து. — ta·ya·*vu* sei·*du*

Sorry.
மன்னிக்கவும். — *man*·nik·ka·vum

Please ...
தயவு செய்து ... — ta·ya·*vu* chey·*tu* ...

Thank you.
நன்றி. — *nan*·dri

How are you?
நிங்கள் நலமா? — *neeng*·kal na·*la*·maa

Fine, thanks. And you?
நலம், நன்றி. — na·*lam nan*·dri
நீங்கள்? — *neeng*·kal

Do you speak English?
நீங்கள் ஆங்கிலம் பேசுவீர்களா? — *neeng*·kal *aang*·ki·lam *pey*·chu·*veer*·ka·la

How much is this?
இது என்ன விலை? — i·*tu en*·na vi·*lai*

I don't understand.
எனக்கு விளங்கவில்லை. — e·*nak*·ku vi·*lang*·ka·vil·*lai*

Accommodation

Do you have a single/double room?
உங்களிடம் ஓர் தன/இரட்டை அறை உள்ளதா? — *ung*·ka·li·tam awr ta·*ni*/i·rat·*tai* a·*rai ul*·la·taa

How much is it per night/person?
ஓர் இரவுக்கு/ஒருவருக்கு என்னவிலை? — awr i·ra·*vuk*·ku/o·ru·va·*ruk*·ku *en*·na·vi·lai

Eating & Drinking

I'd like the ..., please.
எனக்கு தயவு செய்து ... கொடுங்கள். — e·*nak*·ku ta·ya·*vu* chey·*tu* ... ko·*tung*·kal

bill	விலைச்சீட்டு	vi·*laich*·cheet·tu
menu	உணவுப்–பட்டியல	u·na·*vup*·pat·ti·yal

I'm allergic to ...
எனக்கு ... உணவு சேராது. — e·*nak*·ku ... u·na·*vu* *chey*·raa·tu

dairy products	பால் சார்ந்த	paal *chaarn*·ta
meat stock	இறைச்சி வகை	i·*raich*·chi va·*kai*
nuts	பருப்பு வகை	pa·*rup*·pu va·*kai*
seafood	கடல் சார்ந்த	ka·*tal chaarn*·ta

Emergencies

Help!
உதவ! — u·ta·*vi*

Call a doctor!
ஐ அழைக்கவும் ஒரு மருத்துவர்! — i a·*zai*·ka·vum o·*ru* ma·*rut*·tu·var

Call the police!
ஐ அழைக்கவும் போலிஸ்! — i a·*zai*·ka·vum pow·*lees*

Directions

Where's a/the ...?
... எங்கே இருக்கிறது? — ... *eng*·key i·*ruk*·ki·ra·tu

bank	வங்கி	*vang*·ki
market	சந்தை	*chan*·tai
post office	தபால் நிலையம்	ta·*paal* ni·*lai*·yam
restaurant	உணவகம	u·na·va·*kam*
toilet	கழிவறை	ka·*zi*·va·rai
tourist office	சுற்றுப்பயண அலுவலகம்	chut·*rup*·pa·ya·na a·lu·va·la·*kam*

To enhance your trip with a phrasebook, visit **lonelyplanet.com**.

Behind the Scenes

Acknowledgements

Climate map data adapted from Peel MC, Finlayson BL & McMahon TA (2007) 'Updated World Map of the Köppen-Geiger Climate Classification', *Hydrology and Earth System Sciences*, 11, 1633–44.

Cover photograph: Taj Mahal at sunrise, Agra, Amir Ghasemi/Getty Images ©

Illustrations: pp40–1 and pp72–3 by Javier Zarracina; illustrations on pp76–7 and pp200–1 by Michael Weldon.

This Book

This 2nd edition of Lonely Planet's *Best of India* guidebook was researched and written by Anirban Mahapatra, Joe Bindloss, Lindsay Brown, Mark Elliott, Paul Harding, Bradley Mayhew, Daniel McCrohan, Isabella Noble, John Noble, Kevin Raub, Sarina Singh and Iain Stewart. This guidebook was produced by the following:

Destination Editor Joe Bindloss

Senior Product Editor Kate Chapman

Product Editor Alison Ridgway

Regional Senior Cartographer Valentina Kremenchutskaya

Book Designer Wibowo Rusli

Cartographer Hunor Csutoros

Assisting Editors Ronan Abayawickrema, Michelle Coxall, Victoria Harrison, Elizabeth Jones, Jodie Martire, Lauren O'Connell

Cover Researcher Naomi Parker

Thanks to Shona Gray, Chris Hollingworth, Anthony Phelan, Kirsten Rawlings, John Taufa, Juan Winata

Send Us Your Feedback

We love to hear from travellers – your comments keep us on our toes and help make our books better. Our well-travelled team reads every word on what you loved or loathed about this book. Although we cannot reply individually to postal submissions, we always guarantee that your feedback goes straight to the appropriate authors, in time for the next edition. Each person who sends us information is thanked in the next edition, the most useful submissions are rewarded with a selection of digital PDF chapters.

Visit lonelyplanet.com/contact to submit your updates and suggestions or to ask for help. Our award-winning website also features inspirational travel stories, news and discussions.

Note: We may edit, reproduce and incorporate your comments in Lonely Planet products such as guidebooks, websites and digital products, so let us know if you don't want your comments reproduced or your name acknowledged. For a copy of our privacy policy visit lonelyplanet.com/privacy.

Index

A

accessible travel 292
accommodation 292-3
  language 313, 314
activities 18, 20, 248-51, *see also individual activities*
Adivasis 279
Agonda 162
Agra 4-5, 63-83, **65**, **82**
  accommodation 65
  food 83
  itineraries 64
  planning 64-5
  sights 66-82
  tourist information 83
  travel to/from 65, 83
  travel within 83
Agra Fort 78-81
ahimsa 274
air travel 17, 308-9
Ajanta Caves 15, 137-43, **139**
  accommodation 139
  itineraries 138
  planning 138-9
  travel to/from 139, 143
Akbar, Emperor 74, 80, 82, 271, 287
Alappuzha 187-9
Alleppey 187-9
Amber Fort 102-3
amoebic dysentery 296
animals 288-9, *see also individual species*
Anjuna 161, 170-1
antelope 289
Arambol (Harmal) 160
archaeological sites
  Fatehpur Sikri 74-7
  Hampi 210-11, **211**
  Hazrat Nizam-ud-din Dargah 48
  Humayun's Tomb 48
  Jantar Mantar 108
  Mehrauli Archaeological Park 51
  Qutb Minar 44-5
architecture 18, 285-6
area codes 304
art galleries, *see* museums & galleries
arts 286-7
Ashoka, Emperor 268
ATMs 299
Aurangabad 150-3, **151**
Aurangzeb 271
autorickshaws 310
ayurveda
  Jaipur 110
  Kerala 178-9
  Mysuru 202

B

Babur, Emperor 271
Baga 161-2
Bahmani sultanate 270
ballooning 109
Bangalore, *see* Bengaluru
bargaining 299-300
bathrooms 304
bazaars, *see* markets
beaches
  Goa 160-3, 169
  Kerala 180-1, 185
beer 133
Bengaluru 206-9, **207**
bhang lassis 242
bicycle travel, *see* cycling
bin Tughlaq, Mohammed 270
bird-watching 114, 289
birth 278
boat trips
  Kerala 176-7, 187
  Varanasi 242
Bollywood 124-5, 287
Bombay, *see* Mumbai
books 25, 287
Brahma 280
Brahman 280
Buddha 268
Buddhism 268
Buddhist temples
  Ajanta Caves 140-3
  Aurangabad Caves 150
  Bhutia Busty Gompa 223
  Ellora Caves 147-8
  Himalayan Nyinmapa Buddhist Temple 259
  Kalachakra Temple 247
  Observatory Hill 223, 225
  Tsuglagkhang 259
budgeting 17
bus travel 17, 309
bushwalking, *see* trekking
business hours 17, 300-1

C

Calangute 161-2
camel safaris 13, 24, 90-3
Candolim 162
car travel 309
carbon offsetting 308
caste system 278
cathedrals, *see* churches & cathedrals
caves
  Ajanta Caves 15, 137-43
  Aurangabad Caves 150-1
  Ellora Caves 15, 137-9, 144-9
cell phones 16, 304
Chalukyas 269
Chapora 161
Chhatrapati Shivaji Maharaj Terminus 129
children, travel with 32-3
Chinese fishing nets 192
Chola empire 269
choli 278

000 Map pages

churches & cathedrals
  Basilica of Bom Jesus 158
  Church of Our Lady of the Immaculate Conception 166
  Church of St Cajetan 159
  Church of St Francis of Assisi 159
  Sé Cathedral 159
cider 257
City Palace 104-5
climate 16, 22-4, 293, **16**
climate change 308
clothing 278, 303, 305-6
Cochin 189-93, **190**
coffee 208
Colomb Bay 162-3
commission agents 302
Congress Party 275
Coorg 205-6
costs 17
  accommodation 292
  car travel 309
  food 294
credit cards 300, 302
cricket 279
culture 277-9
currency 16, 275, 300
curries 282
customs regulations 293, 298
cycle-rickshaws 310
cycling 249-50

D

dabba-wallahs 131
Dalai Lama 258-61, 265
dance 286
dangers, *see* safety
Darjeeling 12-13, 213-27, **215**, **224**
  accommodation 215
  drinking 226
  food 225-6
  itineraries 214
  nightlife 226
  planning 214-15
  shopping 225
  sights 216-25
  tea estates 216-17
  tourist information 226
  travel to/from 215, 227
  travel within 227
Darjeeling Himalayan Railway 226
Daulatabad Fort 152
deer 289
dehydration 297
Delhi 10, 35-61, **36**, **50**, **55**, **56**, **61**
  accommodation 37, 61
  drinking 57
  food 52-7
  itineraries 36, 46-7
  nightlife 57
  planning 36-7
  safety 58
  shopping 42-3, 51-2
  sights 38-51
  tourist information 58
  tours 51
  travel to/from 37, 58-9
  travel within 59-60
  walking tours 46-7, **46-7**
  women travellers 58
dengue fever 295
Devi 281
dhal 283
dharma 281
dhoti 278
diarrhoea 296-7
disabilities, travellers with 292
diving 186
divorce 278
Diwali 24
dowries 277-8
drinking 21
driving, *see* car travel
druggings 302, 306
drugs 242, 298
Durga 281
Dussehra 24

E

East India Company 271-3
economy 264, 276
electricity 294
elephants 288
Ellora Caves 15, 137-9, 144-9, **139**
  accommodation 139, 149
  itineraries 138
  planning 138-9
  tours 153
  travel to/from 139, 149
emergencies 304
  language 313-14
entertainment 21
environmental issues 289
etiquette 303
events 22-4, 301
exchange rates 300

F

family travel, *see* children, travel with
Fatehpur Sikri 74-7, **76-7**
Festival of Lights 24
festivals 22-4, 301
films 25, 124-5, 287
First War of Independence (Indian Uprising) 273
fishing 251
flora 290
food 19, 21, 282-4, *see also individual locations*
  children, travel with 32-3
  costs 294
  language 313, 314
  safety 297
football 279
forts
  Agra Fort 78-81
  Amber Fort 102-3

forts *continued*
- Daulatabad Fort 152
- Fort Immanuel 189
- Jaisalmer Fort 88-9
- Madikeri Fort 205
- Nahargarh 113
- Ranthambhore Fort 114
- Red Fort 38-41
- Siri Fort 52

G

galleries, *see* museums & galleries
Gandhi, Indira 276
Gandhi, Mahatma 274-5
Gandhi, Rahul 276
Ganesh 281
Ganesh Chaturthi 24
Ganges River 290
gardens, *see* parks & gardens
gay travellers 299
gems 112
geography 288
ghats 232-5
- Assi Ghat 233
- Dashashwamedh Ghat 234
- Hanuman Ghat 233
- Harishchandra Ghat 233
- Kedar Ghat 233
- Mahalaxmi Dhobi Ghat 129
- Man Mandir Ghat 234
- Manikarnika Ghat 234
- Munshi Ghat 234
- Pandhey Ghat 233
- safety 241
- Scindhia Ghat 235
- Trilochan Ghat 235

giardiasis 296-7
gibbons 289
Goa 8-9, 155-71, **157**
- accommodation 157, 163
- activities 164-5
- beaches 160-3
- drinking 163
- food 163
- itineraries 156
- nightlife 163, 170
- planning 156-7
- travel to/from 157

golden langur 289
GST refunds 303
Gupta empire 268-9

H

Hampi 210-11, **211**
Hamta Pass Trek 249
Hanuman 281
Harappan culture 267
health 294-7
- children 33
- food 283, 297
- women travellers 306

heat exhaustion 297
heatstroke 297
hepatitis A 295-6
hepatitis B 296
hiking, *see* trekking
hijras 279, 299
Hindi language 274, 313
Hindu temples 285
- Ellora Caves 148
- Hadimba Mandir 252
- Kailasa Temple 146-7
- Keshava Temple 202
- Manu Rishi Temple 253
- Observatory Hill 223-5
- Sri Chamundeswari Temple 199
- Vishwanath Temple 236

Hinduism 269-71, 280-1
history 266-76
- Aryan civilisation 267-8
- Bahmani sultanate 270
- British rule 271-4
- Chola empire 269
- East India Company 271-3
- First War of Independence (Indian Uprising) 273
- Gupta empire 268-9
- independence 275-6
- Indus Valley civilisation 267
- Mauryan empire 268
- Mughal empire 270-1, 272, 273
- Muslim rule 269-71
- Partition 275
- Portuguese traders 271
- Rajputs 273
- Vijayanagar empire 210-11, 270

HIV 296
Holi 22
holidays 301
hostels 293
houseboats 176-7
Humayun 271

I

immigration 304-5
India-Pakistan Wars 265
Indus Valley civilisation 267
insurance 297-8
internet access 298
internet resources 17, 292, 296
itineraries 26-31, **26**, **27**, **28**, **30**, *see also individual locations*

J

Jain temples 285
- Ellora Caves 148-9
- Jaisalmer Fort 89

Jainism 268
Jaipur 6, 99-113, **101**, **109**
- accommodation 101
- activities 109-10
- drinking 111-12
- food 111
- itineraries 100, 106-7
- nightlife 111-12
- planning 100-3
- shopping 110-11, 112
- sights 102-9, 113
- tourist information 112-13
- travel to/from 101, 113

travel within 113
walking tours 106-7, **106-7**
Jaisalmer 12-13, 85-97, **87**, **95**
accommodation 87
activities 90-3
drinking 96
festivals 96
food 96
itineraries 86
nightlife 96
planning 86-7
shopping 95
sights 88-95
travel to/from 87, 96-7
travel within 97
Jaisalmer Fort 88-9
Jehangir 271

K

Kailasa Temple 146-7
Kali 281
Kashmir 265
Kathakali 182-3
kayaking 188
Kerala 7, 173-93, **175**
accommodation 175
itineraries 174
planning 174-5
travel to/from 175
Kochi 189-93, **190**
Kodagu 205-6
Kovalam 185-7
Krishna 281
kurta 278

L

languages 16, 313-14
Hindi 274, 313
Persian 269
Tamil 314
langurs 289
lassi 240, 242
legal matters 279, 298-9
leopards 289
lesbian travellers 299
LGBT+ travellers 299
literature 25, 287
lungi 278

M

macaques 289
Mahabharata 287
Mahavir 268
malaria 294-5
Manali 14, 245-57, **247**, **254**
accommodation 247
activities 248-51
drinking 256-7
food 253-5
itineraries 246
nightlife 256
planning 246-7
shopping 253
sights 252
tourist information 257
travel to/from 247, 257
travel within 257
mangoes 239
markets
Anjuna flea market 171
Bhuleshwar Market 121
Chandni Chowk 42-3
Chawri Bazaar 43
Chor Bazaar 120
Connemara Market 184
Crawford Market 121
Delhi 42-3
Devaraja Market 199
Krishnarajendra Market 207
Mumbai market district 120-1
Spice Market (Delhi) 43
Zaveri Bazaar 121
marriage 277-8
massage
Jaipur 110
Kerala 178-9
Mysuru 202
Mauryan empire 268
McLeod Ganj 258-61, **259**
measures 305
meat 283
medical services 294
metric system 305
microbreweries 133
mobile phones 16, 304
Modi, Narendra 264, 290
momos 256
monasteries
Ajanta Caves 140-3
Bhutia Busty Gompa 223
Ellora Caves 144-9
Namdroling Monastery 205
Von Ngari Institute 252
Yiga Choeling Gompa 223
money 16, 17, 275, 299-300
money-changers 300
monsoons 16
Morjim Beach 161
mosques
Jama Masjid (Delhi) 48
Jama Masjid (Fatehpur Sikri) 75
Jamali Khamali mosque 51
Quwwat-ul-Islam Masjid 45
motorcycle travel 311
mountain biking 249-50
Mughal empire 270-1, 273, 286
Mumbai 11, 117-35, **119**, **130**, **132**
accommodation 119
drinking 133-4
food 122-3, 131-3
itineraries 118, 126-7
nightlife 133-4
planning 118-19
shopping 120-1, 131
sights 120-9
tourist information 134
travel to/from 119, 134
travel within 135
walking tours 126-7, 128, **126-7**

mundu 278
museums & galleries
  Central Museum 108
  Central Tibetan Secretariat
  Chhatrapati Shivaji Maharaj Vastu Sangrahalaya 128-9
  Crafts Museum 49
  Desert Cultural Centre & Museum 94
  Diwan-i-Am Art Gallery 105
  Himalayan Mountaineering Institute 222
  Himalayan Tibet Museum 225
  Indo-Portuguese Museum 189
  Mattancherry Palace 191
  Men-Tsee-Khang Museum 261
  Museum of History & Heritage 184
  Napier Museum 184
  National Gallery of Modern Art 206-7
  National Museum 49
  Rail Museum 202
  Taj Museum 70
  Thar Heritage Museum 94
  Tibet Museum 259
music 25, 286
Mysore, *see* Mysuru
Mysuru 15, 195-209, **197**, **203**
  accommodation 197
  festivals 204
  food 204
  itineraries 196
  planning 196-7
  shopping 202
  sights 198-202
  tours 198-9
  travel to/from 197, 204
  travel within 204
Mysuru Palace 198, 200-1, **200-1**

N

naan 283
Nahargarh 113
National Gallery of Modern Art 206-7
National Museum 49
national parks & reserves 290
  Ranthambore National Park 114-15
  Singalila National Park 218-21
Navrati 24
Nehru, Jawaharlal 275, 276
nightlife 21

O

Ola 310
Old Goa 158-9
Onam 24
opening hours 17, 300-1

P

painting 287
palaces
  City Palace 104-5
  Fatehpur Sikri 74-7
  Hawa Mahal 108
  Jaganmohan Palace 199
  Jaisalmer Fort 88-9
  Mattancherry Palace 191
  Mysuru Palace 198
  Taj Mahal Palace 128
Palolem 167-70, **168**
Palolem Beach 162-3
Panaji (Panjim) 166-7, **167**
paragliding 251
parks & gardens
  Cubbon Park 209
  Lloyd Botanic Garden 222
  Lodi Garden 49
Partition 275
passports 304
Persian language 269
photography 301
planning 16-17, *see also individual locations*
  books 25, 287
  budgeting 17
  calendar of events 22-4
  children, travel with 32-3
  climate 16, 22-4, 292-3
  exchange rates 300
  India basics 16-17
  government travel advice 296
  internet resources 17, 292
  itineraries 26-31 **26**, **27**, **28**, **30**
  travel seasons 16, 22-4, 292-3
  vaccinations 295
  visas 16, 304-5
plants 290
politics 264-5
population 265
prickly heat 297
public holidays 301
Puranas 287

Q

Qutab Minar 44-5
Qutb ud-din Aibak 269-70

R

rabies 295, 296
Radha 281
rafting 250
Rajputs 273
Rama 281
Ramayana 281, 287
Ranthambhore National Park 114-15
Red Fort 38-41, **40-1**
reincarnation 281
religion 265, 267-8, 277, 280-1
rhinos 289
rock climbing 251
Roy, Arundhati 287
Rushdie, Salman 287

S

safety 301-3
  emergency numbers 304
  solo travellers 303

- swimming 163
- women travellers 58, 279, 305-7

saffron 282
salwar kameez 278
saris 278
scams 302-3
- Delhi 58
- Varanasi 241-2

scenic train journeys 226, 310
seafood 284
Shah Jahan 38, 68, 80, 271
Shiva 281
shopping 20, 42-3, *see also individual locations*
Singalila Ridge Trek 218-21
Singalila National Park 218-21
sitars 237
skiing 250-1
smoking 298-9
snow leopards 289
snowboarding 250
soccer 279
solo travellers 303
spirituality 19
sports 279
street food 123
sustainable travel 308
sweets 284
synagogues 191

T

tablas 237
Tagore, Rabindranath 287
Taj Mahal 4-5, 66-73, 271, **72-3**
Tamerlane, *see* Timur
Tamil language 314
taxes 303
taxis 310
tea 216-17
telephone services 16, 303-4
temples 285-6, *see also* Buddhist temples, Hindu temples, Jain temples
theft 303
Thiruvananthapuram 184-5
Tibetan culture 258-61
Tibetan Handicraft Center 261
Tibetan Institute of Performing Arts 261
tigers 18, 114-15, 289
time 16, 304
Timur 270
tipping 300
toilets 304
tombs
- Akbar's Mausoleum 82
- Bibi-qa-Maqbara 150
- Humayun's Tomb 48
- Itimad-ud-Daulah 82-3

train travel 17, 226, 310, 311-12
travel to/from India 17, 308
travel within India 17, 308-12
trekking
- Kodagu (Coorg) 205
- Manali 248-9
- Singalila Ridge Trek 218-21

Trivandrum 184-5
typhoid 296

U

Uber 310

V

vacations 301
vaccinations 295
Vagator 161
Varanasi 8-9, 229-43, **231**, **238**
- accommodation 231
- drinking 240-1
- food 239-40
- itineraries 230
- nightlife 240-1
- planning 230-1
- safety 241-2
- shopping 237
- sights 232-7
- tourist information 241
- travel to/from 231, 242
- travel within 242-3

Vedas 268, 287
vegan travellers 21, 284
vegetarian travellers 21, 284
Vijayanagar empire 210-11, 270
visas 16, 304-5
Vishnu 281

W

walking, *see* trekking
walking tours
- Delhi 46-7, **46-7**
- Jaipur 106-7, **106-7**
- Mumbai 126-7, 128, **126-7**

water 294
weather 16, 22-4, 293
websites, *see* internet resources
weights 305
wi-fi 298
wildlife watching 23, 288-90
women in India 278-9
women travellers 305-7
- Delhi 58
- sexual assaults 302, 305
- sexual harassment 279, 306
- yoga scams 242

WWI 273-4

Y

yoga 164-5, 171

Symbols & Map Key

Look for these symbols to quickly identify listings:

- Sights
- Activities
- Courses
- Tours
- Festivals & Events
- Eating
- Drinking
- Entertainment
- Shopping
- Information & Transport

These symbols and abbreviations give vital information for each listing:

Sustainable or green recommendation

FREE No payment required

- Telephone number
- Opening hours
- Parking
- Nonsmoking
- Air-conditioning
- Internet access
- Wi-fi access
- Swimming pool
- Bus
- Ferry
- Tram
- Train
- English-language menu
- Vegetarian selection
- Family-friendly

Find your best experiences with these Great For... icons.

 Art & Culture

 History

 Beaches

 Local Life

 Budget

 Nature & Wildlife

Cafe/Coffee

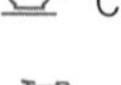 Photo Op

Cycling

Scenery

Detour

Shopping

Drinking

Short Trip

 Entertainment

 Events

Sport

 Family Travel

 Walking

 Food & Drink

 Winter Travel

Sights

- Beach
- Bird Sanctuary
- Buddhist
- Castle/Palace
- Christian
- Confucian
- Hindu
- Islamic
- Jain
- Jewish
- Monument
- Museum/Gallery/Historic Building
- Ruin
- Shinto
- Sikh
- Taoist
- Winery/Vineyard
- Zoo/Wildlife Sanctuary
- Other Sight

Points of Interest

- Bodysurfing
- Camping
- Cafe
- Canoeing/Kayaking
- Course/Tour
- Diving
- Drinking & Nightlife
- Eating
- Entertainment
- Sento Hot Baths/Onsen
- Shopping
- Skiing
- Sleeping
- Snorkelling
- Surfing
- Swimming/Pool
- Walking
- Windsurfing
- Other Activity

Information

- Bank
- Embassy/Consulate
- Hospital/Medical
- Internet
- Police
- Post Office
- Telephone
- Toilet
- Tourist Information
- Other Information

Geographic

- Beach
- Gate
- Hut/Shelter
- Lighthouse
- Lookout
- Mountain/Volcano
- Oasis
- Park
- Pass
- Picnic Area
- Waterfall

Transport

- Airport
- BART station
- Border crossing
- Boston T station
- Bus
- Cable car/Funicular
- Cycling
- Ferry
- Metro/MRT station
- Monorail
- Parking
- Petrol station
- Subway/S-Bahn/Skytrain station
- Taxi
- Train station/Railway
- Tram
- Underground/U-Bahn station
- Other Transport

Mark Elliott

Mark Elliott had already lived and worked on five continents when, in the pre-internet dark ages, he started writing travel guides. He has since authored (or co-authored) around 70 books including dozens for Lonely Planet. He also acts as a travel consultant, occasional tour leader, video presenter, public speaker, art critic, wine taster, interviewer and blues harmonicist.

Paul Harding

As a writer and photographer, Paul has been travelling the globe for the best part of two decades, with an interest in remote and offbeat places, islands and cultures. He's an author and contributor to more than 50 Lonely Planet guides to countries and regions as diverse as India, Belize, Vanuatu, Iran, Indonesia, New Zealand, Iceland, Finland, Philippines and – his home patch – Australia.

Bradley Mayhew

Bradley has been writing guidebooks for 20 years now. He started travelling while studying Chinese at Oxford University, and has since focused his expertise on China, Tibet, the Himalaya and Central Asia. He is the co-author of Lonely Planet guides to *Tibet, Nepal, Trekking in the Nepal Himalaya, Bhutan, Central Asia* and many others. Bradley has also fronted two TV series for Arte and SWR, one retracing the route of Marco Polo via Turkey, Iran, Afghanistan, Central Asia and China, and the other trekking Europe's 10 most scenic long-distance trails.

Daniel McCrohan

Daniel is a British travel writer who specialises in Asia and who has authored more than 40 guidebooks for Lonely Planet and Trailblazer. His expertise lies in China and India, but he has written guides to countries right across the continent, including Mongolia, Russia, Tibet, Thailand and Bangladesh. He also has written numerous British walking guides. Daniel has been a guest speaker at international travel shows, and was a co-host on the Lonely Planet television series *Best in China*. He speaks Chinese fluently, Hindi badly, owns three cycle rickshaws and never uses cars. Find him on Twitter (@danielmccrohan).

Isabella Noble

English-Australian on paper but Spanish at heart, Isabella has been wandering the globe since her first round-the-world trip as a one-year-old. Having grown up in a whitewashed Andalucian village, she is a Spain specialist travel journalist, but also writes extensively about India, Thailand, the UK and beyond for Lonely Planet, the *Daily Telegraph* and others. Isabella has co-written Lonely Planet guides to *Spain* and *Andalucía*, and has also contributed to Lonely Planet *India, South India, Thailand, Thailand's Islands & Beaches, Southeast Asia on a Shoestring* and *Great Britain*, and authored *Pocket Phuket*. Find Isabella on Twitter and Instagram (@isabellamnoble).

John Noble

John has been travelling for Lonely Planet since the 1980s. The number of Lonely Planet titles he's written is well into three figures, on numerous countries across the globe. He's still as excited as ever about heading out to unfamiliar destinations, especially off-the-beaten-track ones. Above all, he loves mountains, from the Pyrenees to the Himalaya. See his pics on Instagram: @johnnoble11.

Kevin Raub

Atlanta native Kevin Raub started his career as a music journalist in New York, working for *Men's Journal* and *Rolling Stone* magazines. He ditched the rock 'n' roll lifestyle for travel writing and has written more than 70 Lonely Planet guides, focused mainly on Brazil, Chile, Colombia, USA, India, the Caribbean and Portugal. Kevin also contributes to a variety of travel magazines in both the USA and UK. Follow him on Twitter and Instagram (@RaubOnTheRoad).

Sarina Singh

Sarina has been an author on 50 Lonely Planet titles, including more than 10 editions of *India;* four editions of *Rajasthan;* three editions of *South India;* two editions of *Pakistan & the Karakoram Highway; Sydney; Mauritius, Réunion & the Seychelles; Aboriginal Australia & the Torres Strait Islands; Delhi; Australia & New Zealand; North India; Africa; Sacred India* and many more. She has also written for dozens of other international publications such as the UK's *Sunday Times* and *Condé Nast Traveller* and the USA's *National Geographic Traveler* and CNBC.

Iain Stewart

Iain trained as journalist in the 1990s and then worked as a news reporter and a restaurant critic in London. He started writing travel guides in 1997 and has since penned more than 60 books for destinations as diverse as Ibiza and Cambodia. Iain's contributed to Lonely Planet titles including *Mexico, Indonesia, Central America, Croatia, Vietnam, Bali & Lombok* and *Southeast Asia*. He also writes regularly for the *Independent, Observer* and *Daily Telegraph* and tweets at @iaintravel.

Our Story

A beat-up old car, a few dollars in the pocket and a sense of adventure. In 1972 that's all Tony and Maureen Wheeler needed for the trip of a lifetime – across Europe and Asia overland to Australia. It took several months, and at the end – broke but inspired – they sat at their kitchen table writing and stapling together their first travel guide, *Across Asia on the Cheap*. Within a week they'd sold 1500 copies. Lonely Planet was born. Today, Lonely Planet has offices in Franklin, London, Melbourne, Oakland, Dublin, Beijing, and Delhi, with more than 600 staff and writers. We share Tony's belief that 'a great guidebook should do three things: inform, educate and amuse'.

Our Writers

Anirban Mahapatra

Anirban is a travel writer, photographer and filmmaker who has authored multiple editions of Lonely Planet's bestselling *India* guidebook, as well as several regional guidebooks. He has written and curated Lonely Planet guidebooks on *Bangladesh, Sri Lanka* and *Bhutan*, as well as designing content models and holding author workshops for Lonely Planet. He has also made videos and documentaries for international television networks, corporates and ministries under the Government of India. When not travelling the world, he lives in Kolkata and Bangkok, where he reads up on Buddhism, listens to the blues and plans his next adventure.

Joe Bindloss

Joe first got the travel bug on a grand tour of Asia in the early 1990s, and he's been roaming around its temples and paddy fields ever since on dozens of assignments for Lonely Planet and other publishers, covering everywhere from Myanmar and Thailand to India and Nepal. Joe was Lonely Planet's Destination Editor for the Indian Subcontinent until 2019. See more of his work at www.bindloss.co.uk.

Lindsay Brown

Lindsay started travelling as young bushwalker exploring the Blue Mountains west of Sydney. Then, as a marine biologist, he dived the coastal and island waters of southeastern Australia. He continued travelling whenever he could while employed at Lonely Planet as an editor and publishing manager. On becoming a freelance writer and photographer he has co-authored more than 45 Lonely Planet guides to *Australia, Bhutan, India, Malaysia, Nepal, Pakistan* and *Papua New Guinea*.

More Writers

STAY IN TOUCH LONELYPLANET.COM/CONTACT

AUSTRALIA The Malt Store, Level 3, 551 Swanston St, Carlton, Victoria 3053 ☎03 8379 8000, fax 03 8379 8111

IRELAND Digital Depot, Roe Lane (off Thomas St), Digital Hub, Dublin 8, D08 TCV4, Ireland

USA 124 Linden Street, Oakland, CA 94607 ☎510 250 6400, toll free 800 275 8555, fax 510 893 8572

UK 240 Blackfriars Road, London SE1 8NW ☎020 3771 5100, fax 020 3771 5101

 twitter.com/lonelyplanet

 facebook.com/lonelyplanet

 instagram.com/lonelyplanet

 youtube.com/lonelyplanet

 lonelyplanet.com/newsletter